W9-BIX-591

AMERICAN ICON

AMERICAN ICON

ALAN MULALLY AND THE FIGHT TO SAVE FORD MOTOR COMPANY

BRYCE G. HOFFMAN

CROWN
BUSINESS
NEW YORK

www.crownpublishing.com

CROWN BUSINESS is a trademark and CROWN and the Rising Sun colophon
are registered trademarks of Random House, Inc.

Crown Business books are available at special discounts for bulk purchases for sales
promotions or corporate use. Special editions, including personalized covers, excerpts
of existing books, or books with corporate logos, can be created in large quantities
for special needs. For more information, contact Premium Sales at (212) 572-2232 or
e-mail specialmarkets@randomhouse.com.

Library of Congress Cataloging-in-Publication Data
Hoffman, Bryce G.
American icon: Alan Mulally and the fight to save Ford Motor Company /
by Bryce G. Hoffman.
p. cm.
Includes bibliographical references and index.
1. Ford Motor Company. 2. Automobile industry and trade—United States—History.
3. Mulally, Alan R. I. Title.
HD9710.U54F636 2012
338.7'629222092—dc23   2011037155

ISBN 978-0-307-88605-7
eISBN 978-0-307-88607-1

Printed in the United States of America

Unless otherwise indicated all photographs are courtesy of Ford Motor Company.

Book design by Leonard Henderson
Jacket design by David Tran

4 6 8 10 9 7 5 3

First Edition

To MSN and MSH,

and to my parents, Ned Hoffman and Billie Crowley,

for a lifetime of support

CONTENTS

AUTHOR'S NOTE

When I first started covering Ford Motor Company for the *Detroit News* in 2005, the automaker was fighting for its life. I had no idea whether Ford would win or lose, but I knew it would be a great story either way—the end of an American icon, or its salvation. For the sake of Ford's employees, its investors, its dealers, the communities it operated in, and the nation itself, I hoped it would succeed. But I would write its story either way.

With that in mind, I kept careful notes from each of the hundreds of interviews I conducted over the next five years. As the Ford beat reporter at the *Detroit News*, I had a front-row seat for most of the events chronicled in this narrative. But I also knew there was much more to this story than had ever been told. When the time came to finally write the Ford story in its entirety, I knew that I would have to conduct many more interviews.

Once it was clear that the company had pulled off one of the most amazing turnarounds in history, I contacted Executive Chairman Bill Ford Jr. and Chief Executive Officer Alan Mulally and told them about my plan to write a book chronicling their epic achievement. I told them that I believed it was a fundamentally positive story that would be that much more compelling if it was told truthfully and in its entirety. To their credit both men agreed, offering Ford's full cooperation with this project. I promised them nothing in return but fairness and accuracy.

Over the next year, I conducted more than a hundred interviews with players large and small in this drama. Many of these were conducted in person, and many lasted for several hours. All of them were conducted with the understanding that I could use any information discussed, provided that I did not attribute it to a particular source. This anonymity was necessary because many of the men and women I interviewed were still employed by Ford Motor Company and were only willing to speak frankly if such protection was guaranteed. Where direct quotes appear, they are excerpted from previously published material. The final chapter is the exception to these rules. I wanted to give Alan Mulally an opportunity to speak directly to you, the reader, and share his thoughts about the events described herein.

With the help of the men and women I interviewed, I have reconstructed relevant dialogue wherever possible. This was done with the utmost care. When dialogue appears in quotes, the wording comes from the speaker, from another participant in that conversation, from contemporaneous notes, or from a transcript. Dialogue that does not appear in quotes is paraphrased or reflects the inability of the participants to remember the exact wording. Where the specific thoughts of an individual are rendered in italics, they come directly from that person or from someone he or she shared those thoughts with at the time.

In the few cases where participants disagreed about the events described in this book, I have done my best to resolve those discrepancies by relying on primary source material. Many of the people I interviewed for this book shared their personal notes, calendars, and other documentary information. My research also benefited from a wealth of primary source material from Ford itself. I was given access to "top secret" company documents, internal memos, and archives. This level of access has never been granted to any other author or reporter. Much has been written about Ford's turnaround and the fall and rise of the U.S. automobile industry in general. The information in this book in some cases contradicts what has already been published. When it does, the reader can be certain that I have rigorously relied on this documentary evidence to establish the facts.

Prologue

O n September 5, 2006, I followed a public relations executive backstage at the media center inside Ford Motor Company's world headquarters in Dearborn, Michigan. My minder knocked, stuck his head in the side door, and waved my colleague, *Detroit News* columnist Daniel Howes, and me through. Inside, the great-grandson of Henry Ford was smiling like a lottery winner. Bill Ford Jr. had just resigned as the automaker's chief executive officer.

"You look happy," Howes observed as Ford took a long swig from a bottle of water handed to him by an aide. Ford laughed.

"You have no idea!" he exclaimed as the world's automotive press shouted into cellphones and pounded away at laptops on the other side of the curtain. "My wife is happy! My kids are happy! I'm happy!"

The man standing next to him was also smiling as he pumped my hand and slapped my shoulder. A few minutes before, Alan Mulally had become Ford's new CEO.

"Doesn't it worry you that the man who you're replacing is doing the I'm-going-to-Disneyland dance?" I asked Mulally.

He flashed what would soon become his trademark grin.

"You don't know much about me yet, Bryce, but let me just tell you one thing," Mulally said. "No matter how bad Ford Motor Company's problems are today, they aren't as bad as Boeing's were on September 12, 2001."

The lanky, gingerbread-haired Kansan was president of the Boeing Company's commercial aviation division. And though few outside the upper echelons of corporate America had heard of him, Mulally was already famous in business circles for having saved the aircraft manufacturer from collapse after the terrorist attacks on New York and Washington five years earlier prompted most of the world's airlines to cancel their orders for new planes. Now, Bill Ford was asking him to save another American icon.

Ford may have been the company that put the world on wheels, invented the moving assembly line, and created the industrial middle class, but its glory days were long past. Together with General Motors Corporation and Chrysler Corporation, it had been a powerful engine of prosperity in postwar America. For half a century, from the 1920s to the 1970s, Detroit's Big Three dominated the U.S. automobile market, accounting for five of every six vehicles sold in the country. That market was still the largest in the world, but their share of it had been declining for decades. During the boom years of the 1950s and 1960s, American automakers had grown fat and complacent as new competitors emerged in Europe and Asia, studied their methods, and figured out how to beat them at their own game. That era of easy profit created a culture of entitlement in Detroit that afflicted management and labor alike — inflating salaries, wages, and benefits until they became the envy of the world. Success was viewed as a birthright, not something that had to be fought for and won. As the Big Three's share of the market had shrunk, they had not. At least not fast enough. They all had too many factories, too many workers, and too many dealers. Generous union contracts negotiated in better times had created enormous legacy costs that their foreign rivals did not have to bear. And none of the American companies had the stomach for the radical reforms that were now necessary just to stay in business. Wall Street had begun a deathwatch, waiting to see which of the Big Three would fail first. Most of the money was on Ford, which had become infamous for lackluster designs, poor quality, and managerial infighting.

Five years before, Bill Ford had taken charge of the company and tried to salvage what was left of its name and his. For a while, it seemed like he might succeed. Quality started to improve. Ford became the first American automaker to bring a hybrid to market. And a few of its products had begun to win praise from critics. But consumers remained wary. Too many of them had bought Fords in the past and were not going to make the same mistake again. Meanwhile, rising gasoline prices were scaring those customers who were left away from the big trucks and sport utility vehicles that were the source of most of Ford's profits. At the same time, Ford found himself unable to overcome an entrenched, careerist culture that resisted all change and put individual advancement ahead of corporate success. In their dark-paneled offices, executives plotted ways to undermine one another's efforts, while on the factory floor, union bosses jealously defended their members' rich benefits and scoffed at attempts to boost productivity. A year earlier, Ford had tapped Mark Fields, president of the company's more successful European division, to lead a restructuring of its core North American automotive business. Fields put together a bold plan to cut the business back to profitability by shuttering factories and slashing jobs. But it was not bold enough. The company was still hemorrhaging money and market share and seemed unable to stanch the bleeding. Japan's Toyota Motor Corporation had just outsold Ford in the United States for the first time.

When Bill Ford took over as CEO in 2001, he had promised that the company would be making $7 billion by 2006. Instead, it was about to post a loss of nearly $6 billion for the third quarter alone—the company's worst quarterly result in more than fourteen years. Investors were losing patience. Once a blue-chip stock, Ford's shares were now trading in the single digits, and its debt had fallen deep into junk bond territory. Analysts had begun to whisper the word *bankruptcy*.

GM and Chrysler had many of the same problems, but most on Wall Street believed those companies were in a better position to address them. The prevailing view was that GM would save itself by better utilizing its immense global assets, while Chrysler's 1998 alliance with German automaker Daimler-Benz AG seemed to offer a different way out of the mess the American automobile industry had become. The analysts had crunched the numbers and concluded that Ford would run out of road first.

But no one had factored in Alan Mulally.

In less than three years, both GM and Chrysler would be bankrupt, and a resurgent Ford would wow Wall Street with quarter after quarter of profits at a time when most companies were still reeling from the worst economic crisis since the Great Depression. Mulally would be heralded as the architect of one of the greatest turnarounds in business history.

But none of it would come easy. Mulally would have to weld Ford's disparate regional divisions into a single, global operation and take a sledgehammer to the ossified fiefdoms that had divided the company for decades. And Ford would be forced to mortgage everything—right down to the Blue Oval itself—to secure the financing necessary to fund Mulally's revolution.

"I was right—Ford's problems weren't as bad as Boeing's," Mulally would later confide in me. "They were much, much worse."

CHAPTER 1

The House That Henry Built

*Business men go down with their businesses because they like the
old way so well they cannot bring themselves to change. One sees
them all about—men who do not know that yesterday is past, and
who woke up this morning with their last year's ideas.*

— HENRY FORD

While many of Ford Motor Company's problems were shared by the rest of Detroit, the Dearborn automaker also faced some challenges all its own. Ford's woes had not begun with the arrival of the Japanese in the 1960s or the oil crises of the 1970s. The company had been struggling with itself since Henry Ford started it on June 16, 1903. It invested massively in game-changing products, and then did nothing to keep them competitive. It allowed cults of personality to form around larger-than-life leaders, but drove away the talent needed to support them. And it allowed a caustic corporate culture to eat away at the company from the inside. These were birth defects that could be traced back to the automaker's earliest days. Henry Ford liked to boast that he had created the modern world. In many ways, he had. But he also created a company that was its own worst enemy.

Henry Ford began that company with a simple vision: "I will build a car for the great multitude. It will be large enough for the family, but small enough for the individual to run and care for. It will be constructed of the best materials, by the best men to be hired, after the simplest designs that modern engineering can devise. But it will be so low in price that no man making a good salary will be unable to own one—and enjoy with his family the blessing of hours of pleasure in God's great open spaces."

Ford made good on that promise with his Model T, a simple, reliable, no-nonsense car that transformed the automobile from a rich man's toy into a means of transportation for the masses.* When the Model T went on sale on October 1, 1908, most cars cost a small fortune. It started at $850—less than $20,000 in today's money. "Even You Can Afford a Ford," the company's billboards proclaimed. But Ford did not stop there.

As demand for these Tin Lizzies grew, the pioneering manufacturer began building them on the world's first moving assembly lines. This cut the average time it took to produce a Ford from thirteen hours to just ninety minutes. But workers got bored on Ford's assembly lines, and turnover was high. So, in January 1914, the company stunned the world by announcing that it would pay workers $5 a day. It was more than twice what most other laborers made at the time. As news spread, tens of thousands of men—particularly in the underdeveloped South—threw down their picks and hoes and headed for Detroit. Ford's $5-a-day wage sparked one of the largest economic migrations since the California Gold Rush and created the industrial middle class. As Henry Ford would later boast, it also made his workers as reliable as his machines. Mass production allowed Ford to cut costs and boost efficiency. He passed the savings on to consumers and made his money on the added volume. Henry Ford claimed that every dollar he shaved off the price of his car bought him a thousand new customers. By 1925, the price of a Model T had dropped to $260—just over $3,000 today—and Ford was making more than 1.6 million of them a year.

It was an impressive figure for the time, but it was nearly 200,000 fewer than the company was making just two years before. Despite the massive price cuts, sales of the Model T were slumping. So was Ford's share of the market, which peaked in 1921 at 61.5 percent. Other automakers, like General Motors, were regularly introducing

---

* The Model T was not Henry Ford's first car, but it was his first real success—the one that propelled his company to the forefront of the automobile industry. Ford sold his first vehicle almost a decade earlier, the handmade "Quadricycle" that he assembled in a brick shed behind his home. Ford Motor Company sold its first car, a two-seat runabout, in July 1903.

new models—each one an improvement over its predecessor. The Model T had seen few updates. It was old technology, yet Henry Ford stubbornly refused to begin work on a replacement. He thought it was all the automobile the average person needed. When his engineers began work on a new prototype anyway, Ford destroyed it with a sledgehammer. But Ford's dealers were clamoring for something new. So was his son, Edsel. By the time Ford finally began work on his new Model A in 1927, demand had fallen so dramatically that he was forced to close his factories and lay off 60,000 workers.

As Ford retooled, General Motors passed it to become the largest automaker in the world. Many thought Ford was finished. But on November 28, 1927, people all over America waited in line for hours outside dealerships for a glimpse of the first new Ford in twenty years. It did not seem to matter that the only thing inside most of the stores was a cardboard cutout. By the end of the day, more than 10 million people—10 percent of the U.S. population—had seen the Model A. It combined the Model T's practicality with something entirely new to Ford customers: style. Thousands placed orders on the spot. Ford's factories surged back to life, unable to keep up with the unprecedented demand for its new car.

Within two years, the company had sold more than 2 million Model A's and its share of the domestic market doubled. Yet once again, Henry Ford rested on the laurels of his phenomenal success as his competitors continued to improve their offerings. The next new Ford would not arrive in showrooms until 1932. By then, other manufacturers were introducing new models every year, and Ford was losing money. Fortunately for the Dearborn automaker, its new flathead V-8 motor was another innovative hit. But Ford would not really begin to diversify its product lineup until after World War II, and even then it would continue to make the same mistake with products like the Thunderbird and the Mustang.

By the 1980s, Ford was fighting for its life once again—this time against new competitors from Japan. Ford and the other Detroit automakers had been ceding sales to the import brands for a decade, and many doubted whether the Big Three would be able to mount a counterattack. Then Ford stunned the automotive world with the most radical new design in years. In 1985, it unveiled the Ford Taurus, a streamlined sedan with rounded corners that featured the tighter suspension and precise steering more typical of European automobiles. Critics said it looked like a jellybean, but it was a hit with consumers and pushed Ford's profits past GM's. The Taurus was so successful that General Motors and Chrysler were soon copying Ford's aerodynamic design, as were the Japanese.

For a while, it seemed like Ford might finally have learned its lesson. It introduced an upgraded version of the Taurus in 1992 that was even better than the original. The Taurus became the bestselling car in America, seizing that title from the Honda Accord. But Ford's investment in the popular sedan soon petered out. In 1997, Toyota's Camry claimed its crown, and the Taurus was soon relegated to rental car fleets. When production finally stopped in 2006, few even noticed.

* * *

Ford's overreliance on a single product was surpassed only by its overreliance on a single man. In the beginning, that man was Henry Ford. Instead of leading a team of managers, Ford preferred to rule his industrial empire like a potentate. He had a good eye for talent and initially tried to fill his court with able executives, but he often drove them away once they began to exert significant influence over his organization. Ford was even unwilling to share power with his own son. Edsel Ford replaced his father as the company's president after the family bought out the other investors in 1919, and he held that position until his death in 1943. But Henry Ford still made all the decisions, large and small, often countermanding any orders his son tried to give. He even rehired men Edsel had fired.

Though Henry Ford did not create Ford Motor Company by himself, he often acted as though he had. James Couzens, the company's first general manager, played the prudent businessman to his mad inventor—at least until he resigned in 1915.

"Mr. Couzens said that, while he was willing to work *with* Mr. Ford, he could no longer work *for* him," wrote another early Ford executive, Charles Sorensen. "The paradox is that but for Couzens and his organization and domination of sales and finance Ford Motor Company would not have lasted long."

William Knudsen, a manufacturing prodigy who helped orchestrate the company's shift to mass production, was also driven away—right into the arms of General Motors. There he became head of Chevrolet, leading it past Ford in factory output by 1931.

"Mr. Knudsen was too strong for me to handle," Henry Ford later conceded. "You see, this is my business. I built it, and as long as I live, I propose to run it the way I want it run."

Instead of capable executives with their own ideas, Ford preferred to surround himself with yes-men and hired guns like Harry Bennett, the éminence grise with reputed underworld connections whom he hired to keep order at the River Rouge factory complex. Bennett was quickly promoted to chief of the Ford Service Department, which under his leadership grew into the largest private police force in the world. Men like Bennett fostered an enduring culture of intrigue and backstabbing among Ford's senior leadership. Employees lived in fear of being fired by capricious managers and thought carefully before answering questions to make sure they gave the expected response, even if it was wrong.

By the 1930s, Ford had become "a dark, almost gothic place, with a shadowy administration, activities shrouded in mystery, and a roster of dubious characters running rampant on the premises," in the words of historian Douglas Brinkley, who also noted the absence of any real corporate structure at the company. "Henry Ford had preferred to receive reports on his company anecdotally, even through espionage, rather than in the numeric rationale of accounting."

The Flivver King, as Ford became known, ran his dominion by instinct and intuition.* The only way anyone in Dearborn knew how much cash the company had was by looking at its bank statements. Ford actually figured out how much money to set aside for accounts payable each month by weighing its bills on a scale. That might have

---

* *Flivver* was a common slang term for an inexpensive automobile. The author Upton Sinclair first referred to Henry Ford as the Flivver King in his critical book *The Flivver King: A Story of Ford-America,* which was published by the United Auto Workers in 1937.

worked for an automotive start-up, but it had long since become a liability—one the U.S. government was not willing to tolerate in a company that, in the 1940s, became a vital contributor to its "Arsenal of Democracy."

As Ford's factories retooled to produce the bombers and jeeps that would help win World War II, the War Department worried about leaving these essential industries in the hands of such a mismanaged corporation. Washington seriously considered taking over the company after Edsel, whom most outsiders viewed as the lone voice of reason inside Ford, died in 1943. Instead, the navy ordered Edsel's son, Lieutenant Henry Ford II, to resign his commission and report for duty in Dearborn. The elder Ford initially tried to prevent his grandson from exercising any real authority, just as he had done with Edsel. But in September 1945, the increasingly enfeebled patriarch was finally persuaded to cede control of the company to his namesake.

Though young and inexperienced, Henry Ford II understood that fundamental changes were needed at the automaker—and needed fast. He personally fired Bennett and the rest of his grandfather's henchmen, replacing them with real businessmen like Ernie Breech, whom he lured away from the far more sophisticated General Motors, and a group of management savants from the Army Air Forces, the legendary Whiz Kids. Together they created a modern corporate structure and instituted disciplined business practices that soon became a model for other companies. At the same time, Ford's new boss ordered his managers to begin treating their employees and one another with respect. He promised that the truth would no longer be punished and encouraged a new openness with the outside world as well. But it did not last. As Henry Ford II grew more confident in his own abilities, he also became more jealous of his position as head of the company. Hank the Deuce, as he was soon nicknamed, began to pit one executive against another. Ford's managers began to worry more about their own careers than the success of the company.

"Henry Ford II's imperial style led to impulsive decisions from which there was no appeal and to a continual shuffling of the executive deck chairs," wrote journalist Alex Taylor III, who began covering

Ford in the 1970s. "The sharp-elbowed company politics were embedded in Ford culture. Old Henry Ford and his thuggish subordinate Harry Bennett had instilled a rule of fear in the 1920s and 1930s that never entirely vanished. . . . Even into the 1980s, executives worried about wiretaps and electronic listening devices that would allow their conversations to be overheard. Unlike at GM, it was rare for Ford executives to hang on to their jobs until retirement; almost everyone was vulnerable to being toppled. The Dearborn company became known as a place where tough guys win."

No one was tougher than Lee Iacocca, the marketing genius who was promoted to president in 1970 after his Mustang revived America's love affair with Ford. But Iacocca created his own cult of personality that threatened to divide the company into warring camps. Henry Ford II began to see Iacocca as a threat to his own authority and fired him in 1978 after learning that he had contacted board members behind Ford's back in an effort to protect his position. Iacocca went on to save Chrysler—at least for a while.

Just when it seemed like the corporate intrigue at Ford was reaching new heights, Hank the Deuce announced that he was retiring. In 1980, he turned the company over to Philip Caldwell, a far more reserved Ford executive who would become the first non-Ford to serve as the company's chairman and CEO. For a time, it seemed as if Ford might become just another boring bureaucracy, like General Motors. But Caldwell's successor, Donald Petersen, quickly ran afoul of a new generation of Fords. Petersen resented the easy ascension of Edsel Ford II and William Clay Ford Jr. to the company's board of directors in 1988 and refused to appoint either of them to a board committee.

"I'm not a caretaker for anybody," he told *Fortune* magazine at the time. "I admire the fact that [Edsel and Bill] are trying very hard to go as far as they can. But being a Ford does not give them a leg up. The principle we must operate on is that selection to top management is based solely on merit."

Petersen spent the next two years trying to hold his ground, but it was a battle he could not win as long the Ford family maintained controlling interest in the company. He resigned in 1990, just as the automaker was entering its most profitable decade ever.

* * *

I once asked a Toyota executive if there was anything he admired about Ford Motor Company.

"Yes," he said after reflecting for a moment. "Their ability to overcome adversity."

The company may have been unable to learn from its mistakes, but Ford was a survivor. It was the Rocky Balboa of the automobile industry—at its best when it was against the ropes. It could take punches and come back swinging. Every time someone wrote Ford off, there it was back in the center of the ring with its gloved hand thrust into the air. But it could not handle success. Like the fictional fighter, Ford kept falling back into its old habits, growing soft and complacent once the danger had passed.

The crisis that Ford faced in 2006 was just the latest in a series of financial disasters that had befallen the company over the past 103 years. The first time Ford almost went out of business was in 1920. Henry Ford loathed debt, but he buried himself under a mountain of it to buy out his early investors in 1919—just as America was slipping into a depression. Inflation was rampant in the wake of World War I, and the company's sales were suffering. But Ford was still spending big on his mammoth manufacturing complex then under construction on Dearborn's River Rouge. As the end of the year approached, Ford had only $20 million in cash and was facing obligations of $58 million in the first four months of 1921 alone. Henry Ford closed his main factory, sacked a quarter of his workers, and sold off their equipment. He took the 125,000 Model Ts sitting outside his plants, loaded them on trains, and began shipping them to dealers along with demands for immediate payment. Until then, dealers paid for cars as they sold them. Not anymore. It was all perfectly legal, thanks to some very fine print in their contracts. By April 1921, Ford had more than $87 million in the bank. The company not only had enough money to stay in business, but also was able to slash prices and surge ahead once the nation's economy began to recover. By the end of the year, Ford was selling more cars than ever before and controlled more than 61 percent of the market.

Eight years later, the world was plunging into an even greater depression. Henry Ford tried to turn back the tide with his own economic stimulus program. Despite declining demand for automobiles, he offered his workers raises—an extra buck a day to spur spending—and dropped the price of his cars to make them easier for cash-strapped consumers to afford. As his competitors' factories sputtered or closed down altogether, Ford's continued to hum. But by 1931, the U.S. car market had shrunk by two-thirds, and even Henry Ford was forced to halt production of his Model A. He closed twenty-five factories, axed 75,000 workers, and even took back the raises of those who remained. As before, these austerity measures allowed Ford to survive, but the company lost $120 million between 1930 and 1933. General Motors, which had not hesitated to cut production and kick its workers to the curb, made it through the Great Depression without losing a cent.

Ford prospered with the rest of the country during the postwar boom, but the U.S. automobile industry was in serious trouble by the 1970s. Ralph Nader's *Unsafe at Any Speed* had destroyed the mystique that surrounded the American automobile—and American automakers—since the days of the Model T. It also helped usher in a new era of government regulation in the United States. Along with the other U.S. car companies, Ford was ordered to make its vehicles safer and reduce tailpipe emissions. Like the others, it tried to pass the cost of these expensive mandates on to consumers, even as America's defeat in Vietnam sent the nation into a recession. As sticker prices began to rise, so did the cost of gasoline. Consumers began searching for cheaper, more fuel-efficient alternatives to Detroit's land yachts.

They found them in the cute compacts that had begun arriving from Japan a few years earlier. Americans started buying imports for their low price and superior fuel economy but soon discovered they were also a lot more reliable than many of the vehicles Ford and the other domestic automakers were producing.

"I frankly don't see how we're going to meet the foreign competition," Henry Ford II warned after the company's shareholders meeting in 1971. "We may be a service nation someday."

After the 1973 oil crisis, the U.S. Congress imposed tough new regulations on automakers, aimed at improving fuel economy. Complying was easy for the Japanese, who were already making the most fuel-efficient cars on the road. But the rules required American automakers to make major investments in new products and new technology.

Then, just when it seemed like things could not possibly get any worse for the Big Three, the 1979 Iranian Revolution sparked a second oil crisis. Those high-mileage Japanese compacts looked more attractive than ever to the motorists stuck in the long lines that soon formed around service stations across the United States.

The 1970s were nothing short of apocalyptic for Detroit's car companies. But for Ford, these challenges were just the beginning of its woes. After reports began to surface of fiery crashes involving its import-fighting Ford Pinto, the automaker was hit by a wave of expensive lawsuits. The company was even charged with murder when three teenage girls burned to death after their Pinto was rear-ended on an Indiana highway in 1978. Meanwhile, other Ford vehicles were being blamed for more than a hundred deaths and nearly 2,000 injuries caused by faulty transmissions. By the end of the decade, Ford's products were widely regarded as the worst on the road. After posting a record profit of $906 million in 1972, the company went into a nosedive that culminated in a $1.4 billion loss in 1980. That was almost as much as Chrysler lost that year, and Chrysler was on taxpayer-funded life support.

Fortuitously, a conservative Henry Ford II had stashed away billions before stepping down as CEO in 1979. When he gave up the chairman's job a year later, the automaker was left without a Ford in the driver's seat for the first time ever.* But this money, along with yet another round of mass layoffs and plant closings, kept the lights on in Dearborn. So did Caldwell, Petersen, and a new generation of

---

* This was not the result of a conscious decision by the Ford family to step back from the company, but rather the result of the simple fact that there was no Ford old enough to lead the company who wanted the job at the time. Hank the Deuce would remain a director and head of the board's powerful Finance Committee until his death in 1987.

executives, who made quality Job One again, negotiated the first concessionary contract with the United Auto Workers, and invested in
new products like the Taurus. By 1983, Ford was back in the black
with a new record profit of $1.8 billion. By 1986, it was making more
money than General Motors. By 1987, it was making more than all of
the Japanese and European carmakers combined.

By the mid-1990s, it seemed like all of Detroit's sins had been forgiven. Gasoline prices were plummeting. Adjusted for inflation, they
were now at an all-time low in the United States. Suddenly, big was
back. All across suburbia, Americans began trading in their family sedans for truck-based sport utility vehicles. What had until then been
niche products for ranchers and other outdoorsy types suddenly became, in the words of veteran auto reporter Paul Ingrassia, "the perfect complement to a Patagonia windbreaker: a fashion statement, the
sports car substitute for soccer moms."

Ford responded to the emerging trend with the Explorer. Launched
in 1990, it took only a few months to become the bestselling SUV in
the world—and one of the biggest moneymakers in the company's
history. By 1995, Ford was selling more trucks than cars.* In 1997, it
introduced the Expedition, an even bigger SUV that generated even
bigger profits. Two years later, the company trumped that with the
Excursion, an SUV so big that it could not fit in many standard car
washes. Or garages. One of the first was sold to a Texas woman who
returned to the dealership the next day with the roof peeled back like
a sardine tin. The salesman asked if she would like a smaller model,
but she insisted on another Excursion and said she would get a bigger garage instead. Environmentalists were less enthusiastic about
the gas-guzzling behemoths. Ford, which now had the worst fleet
fuel-economy average of any major automaker, was attacked by groups
such as the Sierra Club. It suggested the automaker call its new SUV
the "Ford Valdez" instead, in homage to the coastline-defiling Exxon
oil tanker. But with so much money rolling in, it was easy to ignore
the criticism.

---

* The Ford F-Series, first introduced in 1948, was already the bestselling pickup
in America.

Ford's SUV factories, like those of General Motors and Chrysler, had become private mints. They were so profitable that Ford often flew parts in by helicopter when supplies ran low, rather than waste time sending them by truck. Nor did the Big Three have to share their windfall. For the first time in decades, the Japanese were nowhere in sight. They were slow to appreciate the importance of this new segment and would need years to develop credible offerings. In fact, as Detroit cashed in on the SUV craze, its Japanese competitors were struggling to cope with a rising yen that ate into their margins and forced them to raise prices, making their cars even less attractive to consumers now obsessed with trucks.

In 1998, Ford posted a stunning profit of more than $22 billion. It was the most money any automaker had ever made. A big chunk of that came from the spin-off of Associates First Capital Corporation, a financial services company Ford had purchased from Gulf+Western in 1989. But even without that boost, it finished 1999 with earnings of $7.2 billion.

✳   ✳   ✳

As the automaker tried to figure out how to spend all that cash, its founder's heirs were trying to figure out how to put the Ford back in Ford Motor Company.

Though Ford had been publicly traded since 1956, it was still controlled by the Ford family, thanks to some arcane financial prestidigitation. Once Henry Ford wrested control of the company from his original partners, he was determined to keep it in the family. Ford was always afraid that the big banks would somehow find a way to steal the business away from him. The best way to protect the company was to keep it private. But Ford later discovered something he feared more than Wall Street: inheritance taxes. In 1936, he established the Ford Foundation and arranged for most of the company's shares to be transferred to the charity when he died, which he did eleven years later. By 1955, the foundation had become one of the most important philanthropic organizations in the world, a major international force in its own right. The Ford Foundation saw little value in maintaining its ties to the Dearborn automaker and informed Henry Ford II that it intended to sell its shares.* Hank the Deuce could not prevent the move, but his bankers did manage to set up a unique ownership structure that created two classes of shares: Class A, which would trade publicly on the New York Stock Exchange, and Class B, which would be owned exclusively by the Ford family. No matter how many shares of Class A stock were issued, these Class B shares would always wield 40 percent of the voting power.† That gave the family enough votes to veto any decision—or elect a chairman.

At the end of the 1990s, the chairman the family had in mind was William Clay Ford Jr. Known as Billy to the rest of the family and Bill to most of Detroit, his roots in the automobile industry ran deep, even for a Ford. His father, William Clay Ford Sr., was the youngest of Edsel Ford's four children. His mother, Martha Firestone, was the granddaughter of Harvey Firestone, the founder of Firestone Tire & Rubber Company, which had pioneered the mass production of tires and supplied them for Ford's Model T.

The dimple-chinned Bill Ford looked nothing like his gaunt great-grandfather, Henry. He more resembled his softer and better-fed uncle, Hank the Deuce. The first thing most people noticed about the young Ford, besides his bright blue eyes, was his quick intellect and easygoing demeanor. He was personable, quick to smile, and possessed a self-deprecating sense of humor that was entirely unexpected in a man of such means.

Born in Detroit in 1957, Bill grew up in the posh enclave of Grosse Pointe Shores alongside Lake St. Clair. His father was a member of Ford's board of directors and served as vice president and general manager of the company's Continental Division. Bill grew up listening to discussions around the breakfast table about the company and the car business. But by the time he was in grade school, his father's real passion had become football. William Clay Ford Sr. purchased the local National Football League franchise, the Detroit Lions, in

---

* The Ford Foundation's ties to the Ford family and the Ford Motor Company were severed completely in 1976. The automaker's philanthropic arm is now the Ford Motor Company Fund.

† These Class B shares could be traded among the heirs of Henry Ford, but they would convert to regular Class A shares if they were ever sold outside the family.

1963. The team rarely won, but it was not for want of trying. The elder Ford was fiercely competitive, and he tried to instill that same spirit in Bill and his three sisters.

"Everything we did in our house was hypercompetitive," Bill Ford would later recall, describing how cards and trivia games became contact sports in the Ford household. "The most innocent after-dinner game became cutthroat. There were no gracious winners and no good losers."

Bill grew up surrounded by wealth and power. The family would winter at their home at Smoke Tree Ranch in Palm Springs, California. There the young Ford would wave at Walt Disney, who had a place down the street, and wait for his father to return from a round of golf with Uncle Frank—Sinatra, that is. But Ford pushed beyond the comfortable confines of his privileged childhood. He played hockey in a youth league in the blue-collar community of St. Clair Shores—often facing off against kids whose fathers toiled in Ford's factories. He inherited his great-grandfather's love of the great outdoors. Ford's fondest childhood memories were of summers spent at Fontinalis, a private fishing club in northern Michigan where he spent his days casting for trout along the banks of the Sturgeon River.

Like his father and grandfather, Bill Ford attended the prestigious Hotchkiss School in Connecticut, where he could study in the Edsel B. Ford Library or rush the net on the William Clay Ford Tennis Courts. Bill preferred football and hockey, but his sense of family history was strong. It was hard to miss growing up in southeast Michigan, where the Fords were regarded as American royalty. In Detroit, the names of Bill's ancestors adorned not just tennis courts and libraries, but also hospitals, freeways, and, of course, automobiles.

After graduation, his father handed him the keys to a one-of-a-kind metallic green Ford Mustang and sent him to Princeton, where Bill Ford wrote his senior thesis on Henry Ford's relations with the UAW. In college, Ford threw himself into the even tougher sport of rugby with a fearlessness some found almost frightening. By the time he graduated, he had broken several bones. Ford slapped a bumper sticker on his Mustang that read, "In rugby there are no winners, only survivors." But he also studied Eastern mysticism and philosophy, while at the same time managing to get himself elected president of the Ivy Club.

After earning a degree in history from Princeton in 1979, Ford decided to go to work for his great-grandfather's company—the one that made cars, not tires. He wanted to prove himself and was eager to be judged on his own merits, so he showed up for his first day as a product planning analyst with the name William Clay printed on his identification badge. He fooled no one. When 5 P.M. rolled around, Ford looked up from his work and waited for the rest of the employees to leave. He was determined to be the last one out the door. But nobody budged. By 6 P.M., a few of his coworkers were reading magazines. By 7 P.M., one of them decided to order pizza. At 9 P.M., Ford finally pushed back his chair and headed for the door. So did everybody else.

Bill Ford's dedication to Ford Motor Company was evidenced by the simple fact that he showed up for work each day. He certainly did not have to. If he had chosen to spend his days sitting on the beach of a small private island, few would have faulted him for it. By the fourth generation, the heirs of most other industrial fortunes had long since devoted themselves to a life of leisure. After putting in a few years at the company, Ford resumed his education, earning his master's from the Massachusetts Institute of Technology's Sloan School of Management in 1984. Then it was back to work. Bill was named head of Ford of Switzerland in 1987. The alpine nation was not exactly a major market, but the skiing was excellent. A year later, he and cousin Edsel Ford II were elected to Ford's board of directors, where they soon locked horns with Petersen. They won their fight for greater responsibility, and Bill was promoted to head of business strategy for the Ford Automotive Group in 1990. Ten years later, Ford won a different sort of battle with his cousin to become the next head of the Ford family.

Bill Ford was now ready to assume what he and many of his relatives considered his rightful place at the head of Ford Motor Company. However, he bore little resemblance to Detroit's ideal of an automotive executive. Bill dabbled in Buddhism. He played folk guitar. He also had become an ardent environmentalist. Bill believed in global warming and thought his company's cars and trucks were contributing to it. The biggest management challenges he had faced involved his father's football team, and it had one of the worst records in the NFL. Alex Trotman, the wiry Scotsman who had presided over much of the automaker's recent success, considered Bill and Edsel "rich dilettantes ill equipped to meddle with one of the world's largest companies, even if their name was on the building." Trotman seemed to forget that his was not. When the board of directors pushed him to choose Bill Ford as his successor, Trotman resisted. The directors overruled him. Trotman shook his head and left the boardroom, pausing as he passed the young Ford.

"So now you have your monarchy back, Prince William."

*　*　*

Bᵁᵗ Ford's rising son would not rule alone.
      While Ford's board was willing to give Bill Ford a chance, many of the outside directors had their own reservations about his ability to run the company. If nothing else, he was very young—just forty-one when he officially took over on January 1, 1999. Their solution was to divide the office of chairman and CEO into two positions and pair Ford with an experienced chief executive.

The man they chose was Jacques Nasser, a suave and swaggering Arab who had been born in Lebanon and raised in Australia. He was ten years older than Bill Ford and considered one of the company's most talented executives.

The two men could not have been more different. Ford had been born into a world of wealth and power, but had grown into a relatively down-to-earth adult who went out of his way to rub elbows with the common man. Even after becoming chairman, he continued to play hockey on a team that included Ford factory workers. After Princeton, Ford had switched to a particularly brutal variant played outdoors on ponds that added freezing rain and snow to the usual fare of flying pucks and body checks. He tired of stuffy Grosse Pointe and moved his family to a seventeen-acre wooded estate on the Huron River in Ann Arbor, a college town with a slightly bohemian bent about forty-five minutes west of Ford World Headquarters. On weekdays, Bill Ford drove himself to work—in either a new Mustang or an F-150 pickup. On weekends, he Rollerbladed to the local Starbucks. And he remained an outspoken environmentalist, even though his company had become a lightning rod for green anger. Ford's office was decorated with hemp wall covering and undyed cotton curtains woven on a solar-powered loom.

As a poor, dark-skinned immigrant boy in rough-and-tumble Australia, Nasser had grown up battling bullies and scrounging for cash. As an adult, he worked like a man possessed to distance himself from that past, surrounding himself with the trappings of power and wealth. He preferred to travel in limousines, worked seven days a week in an office decorated with polished steel and black leather, and even had his desk placed on a raised dais to compensate for his short stature. After earning a degree in international business from the Royal Melbourne Institute of Technology, Nasser had joined Ford of Australia as an analyst in 1968. Over the next thirty years, he bounced around the world and made his way up Ford's corporate ladder, ultimately becoming head of all automotive operations in 1996. During his ascent, Nasser developed a reputation as an aggressive cost-cutter, earning the sobriquet "Jac the Knife." The board saw him as a fiscal disciplinarian who could make hard decisions without flinching, the perfect counterweight to Bill Ford's youthful idealism.

It all seemed perfectly logical, except for two problems. First, neither man really wanted to share power with anyone. Second, once Nasser became CEO, his fiscal discipline seemed to vanish overnight. Eager to inscribe his name alongside the greats of American capitalism, Nasser succumbed to the irrational exuberance that was spreading like a pandemic through the business world in the go-go days of 1999. He saw what was going on in places like Silicon Valley and wanted a piece of it. He idolized General Electric's Jack Welch, who had become the darling of Wall Street by shifting GE's focus from microwave ovens to financial services, and figured he could do something similar with Ford.

Soon after being promoted to CEO, Nasser received an internal analysis that showed the majority of Ford's profits came from a few truck and SUV plants in the United States. That terrified him, particularly since the Japanese had finally figured out how much money there was to be made in those segments and were getting ready to introduce some gas-guzzlers of their own. But rather than figure out how to diversify Ford's product lineup, he decided to diversify Ford.

Nasser broke open the piggy bank Ford had filled over the past decade and went on a shopping spree. He bought a chain of car repair shops in Britain and a junkyard company in Florida. He invested in dot-coms and inked deals with Microsoft, Hewlett-Packard, and Yahoo! At the same time, he began unwinding Ford's core automotive business. Nasser had the Blue Oval removed from World Headquarters and began replacing seasoned executives with young guns from other industries. He spun off Ford's parts subsidiary, which he renamed Visteon Corporation, and seriously considered getting out of the U.S. car business entirely so that Ford could focus exclusively on the more profitable truck and SUV segments. The only part of the automobile business he thought had potential was the luxury segment. Ford already owned two of the most celebrated brands in the world, Aston Martin and Jaguar. Nasser decided to purchase Land Rover and Volvo, too. He added Ford's own luxury marque, Lincoln, to the mix and created an international house of brands he called the Premier Automotive Group. He even set up a new headquarters for the division in California to put as much distance between it and Detroit as possible.

As Nasser tried to pull the company into the new economy, Bill Ford was pulling it out of the Global Climate Coalition, an industry organization dedicated to lobbying against green initiatives and debunking global warming. Environmentalists applauded the move. Ford was just getting started. In May 2000, he published the company's first "Corporate Citizenship Report," which featured frank assessments of controversial issues like the impact of tailpipe emissions on the climate and the dangers posed to smaller cars by the automaker's big SUVs. Greenpeace invited Bill Ford to deliver the keynote at a green business conference in London. *Car and Driver* editor Brock Yates dismissed the young chairman as "a guilt-ridden rich kid, not a proud tycoon like those who preceded him."

But Nasser had the whole tycoon thing covered. He created a new cult of personality around himself, traveling with a large entourage and constantly upstaging lesser executives at public events. He made sweeping proclamations, ordering all cars to be equipped with analog clocks to give them a touch of class and even changing the hue of blue on the Ford badge on a whim. Nasser once called a meeting of his senior leadership team to outline a new marketing plan. When some of his subordinates began to poke holes in it, he raised his hand to silence the debate.

"This is our new marketing strategy," he said sharply. "If you don't agree with it, I've got somebody from HR who will work out your retirement."

Morale suffered as employees struggled to keep up with the dizzying pace of change at Nasser's Ford and cope with his abrasive personality. It got even worse when he introduced new performance evaluations that assigned letter grades to salaried employees based on a complex set of criteria that gave little weight to experience and favored younger workers. Ford was soon defending itself against a raft of age discrimination lawsuits. Worse, it began to lose the veteran employees who had always been the backbone of the company. These were the men and women whose skills and institutional memory allowed the automaker to bounce back every time it lost its way. They remembered how Ford dealt with past adversities and knew it could again. Now, thanks to Nasser, they were fleeing in droves.

Nasser also alienated Ford's dealers. He came up with a plan to consolidate dealerships in major metropolitan areas into company-controlled superstores. In exchange for giving up their franchises, these dealers would become part owners of these new retail operations. Most felt like Ford was trying force them out of business so it could claim their profits for itself. Some wrote open letters to the company, decrying Nasser's strategy and vowing to fight in the courts if necessary.

Ford began to lose sight of the fundamentals. Quality began to suffer. Corners were cut. Launch dates were missed. Vehicle designs began to slip. However, as long as the company was making record profits, few were willing to challenge the pugnacious Nasser.

But it had all become too much for Bill Ford.

Like most members of the Ford family, he had intense pride in the company that bore his name. The Fords were keenly aware that theirs was the last great industrial dynasty in the United States. They were the custodians of Old Henry's vision. Like him, they had genuine concern for the people who depended on the company for their livelihoods. A month after Bill Ford took over as chairman, a massive explosion ripped through the powerhouse at the Rouge, killing seven workers and injuring many more. Ford rushed to the scene before the fires were even out, followed the wounded to area hospitals, and spent hours consoling grieving family members. He spent the next several days attending the funerals. This was what made Ford different from all the other automakers. It was why many workers still said they worked at Ford's, not Ford.

The idea of Ford employees suing the company hurt Bill Ford deeply. So did the angry letters he was getting from dealers, many of whom he knew personally. He feared that the rapid-fire changes Nasser was making were beginning to do real damage—not only to the company, but to the Ford name as well. He decided to do something to stop it before it was too late.

* * *

In 2000, Irv Hockaday was nearing the end of his distinguished career as the president and CEO of another family-owned company, Hallmark Cards. The bespectacled, white-haired executive with a thick midwestern accent was elected to the automaker's board in 1987 and had been mentoring Bill Ford ever since he joined a year later. Now he listened quietly as his young protégé outlined his concerns about Nasser. Hockaday agreed that the flamboyant CEO was moving faster than many of the directors would have liked, but Hockaday had rarely worried about how the company was being run under the buttoned-down leadership of men like Petersen and Trotman. He was not sure he should begin to now.

"Well, Bill, you know Jac has a world of experience. He's an aggressive guy. He's kind of thinking out of the box," Hockaday said after hearing Ford out. "Relative to his level of experience, you're still kind of wet behind the ears. I wouldn't make a big deal out of it now."

He suggested that they watch and wait. Reluctantly, Ford agreed.

Then the wheels came off. Literally.

In early 2000, the National Highway Traffic Safety Administration began investigating reports of fatal accidents involving Ford Explorers equipped with Firestone tires. The tires were prone to suffering catastrophic failures when driven at high speed in hot weather, causing the vehicle to roll over. That was Ford's take at least. Japan's Bridgestone, which had purchased Firestone in 1988, claimed Ford's SUV was the real culprit. Consumer advocates blamed both companies and also accused them of covering up the problem.

The U.S. government ordered Firestone to recall 6.5 million tires. In an effort to restore consumer confidence, Ford decided to recall 13 million more at a cost of $2.1 billion. As the number of deaths blamed on the problem climbed past 140, both companies became the targets of major class-action lawsuits. They severed their century-long relationship, at least in the United States, and began tearing each other apart in court. All of this litigation would ultimately cost Ford hundreds of millions of dollars. But it would do far greater damage to its brand image.

Meanwhile, America was entering another recession. Ford's sales dropped dramatically—partly as a result of the economy, partly because consumers were starting to notice that its products were slipping. Earnings were down by more than 50 percent at the end of 2000, and 2001 was looking much, much worse. As recalls and litigation ate up what was left of Ford's cash cushion, Nasser's spending began to look downright reckless. Even the Ford Motor Credit Company—long a reliable source of revenue for the parent company—had started to drift. In 1999, Nasser hired a hotshot banker, Don Winkler, to lead the finance company. Winkler thought the business of providing car and truck loans to creditworthy consumers was boring and vowed to turn Ford Credit into "a global auto-finance superpower." Underwriting got fast and loose, and the number of bad loans on the company's books began to increase at an alarming rate.

Bill Ford was no longer the only board member who was worried. When he called Hockaday again, the Hallmark chief agreed the time had come for Ford to share his concerns with the rest of the board. But Hockaday wanted to make sure the young chairman was ready.

He offered to round up a couple of other sympathetic directors for a dress rehearsal.

"Don't take me up on this offer unless you really have your facts straight," Hockaday advised Ford. "Because if you come in with a sort of half-baked emotional presentation, you're going to do yourself more harm than good."

"Fair enough," Ford said.

But he was worried someone might learn of the meeting. Ford had reason to be paranoid. At least one of Nasser's predecessors had tapped Ford's telephone and bugged his car to make sure he was not plotting a coup. Hockaday offered to host the meeting at Hallmark's headquarters in Kansas City, Missouri. He even sent the Hallmark jet for Bill so the trip would not appear on the logbook of any Ford aircraft.

When Ford arrived, he found Carl Reichardt and Robert Rubin waiting for him. Reichardt was the retired head of Wells Fargo; Rubin had been Bill Clinton's Treasury secretary. Both were directors Hockaday trusted—not only to keep quiet, but also to give an honest assessment of Ford's presentation.

All three were stunned by what Bill Ford shared with them. He outlined all of the ways in which Nasser was damaging the company's core business and offered plenty of facts and figures to support his claims. The other directors were deeply impressed that Ford had been able to collect so much data, especially since Nasser had refused to turn over key reports and other documents he had requested. They promised to put the matter on the agenda for the next board meeting.

In July 2001, Ford made his case to the full board in Dearborn. After hearing him out, the other directors asked Ford to leave and called in Nasser.

"You've got an issue here," the board told him. "There are concerns that Bill has and has expressed to some of us, and we think that they are legitimate. We recognize that you're the CEO, but these are concerns you shouldn't ignore."

Nasser remained stoic and offered no defense. The directors called Ford back into the boardroom and addressed both men together.

"You guys need to get your act together, because if you don't, then the board's going to have to step in and resolve the issue," the directors warned them. "It would be better if you could work together to define your roles in a complementary way and leverage your strengths. You better give that a real hard try."

The board granted Bill Ford more authority over the day-to-day running of the business, but Nasser refused to take his concerns seriously. The automaker's finances continued to deteriorate, as did morale. The terrorist attacks of September 11, 2001, delivered a devastating blow to the U.S. economy in general and American automakers in particular. The decline in new vehicle sales that followed made Ford's problems that much worse. The dealers were getting angrier by the month. The board agreed that Nasser had to go. The only question now was who would replace him.

In early October, the heirs of Henry Ford gathered to discuss the future of the company. Bill Ford stood before them and delivered a blunt assessment of the situation. Their company was in trouble. Nasser was destroying everything they and their ancestors had built. Bill told them he had looked up and down Ford's roster and could see no suitable replacement. For two decades, they had let others run their company. Now it was time for a Ford to run Ford again. Bill Ford intended to fire Nasser and replace him as CEO. He asked for their support.

He got it.

By the time Ford's board met two weeks later, the directors had received many phone calls from family members making their feelings clear. Now Bill Ford delivered his own pitch in person. The only way to restore trust in the company was to put a Ford back in the driver's seat. He knew being CEO would require a huge commitment on his part, but Ford assured the directors he was willing to do whatever it took to save the company. The directors were moved by Ford's passionate plea, but many still had doubts about his abilities. It was one thing to run down to the Rouge after an explosion. Managing the day-to-day operations of a multinational corporation was another thing entirely. But they figured he had earned the right to try.

"We were all a bit hesitant," one director confided. "But we all wanted him to succeed."

CHAPTER 2

Broken

The internal ailments of business are the ones that require most attention.

— HENRY FORD

Cheers broke out in Dearborn as word spread that Bill Ford had ousted Jacques Nasser and was taking over Ford Motor Company. Employees actually wept in the parking lot when the Blue Oval was hoisted back up to the top of World Headquarters as a final symbol of Nasser's undoing. Letters of thanks poured in from dealers around the country, and parts manufacturers breathed a deep sigh of relief. Bill Ford had been right. The only thing that could save the company and mend its tattered relationships with workers, dealers, and suppliers was putting a Ford back in the driver's seat.

But not everyone was celebrating. Wall Street had long viewed the Ford family's control of the automaker as an anachronism that prevented shareholders from realizing the true value of their investment, and analysts openly doubted Bill Ford's ability to lead. The $5.45 billion loss Ford reported for 2001 did not help. Nasser and the September 11 terrorists were responsible for most of that, but it marked the end of nine years of steady profits and fueled fresh concern about Ford's future. The company's credit rating was downgraded and its stock tumbled.

Bill Ford did what Ford CEOs had always done when confronted with financial calamity. He cut and cut deep. In January 2002, he announced that the automaker would close five factories in North America and eliminate more than 21,000 jobs. Ford may have been a man of the people, but he had also promised to do whatever was necessary to save his company. That included reducing dividend payments, a move some in the family complained about. At the same time, Ford went after the trappings of executive excess that had come to symbolize Nasser's regime. He fired high-priced consultants, told executives to cut back on conspicuous consumption, and replaced the filet mignon and salmon normally served at lunch meetings with sandwiches. He even got rid of some of the company's jets. More important, he refocused Ford on its core business of building and selling cars and trucks. With the battle cry "Back to Basics," he began extricating Ford from the other ventures that his predecessor had found so much more compelling than manufacturing automobiles. Bill Ford increased product spending, which Nasser had cut to fund his acquisition binge. He ordered a new push to improve quality. And he told veteran engineers that their experience was still valued in Dearborn. He got rid of the bankers who were running Ford Credit into the ground and replaced them with men who understood that its primary function was to support sales. He went to Wall Street and raised $4.5 billion, starred in the company's television ads, and even tried to take on the automaker's notoriously noxious culture.

For years, Ford had hidden its lack of product investment behind cute catchphrases like "cheap and cheerful"—Dearbornese for a barebones compact; "fast follower"—code for a car that was essentially a knockoff of what Ford's competitors already had in their showrooms; and "last in, best dressed"—a rather lame excuse for being the final automaker to enter a particular segment. They were the doublespeak of a company that had learned to justify its own inadequacies, and Ford ordered them banished from the corporate lexicon.

"How do we get back to product leadership?" he asked his designers and engineers. "As long as those phrases are being bandied about, we never will."

He knew Ford could do better. In Europe, it already was. Ford's products were well regarded on the other side of the Atlantic and the company was even making money off them, which was more than Ford could say about most of its North American cars. Sport utility vehicles and pickups were still profitable, but everything else was at best breaking even.

"We have relied far too long on a few home runs," Ford told his team. "We need to hit a bunch of singles, not swing for the fences. We have to make each vehicle profitable."

By the end of 2002, Ford was back in the black.* Warranty costs were down. Ford had climbed two slots in the influential J.D. Powers and Associates initial quality survey and was no longer dead last among the world's major automobile manufacturers. But no one was convinced that Ford had actually turned the corner. The company's stock dropped below $10 a share for the first time in ten years that fall, and Ford's credit rating continued to slide. Bill Ford began to feel like the Rodney Dangerfield of the automobile industry. No matter what he did, he could not seem to get any respect.

✳   ✳   ✳

However, the skeptics were right to be wary. The company may have been making money again, but Bill Ford was struggling.

After sanctioning his coup d'état in October 2001, the board of directors had hoped that—with a little coaching—Ford would rise to the occasion and become a truly effective chief executive. To make sure that he did, the board asked director Carl Reichardt to mentor the forty-four-year-old. Even at seventy, the former head of Wells Fargo was one of the sharpest financial minds in America. He was a titan of the banking industry from the days when it could still be mentioned in polite company, a man Warren Buffett had called one of the best managers in the business. Reichardt was comfortably ensconced on a sprawling ranch in California and planned to retire from the board in six months, but he agreed to come to Michigan and serve as Ford's vice chairman. He would get the company's finances in order, fix Ford Credit, and try to teach young Bill how to run the company.

Assembling the rest of the team proved a challenge—and an urgent one, considering that many of Nasser's top executives had followed him out the door, either on their own or with Bill's boot close behind. What was left of Ford's bench was pretty weak. There was still plenty of talent inside the company, but much of it was buried

---

* Ford earned $284 million from continuing operations, though it lost $980 million when the costs of restructuring and discontinued business were factored in.

beneath a thick layer of executives who were more adept at advancing their own careers than running a car company. They tended to view their high positions as rewards for long service and worried more about enjoying their perks than about the problems facing Ford.

Bill Ford did the best he could. He found an able enough president and chief operating officer in Sir Nick Scheele, a likable Brit who had managed to do what many thought was impossible—make Jaguar profitable, at least for a while. Queen Elizabeth II knighted him for his effort to save the beloved British brand. As head of Ford of Europe, Scheele commenced a promising restructuring and put together a product team that was actually creating some world-class cars. His work on the other side of the Atlantic was far from complete, but none of it would matter if Ford's North American business continued to decline. Ford put an unlikable Brit, David Thursfield, in charge of the company's international operations. The iron-fisted cigar chomper was known for his cutting comments, but he also knew how to cut costs. Ford gave North America to Jim Padilla, an amiable Detroit native who was obsessed with quality. Padilla had a mind for manufacturing but quickly found himself out of his depth when he strayed too far into other aspects of the business.

It was not the strongest team, and Ford knew it. Thursfield and Padilla were soon locked in mortal combat, each convinced that the other was elbowing in on his turf. When one walked into a room, the other left. Soon, lower-level executives were choosing sides and conspiring to undermine the other's efforts. European cars were tweaked so that they could not meet U.S. safety requirements without expensive engineering changes, and cutting-edge technology developed in America was kept from the team in Europe. Scheele at least remained a trustworthy adviser and could be extremely effective when he was focused. Unfortunately, that was not always the case.

Ford got more help a few months later, in May 2002, when Allan Gilmour agreed to come out of retirement and replace Nasser's chief financial officer. Gilmour had already put in thirty-four years at the company, and Bill had worked for him before he retired as vice chairman in 1995. Convincing Gilmour to come back was not easy. After his retirement, he had come out of the closet—a move that proved particularly shocking in an industry that still considered machismo a job qualification. But Gilmour hoped to help his former protégé figure out how to run the company. The board hoped that he, along with Reichardt, would teach Bill how to do it on his own. Both men admired Ford's vision. They wanted to help him realize it. When big decisions were required, they walked him through the various options but tried to leave the final choice to him. But Bill Ford preferred to defer to their experience.

When Ford did make decisions, he had a tough time getting his subordinates to implement them. They would agree with whatever he suggested, then do whatever they wanted. If Ford pressed them, they offered complicated excuses that he lacked the data to refute. But he rarely challenged them. Ford preferred to avoid confrontation. He had promised the board that he would do whatever was required to turn the company around, but after a year as CEO, the burden of leadership was weighing on him. Ford was still interested in the big picture, but he had tired of the details of managing the company's day-to-day operations.

"I can't say I'm having fun yet," he acknowledged in an October interview with *BusinessWeek*.

*   *   *

Bill Ford knew he needed help, and he knew he was not going to find it inside the company. He asked his director of human resources, Joe Laymon, to start looking outside the company.

Joe Laymon was not a typical HR director. He did not spend a lot of time thinking about new ways to track mileage expenses or morale-building exercises. Laymon was an African American, and his father was a migrant farmworker, moonshiner, and civil rights activist from Mississippi. Laymon had picked his share of cotton before earning a master's in economics from the University of Wisconsin in Madison. He went to work for the United States Agency for International Development in Zaire, then took senior positions at Xerox and Eastman Kodak before arriving at Ford in 2000. There he soon became one of Bill Ford's most trusted advisers—and his feared enforcer. Laymon was something of a latter-day Harry Bennett who, like his legendary predecessor, also ran Ford's internal security force. Unlike the brash Bennett, Laymon was a soft-spoken man whose friendly demeanor masked a calculating ruthlessness that other executives roused at their own peril.

"Joe Laymon is a master of the dark arts," one told me. "He knows where all the bodies are buried because he put most of them in the ground himself."

Laymon was also a master strategist who knew what motivated people and how to use that knowledge to his advantage. And he was fiercely loyal to Bill Ford.

In 2003, the two men began putting together a list of possible candidates to lead the top-to-bottom restructuring that Ford now needed to save his company. Their first choice was easy. If the automobile industry had ever bred a rock star, it was Carlos Ghosn. His father was Lebanese like Nasser, but his mother was French and he had been born in Brazil. He joined Nissan Motor Company as chief operating officer in 1999 after France's Renault SA bought a controlling stake in the Japanese automaker, which was then deeply in debt and losing money. Ghosn promised to resign if he could not turn it around. A year later, Nissan was profitable again and Ghosn was promoted to president. He became CEO a year after that, and Nissan became one of the most profitable car companies in the world.

But Ford was still bigger, and Laymon hoped to use that as bait for the ambitious executive. Bill Ford told Laymon to offer Ghosn the position of COO with the promise that he would be promoted to CEO or become a very rich man if he was not. Laymon told his boss that Ghosn would never accept anything less than the top job, but agreed to try.

A few months later, Laymon stood on the sidewalk in front of a trendy Tokyo restaurant wondering why Ghosn had insisted on meeting him outside. That became clear a few minutes later when he noticed a rare commotion down the street. A huge crowd was swarming around an unseen figure, thrusting pens and pieces of paper at the celebrity in the hope of getting an autograph. It was Carlos Ghosn.

I don't know if we have a suite big enough for this guy, Laymon thought as the superstar CEO broke free from the crowd to shake his hand.

It had taken Laymon three trips to Japan to get Ghosn to this restaurant. In the middle of dinner, he reached into his pocket, pulled out an envelope, and slid Ford's offer across the table. Ghosn took a quick glance at it, shook his head, and handed it back to Laymon. He was not interested in working for Bill Ford. He would come to Dearborn. He would save Ford Motor Company. But he wanted to be CEO from the start—and chairman.

"I can't do that," said a stunned Laymon.

Ghosn smiled. "Just tell Bill that I'm his man—provided I'm CEO *and* chairman," he insisted.

Laymon excused himself and went out to call Bill Ford.

"Good news, bad news," Laymon told his boss. "The good news is we got him. The bad news is he wants your job."

Ford told Laymon to get on the plane and come home.

＊　＊　＊

Dieter Zetsche may not have been a rock star, but by the spring of 2003, the mustachioed German was being heralded as a Teutonic Lee Iacocca. In 1998, Daimler-Benz had acquired Chrysler through what the Germans insisted was a "merger of equals." Things did not go well once the Americans recognized the takeover for what it was. In 2000, Zetsche was sent in to save the day and restored Chrysler to profitability after years of losses. Now Chrysler was regarded by many as the strongest of the Detroit Three and was making enough money to offset the growing losses back in Germany.

Laymon's daughter went to school with Zetsche's at the prestigious Country Day prep school north of Detroit. Through that connection, he learned that Zetsche and his family liked living in the United States. He also learned that there was growing discord between the Chrysler chief and DaimlerChrysler's CEO, Jürgen Schrempp. After a couple of meetings at Chrysler's headquarters in nearby Auburn Hills, Laymon persuaded Zetsche to come to Dearborn and meet Bill Ford.

Ford offered Zetsche the COO job, too. He also turned it down. News of the meeting was soon leaked by one of Zetsche's operatives, but with the added twist that Bill Ford had actually offered the German the CEO's position. It turned out that the wily Zetsche had no interest in either job; he was playing Ford to strengthen his hand back in Germany. A few years later, Schrempp was out and Zetsche had his job.

A year after Zetsche turned Ford down, another of the German automaker's top talents was in Laymon's crosshairs. Wolfgang Bernhard was Zetsche's COO at Chrysler. He was only forty-three but was credited with spearheading the cost-cutting effort in Auburn Hills and improving Chrysler's products. Laymon was still trying to convince his boss that he was the right man for Ford when DaimlerChrysler announced that Bernhard would take over its Mercedes-Benz division at the end of April 2004. Laymon shrugged and began looking for the next candidate. But Bernhard was fired a day before he was due to start his new job, the victim of an internal power struggle in Stuttgart. Laymon caught the next flight to Germany, hoping to catch Bernhard on the rebound. He offered Bernhard a similar deal to Ghosn's, albeit less lucrative. The young German was interested and came to Dearborn to meet with Bill Ford. The two men seemed to hit it off, but Bernhard changed his mind when he got back to Germany and found an emissary from Volkswagen AG waiting for him. A few months later, the German automaker announced that Bernhard was joining its managing board and would become chairman of the VW division.

❋   ❋   ❋

As Laymon's list of names got shorter, the litany of Ford's problems grew longer. Ford's U.S. sales fell in 2002, 2003, and 2004. Its market share continued to decline. An incentive war started by General Motors after the September 11, 2001, terrorist attacks undercut both automakers' margins and destroyed the residual values of their vehicles. The company remained profitable, but only because of the revenue generated by Ford Credit.

Reichardt retired for good in 2003, admonishing Bill Ford to do everything in his power to conserve cash and warning that the economy would not keep growing forever. Ford knew Gilmour would not last much longer, either. Scheele decided to hang it up, too, though Bill Ford felt that loss less acutely. Meanwhile Ford's other top executives continued their turf war. Bill knew that one of them had to go before they tore the company apart. Thursfield was more talented, but also more divisive and a lot harder to control. Padilla was already proving the Peter Principle, but at least he could work well with others. Ford announced Padilla's promotion and Thursfield's resignation in April 2004. Gilmour announced his retirement that December. He had already turned the CFO's position over to Donat "Don" Leclair, a dour financial savant who he was satisfied knew at least much as he did about the company's finances. Leclair could be abrasive, though, so Ford hired a leadership coach to work with him. When Gilmour left in February 2005, Bill Ford promoted Padilla again—this time to president—and hoped for the best.

All he got was the same old excuses. When Ford found out that Europe was getting a new version of the Focus compact, he asked why North America was sticking with the old version.

"It's out of sync with our product segmentation," Padilla told him.

What the heck does that mean? Ford thought, suspecting that he was being snowed once again.

"Okay," he said. "Then why can't we converge the two products?"

"The product cycles don't line up," Padilla told him. "They're at different phases. We'll have to wait until the next redesign."

But Ford knew they would still be out of sync then.

This is all a bunch of bullshit, he fumed as he left the meeting. *Nobody will give me a straight answer.*

* * *

Unable to effect the sweeping changes he knew were necessary, Bill Ford resorted to grand gestures that he hoped would somehow jolt the company out of its stupor. Most of these spoke to his own environmentalist leanings and his desire to transform Ford from the poster child of the SUV era to a leader in sustainable technologies.

In 2003, as part of the company's centennial celebration, he unveiled a green makeover of the River Rouge plant, which had long been a symbol of Ford's manufacturing might. Energy consumption was reduced and the world's largest living roof was installed over the enormous factory. A year later, Ford became the first American automaker to bring a hybrid to market and the first company in the world to introduce a hybrid SUV. The Escape Hybrid was a labor of love for Bill Ford. He pushed the project through despite persistent resistance from executives worried that it would be a money loser. They were right, but the same could be said of most of Ford's other products at the time. At least this one would score some points for the company on the public relations front.*

Some progress was being made. Ford's engines were improving, and a new six-speed transmission that it developed with General Motors helped both companies catch up with their foreign competitors — at least in the powertrain race. Ford also began working more closely with Japan's Mazda Motor Corporation. The Dearborn automaker had been a major investor in Mazda since the 1960s and had taken a controlling stake in its Hiroshima-based partner during the Asian economic crisis of the late 1990s. At Scheele's insistence, Ford began leveraging that relationship to gain access to Mazda's superior vehicle platforms. Ford did the same thing with its Swedish subsidiary, Volvo. Soon most of the cars and crossovers sold by Ford in the United States would be based on platforms developed by these two companies. It was a smart move that yielded a significant improvement in the quality and performance of Ford's products, though it did not say much for the automaker's own capabilities.

After Ford's credit rating was downgraded to junk bond status in May 2005, Bill Ford announced that he would forgo all compensation until the company returned to sustainable profitability. He had not taken a salary since taking over as CEO in 2001, but his stock options and other annual compensation were still valued at around $22 million. Now he would give that up as well.

Four months later, in September, Ford stood in the airy atrium of the automaker's most advanced research laboratory and delivered a heartfelt appeal to the company's scientists and engineers, asking them to revive the spirit of innovation that had once been synonymous with Ford.

"We will continue to cut our costs and improve our efficiency, but

---

* Toyota's celebrated Prius was also a money loser from the time it was introduced, in 1997, until the end of 2001.

we cannot win the hearts and the minds of a new generation with efficiency alone," he said. "I need your help more than ever. I need you to question. I need you to challenge. I need you to stop unnecessary processes. I need you to declare that innovation is going to be a necessary ingredient in everything we do."

Ford promised that, by 2010, half of all Ford, Lincoln, and Mercury models would be available with hybrid powertrains. In fact, he said the company would produce a quarter of a million of them a year. It was an absurd goal that Ford would not even come close to reaching.* A month later, the head of Ford's hybrid program resigned in protest.

None of these initiatives did anything to address the fact that Ford's basic business model no longer worked, at least not in North America. The same was true of General Motors and Chrysler, too, and the fact that they all continued to refer to themselves collectively as the Big Three proved that none of them got the joke. There was a lingering sense in Detroit that someday soon the world would wake up and realize that low-quality gas-guzzlers really were the way to go after all, so it was best to keep their options—and factories—open. No one suffered from this delusion more than the United Auto Workers. The union's leadership had spent the last three decades doing everything possible to prevent Ford and other Detroit manufacturers from downsizing their businesses and making their plants more efficient.

By 2005, Ford's North American factories were running at only 79 percent of capacity. The company was actually losing an average of $590 on every vehicle it produced in the region, while Toyota and Honda Motor Company both earned more than $1,200. A big part of the problem was productivity. Fewer than thirty hours of labor went into assembling the average Toyota in North America, while it took nearly thirty-six hours to put together the typical Ford. Yet instead of getting rid of factories, Ford was actually adding more. Five years after Nasser spun off Visteon, Ford's former parts subsidiary was on the verge of collapse and threatening to take the automaker down with

---

* In 2010, Ford actually offered only five hybrid models and sold fewer than 36,000 of them combined.

it. Ford relied heavily on parts from Visteon, and Visteon's U.S. plants were still staffed by Ford workers because the UAW had refused to allow the company to break its contract with them. If Visteon failed, Ford would have to take them all back. It also would be left without a supplier for critical components. To avoid both these nightmares, CFO Don Leclair orchestrated a multibillion-dollar bailout of Visteon in May 2005 that kept both companies limping along. The deal required Ford to take back twenty-four Visteon factories in the United States and Mexico, but it was better than letting them be liquidated.*

The relief that permeated the company in the days following Nasser's ouster was gone, replaced by the sober realization that Ford's problems were bigger than one man. For most employees, the sense of hope sparked by Bill Ford's decision to assume command gave way to a weary fatalism. They updated their résumés and waited for the next round of layoffs. A few continued to rail against the mistakes they saw taking place all around them, but Ford seemed impervious to change. More than one of these frustrated reformers took their case to the press, hoping that exposing Ford's flaws would shame senior management into fixing them. The company leaked like a sieve as sensitive documents were smuggled out as proof. Most of these ended up at the *Detroit News*. Bill Ford's security force tried to plug the leaks by installing software on the company's e-mail network that flagged any message sent to the newspaper. Suspecting that senior executives were the source of some of these leaks, the corporate spooks monitored their cellphone calls and even installed cameras in rooms housing top-secret documents to see who accessed them and when.

Bill Ford knew his company had reached a critical point in its history. If it could not address its fundamental problems, it would not survive. He had tried to find someone to help him lead a global restructuring, but all of his overtures had been rebuffed and none of his

---

* Ford was criticized for the expensive move at the time, but it probably helped save the company. General Motors tried to leave its former parts subsidiary, Delphi Corporation, to its own devices and was still grappling with the fallout years later.

own executives was up to the challenge. Ford decided to narrow his focus and concentrate on fixing the North American automobile business because, if that continued to decline, nothing else would matter anyway. Everything else could wait.

"Our commitment must begin here in the United States," Ford declared in that September speech. "While we're a global company, our greatest challenges and the need for dramatic change are right here—North America."

* * *

As Ford delivered that speech, he was in the process of putting together a team to take on that task. Instead of relying on his top executives, he gathered together less senior managers from around the world who had demonstrated real potential. To lead them, he turned to the company's brightest rising star, Mark Fields.

Fields was a handsome young executive with a wavy mullet and movie-star smile who exuded self-confidence. He was born in Brooklyn, grew up in New Jersey, and still had a bit of its air about him that a Rutgers economics degree and a Harvard MBA could not entirely dispel. Hired by Ford in 1989 after a stint at IBM, he started out in marketing and rose rapidly through the ranks thanks to a quick mind and an evident mastery of management science. Many who encountered Fields thought he was arrogant, but his belief in his own abilities was well founded. After extricating Ford's Argentine subsidiary from a failed marriage with Volkswagen, he was transferred to Japan in 1999 and put in charge of Mazda. He was only thirty-eight, the youngest person ever to lead a Japanese car company.

While Ghosn was making headlines as the savior of Nissan, Fields was working the same magic in Hiroshima, albeit without the media attention. Mazda had no clear idea of what it wanted to be. It had gotten into trouble by trying to match the bigger Japanese automakers with a full family of plain-vanilla models for the masses. But the world did not need another boring four-door sedan. Fields convinced the company to return to its roots and make sporty cars with edgy designs for people who were passionate about driving. The results were a new generation of vehicles that were widely regarded as some of the best in the world and a new tagline, "Zoom-Zoom," that was one of the catchiest in the industry. Mazda stood for something again, and it was soon back in the black. It was a stunning performance, and the lack of notice would have been far less chafing if another gaijin had not been making girls swoon in the streets of Tokyo. It would take Fields a long time to get over that. He was soon reassigned to London, where he was put in charge of Nasser's Premier Automotive Group. In 2004, he became head of Ford of Europe, too.

In each of these postings, Fields made the brands stronger and the budgets leaner. After he arrived in Argentina, he was invited to the company's annual polo tournament. He spent a pleasant afternoon sipping champagne with the Buenos Aires elite, then told his new employees that he hoped they had enjoyed the event, because it was the last one. At Mazda, he had axed 20 percent of the company's workforce—this in a nation where lifetime employment was still the norm. When he took over the Premier Automotive Group, he closed its posh headquarters on London's tony Berkeley Square and moved himself and the rest of the employees to a Ford design facility in Soho.

Bill Ford and the other directors had been following Fields' career closely. They thought his tough-love approach was just the sort of thing the company needed in North America. However, while he was being groomed for the post of president of the Americas—maybe even CEO one day—they were not sure he was ready to take on the company's most dysfunctional division. But they were certain no one else was. So, in late August, Ford picked up his telephone and called Fields in London.

"I really need you here to run the Americas," he said. "This place needs leadership, and you're the guy I'd like to lead it. I need you to help me sort things out."

Fields realized it was a huge opportunity, but he was not sure he wanted to take it. He knew how poisonous the culture inside World Headquarters could be, and he had a pretty good idea just how dire the situation in Dearborn had become. He asked to sleep on it. That night, Fields mulled his situation over a bottle of beer. He was not surprised that Ford was looking for someone else to run the region. Over the past six months, it had become obvious that North America was a rudderless ship with no real plan for the future. He knew the infighting at the top of the house was occupying more time than the problems on the ground. Fields had been insulated from most of this because he was overseas, and he did not relish the idea of being thrown into the thick of it. He thought he could fix North America, but he was not sure the other executives would let him. The next day, he called Ford back and said he was ready to accept the job, provided his boss would promise to protect him.

"Let me build my team, and just keep corporate out of my hair," he told Ford. "Everybody's got to know who's accountable for delivering the Americas, and that's got to be me and my team—not everybody else sticking their fingers into the pot. I've seen that. I've seen what it's done. There's no plan there. There's no accountability."

"Fine," Ford said. "You've got my approval."

He gave Fields a month to wrap things up in Europe and told him to be in Dearborn by October. Then Ford sold Hertz to help finance the big changes he hoped were coming. Ford had acquired the car rental agency back in 1994. The automaker sold it for $5.6 billion, though the deal was actually worth closer to $15 billion once Hertz's debt was factored into the equation.

Fields knew a lot about building brands, but less about building cars. To compensate, Ford paired him with Anne Stevens, a tough-talking manufacturing expert with red hair and an imposing stare. She was lifelong gearhead, an engineer by training who dressed as a boy to sneak into the pits at the local racetrack when she was thirteen. As a married mother of two, Stevens had to fight for every rung of the corporate ladder. She came to Ford from Exxon in 1990 and became the automaker's first female plant manager in Europe in 1995 and its first female vice president of vehicle operations in 2001. With her promotion to chief operating officer of the Americas group, she became one of the most powerful women in the automotive industry.

At fifty-six, she was more than ten years older than Fields and made no secret of the fact that she wanted his job. The two clashed from the start. At an early off-site briefing for senior managers, Stevens made a passionate plea to stop the backsliding on quality.

"We're *never* going to get our customers back if we can't improve quality," she said. "It's the only way we can change the way people look at Ford."

When she finished listing all the ways Ford was failing on this front, Fields raised his hand with a smirk.

"My name is Mark Fields and I have a quality problem," he chuckled.

Stevens glared at him. This was serious stuff, and she thought he was belittling it—and her. But the two managed to restrain their mutual animosity enough to begin work on a plan to salvage Ford's North American car and truck business. Fields promised Bill Ford it would be on his desk in ninety days. With a cross-functional group of fifty managers, he and Stevens began a detailed analysis of Ford's North American automobile business, compared it to the company's far more successful operations in other parts of the world, and tried to figure out what they needed to do differently to stop the long decline in Ford's home market. Key elements of the plan were lifted from the recent turnaround of Ford's Brazilian subsidiary. Others were inspired by the progress Ford was making in Europe.

On November 14, a company holiday, Fields and the senior members of his team came into the office and spent ten hours fine-tuning the details, agreeing on targets and gut-checking one another's assumptions. When they were satisfied they had gotten it right, they began writing it up for the board of directors. Fields called it "The Way Forward," borrowing the Churchillian phrase from a documentary he had watched on the BBC before leaving London. The Ford plan called for idling fourteen factories in North America, including seven assembly plants, by 2012. Closing them would require UAW approval, so that would have to wait until the next round of contract talks. Between 25,000 and 30,000 factory jobs would also be eliminated. Fields hoped to take out about half of these through attrition, the rest through voluntary buyouts that would also have to be negotiated with the union. In addition, Ford would cut another 4,000 salaried positions and reduce the number of corporate officers by 12 percent. Fields set a goal of shedding $6 billion in material costs by 2010 and aimed to reduce Ford's North American manufacturing capacity by 26 percent over the next three years.

But as Bill Ford had said in September, the company could not cut its way back to success. It also needed to reconnect with consumers. Using the same approach to demographic research employed by political operatives in election campaigns, Fields' marketing task force figured out who was most likely to buy Ford's products, who was least likely, and who was still willing to be convinced. That research revealed that most American consumers wanted to buy an American car or truck—far more, in fact, than the roughly 58 percent of them who had purchased a Ford, GM, or Chrysler product the previous year. The catch was that they wanted those vehicles to be every bit as good as the ones being sold by Japanese automakers. Ford would have to redouble its efforts to improve quality in order to meet their expectations, but Fields saw this as a huge opportunity and was determined to seize it. Rather than trying to beat the Japanese at a game they were already winning or out-Korea the Koreans, he wanted to take Ford somewhere those other companies could not follow. To do that, Ford's products needed to do more than just say, "Made in America"—they needed to stand up and sing "The Star-Spangled Banner." Instead of inoffensive appliances, he wanted beefy rides with in-your-face styling that were chock full of innovative features.

Fortunately for Fields, the company had brought in an Englishman to lead a reimagining of Ford's North American product lineup two years earlier. Though he favored tweed suits and ordered his beer by the pint, Peter Horbury shared Fields' vision of what Ford should and could be.* His designs were inspired by things like Conestoga wagons and U.S. Navy fighters. He was determined to capture the American zeitgeist in sheet metal. And he had the ideal flagship for the new Ford—a crossover utility vehicle called the Edge—nearing completion in his design studio.

Fields called this new approach "Red, white and bold." He ordered blue rubber bracelets imprinted with the slogan and passed them out to the other members of his team. He made it clear that these were

---

* Prior to coming to Dearborn, Horbury had been responsible for transforming Volvo's lineup from a series of boring boxes to exemplars of austere Scandinavian design—a feat that earned him wide acclaim in automotive circles worldwide.

not optional fashion accessories. Soon they were being distributed throughout the company. Fields was big on slogans and symbols and vowed not to remove his bracelet until Ford's North American business was profitable again.*

Fields presented his plan to the board on December 7, 2005. He began with an overview of the current business environment, followed by his best guesses about how it would evolve over the next ten years. In retrospect, his assumptions were shockingly naïve: oil prices would remain low except for occasional, temporary spikes; industry volumes in the United States would remain stable at around 17 million units through 2010; there would be moderate growth in the small-car segment, and a gradual shift away from big SUVs to the emerging crossover category. Reality would prove far more harrowing, but at the time these conditions were seen as "challenging." He told the board Ford's biggest challenge was winning back customers.

Fields devoted a big chunk of the meeting to his demographic profiles and brand metrics. The marketing mumbo-jumbo left some board members rolling their eyes, but they got the basic point: Ford needed to stand for something again, and that something was America. Ford also needed to concentrate its investment on those segments where it could really compete and build more products off fewer platforms. That would allow the company to spend more on bodies and interiors, focusing on those parts of the product that the consumer could see and touch and worrying less about what was underneath the skin. By way of example, Fields showed the directors how Ford could build six new cars and crossovers for North America off a single Volvo platform.† This was the same approach Toyota used, and it was part of the reason why the Japanese automaker's material costs averaged more than $1,000 per vehicle less than Ford's. At the same time, Fields proposed eliminating aging vehicles like the Freestar minivan

---

* Fields kept his promise, even though "Red, white and bold" had long since gone the way of "Cheap and cheerful."
† These included the vehicles that would become the Ford Flex, Taurus, and Explorer; the Lincoln MKT and MKS; and a Mercury that was later killed. All of these were, in fact, built off the same D3 platform Volvo had designed for its XC90.

and Crown Victoria sedan, and replacing them with new subcompacts and crossovers, which were lacking in Ford's North American lineup.

"We need to stop planning products to fill plants," he told the board. "We need to match production to the actual demand."

Fields also wanted to roll back incentives, offer clearer pricing, and take other steps to boost the residual values of Ford's vehicles. This would allow the company to offer lower lease rates and make its products more competitive with the imports. Fields closed by going over the specific goals of his Way Forward plan, promising to return the North American automotive business to profitability by 2008 and showing off sales forecasts that projected annual volumes of more than 2.5 million vehicles by 2010.

The board was impressed. Finally, someone was willing to make the deep cuts many of them had long felt were necessary. They commended Fields on his plan and told him to execute it as quickly as possible, because Ford was running out of time.

*   *   *

The formal announcement of Fields' Way Forward plan was delayed until late January 2006 because the company was worried that the grim details of job cuts and plant closures would overshadow important product unveilings it had scheduled earlier that month. But with Bill Ford and the rest of the board behind him, Fields was eager to set his plan in motion. He sounded the first bugle call at the Los Angeles Auto Show on January 4. In a speech to the world's automotive press, he promised that Ford had learned the lessons of its past mistakes and knew it needed to "change or die." Four days later, Fields was back onstage at the North American International Auto Show in Detroit, this time unveiling Horbury's new crossover, which embodied what he was now calling "bold, American design." With an athletic stance and an enormous chrome grille, the Ford Edge certainly did that.

"You are going to see a lot more products like Edge from Ford—products that have a very clear point of view," Fields promised. "It's these sorts of products that will make Ford America's car company. That's what's driving our way forward—a retaking of the American marketplace—and it starts today."

The wraps came off the rest of the Way Forward plan two weeks later.* On January 23, Bill Ford and Mark Fields revealed the details in a speech broadcast live to Ford offices around the world.

"We all have to change, and we all have to sacrifice," Ford told his employees. "The Way Forward contains some strong medicine for our North American business. But it also contains the vision and strategic focus to rebuild the business."

Ford went on to list the things he would no longer tolerate at the company.

"Here is what we will not stand for: incremental change, avoiding risk, thinking short-term, blocking innovation, tying our people's hands, defending procedures that don't make sense, and selling what we have instead of what the customer wants," he said. "In short, we will not stand for business as usual."

It was powerful stuff, but it was lost in the details of Ford's epic downsizing. The *Detroit News* summed up the prevailing reaction with a one-word headline the following day: "Painful."

UAW president Ron Gettelfinger called the Way Forward "devastating news for the many thousands of hard-working men and women who have devoted their working lives to Ford" and promised a showdown with the company when the current contract expired in 2007. Ford's stock leapt more than 5 percent on the news, but many Wall Street analysts remained skeptical. They were still not convinced Ford was cutting deep enough.

*   *   *

Once again, they were right.

By the time Fields' Way Forward was announced, oil prices were back on the rise. By April, the average price of gasoline in the United States was approaching $3 a gallon for the second time in less than a year. As it did, the moderate shift away from trucks and SUVs

---

* The *Detroit News* had actually revealed most of the details in a story that ran the same day Fields presented his plan to the board back in December.

that Fields had predicted in November became a panicked exodus. Since those were the only vehicles Ford sold in North America that were actually making any money, the rapid shift became an existential crisis for the company. In the United States, Ford's sales fell 7 percent year over year, but that was only because of strong demand for its new mid-sized sedans. Ford's truck sales dropped 15 percent, while sales of its once-popular Explorer were down a staggering 42 percent.

When Fields and his team saw those numbers, they knew the Way Forward plan was in trouble. They had factored in the possibility of gas price spikes, but never imagined they would begin three months after the plan was announced. The decline in demand was worse than their worst-case scenario. Prices of raw materials, such as copper and aluminum, were also rising far faster than expected, magnifying Ford's losses. For years, Ford and the other domestic automakers had forced their suppliers to absorb these cost increases. As a result, many of them were now on the verge of bankruptcy and had no choice but to raise their prices as well.

"If this trend continues, we've got a problem," Leclair warned Fields.

In May, it did, despite the launch of an aggressive new marketing blitz. Built around yet another slogan—"Bold Moves"—it was an attempt to strike an emotional chord with consumers and convince them that Ford had found itself again. Because most of Ford's products were still pretty boring, the original plan called for a series of headline-grabbing moves that were actually bold. Ford's advertising agency had come up with a long list of them, including lifetime warranties and carbon offsets for every vehicle sold, but Leclair had rejected all of them as too costly. With no actual bold moves to tout, all that was left was a bunch of television ads showing people jumping off waterfalls, riding bulls, moving to New York, and doing other daring deeds. The whole thing fell flat and left dealers fuming.

June brought more bad news as pickup and SUV sales continued to plummet, taking Ford's stock price and credit rating down with them. Ford was now trading for less than $7 a share, and its bonds were deep into junk territory. The board of directors cut dividend payments in half. The outside directors also cut their own compensation.

In July, Toyota outsold Ford in the United States for the first time ever. By then, Fields had reassembled his Way Forward team and begun work on an even more aggressive downsizing plan. They spent the summer locked in lengthy meetings trying to figure out what else they could cut. More factories would need to be closed, more jobs would need to be eliminated, and Ford would have to abandon its pledge to return its North American automobile business to profitability by 2008. Even with another round of cuts, that was no longer possible. Instead of coming up with another catchy slogan, they simply called the new plan the "Way Forward Acceleration." Most people referred to it a little more ironically as "Way Forward II" and whispered that "Way Forward III" was already being discussed at the top of the house.

As they struggled to go further faster, Fields began running into the same old brick walls that had held back change for so long at Ford. Entrenched executives gave superficial support to his turnaround efforts but often conspired against them whenever his plans ran counter to their own aims. Ford's rigidly regionalized corporate structure made it impossible for Fields to address issues globally. Fields thought his mandate from the board would prove unassailable. When he realized how wrong he was, he appealed to Bill Ford to make good on his promise to protect him. But Bill Ford had not been able to protect himself. Meetings became tense as tempers flared, and the worsening business environment only served to fan the flames.

It all came to a head during an off-site meeting that summer. The company's top executives had cloistered themselves in a conference room at the Henry Ford Museum so that they could work on the accelerated restructuring plan without interruptions. Fields had been fighting with Leclair ever since the CFO vetoed his Bold Moves initiatives. Now Leclair was insisting on even deeper cuts to Ford's advertising budget. Fields refused.

"There's no other alternative," Leclair insisted. "You're going to do this."

"When you run the fucking business, you can do it," Fields fired back. "But you don't run it. You're the CFO. So, I'll take your counsel, but that's it."

"You're going to do this!" Leclair shouted.

Fields leapt out of his chair screaming, "I'm tired of this bullshit!" He was halfway across the table by the time Bill Ford grabbed him. "Cut it out!" Ford demanded.

Scenes like this hampered Ford's progress on the Way Forward II plan. So did the chronic lack of honesty inside the company. The plan's goalposts kept moving as Ford's position in the market deteriorated.

"The budget changed constantly," recalled one executive. "Nobody knew where the money was. Nobody knew how much spending was actually going on. Everyone was trained to pad their budgets and their projected expenses so that they could line them up at the end of the year."

As truck sales continued to tumble, Fields began putting together the biggest production cut in two decades. It called for a 21 percent cut in fourth-quarter factory output, as well as additional cuts to third-quarter production. Ten factories would be idled for extended periods, and some 30,000 workers would be temporarily laid off. However, by the time the cut was announced in September, it was clear that far deeper cuts would be necessary.

Though Fields kept talking about matching production to the actual demand for Ford's cars and trucks, it was now evident that neither he nor anyone else at World Headquarters had the stomach to actually do it. He and his team had tried to take an unflinching look under Ford's hood, but they still suffered from the same failure of imagination that had plagued Detroit for decades. Fields knew that Ford needed to change or die, but he was unable to recognize how deep and sweeping those changes needed to be. Ford did not need bold moves. It needed a top-to-bottom revolution.

And Detroit was not a place that bred revolutionaries.

* * *

The board of directors had already decided it was time to consider other options. Earlier that year, they asked Bill Ford to begin exploring mergers with other automakers and consider selling portions of the company to the private equity firms that were beginning to make discreet inquiries. TPG Capital, then in the middle of a buyout binge, was one of them. So was Jacques Nasser's new employer, One Equity Partners, the private investment arm of JPMorgan Chase. The directors also asked Ford to begin looking at bankruptcy.

For most companies a Chapter 11 filing might have been the next logical step, but Ford's situation was unique. The arcane ownership structure Henry Ford II had created to guarantee his family's continuing control of the company after it went public in 1956 would never survive bankruptcy court. The Ford family would lose their shares along with the other stockholders and would never be able to regain control of the automaker once it emerged from reorganization. The family would not support a Chapter 11 filing, and their ownership of the supervoting Class B shares gave them veto power over any such move. In fact, any merger, sale, or voluntary liquidation of the company required a separate vote of the Class B shareholders.

Bill Ford was hurt by the board's crisis of confidence. He could not sleep. He lay awake at night grasping for a switch that would get Ford back on the right track. He knew where the company needed to go, he just needed to find someone who could take it there. He knew he could not do it alone. In the morning, the bleary-eyed Ford would make the long drive to work, stopping at a Starbucks along the way to fortify himself for another day alone at the top. At World Headquarters, he was spending less time in meetings and more time cloistered in his office. Ford would sit for hours behind the huge burled maple desk that had belonged to his grandfather Edsel, staring out the window at the white smoke billowing out of the enormous Rouge complex. Almost eighty years after the first Model A rolled off the line, it was still turning out the bestselling vehicle in America, the F-Series pickup. But that was no longer enough.

What would Henry Ford think of his company today? Bill wondered. *What would he think of me?*

Bill Ford started making calls to his relatives, suggesting that the time had come to take the company private again. Several of the other Fords agreed, but once Leclair and the lawyers began studying the idea, they realized it would not work. The Fords could come up with enough cash to buy out the other shareholders, but not enough to keep Ford Credit funded. It needed access to the bond markets, and that would become far more costly if Ford went private.

Bill Ford still believed the company could be saved. Other directors were not so sure. Robert Rubin thought the underlying assumptions of Fields' Way Forward plan were still too optimistic and began expressing serious concern about Ford's finances. He questioned whether the automaker still had enough money left in the bank to cope with the increasingly challenging business environment. He would soon resign. Director Irv Hockaday was wary of ruling out anything.

"Bismarck's military strategy was the simultaneous pursuit of diverse options," he reminded his colleagues.

The other directors agreed.

"We want all options on the table," they told Ford.

Reluctantly he agreed to begin an analysis of other alternatives.

In December 2005, Ford had hired his brother-in-law, Steve Hamp, as his chief of staff. The husband of Bill's older sister, Sheila, Hamp had spent the last twenty-seven years at the Henry Ford Museum. He seemed more like a college professor than a businessman, but Hamp had enough management experience to deal with the minutiae that Ford found so frustrating. He also did what he could to help his brother-in-law cope with his increasingly recalcitrant executives. Now, with pressure from the board mounting, Ford asked Hamp to work with Leclair and outside investment bankers to explore the various options.

They established a high-level committee, the Corporate Strategy Leadership Council. Chaired by Bill Ford, it also included Hamp, Leclair, Mark Fields, Joe Laymon, and two other senior executives: Mark Schulz, the vice president in charge of Ford's international operations, and his second in command, Lewis Booth, the head of Ford of Europe and the Premier Automotive Group. It also included Greg Moran, who had recently been promoted to executive director of corporate strategy.* Moran had worked for Bank One and had merger experience. Goldman Sachs and Citigroup served as outside advisers.

---

* Jim Padilla came to one meeting, but relations between him and Bill Ford were increasingly tense, and he was not invited to the next one.

Together they began work on Project Game Plan, a top-secret initiative aimed at figuring out what could still be done to save the company. The team looked at different finance options and tried to figure out how Ford could raise additional cash. They looked at internal restructuring moves. And they not only looked at the possibility of an alliance with another automaker, but actually began discussions with a couple of companies.

Ford's first choice was a three-way tie-up with Renault and Nissan, both of which were now being led by Carlos Ghosn. Talks began that summer, but Ghosn was coy. He was not interested in an alliance. He wanted the whole thing. Toyota, Honda, and South Korea's Hyundai Motor Company were all profiled, but there were no serious talks with any of them. DaimlerChrysler was deemed too much of a mess to bother with. That left General Motors. Ford already had a successful collaboration under way with GM on transmissions. Now it asked the Detroit automaker if it was open to an even broader alliance. In addition to working together on other powertrain components, Ford suggested the two companies explore the possibility of jointly developing vehicle platforms for lower-volume products like small commercial vehicles. Ford also floated the idea of combining the two corporations' back offices, sharing information technology and perhaps even purchasing costs. GM's response to all of these overtures was tepid. The guys in downtown Detroit were convinced they had already passed Ford, and they had no intention of helping it catch up.

Finally, the Project Game Plan team looked at selling Ford's foreign brands. Together, these were worth billions. Proposals were presented to Bill Ford and his senior executives, but no one in Dearborn wanted to part with these prestige properties. The only one they could agree on was Aston Martin. Selling it would generate some cash, but not enough to make a difference.

By the middle of the summer, the mood was somber. The team had graphed Ford's revenue and cash burn rate and came to a sobering realization: The lines did not cross in time. They ran various models, but none of them offered any hope of salvation.

"We are going to run out of cash in eighteen to thirty-six months," Leclair said. "At that point, we will have to make a chapter filing."

Leclair began preparing for that contingency. He and Hamp also began exploring the possibility of a sale to another automaker. It was not the best role for the former museum director. Hamp had little experience with the for-profit world and had no perspective by which to judge Ford's woes. Every problem seemed like a crisis to him. Every hallway conversation seemed to darken his view of the situation a little bit more.

Hamp shared his growing concern with his wife and other members of the Ford family. Many of Henry Ford's heirs were already nervous. They had watched the value of their stock fall steadily since Bill Ford's coup in 2001, from more than $16 a share to less than $10. The tidbits from Hamp took on ever-greater import as they circulated among the family, which was desperate for information. Some began to whisper that the situation was far worse than Bill was letting on. Others worried that he was becoming overwhelmed. In April, Ford finally decided that Padilla was doing more harm than good. He asked him to retire and added the positions of president and COO to his own list of responsibilities. It was too much. Two months later, one of Hank the Deuce's daughters, Anne Ford, sent her cousin a carefully considered e-mail.

"The stock price is terrible," she wrote Bill. "Maybe we ought to bring somebody in to help you."

Anne Ford was not the only one who had begun wondering aloud if Bill was really up to the challenge of running Ford Motor Company. Some of Ford's board members were asking the same question. They were increasingly frustrated with his lack of engagement with the day-to-day operations of the company and his inability to overcome the resistance of his subordinates. A few board members had been advised by their personal attorneys that they could be accused of neglecting their fiduciary responsibility to Ford's shareholders if they did not begin pushing for a change in leadership. Though relations between Bill and the board remained cordial, there were some heated exchanges in executive session when the CEO was not present.

Some said the time had come to force Ford to step aside.

"He is not giving it the 24/7 effort that he promised us. He's not involved in the operational and product meetings. And he's been unable to resolve the internal conflicts," said one director. "You have to have the CEO calling the shots. Bill isn't."

Others argued for more a respectful approach to the man who was, after all, the designated representative of the Ford family.

"At the end of the day, it's their company," said another. "We have to tread carefully."

Bill Ford had accomplished a great deal since 2001. He had taken over a company that was awash in red ink and delivered three years of solid profitability. He had refocused Ford on its core business of building and selling cars and trucks, and had made it the first American automaker to bring a hybrid to market. He had tried to do a lot more, but had ultimately been unable to overcome decades of mismanagement and the ossified corporate culture responsible for it.

As the July board meeting approached, Hockaday decided the time had come for a fatherly chat with the company's top executive. He had been impressed with Bill's desire to lead Ford and had done what he could to support him. Now Ford admitted he was overwhelmed.

"No single individual can run this company effectively under the current circumstances," he told Hockaday. "I need help. Help me get that help."

Hockaday commended Ford for having the self-awareness and the lack of ego to admit that, but he gently suggested that Ford needed something more than a new COO. Bill agreed: The time had come to find a CEO who could save Ford from itself.

＊　＊　＊

On July 12, 2006, less than five years after he had demanded Jacques Nasser's head, Bill Ford once again stood before the company's board of directors and delivered another emotional appeal. This time, he spoke not with the emphatic self-confidence of a rightful heir demanding his throne, but with the strained voice of a man fighting to hold on to his job and his company. When Ford took over as CEO back in October 2001, the company's stock was worth more than $16 a share. Now it was trading for less than $7. Then Ford had been the second-largest automaker in the world, after General Motors. Now it had fallen to third place behind Toyota. Ford had promised $9 billion a year in profits by the middle of the decade. Now Ford was heading toward its biggest loss ever. There was talk of bankruptcy, of selling the company, of parting it out to other automakers or private equity firms. The story of the past five years was written on Ford's face. His easy smile was gone. He looked exhausted. He told the directors that he was tired of showing up at each month's board meeting just to listen to the list of the company's problems read back to him.

"I know what's wrong," he said. "Help me find a solution."

Ford asked the other directors to help him find a new CEO.

"This company means a lot to me. I have a lot tied up in it," Ford said. "But the one thing I don't is my ego."

Though he knew it was coming, Hockaday thought Bill Ford's speech to the directors was one of the most moving he had ever heard in a boardroom. No one ascends to the top of a major corporation without a healthy ego, but those in the automobile industry were oversized even by Fortune 500 standards. It took a big man to admit that he could not save his company, particularly when his name was on the side of the building. In other boardrooms in Detroit, other CEOs were adamantly refusing to admit defeat. They would stubbornly cling to power and take their companies down with them. Bill Ford cared too much about Ford to let that happen in Dearborn.

Laymon made one more stab at Carlos Ghosn. Bill Ford even flew to Paris to meet with him personally, but Ghosn again insisted on having the chairman's title, too. He had clashed with the Michelin family when he worked for the French tire company and would only agree to come to Dearborn if the Ford family had no part in running the company.

As Ford and Laymon flew back from France, the company's directors were going through their address books to see if they could find someone outside the automobile industry who was equal to the challenge. It would have to be somebody who had already proved he could do it—somebody who had not only run a global manufacturing enterprise, but also turned one around. The list they came up with was a short one. The name on the top was Alan Mulally.

CHAPTER 3

The Man on the White Horse

Coming together is a beginning; keeping together is progress; working together is success.

— HENRY FORD

As the head of the Boeing Company's Commercial Airplanes Group, Alan Mulally had spent the past ten years fending off one disaster after another while somehow managing to transform its divisive culture into a model of corporate collaboration. Under his leadership, Boeing had survived an unrelenting assault by Europe's Airbus Industrie, a difficult merger with rival McDonnell Douglas, and the collapse of sales that followed the terrorist attacks on New York and Washington, D.C., in 2001. Mulally turned what could have been a fatal blow to the aerospace giant into an opportunity to fundamentally transform the company into a leaner, more profitable enterprise. By 2006, Boeing's commercial jet division was well on its way to record sales, revenue, and earnings. Mulally credited it to a team-based approach he called "Working Together." And he had learned many of its principles from Ford Motor Company.

Mulally's success at Boeing was already making him something of a corporate celebrity, but he hardly acted the part. He looked like an older version of Richie Cunningham, the wholesome protagonist on the television sitcom *Happy Days*. Mulally had the same reddish-blond hair, the same pointed chin, and the same gee-whiz grin—only Mulally's suggested he knew more than he was letting on. It was the only hint that there was more to him than his aw-shucks, backslapping demeanor suggested. It was as though he had an ace up his sleeve that he was only barely managing to conceal. Otherwise he came off like an overgrown Boy Scout, seasoning his conversations with words like *neat, cool,* and *abso-*LUTE-*ly*. While most high-level executives favored tailored suits and expensive cuff links, Mulally's trademark couture at Boeing was a red Windbreaker. His idea of dressing up was a blue blazer and tie. Instead of an expensive Mont-blanc pen, he used cheap retractable ballpoints he could buy by the box. He drew a smiling jumbo jet under his name whenever he signed anything.

The *Seattle Times* called him "Mr. Nice Guy." Mulally's lack of pre-tension was evident in his dealings with other people. At formal events, he showed little interest in the rich and powerful, preferring to mingle with those less interested in comparing résumés or other measurables. He asked more questions than he answered and seemed genuinely interested in what people had to say, be they world leaders or waitresses. Mulally made a point of remembering something about everyone he met and would often astonish underlings by recalling some scrap of information about their lives they had shared with him months or years before. He was also big on hugs, and had even been known to plant pecks on the cheeks of both men and women when he was in a particularly exuberant mood. All of this made Mulally adored by subordinates. It also kept his rivals off balance. They could never quite figure out how much of it was an act. And Mulally liked to keep it that way.

The truth was that Mulally's character was an odd mix of guileless-ness and relentless determination that was born of an austere child-hood and a lifelong desire to write his name across the sky. Mulally's interest in aviation was not the product of the usual schoolboy fasci-nation with flight, but an attempt to lash himself to something really big and important that would take off like a rocket and leave his hum-ble beginnings in Lawrence, Kansas, lost in a plume of prairie dust.

Mulally's parents met at a USO dance there in 1943. A month later they were married and his father was on his way to the Pacific. Mrs. Mulally followed him to his base in Oakland, California, when she found out she was pregnant. Alan was born there—the first of four children, and the couple's only boy—but returned to Kansas with his mother a few days later. His father joined them there after the war, taking a job as a postal worker. The Mulallys were not poor, but they were far from well-off. Alan grew up in a series of small ranch homes, a somewhat nerdy kid with a crew-cut and off-brand jeans who dreamed of bigger things. He used to sit in one of the front pews at the Plymouth Congregational Church so that he could study the pastor and learn the secret of his sway over the congregation. As a child, Mulally delivered the local newspaper and *TV Guide*. As soon as he could afford it, he made a down payment on his first bicycle at Montgomery Ward so that he could take on longer routes. It cost $57 and Mulally rode back to the store every week to make a $1.25 payment. In high school he upgraded to a motorcycle and started a lawn-mowing business, building a trailer for his bike so that he could tow his equipment. Instead of football, he went out for gymnastics. It did little to improve his social standing on campus, though he finished second in the state. But Mulally continued to search for something bigger and more important.

He finally found what he was looking for on his family's black-and-white television in September 1962 when he watched President John F. Kennedy call on his generation to go to the moon. Mulally took it as a personal challenge—one worthy of his lofty ambitions. He enrolled at the nearby University of Kansas, joined the Air Force ROTC, and started studying physics and calculus as he plotted his path to the stars. But a routine physical revealed that Mulally was color-blind and put an end to his dream of becoming an astronaut. Mulally shrugged it off and switched his major to aeronautical and astronautical engineering. If he could not go to the moon, he could still build the rockets that would take other men there. At the same time, Mulally was beginning to demonstrate the charisma and leadership skills that would serve him so well later in life. He joined the Kappa Sigma fraternity and became president of the Lawrence chapter. At night he managed a small convenience store, Dylan's Quick Shop. The owner told Mulally he would never amount to anything, but his professors were more encouraging. His graduate adviser, Jan Roskam, thought Mulally was a born leader with a knack for getting people to work together. At the school's annual engineering exposition, Mulally not only did much of the organizing, but also made sure everyone had fun at the event. Roskam told Mulally that he had a rare gift for an engineer—people skills—and suggested that he think about management. The professor, who consulted for Boeing, also talked Mulally into going to work for the aerospace company instead of NASA.

Mulally toyed with the idea of becoming a professional tennis player first. He was that good. But after earning his master's in 1969, Mulally headed for Seattle. Airliners were not nearly as sexy as rockets, but he soon found himself enamored with the idea of jet travel and its ability to make the world a smaller place. Just as Roskam predicted, Mulally was quickly promoted to management. But his first employee quit after Mulally kept redoing all of his work and showing him his mistakes. The young boss realized that his job was not to show his subordinates how much smarter he was than they were, but to bring them up to his level. It was a valuable lesson, and one he never forgot. As he honed his management skills, Mulally kept asking for more responsibility and getting it. He worked on every Boeing jetliner program from the 707 to 767. By the early 1980s, Mulally was being eyed for a senior position. Boeing sponsored him for a Sloan Fellowship at MIT, where he earned a second master's in management and only missed Bill Ford by a couple of years. Mulally's career advanced quickly after that. He led the cockpit design team for the 757 and 767 programs, creating the first all-digital flight deck for a commercial aircraft. But it was on the pioneering 777 program that Mulally really made a name for himself.

Ford CEO Donald Petersen was a member of Boeing's board of directors in the late 1980s when Mulally was named chief engineer for the important new jet program. Petersen suggested that Mulally study Ford's work on the Taurus and offered to introduce him to Lew Veraldi, the man who led the development group Ford called "Team Taurus." Veraldi was a visionary product development executive who, when given the task of designing a car that could take on the Japanese, had assembled a team that included almost every Ford function to make sure they got it right. In addition to the usual designers and engineers, there were representatives from manufacturing on hand to offer insights from the assembly line, purchasing staff to add input from suppliers, and marketing people who talked to dealers and found out what their customers really wanted. Veraldi even worked with major insurance companies to figure out how to make the car cheaper for customers to repair after a collision. As a result of this innovative approach, the Taurus not only became the bestselling car in America, but also came in nearly $500 million under budget—unheard-of at a company famous for its cost overruns.

Ford promptly forgot most of what it learned from Veraldi and Team Taurus, but Mulally did not. He blended it with other lessons he picked up on Toyota's assembly lines during visits to Japan and applied it all to the Boeing 777 program after he was promoted to general manager in 1992.

By then the new jet had become a make-or-break gamble for the aerospace giant. All over the world, airlines were passing on Boeing's aging 747 and buying newer models from its rival, Airbus. The company was losing market share and desperately needed a new plane, but the entire industry was in the midst of a deep recession. One of the most complicated machines ever built, the 777 would push the envelope on aeronautical science and would cost an estimated $5 billion. It was a huge risk but Boeing had no choice. The company staked its future on the program and asked Mulally to lead it.

He assumed command of a team of ten thousand and a supply chain that stretched over four continents. The program was already behind schedule, a victim of the same sort of corporate infighting that had plagued Ford. To cut through it, Mulally and his boss, Philip Condit, instituted a new policy of enforced cooperation and transparency. This was Working Together, and it required the top leaders of each discipline and function to meet every week to go over their progress, discuss problems, and figure out how to deal with them as a team.

"It was a point of conflict to begin with. You know, an engineer with pride wants to find the solution to his problems. And it's not a natural thing to go out and explore publicly the particular problems you have," said Ronald Ostrowski, who became chief engineer of the program after Mulally was promoted to general manager. "There was resistance at first."

Mulally overcame it by inviting a documentary crew to film the entire process. He knew the cameras would keep everyone on their best behavior.* It worked.

At about $100 million a plane, Mulally would have to sell some 200 of the new jetliners to save Boeing from ruin. A year after United Airlines took delivery of the first one in 1995, the order tally was already approaching 300. Boeing logged its 500th order four years after that. The 777 would become one of Boeing's most successful—and profitable—aircraft ever. It would also make Alan Mulally a star.

When Boeing merged with McDonnell Douglas in 1997, he was given the unenviable task of weaving together the two companies' space and defense businesses. Some in the industry wondered if that was even possible, particularly for a man with no military background. But Mulally did it. Then he was called on to save Boeing once again.

Despite the success of Mulally's 777, the company found itself in serious trouble by 1998. Banking on the success of the new wide-body, the commercial aviation division had launched an ambitious growth program with the aim of doubling production. Instead, Boeing's supply chain collapsed and work at its factories stopped completely. The company reported its first loss in fifty years. The group's president, Ron Woodard, was fired, and Mulally was tapped to replace him. Mulally began a radical reformation of the Commercial Airplanes Group. Declaring that "you can't manage a secret," he ordered his senior managers to compile every possible piece of data about the company's operations, organize it all into easy-to-read charts and tables, and present their findings in daylong problem-solving sessions held every Thursday. Based on this information, Mulally and his team quickly developed a restructuring plan. They streamlined every aspect of the group's operations, cut thousands of jobs, and outsourced work that did not have to be done in-house. A year later, the division was profitable again and setting new production records.

Mulally was named CEO of the commercial aircraft division in 2001, just a few months before terrorists hijacked four of its planes and used them to attack the World Trade Center and the Pentagon.

---

* The result was *21st Century Jet: The Building of the 777,* which became a popular PBS documentary.

The attacks would prove devastating to Boeing as well. Over the next several months, half of Boeing's orders were canceled or delayed. Airbus soared past Boeing to become the largest commercial jet manufacturer in the world. Mulally responded by slashing Boeing's workforce in half and outsourcing even more production. He also streamlined the company's product portfolio, canceled programs that no longer made sense, and used the money he saved to invest in the most advanced commercial airliner ever: the Boeing 787.

Dubbed the "Dreamliner," this was a paradigm-shifting plane that promised to make air travel easier, cheaper, and less damaging to the environment. The 787 was designed to be 20 percent more fuel-efficient than the 767, which carries about the same number of passengers. That translated into lower greenhouse gas emissions and operating costs for the airlines. The 787 was also designed to break the hub-and-spoke model—which had long dominated civilian air transportation, to the chagrin of passengers everywhere—by encouraging more point-to-point flights. The airlines were impressed, and Boeing was soon on the rebound as airlines lined up to place orders for the new jet. Mulally's promotion to CEO of the entire company seemed only to be a matter of time.

That job now belonged to his mentor, Philip Condit. But at the end of 2003, Condit was forced to resign in the wake of a controversy involving U.S. Air Force contracts. Less than two years later, his replacement, Harry Stonecipher, was also forced to resign after it was discovered that he was having an affair with another Boeing executive. Neither of these scandals had anything to do with Mulally, and it was assumed that he would be named Boeing's new chief executive once the board had a chance to catch its breath. But Boeing's biggest customer, the U.S. Department of Defense, was getting tired of the headlines. The Pentagon told Boeing to bring in someone from outside the company to make a clean break with the past. That man was Jim McNerney, then chairman and CEO of 3M and the former head of General Electric's aircraft engine division. Mulally, who was about to turn sixty, had been passed over.

If Mulally was devastated, he did not show it. He seemed to shrug it off just as he had the news of his color blindness. However, there

were plenty of other people who were openly indignant on his behalf. One of them was Tom Buffenbarger, the president of the International Association of Machinists and Aerospace Workers. He had
led strikes against Mulally and accused him of coming at his members "with a meat cleaver" after September 11, but he said Mulally
deserved the top job at Boeing and called the decision to pass him
over "a crime."

*   *   *

M ulally was used to getting calls from corporate headhunters interested in his obvious managerial gifts. He usually dismissed
them out of hand. He was only interested in building airplanes. But
this call was different. This one was from Ford Motor Company. It
came not from a headhunter, but from board member John Thornton
himself.* And Thornton was calling to tell Mulally that William Clay
Ford Jr. wanted to talk to him about running his company.

*Bill Ford, the great-grandson of Henry Ford himself, wants to speak to
me,* he thought as he hung up the telephone. *What an honor!*

The Mulallys' home was being remodeled, so he had moved his
family into a small apartment. Mulally had claimed a tiny bedroom as
his home office, and he sat there now, staring up at the ceiling, awed
by the opportunity that had just been presented to him. Ford Motor
Company. If there was a more powerful symbol of American manufacturing might, he could not think of it. Ford was the company that
brought the automobile to the masses, created the moving assembly
line, and lifted factory workers out of poverty. Mulally thought back to
the old Ford pickups that were as much a part of the landscape of his
youth as the Kansas prairie itself. Like Boeing, Ford was a legendary
name associated with legendary products. Boeing had its B-17 and
747; Ford had the Mustang and the Thunderbird. America would not
be America without Bill Boeing and Henry Ford. After a few long moments, Mulally emerged from his reverie, stood up, and opened the
door. His wife and son were standing outside.

---

* It was Thornton, the former president of Goldman Sachs, who first suggested
Mulally as a candidate for the CEO's job at Ford.

"That was Ford!" Mulally beamed. "They want me to run the company."

The Mulally clan quickly swung into action. His son Googled "Ford" on the home computer while his siblings away at college began their own research efforts. They scoured the Internet for information about the company and the Ford family, forwarding everything to their father. Mulally spent the next several days learning everything he could about the automaker. He printed out the latest financial data, product photos, and scores of recent articles. As he leafed through it all, his initial enthusiasm waned a bit. Ford may have once been a great company, but it was in deep trouble now. Reviving it would be a herculean task. But if he pulled it off, he would be a hero. And he would be a CEO.

But how can I leave Boeing? Mulally asked himself.

Boeing was his baby. Mulally had nursed it through the ups and downs of the business cycle and an array of unprecedented challenges. After slogging it out with archrival Airbus, Boeing was about to deliver a decisive blow with its best airplane yet. How could he walk away before it was finished? Mulally was still weighing that question when Bill Ford called and asked him to come to Dearborn to hear his pitch in person.

✳   ✳   ✳

On Saturday, July 29, 2006, Ford sent a Gulfstream V to pick up Mulally in Seattle. On the way to Michigan, he pored over the thick file of data he had collected on the company. The research he had been doing on Ford since that first phone call had generated a myriad of questions; he was about to meet the man who he hoped could answer most of them. Mulally began writing his questions out on the back of a copy of Ford's most recent annual report.

The plane landed at Willow Run Airport, which had been built by Ford during World War II when the company was in the bomber business. When Mulally stuck his head out into the humid summer air, he found a driver waiting for him next to a Ford Expedition. The man took his bag and opened the rear door, but Mulally climbed into the front passenger seat. As the big sport utility vehicle navigated the winding road through the woods near Ann Arbor, Mulally found himself growing excited. He tried to temper his enthusiasm.

I'm just here to gather information, Mulally reminded himself. *I'm not deciding anything.*

They pulled up to Bill Ford's gate at noon. Mulally admired the leafy estate. He recognized that he was in the domain of the truly rich. But as the Expedition pulled up to the front door, he was surprised to see the lord of the manor emerge from the front door in shorts and a polo shirt, accompanied by his wife, Lisa. Mulally surprised the Fords by greeting them with big hugs. Bill gave Mulally a brief tour of the grounds, then invited him inside. The two men sat down on couches in the spacious living room and started with football. They both knew Tod Leiweke, the CEO of the Seattle Seahawks. But they soon got down to the business of the business itself.

Ford started by outlining the history of his company, from its founding by Henry Ford, through the heady days of Hank the Deuce, to the debacle that was Jacques Nasser, culminating in his own frustrated efforts to save it. He talked about the competitive landscape—railing against Toyota, which he accused of working with the Japanese government to manipulate the yen in order to boost exports and of other devious practices. He told Mulally that the upcoming 2007 contract negotiations with the United Auto Workers would be critical to the company's survival, and outlined the concessions he hoped to wrest from the union: wage cuts, more competitive work rules, and an end to the infamous jobs banks, where idled workers continued to collect pay and benefits—sometimes for years—while waiting for new positions to open up. If Ford could not get these concessions, it might have to move most of its production to Mexico.

Mulally seemed hooked. Clearly there were a lot of challenges facing the storied automaker. And he had a lot of questions that needed answering before he would consider taking charge of such a troubled company. But here was a chance to fight for the very soul of American manufacturing.

If I'm going to do this, I'm going to need to know everything, he thought. So Mulally began his interrogation.

"Why are there so many brands?"

"What is the strength of the dealer network?"

"Why all these different regional organizations?"

"Why aren't you leveraging your global assets?"

Ford was a little taken aback by Mulally's intensity, but he answered every question Mulally put to him. He told Mulally about Nasser's dream of building a house of brands. He acknowledged there were too many dealers, and told Mulally about his push to globalize product development.

"Until we do that, nothing else is going to work," Ford said. "Our costs are going to be too high. Our product cadence is going to be too slow. We're just going to fall further and further behind."

"Why haven't you done it already?" Mulally asked.

Ford explained that he wanted to, but was getting pushback from his executives, who saw it as a threat to their regional fiefdoms. If Mulally took the job, he would have to find a way to overcome that resistance.

"That will be the enabler to get everything else done," Ford told him. "If you can't do that—if we can't get that—then we'll just be whistling past the graveyard."

The internal politics of Ford troubled Mulally. He asked Bill Ford for more details. Ford grabbed a piece of notebook paper and sketched out the company's organizational structure in black pen—a family tree of sorts that listed the head of each division and showed who reported to whom. All of the lines seemed to run through Ford's chief of staff, Steve Hamp. Mulally was shocked to see how few people reported to Ford directly.

He is too insulated, Mulally thought as he studied the paper. Mulally was even more surprised to learn that Hamp was Ford's brother-in-law.

Ford continued his unflinching assessment. The automaker was in deep trouble. It was being pulled apart by internal and external forces. The board of directors was actively considering selling Ford or finding another automaker to merge with. The chief financial officer, Don Leclair, was pursuing his own agenda.

"The operating people are on quicksand," Ford told Mulally. "I need help."

Mulally had realized that Ford's problems were serious, but did not know they were this bad. Bill Ford was clearly in over his head, and he did not try to conceal it. Mulally was moved by his self-awareness and candor but worried about the dire portrait Ford was painting of the company. If the automaker still had a chance to save itself, this was its last.

Bill Ford had some questions of his own, of course. He asked about Mulally's background, his experiences at Boeing, how he coped with crisis. He asked Mulally to describe his management style. Mulally explained how, at Boeing, his entire leadership team was expected to participate in a lightning-fast analysis of the entire business every Thursday morning. Each of his direct reports delivered a brief update on the status of his or her division or function, highlighting anything that had changed since the previous week's meeting. It was the centerpiece of his management philosophy, and he would use it in Dearborn if he came there, too.

"This is going to be a culture shock," Ford cautioned.

What does that mean? Mulally wondered.

Still, as the afternoon shadows lengthened, Mulally found himself becoming increasingly enamored with both Ford the man, and his company. The automaker faced huge challenges, but Mulally thought he knew how to overcome them. And there were at least a few bright spots, as Bill Ford was quick to point out.

"We have good people," he told Mulally. "They just need a leader who can guide them and inspire them."

As the conversation continued, the two men found themselves finishing each other's sentences. By dinnertime, Mulally noticed that he had started to use the word *we* instead of *you* in reference to the automaker. He tried to stop, but found it harder and harder not to become personally invested in it all. But he had one more question. Mulally said he believed that nothing short of a sweeping restructuring of the entire corporation could save Ford Motor Company. If Bill Ford was going to retain the position of chairman, Mulally needed to know he had the stomach for what lay ahead.

"Are you absolutely committed to this?" he asked.

"I am," Ford assured him. "And so is the Ford family."

Ford had a similar question for Mulally.

"Can you tell Jim?" he asked, referring to Boeing's CEO, McNerney. "What will Jim do?"

Mulally did not answer.

That night, Bill and Lisa Ford took Mulally out to dinner in Ann Arbor at Eve, a nouvelle French American restaurant that was a favorite of area foodies. Mulally was impressed by the cuisine and by the royal treatment he was afforded as a guest of the Fords. He was even more impressed by the fact that Bill Ford, who had a squadron of drivers at his disposal, drove himself. Everyone seemed to recognize the Fords when they walked in, and many of the other diners stopped by their table during the course of the evening to pay their respects.

The experience was a little more harrowing for Ford, who spent much of the night worrying that someone might recognize Mulally and wonder why the two men were dining together. But he was also becoming more convinced by the minute that this was the guy who could save his company. Mulally was clearly a born leader with an innate charisma that Ford found inspiring. He had been through hell at Boeing and came out smiling. He was not a car guy, but he knew enough about manufacturing to grasp the complexities of Ford's situation. And he seemed to agree with Ford's own assessment of what the company needed to become. Lisa Ford was impressed with Mulally, too. When their guest excused himself for a few minutes, she leaned over to her husband and whispered, "He seems too good to be true."

"I know!" said Ford, certain he had found his man.

Mulally was pretty convinced himself. He had long since given up his struggle to avoid the *we* word. As they drove back to his hotel, he could not help noticing how many of the cars on the road were Fords.

When they reached the Campus Inn in Ann Arbor, the two men shook hands. Ford asked Mulally if he wanted to continue the discussion.

"I do," Mulally said eagerly.

Ford suggested he meet with some of the board members next. Mulally agreed. Ford told him the company's vice president of human resources, Joe Laymon, would handle everything from here on out, but he also gave him his personal cellphone number.

"Call me if you need anything," Ford said.

By the time Mulally got back to his hotel room, his mind was buzz-ing. He sat down at the desk, took out a blank sheet of paper, and started writing down everything he could remember in a long stream of consciousness, starting with his arrival in Michigan. He noted the temperature—95 degrees. This was definitely not Seattle. Then he moved on to his impression of the Ford family ("Bill, Lisa . . . great kids . . . two dogs . . . a tutor"), their residence ("Elegant house . . . two stories . . . wood paint . . . gated . . . woods"), and his host's lifestyle ("Detroit Lions . . . drives himself . . . sports with kids").

Then he moved on to the company.

"Stock at $6," Mulally noted. "Great opportunity."

He jotted down what he could recall from the discussion of Ford's challenges: "UAW . . . product development . . . global produc-tion . . . Mexico . . . insular industry . . . CFO has own plan . . . need to save cash . . . need acceptance of reality."

Next to Bill Ford's name, Mulally wrote just three words: "Not tough enough."

As he scanned the rapidly filling page, Mulally thought about how similar all of this was to the issues he had faced over the years at Boeing. The automobile industry might have its quirks, but it was fundamentally similar to the aerospace business. Mulally had dealt with unions before. He knew how to globalize product development and production. He had ridden out more than one business cycle. It was all familiar territory, and he knew he could navigate it as well as anyone else. Maybe better. Mulally could lead Ford just as surely as he could have led Boeing—if he had been given that chance. He had only two real questions left, ones Bill Ford could not answer.

Is there enough money left to save Ford Motor Company? he asked him-self. *Can I still make a difference, or is it too late?*

He picked up his pen again.

"Want to take the next step," he wrote.

In his mind, Mulally already had.

"We must change to grow and survive . . . we are not competi-tive," he continued. "We have to take action . . . take down produc-tion . . . get back to profitability . . . embrace the future."

By the time he turned out the light, Mulally had filled the entire page. At the bottom, he added one more line: "We just need to act on the reality. We'll be back."

Mulally continued his meditation on the plane ride home, sketching the broad outlines of a plan to save Ford. He started with his goals. On a piece of a notebook paper, he wrote, "Make the best cars in the world" and "Profitable growth for all." Then he listed what he would later call his "Four P's": "performance," "product," "process," and "people." Beneath that, Mulally wrote, "Leadership counts."

Next he outlined the business environment as he saw it. He noted that Ford had too much capacity, was struggling against downward pricing pressure and "great competitors." He also identified "auto culture" as a problem he would have to overcome.

On another page, Mulally listed the key metrics he would want tracked in his weekly business plan reviews: revenues, expenses, research-and-development costs, operating costs, earnings, and cash-on-hand.

When he was done, he wrote, "Wow! What fun!"

✳   ✳   ✳

Once he got back to Seattle, Mulally called John Thornton.

"Why do you want me?" he asked the Ford board member.

"We need somebody with vision," Thornton told Mulally. "But we also need an operating guy who can drive it home."

As they talked, Mulally wrote two phrases on his notepad: "compelling vision" and "ruthless execution."

Those were what Ford needed. Those were what Thornton thought Mulally could deliver.

Thornton invited Mulally to Aspen, where fellow board member Irv Hockaday had a home. It would be a discreet place to meet for a more in-depth discussion. Thornton was going there for an Aspen Institute function and no one would think anything of Mulally jetting off to the trendy vacation spot for the weekend.

They met for lunch on August 6. Mulally peppered Thornton and Hockaday with questions throughout the meal, just as he had done with Bill Ford. They fired back with questions of their own.

They were particularly keen to learn how Mulally intended to better integrate Ford globally. Mulally pulled out a copy of the organization chart from Boeing and slid it across the table. It was a matrix that divided the commercial aircraft division into regional business units and functional departments. Mulally told them he would implement the same management structure at Ford.

Both men studied the chart and nodded.

If Hockaday and Thornton had any doubts that Mulally was the right man for the job, they evaporated over lunch. By the end of the meal, they had switched to selling mode.

"Alan, if the board offers you this job and you take it, you need to understand that there are no sacred cows," Hockaday told Mulally. "Any friends of Bill that are in the wrong positions or you conclude are not the right guys, you can get rid of them—and Bill will confirm that."

Mulally shook his head.

"That's not an issue, because I'm not going to have to get rid of many people," he replied.

Mulally's response was a little worrisome to Hockaday and Thornton. They believed the time had come for a little bloodletting at the top of the house in Dearborn. It was concern about the weakness of Ford's bench that had prompted them to look outside the company for a CEO in the first place.

"How do you come to that conclusion?" Hockaday asked.

Mulally responded by outlining his system of weekly meetings for them, just as he had for Ford. He told them this approach enforced extreme accountability on a weekly basis and left no hiding place for anyone who was not entirely committed to executing his part of the business plan.

"It's likely that a lot of people at Ford aren't used to that, and they will self-select out," Mulally said. "I won't have to do it."

Hockaday was impressed and offered Mulally one more enticement.

"If you think, Alan, that you need the chairman title to get the job done, Bill is willing to consider that," he said.

Once again, Mulally shook his head.

"I won't take the job unless Bill stays as chairman," he said to the surprise of both directors. "Bill has the name. I'm sure he has the magic with the employees, and probably with the dealers. He can do things that I wouldn't be able to do because of who he is and the way he is. I'm going to be so busy if I take this job that I'll need him in that job."

Mulally left Aspen confident that he would have the board's support if he came to Ford. Hockaday and Thornton just hoped Laymon could seal the deal.

* * *

As he flew out to Seattle, Laymon was not sure he could. The steely-eyed HR chief had done his homework. Mulally was nothing if not loyal. Prying him away from Boeing would be hard. He also had a lot invested in the local community. Mulally and his wife were part of Seattle society. They were in the process of creating their dream home on Lake Washington's tony Mercer Island, and Mulally had not given any indication that they were willing to relocate to Michigan.

The challenge, he thought, *will be extraction.*

Laymon was prepared to do whatever was necessary to bring Mulally back to Dearborn, but he also wanted to make sure he was worth the effort. He knew Bill Ford and the board were already convinced, but as the head of human resources, he felt he had an obligation to vet Mulally himself, just as he would any other candidate.

The two men met for the first time in Laymon's suite at the Four Seasons Hotel. Laymon took an instant liking to Mulally. Like everyone else, he found his charisma irresistible. But he was determined to put Mulally to the test. Laymon bombarded him with questions, poking and prodding to see if he could raise his ire. Ford's World Headquarters could be a shark tank, and the last thing he wanted was a CEO who would crack during his first staff meeting and set off a feeding frenzy. Mulally never lost his cool. Laymon threw curveballs, knuckleballs, and sliders, but Mulally hit them all out of the park. They talked about his management process. Laymon said he was not sure it was transferrable to Ford. Mulally convinced him that it was.

After several hours, they took a break and went for a walk

downtown. Laymon thought it was a calculated move on Mulally's part, to show Laymon how well loved he was by the good people of Seattle. If it was, Mulally could not have scripted it better. Every ten or twenty steps, they ran into somebody who recognized him. Laymon was not impressed by Mulally's local celebrity: he was impressed that it was not just businesspeople who came up to him on the street but maintenance workers and students, and Boeing employees. And Mulally greeted all of them with the same enthusiasm. Laymon knew that was rare for someone of his stature. He thought it would play well at Ford, where even jet-setters like Hank the Deuce had been at ease with the lowliest line workers. But it also compounded Laymon's concerns about getting Mulally to Detroit.

He started working on a plan as they walked.

There is no way I'm going to get this guy to leave Seattle. He's an icon in the community. Even if he takes the job, he's never going to sell his house here because, when he leaves Ford, he's taking his ass right back to Seattle, Laymon mused. *I'm going to have to set him up with a condo in Dearborn and a plane for him and his family. Some of the shareholders aren't going to like that, but we can make it work. And besides, I won't have to worry about him spending his days at Bloomfield Hills Country Club or going to lunches in downtown Detroit. We'll park him a mile from the office and work his ass off.*

Laymon stopped and turned to Mulally.

"What if we let you and your family use a corporate jet? Would that work for you?" Laymon asked.

Mulally loved the idea.

But when he returned to Dearborn, Bill Ford was less thrilled with Laymon's offer.

"You promised him what!?" he asked. He reminded Laymon that the media was already hounding Ford Americas president Mark Fields for his personal use of Ford's corporate jet. Fields had only agreed to return to the United States if his family could stay in Florida. His two sons had been following him around the world for years, and he wanted to make sure they spent a little time in America before going off to college. Fields had just bought a home on the water in Delray Beach when Bill Ford called and asked him to come to Dearborn. He told his boss that he did not want to have to move his family again. Bill Ford agreed to let Fields use a company plane to commute back and forth from Florida each week, but he regretted it as soon as the media found out. Now Ford was worried that Laymon was repeating that mistake. But Laymon persisted.

"I think we have a chance with Mulally," Laymon told Ford calmly. "If he says no because of that, what are you going to do?"

"Okay," said Ford. "Keep after him."

* * *

The truth was, Bill Ford could not contain his excitement about the Boeing executive. Though he knew better than to say anything before making Mulally a formal offer, he started whispering to his closest confidants that he had finally found the man who could save his company.

"This guy is a turnaround expert. He's done it before at Boeing," Ford told his vice president of communications, Charlie Holleran. "That's what we need. I've never turned around anything."

Holleran was a heavyset, white-haired Irish American from Scranton, Pennsylvania. Give him a badge and a desk, and he could have been precinct sergeant. With a helmet and a hose, he could have passed for a fire chief. He was Bill Ford's personal, one-man damage control squad. And that meant he knew more than most at the company just how much his boss needed help. Holleran was relieved to hear that Ford might finally be getting some.

Getting the board to green-light a deal with Mulally required little effort after Hockaday and Thornton shared their impressions with the other directors. Though they were aware of Ford's previous, unsuccessful efforts to recruit a new chief executive, Mulally's name was the first one presented to the board as a serious candidate. Because most of the board members were not "car guys," none of them objected to hiring someone from outside the industry. In fact, some thought that made him a more desirable candidate. After all, it was the car guys who had screwed everything up in the first place.

* * *

B efore Mulally would agree to talk terms, he called Bill Ford with one more question. He had been thinking about what Ford had told him about some of the board members wanting to dismantle the company. Mulally wanted to make it clear that if he came to Dearborn, it would be for only one reason.

"I'm not coming to take it apart. I'm coming to take it flying," he told Ford. "I just want to know that that's what you want to do. Because I want to create a viable business—not only for Ford, but for the good of the United States."

Ford told Mulally that was what he wanted as well.

"I will back you one hundred percent," he promised Mulally.

Once more, Mulally asked Ford if he understood what would be required. Mulally was working on a plan. It would mean painful sacrifices. As they had agreed, consolidating Ford's global operations to better leverage its worldwide assets and achieve real economies of scale would be Job One. But Mulally also wanted to sell off the foreign brands and eliminate both Mercury and Lincoln. He wanted to trim the dealer base, close more plants, and move more manufacturing to Mexico. The latter was important, because Mulally feared the upcoming contract negotiations with the UAW might get ugly—particularly since he would reject any deal that did not make Ford competitive with the foreign transplants. He wanted to reduce the automaker's dependency on its domestic plants ahead of a possible strike, which he urged Ford to begin preparing for immediately. Finally, he wanted to borrow money. A lot of it. The top-to-bottom restructuring he was planning would not be cheap, and Ford needed to up its investment in new products at the same time.

"You've been going out of business for thirty years," Mulally said. "This is how to get back in it."

"Let's get to work," Ford said. "The fourth quarter is really ugly."

* * *

O n Friday, August 18, Laymon flew back to Seattle with a formal offer. He was no longer worried about landing Mulally. Laymon had been working his connections and knew that Mulally and

McNerney were not getting along. More important, Mulally had convinced himself that he could save Ford.

This time Laymon booked a suite at the Fairmont Olympic Hotel and met Mulally for dinner downstairs at Shuckers Oyster Bar. The carved oak paneling and tin ceiling made it a cozy place to discuss business. Laymon was confident the letter he carried in his pocket would seal the deal, and he made a big show of slowly withdrawing it and presenting it to Mulally. When Mulally opened the envelope, he was visibly impressed. He accepted Ford's offer on the spot—tentatively. He wanted to review it with his financial adviser before signing. Laymon smiled. He had two other offers in his pocket. The one he had handed Mulally was the second best of the three.

"No problem—but be careful," Laymon said, urging Mulally to think hard before breaking the news to Boeing. "They'll counter. They'll throw money at you. Jim is going to offer you shared governance rights, dependent on board approval. But, Alan, you cannot accept that until you have it in writing."

Mulally assured Laymon his mind was made up.

On the way back to the airport, Laymon called Bill Ford.

"We've got our guy."

* * *

However, Laymon's initial concerns turned out to have been well-founded. For Mulally, leaving Boeing would prove easier said than done. Boeing had moved its corporate headquarters to Chicago, though the Commercial Airplanes Group remained based in Seattle. Mulally waited for Jim McNerney's next visit to tender his resignation in person. But as Mulally walked down the hall to his boss's office, the aeronautical engineer found himself regretting his decision to leave the plane maker a little more with every step.

I love Boeing. I love airplanes, he thought. *My work here is not finished.*

Even though it had yet to fly, Mulally's 787 Dreamliner was already being heralded as a game-changer. Moreover, once it was done, he still had one more aircraft to build to complete his planned transformation of Boeing's lineup—the replacement for the aging 737. As

Laymon had predicted, McNerney did not make Mulally's decision any easier. When Mulally told him that he had been offered the top job at Ford and was thinking of taking it, the Boeing CEO shook his head.

"Alan, you're crazy," he said. "Ford is a dying company in a dying industry in a dying town."

By now Mulally knew the depth of Ford's woes better than just about anyone outside Dearborn. He had convinced himself that he could overcome them. But as he listened to McNerney, he wondered if anyone really could.

Maybe it is too late, he thought.

Mulally knew that if he accepted the job at Ford and failed, no one would remember that he was the guy who had saved Boeing.

McNerney asked Mulally if he was happy at Boeing. He could understand that Mulally felt bad about being passed over for CEO, but McNerney told him the game was not over yet. Perhaps there was something that could be done to allow him to play a bigger role in running the entire company. He was willing to consider a different management structure. It would be up to the board of directors, of course, but there was a meeting coming up in a few days. Who knew what the future held?

*   *   *

Bill Ford's cellphone rang just after 7 P.M. on Friday, August 25. When he saw that it was Alan Mulally calling, he smiled. He was already counting the days before his new CEO took over. He hit the "Talk" button.

"Hey, Alan!" Ford said brightly. "What's up?"

"Bill, I am honored that you asked me to serve," Mulally began, his voice quavering slightly.

Ford's heart sank as he heard Mulally's regretful tone.

"Working together with you would be really neat," Mulally continued. "But I'm going to stay at Boeing."

He waited for Ford to respond, but there was only silence. After a few long moments, Bill Ford composed himself and calmly asked, "Is there anything I can do? Is there anything you're not satisfied with?"

"No, I love the opportunity. I love the idea of working with you. I love everything I've learned about Ford," Mulally said. "I think we could do it. But there's one more airplane that I want to make."

There was another awkward pause.

"Well, if anything changes, please give me a call," Bill Ford said amiably. "We really want you to come, and we really think you could make a difference."

As soon as he hung up the phone, Mulally regretted making the call.

*   *   *

B ill Ford may have taken Mulally's rejection gracefully, but he was dying on the other end of the line. He would later call it one of the darkest moments of his life. There were no other names on his list. For the past five years, Bill Ford had been trying to find some-one to help him save his company before it was too late. As he stared at his cellphone, he realized that there was nowhere left to turn. He called Laymon.

· The HR director was eating dinner at home with his family when the phone rang. Laymon had been spending a lot of time in Seattle trying to woo Mulally, and was planning a big weekend with the wife and kids to celebrate his catch.

"We lost Alan," Ford said as soon Laymon answered.

Laymon smiled. Both men were world-class practical jokers and prided themselves on their ability to yank each other's chains.

Shit, he thought. *You've gotta come up with a better one than this.*

"Sure we did," he chuckled.

"No, Joe, we did," Ford insisted. "And you cannot call him. He doesn't want to talk to you."

Laymon suddenly realized his boss was serious.

After he got off the phone with Laymon, Ford set up a conference call with his board of directors. They were all disappointed.

"Let me take a crack at him," Thornton said.

Later that night, Ford called Charlie Holleran and gave him the bad news. Holleran was with his lieutenant, Jon Pepper, a former *De-troit News* business columnist who handled press for Bill Ford and corporate communications. When Holleran got off the phone, he told Pepper everything. Later that night, the two men sat in a piano bar near Dearborn, doing their best to drown their misery with martinis. They both knew Bill Ford was out of options.

"What the fuck are we going to do now?" Holleran sighed.

*　*　*

J ohn Thornton called Mulally the next day.

"Alan, you've done everything you can for Boeing, and you should feel good about it," he said. "But a great American company needs you. This is about America and our competitiveness."

Mulally admitted that he was already regretting his decision. Thornton hung up and called Bill Ford.

"It's not over," he said.

Ford immediately called Laymon.

"Get back to Seattle right away," he said. "Stay there until you get Mulally. I don't care if you have to buy a house out there. If you can't get him to sign, don't bother coming back."

Laymon already had a bag packed. He headed for the airport.

However, once he arrived in Seattle, Mulally refused to see him. But Laymon was nothing if not persistent. He kept calling the apartment and finally persuaded Mulally to meet him at his hotel Sunday afternoon, just before the Boeing board dinner.

"I'm not here to change your mind," Laymon told him as they sat down. "I'm just here to help you with your conversation."

"What do you mean?" Mulally asked.

Laymon told him he knew exactly what was going to happen during Boeing's board meeting.

"It's going to be one of the toughest damn conversations you've ever had. McNerney's going to make this presentation about your matrix organization and how you sold all these damn planes, and you're going to look like a hero. Then they're going to go into executive session, and he's going to come out of there, and he's going to give you every dollar I gave you—plus one. He's going to beat our offer. He's going to then tell you that he proposed to the board that you should be one of the top guys—COO—but the board wouldn't let that happen," Laymon said. "So, you can say, 'Thank you for the money.' You're much better off. You can stay in Seattle. Or you can say, 'I just got fucked, and it doesn't feel too good.'"

Mulally said he doubted things would turn out that way. Boeing respected him too much. Laymon smiled at his naïveté.

"Alan, let's just play through this for a minute," he continued. "If you're right, you're going to be COO, on the board, with a hell of a lot more money—and you don't have to move. If you're wrong, you've got a lot of money, and you have some pride. You can run a Fortune 10 company *today*. You can be a CEO *today*. Boeing isn't the only company in the world that you can run that deserves your leadership. That's the extremes. If I'm right, he's going to fuck you. If you're right, I'm going to give you the most expensive glass of champagne I can find, and we're going to celebrate. But we have to prepare for both extremes."

Mulally promised Laymon he would call him and let him know how things went.

"I'm not going anywhere," Laymon said. "I'm staying right here and waiting for you."

* * *

Boeing's board of directors met on Monday and Tuesday. What happened inside the boardroom depends on whom you ask. But one thing is certain: By the time he met back up with Laymon on Wednesday, Mulally had changed his mind again. Bill Ford's emissary could tell things had not worked out the way Mulally had expected. He looked dejected, but Laymon had just the thing to cheer him up. He reached into his pocket and handed Mulally another envelope. It was the best of the three offers.

"Since they bettered my offer, I'm going to better their offer," Laymon said.

Mulally opened the envelope and studied the numbers. He was blown away.

The package Laymon had put together for Mulally included a base salary of $2 million, which was prorated to $666,667 for the remainder of 2006. It also included a $7.5 million signing bonus and another

$11 million to make up for the deferred compensation that Mulally would be walking away from when he left Boeing. With stock grants and options, the total package was worth more than $28 million. Mulally's total compensation at Boeing the previous year had been worth less than $10 million. Even without the one-time up-front payments, he stood to make nearly twice that amount at Ford annually. In addition, the company would pay for Mulally's housing in Michigan for the next two years and grant him personal use of a company aircraft. Finally, the offer included a golden parachute clause that would pay Mulally more than $27.5 million if Ford was sold or merged with another automaker during the next five years.*

The dream home on Mercer Island was about to get a whole lot dreamier.

"I'll be disappointed if, when all is said and done, you aren't the industry's first half-billion-dollar guy," Laymon told Mulally.

Mulally was grinning even more than usual. They shook hands and opened a bottle of champagne. There were still loose threads that needed to be tied up. For one thing, Mulally had to tender his resignation, and McNerney was already on his way back to Boeing's corporate headquarters in Chicago. Mulally decided to go there to break the news to him in person.

Once again, Laymon coached Mulally on how to negotiate the meeting with McNerney.

"Tell him, thank him, shake his hand, and leave," Laymon advised. "Tell him that we're announcing Tuesday. If he wants to get his PR people in contact with us, we can do that."

The press conference was a ploy on Laymon's part to keep Mulally from changing his mind again. He wanted to push the deal past the point of no return as quickly as possible.

When the bottle was empty, Mulally stood up and wished him a good trip back to Michigan.

---

* The golden parachute actually had a double trigger. Not only would a merger have to close, but Mulally would also either have to lose his job or have his compensations reduced significantly in order for him to receive this payment.

"Nope, I'll wait for you," Laymon said. "I can't let you go to Chicago without me."

He had let Mulally get away once; he was not going to let it happen again.*

✴ ✴ ✴

Jim McNerney was surprised when Mulally arrived at Boeing head-quarters on September 1 and asked to speak with him. McNerney thought everything had been resolved when he left Seattle. Mulally sat down and told him he had changed his mind; he was leaving to take the CEO job at Ford. McNerney scoffed at Mulally's indecisiveness. Laymon had warned him to expect that, and had reminded Mulally that McNerney had done the same thing before taking the job at Boeing.

"Jim, I'm going to do just what you did," Mulally said. He stood up, shook McNerney's hand, and left for Midway Airport.

Laymon was waiting for him there in a meeting room, pacing the floor with Mulally's contract in his hand. Mulally sighed as he sat down at the table. Then, with a decisive flourish, he signed the document. For once he omitted the smiling airplane.

"I've got to call my wife," Mulally said when had finished, reaching for his phone.

"No, you've got to call Bill first," Laymon told him. He dialed his boss's number and put him on speakerphone.

"Do you still want me to come?" Mulally asked Ford playfully.

"Yes!" Bill Ford almost screamed into the phone.

---

* Mulally would fly to Chicago on a Boeing jet, but the two men agreed to rendez-vous at Midway Airport.

CHAPTER 4

The Boldest Move Yet

Failure is only the opportunity more intelligently to begin again.

— HENRY FORD

On Tuesday, September 5, 2006, the man hired to save Ford Motor Company pulled up to its world headquarters at One American Road in Dearborn in a Land Rover driven by Joe Laymon. Charlie Holleran was in the truck with them. The plan had been to drive into the executive garage and sneak Mulally into the building without anyone noticing. But when Mulally saw the slab of sky-blue glass that housed Ford's corporate offices gleaming in the late summer sun, he asked Laymon to pull into the main driveway so that he could take it all in. Locals called it the Glass House. A semicircle of flags flapped at its base, each one representing a country where Ford operated. Mulally asked Laymon to circle the parking lot so that he could see all forty-two of them, starting with that of the United States and then following the alphabet to Venezuela. It looked like the United Nations had been picked up and replanted in the middle of Michigan. When it opened in 1956, the edifice was a sparkling tribute to the bright future Ford had come to view as its birthright. To the employees who labored inside, it had since become a reminder of better days that were unlikely to be repeated. But to Mulally, it retained its magic. Mulally tended to see things in epic proportion, and this was no exception.

There it is, he thought. *An American and global icon!*

Mulally had saved Boeing. If he could save Ford, too, he knew he would be regarded as one of the greatest business leaders of his era. Maybe of all time. Mulally had been rolling that thought over like a shiny stone ever since Ford had surprised him with that first phone call. More than the money, this was what had convinced him to come to Dearborn—this and the desire to make a difference that had driven him since that day forty-four years before when President Kennedy had challenged his generation to do what was hard. Mulally knew that everything he had accomplished would mean little if he failed now. Instead of being remembered as the guy who saved Boeing, he would be the guy who lost Ford. But Mulally banished that thought from his mind as he looked up at the big Blue Oval that crowned the edifice.

"Okay," he said. "I'm ready."

* * *

Only a handful of people inside World Headquarters knew he was coming.

Bill Ford had begun notifying his senior executives on Friday, September 1, starting with Chief Financial Officer Don Leclair, and then the heads of Ford's American and international operations. Mulally followed up with calls of his own over the weekend. Ford knew the news would be particularly disappointing to Mark Fields, who was widely viewed as his heir apparent. He was also the man who had been tapped to fix Ford a year earlier. Fields was only forty-five—still young enough to have a shot at the top job once Mulally was done. But the decision to bring in an outside turnaround expert could be seen as an indictment of his own ability to address Ford's woes.

"Mark, this is the guy who can make you a CEO," Ford told him. "I really need you to support him. I think he'll provide the right leadership for the company and help you and your team be successful in continuing the turnaround."

In truth, Fields was not really surprised. He had noticed the tension at recent board meetings and assumed something was going to have to change soon. He may have been disappointed, but he was also amazed that Ford was willing to put aside his ego and ask for help. So he Googled "Alan Mulally" and started reading up on his new boss.

Mark Schulz, vice president of Ford's international operations, thought he, too, was in line for the chief executive's job. When he got the call about Mulally from Bill Ford, he felt slighted. Though he understood why the board might like the idea of an outside CEO, he took it as a snub to the company's senior leaders. The message it sent was that none of them was up to the challenge. Now, he realized, he would never have the chance to prove the board wrong.

More executives were notified Tuesday morning. Most were surprised by the news initially. Some said they saw it coming. All of them were moved by Bill Ford's apparent lack of ego, even if it defied the rules of their world. Power was an end unto itself in the automobile industry, and the idea that someone of Ford's stature would voluntary give it up was almost unimaginable.

✳   ✳   ✳

At 2:20 P.M., Laymon finally pulled into the garage beneath World Headquarters like a smuggler, his eyes darting down the rows of washed and waxed Jaguars and Land Rovers that were the preferred rides of Ford's executives to make sure none of them was around. Mulally noted the lack of Fords and Lincolns.

Bill Ford was waiting when they pulled up to the entranceway. He was a little surprised to see his new CEO emerge from the Land Rover wearing a blue blazer, olive slacks, a blue button-down shirt, and a yellow tie. This was Dearborn, Michigan, not Silicon Valley. Men still wore suits to work here, as Ford's own bespoke gray one ably demonstrated. But Mulally was about to establish a new normal. He was wearing what would soon be recognized as his customary uniform. In the days to come he might mix it up a bit with a white shirt and red tie—maybe even gray trousers—but Mulally would not put on a suit, even when he visited the White House.

Waiting next to Bill Ford was Karen Hampton, a young communications executive who would become Mulally's media handler and minder. She slapped a Blue Oval pin on his lapel and led the two men upstairs for a photo shoot in the company lobby. Once again Mulally was overcome by a sense of history and felt a lump in his throat as he surveyed the Model Ts, Mustangs, and other vintage Fords that filled the marbled main floor. He smiled at a portrait of Henry Ford. Curious employees walked by wondering who the grinning guy was posing with Bill Ford. Holleran knew it was a risk for them to be seen together before the news was announced, but he needed to get pictures for the press packets his team was putting together upstairs. Mulally, however, had little tolerance for secrets. He wanted to shake hands with everybody who walked by, introduce himself, and ask them what they thought he should do to fix the company.

When they were done, the group hurried into the executive elevator and rode it to the twelfth floor. Mulally followed Ford to his office, which occupied the southeast corner. He pointed to Mulally's own office just a few steps away in the northeast corner. The two suites were separated only by a waiting room.

"I'll be right here when you need me," Ford promised.

The company's senior executives were crammed into Bill Ford's private conference room. The overseas chiefs were listening in on speakerphone. At 3:30 P.M., Ford and Mulally walked in and the room fell silent. Ford explained that he was resigning as CEO and introduced Mulally as Ford's new chief executive. As he talked, all eyes were on the Boeing executive. Mulally did his best to smile back, despite the growing intensity of their stares. He had never felt so scrutinized. Mulally thought about shouting, "Boo!" and then telling the serious-looking executives, "Don't worry—it's going to be okay." But he restrained himself.

Fields eyed Mulally's outfit.

He's here to meet the press and he's wearing a sport coat, the dapper executive thought acidly. *Well, this is sure going to be different.* Fields' first impression of Mulally was that he was a bit corny. And he was not the only one who felt that way. Mulally's farm-boy demeanor surprised many in the room.

He doesn't look like he'll be a hammer, thought Ford Credit CEO Mike Bannister. He had gotten the news that morning and Googled Mulally before heading over to Bill Ford's conference room. Bannister was hoping for somebody with a bit more gravitas. He was fed up with the infighting in Dearborn and thinking about quitting. He liked Mulally but wondered if he was tough enough to do what needed to be done.

Mulally seemed more like a politician to Mark Schulz, who was put off by his backslapping and arm squeezing.

"Why did you leave Boeing?" he asked.

"This is an opportunity for me to help another American and global icon," Mulally replied.

At least one person rolled his eyes.

It was not a warm reception. Ford's senior executives were products of a cutthroat corporate culture. Like courtiers of old, they were accustomed to smiling at the new king even as they plotted his demise. Mulally was an outsider whose very presence testified to the fact that Bill Ford had lost all confidence in his management team. It did not take long for someone to note that Mulally knew nothing about the automobile industry.

"We appreciate you coming here from a company like Boeing, but you've got to realize that this a very, very capital-intensive business with long product development lead times," quipped Ford's chief technical officer, Richard Parry-Jones. "The average car is made up of thousands of different parts, and they all have to work together flawlessly."

"That's really interesting," Mulally replied with a smile. "The typical passenger jet has four *million* parts, and if just one of them fails, the whole thing can fall out of the sky. So I feel pretty comfortable with this."

That shut them up, but Mulally got the message.

They don't believe I can do this, he realized. *I need to convince them that I get this.*

❊　　❊　　❊

Ford's executives were not the only ones who needed convincing. As Mulally met with his new leadership team upstairs, Holleran was meeting with his own team a few floors below in the communications department.

On the previous Wednesday, Holleran had summoned three of his top managers—Hampton, Jon Pepper, and Oscar Suris, a former *Wall Street Journal* reporter who was in charge of corporate media relations—to his office to let them know what was about to happen. They spent the rest of the week putting together the press releases and internal memos announcing Bill Ford's decision.

Over the weekend, Holleran and Laymon flew out to Seattle to prepare Mulally for the announcement. First they played a round of golf. Mulally was an avid golfer. So was Laymon. But the HR chief was also a student of human nature, and he spent most of his time on the course watching Ford's new CEO closely. He noticed that Mulally learned from his mistakes, adjusting his swing whenever he hit a less-than-perfect shot. Mulally was also friendly with the beverage cart vendor—not at all condescending or aloof. And when someone hit a particularly bad shot and got frustrated, Mulally slapped him on the back and said, "Well, look how far down the right side you are."

We got lucky, Laymon thought. *This guy is the real deal.*

After eighteen holes, the group sat down to discuss the upcoming announcement. Mulally told Holleran that he had come up with a plan for dealing with the media.

"We already have one," Holleran said, sliding a thick binder across the table. Mulally opened it.

"Holy shit!" Mulally said as he thumbed through the pages, which contained not only the answers to every question he was likely to be asked but also detailed plans for staging the event. It covered everything, right down to where the press photographers would be corralled to control the composition of their shots.*

"Every picture that's taken is going to include you and Bill, because we don't want a palace coup as the story," he explained.

"Is all this necessary?" Mulally asked.

"This isn't Seattle. It isn't even Detroit. It's the world. This is the Ford Motor Company, and every burp is news," Holleran told him. "There's a reason that the *Wall Street Journal*, the *New York Times*, and all the wire services have offices in a decaying city. This is the linchpin of the economy, and you're going on center stage."

Holleran's team had been setting that stage for days. They drafted memos for Bill Ford to send out to employees bemoaning the lack of honesty at the top of the company and calling for fundamental

---

* This was the work of Ford's director of strategic communications, Josh Gottheimer, who learned such tricks when he was a special assistant to then-president Bill Clinton.

changes in the way the corporation was run. Then they leaked these to the press. The idea was to paint a portrait of Bill Ford as a man looking for a lever with which to pry his company out of the rut it had been stuck in for too long. That way, the hiring of a new CEO would be seen as something Bill Ford did, rather than something that was done to him.

Ford's PR team knew that reporters would be looking for quotes from outside sources come Tuesday, and they wanted to make sure those were positive, too. That weekend, they had Bill Ford call David Cole, the chairman of the Center for Automotive Research in Ann Arbor and the most quoted industry pundit in America. Holleran knew that Cole would be the first person most reporters called for a reaction once they heard the news.

"We're going to bring in a new CEO," Ford told Cole. "I'm really enthusiastic about this guy, because he's done it before. He's coming from Boeing. His name is Alan Mulally. You'll like him."

Unlike most people in Detroit, Cole knew all about Mulally. Cole was a Boeing shareholder and had followed his efforts to keep the company flying. Cole also knew that the aerospace business was at least as complex as the automobile business. Mulally called Cole himself a few minutes before Tuesday's press conference and worked his own magic. When the reporters started calling a few minutes later, Cole had nothing but good things to say about Ford's new CEO.

Holleran and Pepper even figured out a way to bend the nation's most influential financial organ to their will. The *Wall Street Journal*'s top investigative reporter, Monica Langley, was already working on a piece about the automaker. They were worried it was going to be an indictment of Bill Ford's leadership but had agreed to cooperate with her because they knew she was talking to board members and would end up with a story either way. Her piece was slated to run a few days after Mulally's hiring was announced. They decided to call her and offer her the scoop. If she had it, the only thing her story could be about was Alan Mulally. Langley might hurl a few barbs at Bill Ford in the process, but she would also have to give him credit for having the courage to step aside. But they needed Bill Ford's approval to let her in on the secret, and Ford was nervous about letting anyone in the press know ahead of time.

"Bill, it's the best way to get this story told," Holleran told his boss. "The *Journal* will set the tone for the rest of the national coverage."

In the end, Ford agreed. At eight o'clock Tuesday morning, Langley received a call from Pepper. He told her that Ford was about to make an important announcement and offered to fill her in if she agreed not to release the story until the press release went out on the wire. She was reluctant, but Pepper told her she would have hours to work on her story before the rest of the media even knew about it. Langley agreed. Like David Cole, she received a call from Mulally Tuesday afternoon.

✱   ✱   ✱

The press release went out as soon as the markets closed, just after 4 P.M., as did an e-mail from Bill Ford to his employees around the world. In both, Bill Ford described the challenges facing the company and the reasons for his decision to step aside.

"While I knew that we were fortunate to have outstanding leaders driving our operations around the world, I also determined that our turnaround effort required the additional skills of an executive who has led a major manufacturing enterprise through such challenges before," he wrote in his message to employees. "After dealing with the troubles at Boeing in the post-9/11 world, Alan knows what it's like to have your back to the wall—and fight your way out with a well-conceived plan and great execution. He also knows how to deal with long product cycles, changing fuel prices and difficult decisions in a turnaround."

Ford stressed that his own commitment to the company remained unchanged.

"Let me assure you: I'm not going anywhere," Ford continued. "As executive chairman, I intend to remain extremely active in the direction of this company. I'll be here every day and I will not rest until a prosperous future for this company is secured."

Throughout Dearborn and around the world, Ford offices fell

silent as employees read the message. Murmurs ran down the assembly lines in factories on six continents.

Meanwhile, dozens of reporters and photographers rushed to Ford World Headquarters for the 5 P.M. press conference. Inside the media center, cameras clicked and flashes popped as Ford and Mulally fielded questions beneath a big Blue Oval. Most of the reporters wanted to know just who was in charge in the Glass House now.

"This is a partnership," Ford said. "Alan is going to be CEO, and I'm going to be executive chairman, and we're going to be working closely on all of these issues."

Mulally was also asked if his experience in the aerospace business was transferable to Detroit.

"The fundamentals between these two industries are exactly the same," Mulally insisted, holding both companies up as icons of American manufacturing. "Some people think the United States can't compete in the design and production of sophisticated products. I personally think we can."

He said he had demonstrated that at Boeing, and he promised to do the same at Ford.

Then someone asked Mulally what type of car he drove.

"A Lexus," he said without even a hint of embarrassment. "It's the finest car in the world."

"That's being keyed now as we're sitting here," Ford quipped, referring to the practice of scratching a vehicle's paint with a car key.

The always-personable Bill Ford had a way of turning press conferences into laugh-fests, a rare quality in a town where most executives took themselves far too seriously. This one was no exception. When a reporter observed that Mulally was sixty-one and noted that most Ford executives retired by sixty-five, Ford threw out another zinger.

"Doesn't he look great for sixty-one?" he said. "This place will change that."

* * *

The next morning, Ford and Mulally addressed employees in a town hall meeting at World Headquarters that was broadcast to the company's facilities around the world. As Ford mounted the stage, he received a standing ovation from the workers in the auditorium. Mulally did, too, but there was less enthusiasm in their applause.

Both men reiterated what they had said the day before. Bill Ford talked about the need to have someone at the top who had "been through the wars, and has the scars to show for it and came out victorious." Mulally said he was honored to be asked to lead such a storied company. Then they opened the floor to questions.

The first came from a woman who nervously asked about the epic downsizing Mulally had presided over at Boeing. She was not alone in her concern; many in the company were worried that what Ford had hired was not so much a CEO as a hatchet man. Mulally did his best to reassure her, explaining that the cuts he had made at Boeing were the direct result of the 2001 terrorist attacks, which had forced the aircraft manufacturer to slash production by more than 50 percent.

"We had to take dramatic action just to survive as a company," Mulally told her. What he did not say was that Ford would have to as well.

Another employee asked for the specifics of his turnaround plan. That was still a work in progress, Mulally said, but he thought the company's recent restructuring moves were a good start.

"Matching the capacity to the demand right now is just critical," he said, adding that improving quality and productivity while continuing to invest in new products would also be essential. "I'm building on what you've done to get us to this place."

Mulally was asked if he was going to bring in his own team of executives.

"My team is right here," he said with a smile.

The senior executives sitting in the front row smiled back, though few of them believed Mulally meant it. If the past was any guide, many of them would soon be looking for jobs. But Ford's recent past was nothing to Mulally but a cautionary tale. It was a new day in Dearborn, as Mulally made clear when one executive, Linda Dunbar, asked if her strategic planning group would play a bigger role in his regime.

Mulally shook his head.

"You don't want somebody on the side doing the strategy," he said, nodding toward the front row. "It's us. That's the number-one thing. It's not going to be a strategy department. It's going to be our team. It's going to be the leadership team that decides where we are going."

Dunbar's group would be dissolved a few months later.

A Jaguar–Land Rover employee called in from Britain to ask Mulally what he intended to do with Ford's European brands. The man could not help but notice that Boeing had only the one brand. Mulally said he was looking forward to having a discussion about Ford's brand lineup. That did not exactly reassure the folks in England.

An engineer in Dearborn asked Bill Ford if his family was prepared to give Mulally a free hand.

"I wouldn't have been able to attract someone of Alan's caliber if his hands were tied," he replied. "Alan's the CEO. He's going to make the changes that he feels he should make and wants to make, and I'll support him."

Ford made it clear that his decision to bring in an outside CEO meant the end of business as usual at the company.

"Everybody here has not always been on the same page, and we have not had alignment always throughout the organization. It's frustrated me enormously," he said. "That's been an inhibitor in the past, and it's time for it to change."

＊　＊　＊

The executives at Ford tried to learn everything they could about their new CEO.

Fields started calling friends who knew Mulally, or at least knew of him. Everybody told him the same thing: He was an excellent leader who believed strongly in teamwork, execution, data, and delivering on commitments. One of them sent Fields a video—a clip from the PBS documentary that showed Mulally's team stress-testing the wing for the Boeing 777. When it passed, a jubilant Mulally hugged all of his coworkers. He looked like he might kiss a couple of them. The scene raised the eyebrows of the tough, Jersey-born product of Detroit's macho car culture.

I was right, Fields thought. *This is definitely going to be different.*

Other executives did their own research. E-mails from Boeing executives describing Mulally's management style made the rounds. Some Ford executives found out that Mulally had written the introduction to a book on teamwork called *Working Together* and ordered copies. More than a few updated their résumés and waited for the guillotine blade to fall. No one was willing to acknowledge that he had been part of the problem. But most feared they would be found guilty by association and sent packing with the rest of the old guard.

It did not take long for the first executive to "self-select" out, just as Mulally had predicted.

Anne Stevens had grown tired of bickering with Fields. She was already headed for the exit before Mulally's hiring was announced, but this was her last straw. The highest-ranking woman in the automobile industry was determined to be CEO herself one day. She was fifty-six and already behind Fields in the queue, so she decided that was never going to happen at Ford. The automaker announced Stevens' retirement on September 14.*

The world outside Ford was trying to figure out what to make of Ford's new CEO as well. Holleran's media plan had worked. The coverage of Mulally's hiring was overwhelmingly positive. But not entirely.

"Ford and the Detroit auto industry have a history of expelling outsiders the way the human body expels foreign objects," wrote Daniel Howes in a column in the *Detroit News* that appeared the following morning. "Things get all furious, nasty and infectious until the interloper leaves or is removed, while those who remain vow to 'never again' make the same mistake."

After Bill Ford read it, he called and canceled his subscription. It would be months before he would renew it—or talk to Howes again.

Ford's factory workers did not take the news well, either. The talk on the assembly line the next day was about all the machinists who lost their jobs under Mulally at Boeing.

As it turned out, they had reason to worry.

---

* Stevens would soon reach her goal, taking a job as CEO of Carpenter Technology Corporation. Three years later, she would be out of a job once again, and a year after that her face would appear on the cover of the *Wall Street Journal*, illustrating a story on down-and-out executives looking for work.

✳ ✳ ✳

L ess than two weeks after Bill Ford announced that he was stepping down as CEO, reporters were again summoned to the Glass
House. This time the news was grim. But in keeping with Mulally's
new spirit of transparency and honesty, it was delivered without the
customary spin. Though Fields was still sporting his infamous mullet,
his usual Jersey-boy swagger was noticeably absent when he took the
stage. His Way Forward plan had not worked. It had been derailed by
the collapse of the truck market and rising raw materials costs. The
original plan was supposed to restore Ford to profitability by 2008.
Now he conceded that goal was unreachable. The company would not
be able to return to profitability until 2009, and then only by making
even deeper cuts.

"The fundamentals of our Way Forward plan have not changed. It's
our timetable that has changed—and changed dramatically," said a
chastened Fields. "It is now clear that we were too optimistic in January about our ability to stabilize our market share given the quicker
than expected shifts in the marketplace. The simple fact is that the
business model that served us in North America for decades no longer works. We must change to a new business model that delivers
greater bottom-line contributions from cars and crossovers, continued leadership in pickups, new products that drive revenue and actions that more rapidly reduce costs to achieve profitability."

With that, Fields announced his Way Forward acceleration plan.
It called for shuttering two more factories, bringing the total number
of plants now slated for closure by 2012 to sixteen.* In addition, all
of the factories Ford took back as part of the 2005 bailout of Visteon
would be sold or closed by the end of 2008. A third of the company's
North American salaried workforce would be eliminated, translat-
ing into the loss of another 14,000 jobs on top of the 30,000 already
cut. Ford had reached an agreement with the United Auto Workers

---

* Those two factories were Ford's Maumee Stamping Plant in Ohio and Essex
Engine Plant in Windsor, Ontario. The new plan also accelerated the timetable
for the previously announced plant closures.

to offer voluntary buyouts and early retirement packages to all union members. Fields said the company now hoped to eliminate between 25,000 and 30,000 factory jobs over the next two years. Ford would also suspend dividend payments indefinitely.

"These actions have painful consequences for communities and many of our loyal employees," Bill Ford said. "But rapid shifts in consumer demand that affect our product mix and continued high prices for commodities mean we must continue working quickly and decisively to fix our business. Mark Fields and his team deserve credit for the accelerated Way Forward strategy, which puts us on an even faster product-driven path to success. Alan Mulally's experience in turning around a major industrial company will help guide the implementation of these measures as he assumes leadership of the company."

* * *

Mulally had reviewed the plan with Fields and his team before the presentation. As Fields went over the details with his new boss, he wondered if it had all been for naught.

"Alan, we're going to the board with this tomorrow. Our intent, once we get the board approval on this, is to announce it on Friday," he said. "But you're the new CEO. If you want us to put a hold on this and not announce it, that's your prerogative. I'm perfectly prepared to do that."

"No," Mulally said. "You guys should go ahead. We'll improve it as we go."

However, he did make a few changes. Mulally pointed out that Fields' plan was all about cutting costs and did little to address the more fundamental problem: Ford was not making cars that people wanted to buy. Mulally knew Ford had to stop losing money, but he also knew that was only part of the equation. It also needed to give consumers a reason to believe in the Blue Oval again. He told Leclair and Fields that he was working on a plan to radically simplify Ford's global product lineup. Instead of spreading its new product dollars thin across scores of different nameplates, Mulally wanted to focus Ford's investment on a few key vehicles and make those products truly world class. He explained how a similar approach had paid off at Boeing. It would work at Ford, too—but only if the company was prepared to really invest in those products. Mulally pointed out that all of the buyouts and severance packages required by Fields' plan were going to add up, and he wanted to make sure there would still be enough cash left in the company's coffers to pay for a showroom full of game-changing cars and trucks.

"Do we have enough money to restructure ourselves, and get back to profitability and accelerate the development of new products?" he asked.

Leclair told him the finance team was already working on a plan to ensure Ford had the money it needed. Mulally told him to aim high.

✳ ✳ ✳

The two-day-long September meeting was Mulally's first opportunity to address the entire board of directors. Following the formal introduction of Mulally by Bill Ford, one board member after another told Mulally how happy they were that he had decided to join the company. But they also made it clear that they expected a lot from him. Then they asked what he thought of Ford so far.

Mulally paused for a moment before answering. Here was a chance to begin the discussion about simplifying Ford—the central theme of his turnaround strategy. At the same time, he knew he had to tread carefully, because these were the same people who had presided over the acquisition of Ford's foreign brands and approved the hodge-podge of disparate products the company was selling around the world. Nonetheless, Mulally knew an opening when he saw one and took it.

"We have a lot of brands. We have a lot of nameplates. We're known in the U.S. as a big truck and SUV company—and for the Mustang. We have very complex product offerings," he told the directors. "I think there is a tremendous opportunity to simplify, consolidate, and focus Ford."

Mulally wanted to say more but checked himself out of fear of going too far too fast. Then he noticed the smiles and nodding heads. Several of the directors agreed with his assessment. They asked what he thought of Fields' plan.

"This is a good start," he said. "We have the key elements in there. But we need to further develop this."

Saving the company would require even deeper cuts, Mulally told the board. It would also require a fundamental reorganization to better utilize Ford's global resources. He needed to come up with a new leadership structure to ensure greater accountability and force everyone to work together toward a common set of goals. And none of these steps would mean anything if the company did not accelerate the development of new products. He asked the board to pledge its support for these moves once he had worked out the details. The board agreed with Mulally's assessment and promised to back whatever changes he felt were necessary. The directors approved Fields' proposal with the understanding that Mulally would prepare a more aggressive plan by the end of the year.

They will back me one hundred percent, he realized as he left the meeting. *Now I just need the support of the Ford family.*

✳ ✳ ✳

The descendants of Henry Ford flew into Dearborn on September 18 to eyeball their new CEO. They met with Mulally at Greenfield Village—the nineteenth-century fantasy town their ancestor had frozen in time and later turned into an educational theme park to commemorate the world his automobiles had left in the dust.

Mulally was so excited about meeting all the Ford heirs in person that he actually printed out a family tree beforehand and brought it with him so that he could figure out who was who. He asked the family members to autograph it for him. Touched by Mulally's enthusiasm for Ford's illustrious past, they obliged. But they were a lot more interested to hear what he thought of Ford's future. They asked Mulally to explain how he had brought Boeing back from the brink, and what he thought of Ford's chances for survival.

"I've been through it, and I think we can do it here," Mulally assured them. "Here's what we have to do: We have to deal with the reality of today and then develop a growth plan for the future."

He told them that he was still working out the details of his plan but had already concluded that Ford needed to simplify its brand lineup and product offerings. The company needed to focus on the things its customer really wanted, not what the engineers or bean counters wanted. And Ford needed to develop a point of view about the future instead of just reacting to its competitors.

As he left, one family member after another shook his hand and told him how happy they were to have him in charge of the company.

* * *

Before heading back to Seattle to wrap things up at Boeing, Mulally sat alone in his new office at the top of World Headquarters and took in the view. To his right he could see the futuristic Ford-built tower in downtown Detroit that now housed General Motors' world headquarters. On the horizon in front of him was the hazy outline of Chrysler's copper-colored edifice in Auburn Hills.

"I've got them right where I want them," he told a visitor with a laugh.

The men in charge of those companies were having a good laugh of their own at Mulally's expense. The conventional wisdom in Detroit held that outsiders were incapable of understanding the complexities of the automobile business. Bill Ford's decision to hire an aeronautical engineer to save his car company spawned plenty of jokes during those early weeks. There was a lot of snickering about flying cars and the return of tail fins. "He has no idea how we do things in Detroit" was the common refrain at Ford's crosstown rivals, as well as within Ford itself. And Mulally knew it.

They're right. I don't know how they do things in Detroit, he thought. *But I do know it doesn't work.*

CHAPTER 5

The Revolution Begins

We do not make changes for the sake of making them, but we never fail to make a change when once it is demonstrated that the new way is better than the old way.

— HENRY FORD

When Alan Mulally returned to Dearborn the following week, he took one look at his crowded schedule and shook his head.

"That doesn't work for me," he said.

It was "meeting week" at Ford Motor Company, the time each month when Ford's senior executives sat through one agonizing caucus after another, each devoted to a different issue or facet of the company's operations. There were meetings to discuss Ford's finances, meetings to discuss sales, meetings to discuss new products. Mulally thought about canceling them all on the spot, but decided to endure one complete cycle to better understand the pathology of Ford's illness.

During the sessions he attended, Mulally asked probing questions and demanded yes-or-no answers. He brooked no equivocation and was not interested in the long-winded explanations that most of his managers felt compelled to offer. What he did demand was transparency and honesty. Mulally found both in short supply. It did not take long for him to realize that the truth came in many flavors at Ford.

Even when he tried to focus on the data, he found that different sources offered different numbers for different audiences. For example, when estimating demand for a new product, inflated figures were often given to suppliers to help win lower prices while a more conservative figure was offered to analysts so that Ford would look good when it exceeded their expectations. The same thing happened internally. Executives offered exaggerated sales estimates for proposed products to the finance staff in order to win approval for their programs.

Mulally was not officially due to take over as CEO until October 1, but this was just too much for him. Since Ford's executives seemed to like meetings so much, he asked his secretary to schedule one more. When he had them all together, Mulally started laying down his law.

"There are too many meetings," he told them. "When do you have time to think about the customer?"

Nobody answered. From now on, Mulally continued, there would be only one corporate-level meeting—his "business plan review," or BPR. It would be held every week on the same day, at the same time, in the same place. Attendance would be mandatory for all senior executives. All would be expected to personally deliver succinct status reports and updates on their progress toward the company's turn-around goals. This would not be a forum for discussion or debate. Any issues that required more in-depth consideration by the entire leadership team would be taken up in a "special attention review," or SAR, immediately following the BPR. The idea was to keep the main meeting focused on the big picture. And Mulally stressed that, when there was discussion and debate in the SAR, it would be based on business realities, not politics or personality. That was the old Ford, he said. The new Ford was all about the numbers.

"The data sets you free," he said with a smile.*

Mulally had developed this business planning process at Boeing. It was based on the system the aircraft manufacturer used to manage product programs, but he had evolved it into a framework for managing the entire organization. All of the data from every business unit and function was distilled down to a set of tables, charts, and graphs and presented in a series of PowerPoint slides. Mulally was still an engineer at heart. He had approached the task of running Boeing's

---

* Mulally's emphasis on facts and figures was reminiscent of the data-driven regime the Whiz Kids introduced at Ford after World War II. This group of U.S. Army Air Forces veterans applied the same statistical methods they had used to manage the air war over Germany and Japan to the business of making automobiles.

commercial aircraft division as an engineering exercise. The BPR process was the algorithm he had developed to solve it. He believed the same system could be used to run any complex, global enterprise. Ford would be the test of that hypothesis. He gave each executive a set of slides from Boeing to use as templates until they understood the process and could develop their own. He told them to fill in the blanks with the real data and be ready to present it the following Thursday. And he told them to be ready for action.

"We are the decision makers," Mulally said. "We need to make decisions and not pass the buck."

*　　*　　*

When he was not admonishing his new executives, Mulally blew through the Glass House like a Kansas cyclone, shaking hands, memorizing faces, and leaving everything changed in his wake. He would stop people in the hallway and ask them what they did and what he could do to improve the company. Instead of eating in Ford's famously posh executive dining room, he took his lunch in the company cafeteria. He stood in line with his plastic tray and chatted up accountants. He would sidle up to a table full of sales analysts and ask if he could join them. For Mulally, an open door was an invitation to pop his head in and see what was going on inside. More than one meeting came to an abrupt halt when someone noticed him standing in the doorway.

"What are you guys talking about?" he would ask as he made his way around the table, shaking hands and squeezing shoulders. Mulally would listen in for a few minutes and then continue on to wherever he was going, leaving behind a roomful of open-mouthed employees.

Ford's ranks were full of men and women who had tried unsuccessfully to draw management's attention to inefficiencies in their departments, shortcomings in Ford's business strategy, or ways its products and processes could be improved. Now they found somebody who was willing to listen. Mulally was inundated with e-mails but responded personally to every message. His own notes were peppered with smileys. If an e-mail really caught his eye, he might even follow up with a telephone call. These quickly became the stuff of water cooler conversations throughout the company.

One Ford engineer, James Morgan, took a gamble and showed up at Mulally's office with an armload of engineering schematics. Like Mulally himself, Morgan was a student of the Toyota product development system. He had even written a book about it, and he wanted to show Ford's CEO just how much Ford still had to learn. Morgan unrolled drawings for more than a dozen different hood structures on Mulally's conference table. Mulally leaned over them, studying each one closely as Morgan showed him how each was structured in a different way. They even used different latches. Mulally may not have been a car guy, but he knew how to read engineering schematics. They told him everything he needed to know about the company's lack of engineering discipline. He asked Morgan if there was a way to reduce this complexity. There was, Morgan told him. Mulally put him in charge of that effort and asked for regular updates.

Instead of being discouraged by Ford's inefficiency, such discoveries actually came as a relief to Mulally.

"I look at that as nothing but opportunity," he said. "If you were a lean machine, doing a turnaround like this would be terrifying. But this is a very complex place, and there's a lot of opportunity to consolidate and simplify."

But Mulally was dismayed by his first visit to the company's Product Development Center, a sprawling redbrick campus located a few minutes from World Headquarters. There, Ford's head of product development for North America, Derrick Kuzak, was waiting to show off the company's lineup. Kuzak and his staff had parked every vehicle Ford sold in North America beneath the domed ceiling of Ford's private showroom and waxed them until they were sparkling in the bright spotlights. The first thing that struck Mulally when he walked in was how big most of the cars and trucks were. There were almost no compacts, and not a single subcompact. He noticed that something else was missing as well.

"Where's the Taurus?" Mulally asked.

The product guys looked at one another.

"We killed it," Kuzak said.

"You killed it?!" Mulally asked incredulously. "Wasn't it the best-selling car in America?"

"At one point," Kuzak said. "But we didn't maintain our investment in it. People stopped buying them. The only customers we could still sell them to were rental car agencies. The plant that made them is going to be closed at the end of the month."

"But it was such a great brand," Mulally said. "Why didn't you just make a new one?"

Kuzak told him that Ford's marketing staff had concluded the Taurus nameplate was irrevocably damaged. The car's replacement was the Fusion. And it was selling well, he pointed out.

That may be, Mulally thought. *But you don't spend millions of dollars building a brand and then walk away from it. That is one mistake that is not going to happen again under my watch.*

Mulally started driving a new Ford home every night, and showed up the next morning eager to share his thoughts about it. The Ford Fusion did impress him. Mulally had not paid much attention to Ford vehicles as a consumer, and he was surprised to find a car this good in the company's lineup. But other vehicles, such as the uninspiring Ford Five Hundred, made him realize how much work there was still to be done. Once he had worked his way through all Ford's cars and trucks, he asked the company's fleet manager to start providing him with competitors' vehicles so that he could see how they compared. His first request was for a Toyota Camry. Mulally had owned a couple before trading up to a Lexus and wanted to see how the Japanese automaker had improved them since then. He was stunned to learn that there were no cars from other automakers in Ford's fleet. While the company purchased Camrys for evaluation and engineering teardowns, none of the executives had ever asked to drive one. Mulally told his fleet manager to go shopping, and he ordered his senior managers to start driving Volkswagens and Hondas home instead of their Jaguars and Land Rovers.

Everything Mulally did seemed downright subversive in an industry that celebrated power and privilege. In Detroit, CEOs did not dine with their employees, nor did they seem to care much about what their employees thought. And they certainly did not drive Japanese cars home. In fact, they rarely drove at all. That was what chauffeurs were for.

But Mulally was just getting started.

* * *

The real revolution began on Thursday, September 28, 2006.

At 8 A.M., Ford's senior executives gathered in the Thunderbird Room on the eleventh floor of World Headquarters for their first BPR meeting. There, beneath black-and-white photographs of Henry Ford and his Model T, the latter-day leaders of the Ford Motor Company gathered around a large round table like knights in some modern staging of the tales of King Arthur, with Mulally in the title role. To his surprise, many arrived trailing adjutants and subalterns armed with thick three-ring binders that presumably contained the answers to every conceivable question the new CEO might ask their bosses. Mulally thought he had made it clear that executives were responsible for their own presentations.

"You're welcome to bring guests," he announced as they filed into the room. "But they won't be allowed to speak or answer questions."

Nervous glances were exchanged among the executives. They were used to deferring tough questions or demands for details to their subordinates. But Mulally reminded them that they were in charge of the company and were expected to know their areas inside and out.

"If you don't know the answer to something, that's okay, because we'll all be here again next week," he said with a smile. "And I *know* you'll know it then."

As the executives took their places in black leather chairs around the cherry table, Mulally called their attention to a list of rules posted on the wall. There were ten of them:

- People first
- Everyone is included
- Compelling vision
- Clear performance goals
- One plan
- Facts and data

- Propose a plan, "find-a-way" attitude
- Respect, listen, help, and appreciate each other
- Emotional resilience . . . trust the process
- Have fun . . . enjoy the journey and each other

Like the slide templates, these rules had been imported from Boeing. Yet they seemed tailor-made for Ford. As he went down the list, Mulally added a few specifics to underscore these points. There were to be no side discussions, no jokes at anyone else's expense, and no BlackBerrys.

These regulations would prove particularly onerous. At Ford, meetings were political theater; side discussions where the real business of the company was conducted. They were where deals were cut and truths too painful to put in a PowerPoint presentation were shared. From now on, Mulally insisted, there would be no more secrets. The BPR and the SAR would shine a light into the darkest corners of the company. Everything would be illuminated.

Making jokes at the expense of others was a regular pastime at Ford—one some of the executives sitting in the Thunderbird Room that morning had spent decades mastering. They had not gotten where they were just because they were the best or the brightest, but because they knew how to dish it out and how to take it. In a company like Ford, the weak went to the wall; only the strong survived. Now they were being told they were all on the same team, and Mulally expected them to act like it.

The rule on BlackBerrys struck several of the executives as particularly condescending. They all carried them, and most spent the better part of any meeting glued to them—reading e-mails, checking sports scores, or playing BrickBreaker. This was disrespectful to whoever was speaking, Mulally told them. The whole point of the BPR was to maintain a laserlike focus on the facts of the business, and Mulally meant that literally.*

---

* It took several weeks for the BlackBerry rule to sink in. During the next few BPRs, several executives neglected to turn off their devices. When they got a message, the electrical signal would generate static in the teleconferencing system. Mulally would grimace and scan the table, trying to identify the offender.

Those facts would be displayed on a large screen that dominated the western wall of the room. Mulally took his place at the table directly opposite the screen and looked around the table. There was Chief Financial Officer Don Leclair, Ford Credit CEO Michael Bannister, Ford Americas president Mark Fields, and the head of the company's international operations, Mark Schulz. Human resources and labor affairs boss Joe Laymon was there, as well as Charlie Holleran, the vice president of communications, and Ziad Ojakli, head of corporate affairs and government relations. Also present were marketing director Hans-Olov Olsson and Ford's general counsel, David Leitch. The "guests" were given chairs along the northern, southern, and eastern walls.*

A microphone was mounted in front of each executive. In future meetings, those unable to attend in person would be connected through Ford's teleconferencing system at its European or Asian headquarters. A camera would broadcast the image currently being displayed on the main screen or the face of whoever was speaking to those remote facilities. When people there spoke, they would appear on smaller screens set into a circular opening in the center of the table in the Thunderbird Room. Blinds, flanked by light blue curtains, were shut to keep out the glare.

"Okay, Jackie, let's have the first slide," Mulally said, addressing the woman who ran the show with two assistants from a control booth behind the eastern wall. The agenda for the meeting was displayed on the screen. Mulally would go first. He walked the other executives through the rest of the schedule.

"Next slide," Mulally said.

What followed was a series of projections that outlined the purpose of the meeting and detailed Mulally's emerging plan for the company. One of the first was titled "Our Creating Value Road Map." In its center was a blue oval marked "Vision." Mulally defined this vision for those in the room as "People working together as a lean,

---

* The number of people included in each meeting would expand considerably as Mulally implemented his matrix organization. New rules on guests would also be implemented. More details of the final BPR process will be presented in chapter 20.

global enterprise for automotive leadership." By *leadership,* he said, he meant being viewed as second to none by customers, dealers, suppliers, employees, and investors. Mulally pointed out that there were plenty of ways to measure Ford's standing with each of these constituencies. Right now it was dismal. Together they were going to change that, he told his executives. The central oval was surrounded by three more ovals, labeled "Business Environment and Opportunities," "Strategy," and "Plan." Arrows connected these three, as each one depended upon the other two. The external environment represented by the first had to inform Ford's strategy. That strategy would provide the foundation for the company's actual plan, which would be made up of measurable goals. That plan would in turn help Ford understand how to react to the challenges and opportunities of the business environment.

The mechanism for monitoring all of this was the BPR itself, Mulally explained. Each week, the entire team would review the business environment, examine the company's progress against the backdrop of the plan, and make whatever adjustments were necessary in the SAR.

"This is the only way I know how to operate," he said. "We need to have everybody involved. We need to have a plan. And we need to know where we are on the plan."

It was a lot to take in, and the idea of doing it every week was more than some of the executives could take. They began plotting end runs around Mulally before his presentation was even finished.

When Mulally was done, he asked Leclair to go over Ford's finances. The company was facing a projected loss of more than $12 billion for the year, Leclair told the room. It would be the worst loss in Ford's history. And 2007 was not looking much better. Mulally was not surprised. Bill Ford had warned him that the situation was dire. He was reminded of a quote he had read from the Grateful Dead's Jerry Garcia: "Somebody has to do something, and it's just incredibly pathetic that it has to be us."

In this case, "us" was Mulally himself.

This company has been going out of business for thirty years, he thought as he studied the numbers. *These guys did study after study that showed that something had to be done, and yet they chose not to do it. None of them was ever going to stand up and say, "This is how it's got to be."*

One by one, the assembled executives stumbled through their slides. It was clear that several sets of numbers were still in play, despite Mulally's admonition. He told them he expected all of them to get their facts straight by the next BPR meeting. As in the other meetings he had already attended, Mulally hammered home his twin themes of honesty and accountability. He was affable enough. He never stopped smiling. He did not argue. He preferred to listen and let people dig their own graves. Much of what Mulally heard during those first few meetings was nothing but bovine scatology. But he had a built-in BS detector and a knack for exposing it. Mulally knew that once people had embarrassed themselves a couple of times in front of their peers, they would think twice about lying to him again.

When it was Mark Schulz's turn, the president of Ford's international operations asked if his chief financial officer could do the presentation.

"No," Mulally told him. "I expect each business unit leader to do their own."

Schulz frowned. He did his best to muddle through a presentation for which he was obviously unprepared. After a few minutes Mulally had heard enough.

"Okay," he said.

Schulz kept on talking.

"Good," Mulally said. "Check."

Schulz continued.

"Okay," said Mulally.

Schulz still did not get the hint. Several other executives could see that Mulally was turning red, but Schulz was not one of them.

"Okay!" Mulally snapped.

Schulz stopped mid-sentence and looked around the table. The other executives looked down, intently studying their printouts.

Mulally's staff quickly realized that their new boss often used code words that they ignored at their own peril. *Okay* was one of them. The first *okay* translated as "Thanks, I've heard enough. Let's move on." The second *okay* meant "You are starting to get on my nerves." The third *okay* could be roughly translated as "If you don't shut up right this second, you're fired!" *Check* meant the same thing as *okay*. There were also the three levels of the question *Really?* The first *really* was Mulally-speak for "That's really interesting, if it's true." The second *really* meant "I think you're full of crap." The third *really*—another place nobody wanted to go—translated as "Are you sure you don't want to retract that statement before it permanently affects your status at the company?"

Much of the discussion among executives in those early weeks was devoted to deciphering these codes.

* * *

Schulz walked out of the first BPR meeting chafing at Mulally's new order.

To him there was nothing special about Mulally's process. It was just a different way of looking at the same data—no better or worse than half a dozen others he could think of. If anything, he thought it was overly simplistic. Schulz also worried that preparing for each week's BPR session would be a huge drain on his time. Then there was Mulally's mandatory attendance requirement. In their first one-on-one meeting, Schulz told Mulally that he spent most of his time away from Dearborn. He worried that these Thursday meetings would get in the way of the important work he was doing in Asia. He was spending a lot of time in China trying to secure government support for a new factory in Shanghai. He told Mulally that his weekly meetings would interfere with that work.

"That's okay, you don't have to come to the meetings," Mulally said with a smile. "I mean, you can't be part of the Ford team if you don't—but it's okay. It doesn't mean you're a bad person."

Schulz called in sick to the next BPR and sent his controller in his place. He said he had injured his foot and required surgery, but some of the other executives thought he was really just afraid of another showdown with Mulally. Many of them were beginning to realize that they had underestimated the grinning Kansan. Mulally's down-home persona was like a velvet glove hiding the proverbial iron fist, and they were beginning to feel its squeeze. The sort of accountability and transparency Mulally demanded was unprecedented inside Ford. And Mulally's BPR ground rules made them feel like ill-mannered children. Ford's senior executives were used to trumpeting their successes, not dissecting their failures. Those had been swept under the rug as quickly as possible. The executives also were accustomed to running their divisions as they saw fit. Mulally's insistence that each area of the organization be run using common practices and principles was not only jarring, but also a direct threat to their personal authority.

Schulz was not the only one who thought the whole thing was a big waste of time. Fields, too, tried to get out of the weekly sessions.

Ever since he had been called back from Europe, Fields had jealously guarded his calendar. He thought that most of the corporate meetings he was required to attend were essentially useless. Despite Mulally's assurances that his Thursday BPRs were the cure for this cancer, Fields saw them as one more symptom of the same disease. Fields came to his first one-on-one with Mulally armed with a printout showing how his time was divided. He handed it to Mulally and showed him how most of it was already being spent in meetings. Fields told him he needed to spend more time in the trenches.

"Listen, Alan, one of the most important things I need to spend time on is in the business unit, not getting distracted," Fields told him. "I really don't want to do this."

Mulally stared at him across the desk. "Trust the process," he told Fields.

Do I have a choice? Fields thought. But instead of continuing the debate, he gave Mulally an update on the status of the Way Forward acceleration.

A few of the old guard thought they could wait Mulally out—pay lip service to his reforms, but drag their feet and bide their time. Eventually, they figured, he too would succumb to Ford's noxious culture. But most could see that Mulally was different. He was far more interested in the details of the business than any senior executive had the right to be in the ancien régime, and he missed nothing. Executives had been accustomed to dealing only with the big picture. Now they were being asked to explain the minutest details of their divisions. They might chafe against that, but they could see he demanded nothing of them that he did not demand of himself.

* * *

Mulally's energy was impossible to ignore. The atmosphere on the twelfth floor crackled with it, as though Bill Ford had unleashed some force of nature inside the building. Even the executive chairman was not immune from it.

Company protocol required any executive who wished to speak with Bill Ford to enter his outer office, quietly ask his secretary if he was seeing visitors, and then wait outside while she slipped into his private chambers and checked. Mulally had no patience for that. One morning, as Ford was freebasing espresso and fretting about the Detroit Lions, his new CEO simply strode down the hall, opened the glass door to Ford's outer office, waved at his secretary, and blew past her before she could even object. Ford was slightly flustered the first time it happened, but after a while he got over it. Mulally showed up for work each morning bristling with new ideas, and Ford was often the only person he could bounce them off.

"You know what would be neat?" Mulally would say, before outlining his latest brainstorm.

It put Ford in a somewhat awkward position. Most CEOs did not stick around after admitting defeat. But this was his company, and he still had a major role to play in running it. However, Ford was also determined to stay out of Mulally's way. As Mulally's new order took hold, more than one executive tiptoed to Ford's office to lodge a complaint against the new CEO's intrusion into his affairs. Ford would cut each of them off before he could finish his lament.

"If you have an issue, take it up with Alan," he said to each one. "I agree with everything he's doing."

* * *

On October 23, Ford released its financial results for the third quarter—the first since Mulally joined the company. Ford posted a net loss of $5.8 billion for the months of July, August, and September—its worst quarterly loss in fourteen years.*

"Let me make it clear: these results are unacceptable," Mulally said during a conference call with analysts and reporters that morning. "We know where we are with our business, and we know why we are where we are. We are committed to moving from here to create a viable business going forward. As I have examined our performance, I clearly see the opportunities that will allow us to do so."

It was just the sort of honesty and transparency Mulally demanded of his subordinates. He led by example. He arrived early and often worked seven days a week. With his family back in Seattle, he spent his nights poring over reports from Ford's operations around the world.

Early on, a friendly competition developed between Mulally and two of his executives, Don Leclair and Michael Bannister, to see who would be the first one into the office each morning. Getting there first had long been a badge of honor for the finance guys—a way of establishing that they were the ones who really ran the place—and no CEO was going to deny them that pleasure. Each morning, they would get up a little bit earlier and drive a little bit faster. But Mulally was always at the office first. Bannister gave up when he realized that 5:30 A.M. was still too late.

You guys can win this one, he thought. After all, Mulally just lived a few minutes away from World Headquarters. Ford had given him a luxury condo in the gated Tournament Players Club of Michigan, a private golf community built around a Jack Nicklaus–designed course a mile from the Glass House.

Leclair refused to give up, despite the fact that he lived one county over in Plymouth. To arrive in Dearborn by 5:30 A.M., he had to get up at 4:30 A.M. at the latest. But that was the sort of person Leclair was—a fact not lost on Mulally.

Though he had worked at Ford for thirty years, Leclair was in some

---

* Ford would later restate this as a loss of $5.2 billion. Either way, it was its biggest quarterly loss since the first quarter of 1992, when the company lost $6.9 billion.

ways as much of an outsider as Mulally. While most of Ford's top executives favored loud talk and expensive suits, Leclair was a quiet midwesterner who spent most of his days alone in his office with his shoes off. They wore their cocky overconfidence like pinkie rings. Leclair knew just how bad things were and showed it. They would dismiss dire predictions with a wave of the hand and a reminder that Ford always triumphed in the end. Leclair checked his numbers, checked them again, and saw that time was running out.

Leclair's pessimism and drab personality left him with few friends at the company. But if his fellow executives thought little of him, Leclair thought even less of them. He knew he was the smartest guy in the room, and tended to act like it. As Bill Ford had warned Mulally in their first meeting in Ann Arbor, Leclair was pursuing his own agenda with little regard for what anyone else in the company thought.

But Mulally appreciated Leclair's honesty, as well as his grasp of the minutiae of the business. His knowledge of Ford was encyclopedic. Leclair did not just know finance; he recalled the details of every product program and engineering decision, as well as who was responsible for each one. Mulally's BS detector had been going off like a smoke alarm since he walked into his first BPR meeting. With Leclair, however, it was silent. He was the first person with whom Mulally felt like he could have a genuinely frank conversation.

Mulally called his new CFO into the office on a Sunday for the first of many weekend one-on-ones between them. They spent five or six hours going through all of the company's finances. Leclair walked him through the entire business. Everything Mulally heard confirmed his worst suspicions about the state of the company and reaffirmed the underlying theses of his preliminary plan. At the end of the day, Mulally outlined the major points of his strategy for Leclair. He told Leclair that the BPR process was essential to making it all work.

"We've got to get everybody at the table," he said. "We can't do this with just five or six of us. We need everybody."

Mulally had shared all of this with the board of directors, but Ford's executives were all still wondering what the new boss really had in mind. Leclair seemed visibly moved by the vision of the company that Mulally offered.

"We've never had a CEO who knew what to do," Leclair told him. He pledged his support but warned Mulally that many of the other executives would fight this.

"They all don't get it," Leclair said. "None of them are qualified for the jobs they have."

"I'll take care of that," Mulally assured him.

Mulally paid close attention to what Leclair had to say, both at that meeting and during their many subsequent discussions. In the coming weeks and months, the two men would spend hours together in Mulally's office—going over the books, dissecting each line item, and stress-testing each projection. But Mulally was worried about how negative Leclair was. He was not convinced anybody could save Ford, and his pessimism would only increase as the company's finances deteriorated. However, Mulally's biggest concern about his hardworking CFO was Leclair's apparent inability to work with the rest of the leadership team.

Don knows the business better than anybody, Mulally thought as he listened to Leclair. *But he's not a team player, and he never will be. He's smart, but he can't join me in pulling everyone together.*

As a result, Mulally knew Leclair's days at Ford were numbered. But he was determined to draw out as much knowledge from his CFO as he could before the situation came to a head.

Mulally was quick to appreciate the immense—and too often untapped—pool of talent that surrounded him at Ford. When he found someone who knew what was going on and was not afraid to say so, he brought that person to his office and listened—sometimes for hours—as he explained the flaws in some aspect of Ford's operations and suggested ways these problems could be fixed.

Another early member of Mulally's brain trust, George Pipas, was a veteran sales analyst and forecaster who was getting ready to retire. After watching Ford's share of the U.S. car market decline for the better part of three decades and spending most of that time whispering under his breath about ways to stanch the loss, he had bought a house on Hilton Head and was getting ready to put Ford's woes and Michigan's harsh winters behind him. Mulally called him in South Carolina and asked him to get back to Dearborn as soon as he could.

"I really want to understand the history," Mulally told Pipas when they finally met. "What do we need to do from a product standpoint to create a business that's going to grow?"

The two men spent the better part of a week closeted in Mulally's office, starting early, working late, taking their meals at his conference table. Pipas held nothing back. He walked Mulally through every aspect of the automobile business. He outlined the vehicle segments, from subcompacts to full-size pickups. He guided him through the competitive landscape, detailing each automaker's strengths and weaknesses. He explained how Detroit's foreign rivals had outmaneuvered the Big Three, and he charted Ford's own dramatic decline. They talked about the seasonality of demand, Ford's addiction to pickups and sport utility vehicles, its failure to maintain investment in key products like the Ford Taurus, and its confusing array of nameplates and options. In the end, Mulally asked Pipas to rethink his retirement. He told him he could telecommute from South Carolina as long as he agreed to come back to Dearborn each month and brief him on the sales results. Now that Ford had a leader who listened, Pipas was happy to stay.

Mulally continued to rely on Joe Laymon and Charlie Holleran as well. But he knew their real loyalty was to Ford the man, not Ford the company.

Holleran walked Mulally through the media landscape, explaining which publications and programs were important to Ford and why. The press coverage surrounding Mulally's hiring had been predominantly positive, but Holleran warned him that the honeymoon would be over soon. He told him to stay on message and start preparing for the tough questions that were bound to come.

Before Mulally's first day in Dearborn, Laymon went over the corporate roster with Mulally. He offered two assessments of each executive—an objective one and his own uncensored view, which was often quite cutting. But Laymon advised him to move slowly with any reshuffling.

"You can't change the team you have for a while," he cautioned. "You don't know how to build a car."

Mulally agreed, but insisted on one change: He wanted Steve Hamp out. Mulally neither needed nor wanted a chief of staff. He thought the position added an unnecessary layer of insulation between a CEO and his executive team. And he certainly did not want one who was the executive chairman's brother-in-law.

"You've got to tread very carefully," Laymon warned Mulally. "Steve didn't hire himself. He was put here by certain members of the family. He and Bill have struggled, but he is the chief of staff."

"My team reports directly to me," Mulally replied. "Before I get there, you've got to tell Bill that."

But Laymon warned Mulally that moving against Hamp could turn the family against him before he even started. He told Mulally to give him a chance. However, Hamp's negativity was something Mulally could not abide. Like Leclair, Hamp remained pessimistic about Ford's future and missed no opportunity to share his views. Bill Ford was losing patience with his brother-in-law, too. A few weeks after Mulally started, the two men had a frank discussion about Hamp. When it was over, Ford summoned Laymon to his office.

"Hamp has to go," Ford told his human resources director. But he reminded Laymon that this would be a delicate operation. Ford had not moved against his brother-in-law previously out of fear that it would deepen the rift in the family. Hamp and his wife had their allies. They could still make trouble for Bill and his new CEO.

"Do your magic," Ford told Laymon. "Just make sure it's tight."

Laymon drafted an exit agreement that included some of the strongest nondisparagement language he had ever written. It also included generous compensation. On October 12, the automaker announced that Hamp was leaving the company and that the position of chief of staff was being eliminated. Hamp's departure still created a stir in the Ford family. But Bill and Edsel were able to keep it from blowing up—at least for the time being.

* * *

Mulally would have to work to keep more talented executives from following Hamp out the door.

The first BPR meeting had been a bit overwhelming for Ford Credit chief Michael Bannister. He had not been expected to know much about the rest of the company's operations, let alone the rest of the automobile business. Though he struggled to decipher the dizzying array of acronyms and technical terms that were being thrown around by his colleagues, Bannister was fascinated to find out what was really going on in the rest of the company. However, it only confirmed his suspicion that Ford was a wreck. He found Mulally's approach inspiring, but he was already thinking of retiring and was not sure he wanted to wait around and see how long the well-meaning CEO would last.

A bespectacled moneyman with a Tennessee drawl, Bannister had been working at Ford Credit since 1973. The company's lending arm was founded in 1959 to support the sale of Ford's vehicles, providing financing to customers and dealers alike. That started to change in the late 1990s when first Alex Trotman, then Jacques Nasser began bringing in outside financiers who treated it more like a stand-alone banking enterprise. They focused on maximizing profits instead of moving metal. Bannister was in Europe at the time, largely insulated from the big changes going on back in Dearborn. When Carl Reichardt came on board to help Bill Ford, he put Bannister in charge of Ford Credit's international operations and taught him a more disciplined approach. After the North American credit business started to spin out of control, Reichardt asked Bannister to come back and take over the entire operation in 2003. It did not take him long to get Ford Credit back on track. In fact, it had become the only reliable source of profits in the entire enterprise.

Bannister wanted to believe in Mulally, but he had yet to see anyone stand up to Ford's culture and win. Still, he liked the new CEO's approach and decided to hold his own BPR at Ford Credit a few days after Mulally's first one. It followed the same pattern as Mulally's Thursday meeting, and it was just as much of a shock to Bannister's staff. But they quickly saw the value of it. Over the next weeks and months, first one executive, then another began holding weekly BPRs in their own departments and business units. Some did it to score points with the new boss, at least initially. Others, like Bannister, did it because they saw the value of Mulally's data-driven approach. Mulally could tell the difference, and he counted Bannister as one of his first converts. But word got back to Mulally that Bannister was getting ready to quit. So Mulally decided to pay him a personal visit.

Mulally showed up unannounced in the middle of a United Way fund-raiser. All the employees were enjoying a catered lunch and most of Ford Credit's executives were locked up in a mock jail. The subsidiary's chief counsel was sauntering around the office in a pirate uniform, complete with eye patch. Bannister was more than a little embarrassed, but Mulally just laughed and commended him for keeping his employees engaged with the community. Then he asked if they could speak in private.

"How are things going at the credit company?" Mulally asked as Bannister closed the door to his office.

"We have our fair share of travails, but not anything that we can't handle," Bannister replied.

Mulally nodded.

"I understand what you do. I understand what you want to do. Now my question is, are you going to stay or not?"

The frank question caught Bannister off guard, but he liked Mulally's directness. It was something he had found in short supply in Dearborn. He looked Mulally in the eye, trying to read the depth of his commitment. He liked what he saw.

"If you are going to come, and stay and make a success out of the company, I'll stay," Bannister said.

"That's the plan," Mulally said, grinning.

* * *

Bannister was still there when Mulally walked into the Thunderbird Room a few days later. The first BPR meeting had lasted only until 3 P.M. There was more to go over, but Mulally was worried his new team was already overwhelmed. The second BPR would last all day.

He had given the executives a week to digest the basic concept and correct their numbers. Now Mulally introduced them to his color-coding system. Anything that had changed from the previous week would be highlighted in blue. The data itself would be presented in the form of bar charts, starting with the actual results for the most recent period and continuing five years out. Those projections would be updated constantly as new information became available. The BPR system was a two-track process, Mulally explained.

"We're going to be checking our progress against the plan," he told the team. "But, at the same time, we're also going to be working on a *better* plan. It's all about continuous improvement."

The plan goals would be displayed as blue bars, while the current forecast for each period would be plotted as a red diamond. That made it easy to see if the forecast for any given piece of data—whether it be Brazilian sales, European marketing costs, or U.S. profits—was on plan, off plan, or ahead of plan. Similarly, the status of every program or project would be displayed as a colored box: green for those that were on track or ahead of schedule, yellow for those with potential issues or concerns, and red for those that were behind schedule or off plan. Any change in status would be reflected by a two-color box divided by a diagonal line—the top color showing what it was the previous week, the bottom color showing what it was now.

The point of the color codes was to make it clear what had changed since the previous meeting and where potential problems existed. Mulally encouraged the executives to apply the colors honestly.

"The neatest thing about this process is that we're going to get back together next week," he said. "I just want to know that you know what's happening, because I'm going to see you again next week—and I *know* you're going to make progress by then."

Mulally used those early BPR meetings as a bully pulpit to drive accountability, enforce cooperation, and ensure execution. If any of the executives in the Thunderbird Room still doubted that he was serious about changing Ford's culture, those sessions quickly dispelled their illusions. If Mulally's tactics seemed harsh, they needed to be. Having correctly diagnosed the disease that plagued the automaker, he set out to eradicate it with a surgeon's skill. Yet as hard as he could be on the senior executives, Mulally also went out of his way to encourage each one of them and let them know that he was not blaming them for the faults he was finding with Ford.

"You *have* a problem," he would say, with a squeeze of the arm and as smile. "*You* are not the problem."

Mulally also worked hard to make each executive feel a part of a team—a team that could win. At the end of one meeting, Mulally got up and walked to the screen. It displayed a financial chart showing a long, steep decline followed by a modest rise at the end. It looked bad, he acknowledged, but he told the team he had seen worse at Boeing.

"Guys," he said, pointing to the trough, "let's get to the bottom as quick as we can, because let me tell you, the ride up is a lot of fun."

✳   ✳   ✳

By the end of October, Mulally had finished explaining the BPR process and the meetings were going a lot more smoothly. Instead of taking the better part of each Thursday, they were now over in a few hours. But Mulally was frustrated. He had explained the BPR process and had explained the color codes. He had assured the team that this was a safe environment. Yet all the charts remained green. By October 26, Mulally had seen enough. He stopped the meeting halfway through.

"We're going to lose billions of dollars this year," he said, eyeing each executive in turn. "Is there anything that's *not* going well here?"

Nobody answered.

That was because nobody believed Mulally when he promised that honesty would not be penalized. In the past, high-level meetings were arenas for mortal combat at Ford. Executives entered the room with keen eyes, searching for flaws in one another's plans. They examined their own presentations beforehand like generals surveying their lines for weak points. They were sure Mulally was just trying to set them up, and none of them was foolish enough to fall for such an obvious trap.

But Mark Fields was beginning to feel like a man with nothing to lose. The Glass House was rife with rumors of his impending demise. He was the most obvious threat to the new CEO, so it would be only natural for Mulally to take him out. That was how things had been done in Dearborn for as long as anyone could remember.

Those thoughts were weighing heavily on Fields' mind as he prepared his slides for the next BPR meeting. When he got to the one showing the status of the North American product programs, he paused. As usual, they were all green. He stared at the line for the new

Ford Edge, which was due to launch in just a few weeks. Production had already begun at the company's factory in Oakville, Ontario. But there was a problem.

The day before, Fields had received a call from Bennie Fowler, Ford's quality chief. His people had already signed off on the Edge, certifying that it was okay to begin shipping the cars to dealers. The first ones were already being loaded onto train cars in Canada as they spoke. Now Fowler informed Fields that a test driver had reported a grinding noise coming from the suspension. Technicians had examined the vehicle in the field but had been unable to figure out what was causing the problem.

"We don't know what it is," Fowler told Fields. "But we need to hold the cars until we find out."

The Edge was Ford's next big thing—its first true crossover, aimed squarely at the heart of the industry's hottest new segment. Fields knew that delaying the launch might bring down the as-yet-unfathomed wrath of their new CEO. Then again, shipping a vehicle with a potentially serious problem was certain to do that. It was the end of the year, the time when Ford executives traditionally pulled out all the stops and cut whatever corners might be necessary to hit their sales targets. But that was the old Ford. Mulally had already made it clear that he did not want any vehicles shipped that were not ready.

"Okay, let's hold the launch," Fields told Fowler. "I don't like it. But I want to be safe, rather than sorry."*

It was a tough decision, but Fields now faced an even tougher one. It was one thing to delay a launch; telling everybody about it in the Thursday meeting was something else entirely. Before Mulally, it would have been like throwing chum into shark-infested waters. Fields' colleagues would have ripped him to shreds. Besides, he reckoned, maybe the noise would turn out to be nothing and the new crossovers would be on their way to showrooms before anyone outside his own team even noticed the delay. Then again, maybe not.

---

* Fields' decision was reminiscent of Ford's decision to delay the launch of the Ford Escort in 1980 because unresolved issues with the vehicle would have flown in the face of the company's new motto: "Quality Is Job One."

Late that Wednesday, Fields was going over his slides with his head of manufacturing, Joe Hinrichs. When the product program slide popped up on the screen, Hinrichs looked stunned. He pointed to the red box next to the Ford Edge.

"Are you sure you want to show that?" Hinrichs asked.

"Joe, is it red?"

"Yes."

"Well, we're going to call it like it is," Fields said.

*   *   *

As his turn approached the next day, Fields figured he had a fifty-fifty chance of walking out of the room with his job. By now, he assumed there was a good chance he was going to lose it anyway.

Somebody has to figure out if this guy is for real, he thought as he studied Mulally, trying to divine his mood. *If I go out, it might as well be in a blaze of glory.*

Fields began with his overview of the business environment in the Americas. He called for the slide showing the region's financials. Then there it was—the product program slide. Fields tried to be nonchalant.

"And, on the Edge launch, we're red. You can see it there," he said, pointing at the screen. "We're holding the launch."

There was dead silence. Everyone turned toward Fields. So did Mulally, who was sitting next to him.

Dead man walking, thought one of his peers.

I wonder who will get the Americas, another mused.

Suddenly, someone started clapping. It was Mulally.

"Mark, that is great visibility," he beamed. "Who can help Mark with this?"

Bennie Fowler raised his hand. He said he would send some of his quality experts to Oakville right away. Tony Brown, Ford's vice president in charge of purchasing, said he would contact all of the relevant suppliers and ask them to check their components.*

---

* The problem was quickly resolved, and the Ford Edge began shipping in early December.

Now we're getting somewhere, Mulally thought.

However, when the team reconvened the following Thursday, Fields was still the only one willing to admit that he had a problem. The rest of the slides were still green. The truth was that many of the other executives were surprised to see him at the meeting. They assumed he had been taken out back and summarily executed when no one was looking. Some expected the ax to fall during this week's session. But when that meeting ended with Fields still in charge of the Americas, most of his peers had reached the same conclusion he had: Mulally was true to his word. He said he wanted honesty and he meant it. It was not a trap.

A week later, everyone's slides were splattered with more red than a crime scene. There was plenty of yellow, too.

As Mulally stared at the rainbow of colors, he did not know whether to laugh or cry.

Now I know why we're losing so much money! he thought. *But they trust me. They trust the process. We finally have it all out in the open. Now we can start fixing it.*

Mulally would later call this the defining moment in Ford's turnaround. He had always believed he could save Ford Motor Company. After that meeting, he knew he would. All he needed was a plan.

CHAPTER 6

The Plan

Progress is not made by pulling off a series of stunts. Each step has to be regulated. A man cannot expect to progress without thinking.

— HENRY FORD

Alan Mulally began working on his plan to save Ford Motor Company on the plane ride back to Seattle after his first meeting with Bill Ford. He had fleshed it out since then, but its broad outlines remained the same: Ford needed to drastically downsize its automotive operations to match the real demand for its products, overcome its dysfunctional corporate culture, and negotiate new labor agreements with the United Auto Workers to close the competitiveness gap with its foreign rivals in the United States. But Mulally was also working on what he called his "better plan," to ensure the company's long-term success and prosperity. Right now that included things such as globalizing product development and creating a new generation of cars and trucks that people actually wanted to drive. Finally, he had to figure out how to pay for it all.

Mulally knew he still had a lot to learn before he could finalize his plan, and he threw himself at that task like a senior before finals week. Even as he assembled his brain trust inside the Glass House, Mulally cast a wide net outside the company in an effort to learn everything he could about the automaker and the automobile industry as a whole.

I've got to make some big decisions, he thought. *I need to know what people are thinking about Ford.*

So Mulally started making telephone calls. He rang up industry experts like David Cole at the Center for Automotive Research and talked to Ford's financial advisers at Goldman Sachs. He even called veteran journalists like *Forbes* columnist Jerry Flint, who had been covering Detroit for nearly fifty years. It took a while for Mulally to convince the cantankerous old reporter that his call was not a prank. Mulally commissioned studies from consulting firms like Deloitte, Booz Allen Hamilton, and Common Ground. He read analysts' reports, clipped newspaper articles, and even cut out cartoons that he thought summed up the situation. He took copious notes and collected everything in white three-ring binders. The material from Common Ground alone filled a five-inch binder. Mulally read each one cover to cover. He also read old financial reports, white papers, and internal studies that his predecessors had ignored.

After seeing how poorly Ford's products fared in *Consumer Reports*, Mulally grabbed Ford's head of engineering for North America, Paul Mascarenas, and Doug Szopo, the head of product planning, and flew to the magazine's test facility in Connecticut. On the way, he told the two men to keep their mouths shut during the visit.

"We're going there to listen," Mulally told them. "We're not going there to rationalize the feedback that we're getting."

They nodded. But they had a hard time remaining silent when the head of *Consumer Reports'* automotive testing division, David Champion, lit into the new Ford Edge.

"It is disappointing," Champion told Mulally. "The interior fit and finish is poor, the steering woolly, and the design of the tailgate makes it very hard to lift."

Mulally thanked Champion for his honest feedback. By the time the Ford jet landed back in Detroit, Mulally and his traveling partners had already had a long discussion about how to address these issues.

Champion may have offered more specifics, but Mulally was hearing the same things from everyone he talked to. Ford had let itself go. The company made good cars and crossovers in Europe, but most of the products it sold in the United States were boring and uncompetitive. Consumers thought of Fords as unreliable gas-guzzlers—if they thought about them at all. Suppliers hated working with the company because it always provided inflated production estimates. Dealers felt like they were being lied to about the fate of the Mercury brand. Investors winced every time they looked at the company's stock price.

And employees were bitter over the endless stream of layoffs, angry about the extra work those cuts shifted to their shoulders, and worried about their futures.

But Mulally learned that people also wanted Ford to succeed. There was still a lot of love for the iconic brand. Many harbored fond memories of better days and better products. More worried about what the failure of Ford would say about America itself. It had taken the automaker decades to destroy the goodwill created by the Model T, the Mustang, and the $5-a-day wage. Mulally was convinced that consumers would forgive and forget, if only they were given a reason to believe in Ford again.

✳ ✳ ✳

Mulally also studied the competition. The chief executives of General Motors and Chrysler had both called to congratulate him shortly after his arrival in Dearborn, but he had yet to meet either one in person. Now, as he gazed out his window at the Renaissance Center—the futuristic cluster of cylindrical towers that dominated the Detroit skyline and served as GM's headquarters*—Mulally decided it was time to pay a visit to America's largest automaker. On October 13, 2006, he arrived at the Renaissance Center for a meeting with GM CEO Rick Wagoner.

Wagoner, like so many other Detroit executives, had worked his way up through the ranks in the company's finance department and now took obvious pleasure in his own authority. Tall and imposing, Wagoner had captained his high school basketball team in Richmond, Virginia, and went on to play at Duke University. After earning an MBA from Harvard Business School, he took a job at General Motors in 1977. In Detroit, Wagoner soon found himself on the fast track. By 1992, he was already CFO. And he was only thirty-nine. By age forty-eight he was CEO. Wagoner was a good manager, but he also benefited from a strong economy and an insatiable hunger for GM's

---

* The Renaissance Center had actually been built by Henry Ford II in the 1970s as part of a largely unsuccessful effort to revive the city's faltering economy. Ford had long since moved out, and GM purchased the building for pennies on the dollar in 1996.

big sport utility vehicles. Some questioned whether GM really needed another insider at the top, given its inability to overcome its own historic weaknesses.

"An outsider could never come in here and figure it all out," Wagoner insisted.

That was in 2000. Over the next six years Wagoner made some impressive gains. He started globalizing product development while Bill Ford was still fighting to convince his own team to even consider such a move, and he led the company's lending arm—the General Motors Acceptance Corporation, or GMAC—into the home mortgage business in time to cash in on America's housing boom. Wagoner knew GM had problems, but the company was making money, and he was content to move slowly.

"[Wagoner's] strategy, in effect, was a big bet on continued cheap oil," wrote journalist Paul Ingrassia. "By coincidence, in June 2004, *National Geographic* magazine carried a cover story titled 'The End of Cheap Oil.' One GM executive showed the story to Wagoner and suggested GM might be relying too heavily on trucks and SUVs. Wagoner retorted that the same faulty thinking had made GM the last company in Detroit to cash in big on the truck boom, and he wasn't about to repeat that mistake."

Now GM too was paying for its overreliance on pickups and SUVs. But reality had done little to diminish Wagoner's self-confidence. Though privately dismissive of Mulally, he received his guest graciously, welcoming him to Detroit and the automobile industry.

"We're fierce competitors, but we have a lot of things in common," Wagoner told Mulally, explaining how the two companies had historically collaborated on certain issues relating to government regulation of fuel economy, emissions, and safety. "I hope we can continue to work together in the future."

Mulally assured Wagoner that nothing would please him more. After all, he still had so much to learn about the automobile industry. Wagoner smiled smugly. He would be happy to school the novice CEO. So Mulally began firing off a barrage of questions about everything from business cycles and product strategy to the upcoming negotiations with the United Auto Workers and the U.S. Environmental

Protection Agency's efforts to raise corporate fuel-economy averages. He sounded like a man struggling to negotiate unfamiliar terrain. It was a calculated ploy worthy of Mata Hari, and Wagoner fell for it entirely. He was more than happy to play the wise master to Mulally's naïf. He went out of his way to demonstrate his knowledge of these issues and others that Mulally had not dared ask about. It was a good thing Mulally was already becoming famous in Detroit for his grin, because as he listened to Wagoner talk, he could not help but smile.

These guys don't have a clue, either, he thought. *They're in the same place we are. They have all the same problems that Ford does.*

As he was leaving, Mulally told Wagoner he would like to be able to call him in the future if he had more questions. He was just trying to be polite, but Wagoner took it as another sign of weakness. He would later claim publicly that Mulally had sought his help as he struggled to understand the industry in those early days. The truth was, Wagoner had been played so well he did not even notice.

Mulally did not need to study Ford's archrival, Toyota. He had been a keen student of the Japanese automaker for years.

"They make products that people want, and they do it with less resources and less time than anybody in the world. They're a magical machine," he said in an early interview. "This system of continually improving the quality, putting the variations into the product line that people want and doing it with minimum resources and minimum time is absolutely where we have to go. If you look at Ford, it's the antithesis."

❋   ❋   ❋

At the same time, Mulally was discovering that at least a few things in Dearborn were worth keeping.

He had granted tacit approval to Fields' Way Forward II plan shortly after accepting the job in Dearborn, assuming it would serve as a stopgap until a new and better plan could be developed. Now that Mulally had the opportunity to study it with a better understanding of the company and its problems, he realized that Fields' new plan was fundamentally sound. If implemented correctly, it would reduce Ford's North American production capacity by 26 percent over the next two years, reducing its installed maximum annual production capacity to 3.6 million units by the end of 2008. That was still more vehicles than Ford's sales forecasters thought the company needed, but the gap was much narrower than it was now. Moreover, that figure assumed each factory would be running two shifts. If as many UAW members took buyouts as the company hoped, the actual capacity would be closer to 3 million units—about equal to projected sales. The plant closures and job cuts were also expected to reduce Ford's annual operating costs by $5 billion. At the same time, Fields' plan promised to accelerate the introduction of new cars and crossovers. Some 70 percent of Ford, Mercury, and Lincoln products by volume would be new or significantly upgraded by the end of 2008.

This is a good foundation, Mulally thought.

But he was wary. Fields and his team had let the market get away from them once. Mulally wanted to make sure they did not let that happen again. He directed the North American team to flyspeck their progress on cutting costs, boosting factory utilization, and stabilizing market share. Mulally was sure the Thursday meetings would keep them honest—and keep him up to date.

"Deliver the plan," he told Fields.

Mulally was also impressed by a new approach to design and engineering that the company had started rolling out a year earlier. Ford was still developing different vehicles for different regions, but at least it had begun using a common system in each part of the world— one that promised to save both time and money. It was based on the system used by the company's Japanese subsidiary, Mazda, but also incorporated best practices from Volvo and Ford's North American and European divisions.

Mazda's system was similar to the one used by Toyota, which was widely recognized as the best in the world. At American automobile companies, design was art and engineering was science. Designers wore black shirts, Italian shoes, and sported enormous wristwatches that cost more than some of the cars they had created. Engineers favored khakis and plaid shirts with pocket protectors and wore their cellphones on their belts. The two usually met at arm's length, if they met at all. Mazda's system forced them to work together, often side by side in the same studio. It also gave other functions such as manufacturing, purchasing, and even sales a seat at the drafting table. The point was to prevent costly and time-consuming revisions of the initial design. When these groups worked independently, mistakes occurred. A designer who knew nothing about thermodynamics might create a great-looking grille only to discover that it did not allow enough air to flow into the engine compartment. An engineer with no knowledge of ergonomics might develop an exhaust system that worked perfectly but was impossible to install. By including people from each of these disciplines in the design process, Mazda had been able to dramatically reduce such missteps.

The system was remarkably similar to the approach employed by Ford's own Team Taurus, which had so impressed Mulally in the 1980s. He could not help but wonder why Ford's product team had to relearn all this from the Japanese, but he was glad they were. The new system they had come up with also incorporated Volvo's virtual design system, Ford of Europe's superior industrial processes, and the more advanced computer-aided design and engineering systems used by the company in North America. The resulting amalgam allowed Ford to simulate every aspect of a new vehicle—from its ride and handling to the manufacturing steps required to build it—before work on the first prototype even started. The result was dubbed the Global Product Development System, or GPDS, and it promised to dramatically reduce both engineering costs and development times. It was already helping Ford bring new cars to market faster and for less money.

GPDS was just being rolled out when Fields took over Ford's Americas group in the fall of 2005. It was first used to make last-minute changes he ordered to the new Ford Fusion sedan. The first vehicle to be entirely developed using it was the Ford Flex crossover.* It was still a work in progress when Mulally arrived in September 2006, but the benefits of the new system were clear. It had already reduced the number of engineering changes required for each new part by 50 percent.†

---

* The Ford Edge and Lincoln MKX crossovers were pilot programs for GPDS, but work on them had already begun when it was implemented.
† Before GPDS, the total number of engineering changes for each part had averaged between ten and fifteen, depending on the type of vehicle.

These were precisely the sort of efficiencies Mulally was looking for, and the system's team-oriented approach matched his own management philosophy perfectly. Moreover, it used many of the same digital design tools as Boeing, which had adopted a similar system during the development of Mulally's 777.

Mulally was just as excited to learn about a still-secret collaboration between Ford and Microsoft Corporation that promised to make the automaker a technology leader once again. It would allow motorists to talk to their cars, and Mulally thought that was just the sort of thing that could convince consumers to take a second look at the Blue Oval.

As Mulally studied all of these efforts, he was reminded of the old Buddhist maxim: "The teacher will appear when the student is ready." Such efforts spoke to the untapped talent still latent in the struggling automaker. By themselves, these measures would never have been enough to save a company so fragmented by internal strife and paralyzed by its own poisoned culture. But they were all things Mulally could build on as he constructed his own plan.

*   *   *

Mulally also looked to Ford's past for inspiration. As he learned more about the automaker's illustrious history, he became convinced that the key to Ford's future was a return to the principles that had made it so successful in the early days, when Henry Ford was still sitting in the chair he now occupied. The company that Ford founded had changed the world and created hitherto unimagined prosperity for generations. That was the result of not one man, one idea, or one vehicle, but the work of many men and women inspired by many great ideas who had together created many great cars and trucks. Over the subsequent decades, the company had lost its way, but Mulally was convinced he could help Ford find it again.

In between meetings, he dug through its corporate archives like a miner convinced that gold was close at hand. Mulally hit pay dirt when he came across an old advertisement Henry Ford had taken out in the *Saturday Evening Post* on January 24, 1925. In a style reminiscent of Norman Rockwell and Maxfield Parrish, it depicted a young, windblown couple standing atop a grassy hill, their trusty Model T visible in the background. Their children play at their feet as the man and woman gaze optimistically across rolling farmland bisected by a road filled with automobiles, to a hazy horizon over which looms the smoky outlines of Ford's new River Rouge factory. The caption read, "Opening the highways to all mankind." Beneath it, Henry Ford outlined his vision for the company's future.

"An organization, to render any service so widely useful, must be large in scope as well as great in purpose. To conquer the high cost of motoring and to stabilize the factors of production—this is a great purpose. Naturally it requires a large program to carry it out," it stated. "In accomplishing its aims the Ford institution has never been daunted by the size or difficulty of any task. It has spared no toil in finding the way of doing each task best. It has dared to try out the untried with conspicuous success."*

This was exactly what Mulally had been looking for—a polestar to guide his transformation of Ford, a touchstone that he could return to in times of doubt. Everything came together for him in that image. He grabbed a pen and a pad of paper and began writing in his usual stream-of-consciousness style:

✓ *Pull all the stakeholders together around a compelling vision: Opening the highways to all mankind*
✓ *Form a tight working-together relationship with Bill, the board and the family*
✓ *Respect the heritage*
✓ *Join the Ford team*
✓ *Respect and reach out to all the stakeholders*
✓ *Implement a reliable discipline and responsible business plan process*
✓ *Include everyone*
✓ *Make it safe*
✓ *Every week, every month, every quarter*

---

* For a reproduction of the complete advertisement, see the photo insert.

- ✓ *Continuous improvement*
- ✓ *Organize to deliver the plan — the matrix organization*
- ✓ *People working together*
- ✓ *Great products . . . Strong business . . . A better world*
- ✓ *The best-designed vehicles in the world*
- ✓ *Aggressively restructure*
- ✓ *Accelerate the development of new products*
- ✓ *Obtain financing and improve the balance sheet*
- ✓ *Change the culture*
- ✓ *Share our story*
- ✓ *Tell the plan*
- ✓ *Shape the business*
- ✓ *Consolidate and integrate*
- ✓ *Laser focus*
- ✓ *Divest all the non-core brands*
- ✓ *Complete family of small, medium and large cars, utilities and trucks*
- ✓ *Best-in-class*
- ✓ *Streamline the brands*
- ✓ *Fewer dealers*
- ✓ *Reduce the inventory*

When Mulally was finished, he grabbed another sheet of paper and outlined his personal goals:

Alan Legacy

- *Clear, compelling vision going forward*
- *Survive the perfect storm — commodities, oil, credit, CO_2, safety, UAW*
- *Develop a profitable growth plan, global products and product strategy*
- *A skilled and motivated team*
- *Reliable ongoing BPR process*
- *A leader and leadership team with "One Ford" vision implementation tenacity*

Here, on two pieces of paper, Mulally had created the framework of a comprehensive plan to save Ford Motor Company. Many of its elements might have seemed obvious to an outsider, but in Dearborn it read like a radical manifesto. And Ford's new chief executive was ready to begin promulgating his doctrine. In fact, he had already started.

✸ ✸ ✸

The day that he went to visit GM's Rick Wagoner, Mulally sent the following e-mail to Ford's employees around the world:

> From: Alan Mulally
> Sent: Friday, October 13, 2006 11:07 AM
> To: The Ford Team
> Subject: First Impressions
>
> I've been on the job—officially anyway—for two weeks. In that time I've had a lot of interaction with people, but I realized there will never be enough hours in the days to see and talk to everyone. So I thought I would write to all of you with some initial thoughts and impressions.
>
> Perhaps not surprisingly, I've spent a lot of time with our leadership team reviewing our plans, asking questions, and evaluating our prospects. Bill Ford was completely candid about the challenges we face, so I came into this with my eyes wide open. We have some very big decisions to make about what kind of business we need to become. And, as you well know, this is an extraordinarily gut-wrenching time at Ford Motor Company, particularly as we become smaller in some of our core areas, such as North America. Some very good and loyal people are going to leave this company between now and next summer, and that's going to be tough on everyone.
>
> And yet, people are the reason I'm so excited about being here. I've met so many Ford Motor Company employees who want to work together to help this company find its footing again

and grow. They are bursting with ideas, and they share them with me when they send me e-mails, stop me in the hallway or run into me in the cafeteria. They want me to know how great this company has been in the past, and how it turned around its fortunes just when the future seemed bleakest. Ford people know the talent that we have in our product development area, and the great resource we have in our dealer networks. And they know we can restake our claim as history's best example of a company that enriches the lives of all its stakeholders: investors, customers, dealers, suppliers, employees, our union partners and the countries and communities in which we live.

It wouldn't take anyone very long to realize that Ford people are winners by nature. The sense of pride in the value Ford has always created in more than a century is obvious and justified. And it is encouraging that there are so many areas of excellence we can point to within our company right now. But pockets of success aren't enough. Not today. Not in this competitive environment. We need success across our entire enterprise. To get there, we need to have a universally agreed to and understood business plan. It needs to be a single plan, and it needs to work for the entire company. Competitors may try to "divide and conquer" us; I'm determined we are not going to do that to ourselves. So we need to set such a plan in place and ensure that everyone knows how we're doing against it. We need to agree on the urgent issues, and we need to work together as never before to achieve our objectives.

I've started weekly Business Plan Reviews with the senior leadership team. Together we look at one set of data on one screen. We talk to each other with candor and respect. We are all determined to get to one plan for our company. We will all participate, and we will all support each other's efforts to succeed. I don't yet know everything I need to know about Ford, but I do know that this is the only way I can work.

There are lots of details to come, but I can tell you with certainty that our plan will be built around three priorities:

- PEOPLE: A skilled and motivated workforce.
- PRODUCTS: Detailed customer knowledge and focus.
- PRODUCTIVITY: A lean global enterprise.

With these as priorities we will build our business model with a clear view of our competitive environment and our own financial circumstances. And together we will answer the most fundamental questions. What are the critical elements needed for a compelling business plan? How accurate are our assumptions? How do we get losses behind us and once again create profitable growth for all?

I know that the people of Ford have been through some tough times in the past few years. I wasn't here to share that with you, but I am here now to help move us forward. For me it is at once the most humbling and exciting prospect of my professional life. But I can tell you from previous experience that as demoralizing as a slide down may be, the ride back up is infinitely more exhilarating. And there is no better feeling than knowing that your personal contribution is helping to move this great enterprise forward again.

Everyone loves a comeback story. Let's work together to write the best one ever.

Thank you!

It was the opening salvo in Mulally's battle for the hearts and minds of Ford's employees. But they were not the only ones he needed to reach. Mulally also wanted to speak to Ford's suppliers, dealers, and investors—and of course the car-buying public.

To do that, he would use the media.

*　*　*

On November 10, Alan Mulally arrived at the *Detroit News*, flashing his trademark smile at copy editors and cop reporters as he and his entourage made his way through the newsroom like a veteran campaigner looking for an endorsement. He dropped into a large black leather chair in the editorial conference room across the table from several senior editors and members of the autos team, leaned back, and started explaining how he was going to save Ford.

It would start with a global reorganization of the entire enterprise.

"There's not one Ford: there's Ford of North America, there's Ford of South America, there's probably three Fords that make up Ford of Europe. There's Australia, there's China, India—there's a lot of Fords, and they're operated very separately as business units," he said. "We've got to go from where we are to leverage our global assets to compete as one company going forward."

Mulally wanted to weld Ford's disparate regional divisions into a single, global operation capable of competing with the best in the world. But the corporate structure was not the only thing he wanted to streamline.

"We are going to rationalize the brands, rationalize the product lines," he said, explaining how he had taken a similar approach at Boeing, reducing its aircraft offerings from more than a dozen models to just four. Ford could get a lot more for its money by building more cars and trucks off of common platforms and sharing more parts and components between them. Some initiatives had already been launched in this direction before he was hired, but he wanted to see these efforts deepened and expanded.

He called on the United Auto Workers to help him close a labor cost gap with Ford's foreign rivals.

"You can't compete with a $3,400 [per vehicle] disadvantage," he said. "We have to deal with reality."

Ford needed to match production to the actual demand for its cars and trucks. People in Detroit were too obsessed with market share; he pointed out that some of the most profitable car companies in the world were also some of the smallest.

"We're not going to chase market share," Mulally vowed. "We're not going to put out vehicles where demand is not there and then discount and make it even worse. It's the most important thing in the business that you always deal with the reality in the marketplace and match the capacity to demand. Because if not, it just gets worse."

And Mulally made no secret of the fact that the clock was ticking.

"We have got to turn around North America and be profitable by 2009," he said. "Because if not, you just keep losing cash and pretty soon you run out."

* * *

S traight talk like this was unheard-of in Detroit. The American automobile industry had mythologized itself for so long that lying
had become a virtue. The Big Three could not fail for the simple reason that they were Big Three. In this city, two plus two always equaled
five. But Mulally was not from Detroit. Bill Ford's decision to hire an
outsider to save his company suddenly made a whole lot of sense.

Mulally understood why Ford had developed the way it had. As the
world's first mainstream manufacturer of automobiles, Henry Ford's
company had grown organically. Ford was pulled to places such as
Australia and Brazil by the clamoring demand for its Model T, not
pushed there as part of a corporate strategy to gain new markets. Offices were opened around the world to handle orders for cars shipped
from Michigan or Ontario. These gave way to warehouses where
Model Ts were assembled from parts manufactured in the United
States, which in turn yielded to full-scale factories once domestic demand justified the investment.

Henry Ford tried to create some order out of this chaos in 1928
by establishing foreign subsidiaries in the major markets. These were
largely autonomous. They needed to be in a world that still communi-
cated by telegraph and traveled by steamship. After World War II, the
automaker realized that that system no longer made sense and tried
to create a more integrated global organization, but it was only partly
successful. While Henry Ford II and his team managed to pull the
company's worldwide operations together on the same balance sheet,
much of the decision making was still left to the regional divisions.
Alex Trotman's Ford 2000 plan had tried to eliminate these regional
organizations altogether. Trotman replaced them with vehicle centers
that were given global responsibility for specific segments like small
cars and trucks. But a huge amount of local knowledge was lost in
the process and employees chafed at this top-down approach. It only
got worse under Nasser, who ordered each of these vehicle centers to
negotiate their own sourcing deals with suppliers. Instead of saving
money by buying in volume, his plan drove costs higher and further
eroded Ford's profits.

What Mulally wanted was a dialogue between Dearborn and the rest of the company that would create consensus. Mulally understood that Ford's global operations were too complex to be run centrally out of Dearborn, but he also appreciated the tremendous cost savings and efficiencies that could be gained by eliminating duplicate efforts around the world and creating real economies of scale.* During one of his first press conferences, Mulally was asked if Ford was considering a merger.

"Yes," he said. "We're going to merge with ourselves."

As an aeronautical engineer, streamlining was as dear to Mulally as pork to a politician. He had spent his entire professional life figuring out how to reduce drag and improve aerodynamics. Now he began applying these same principles to Ford's product portfolio. He asked for a chart showing every car and truck the company made around the world. To his dismay, none existed. So Mulally went to the websites of each of Ford's divisions and printed out pictures of all of their offerings. Then he asked his secretary for scissors and glue. When she brought them, she found Mulally sitting at his conference table with printouts spread all over it. He took the scissors and started cutting out pictures of each vehicle made by Ford and its subsidiaries. Then he divided them by region and started pasting them together on pages like a kid working on a school project. When he was finished, Mulally counted them all. Ford and its subsidiaries were making and selling ninety-seven different nameplates around the world.†

Way too many, Mulally thought as he studied his handmade charts.

He picked up the scissors and started cutting again.

Mulally would later share his charts with Ford's board of directors.

---

* Mulally liked to contrast Ford's organic development to that of Toyota, which had focused solely on the domestic Japanese market until the late 1950s, when it began exporting internationally as part of a calculated growth strategy. Unlike Ford, Toyota expanded as single, global entity. Though it would go on to establish product development and manufacturing facilities around the world, Toyota's operations remain centralized in Japan. While Mulally found inspiration in Toyota's model, it was actually closer to Trotman's Ford 2000 strategy than Mulally's own plan—a fact that would come back to haunt the Japanese automaker later.

† This figure included Ford's European luxury brands and Mazda.

Before their December meeting, he commandeered a conference room and mounted blowups of them on the wall. When the directors had gathered at World Headquarters, he ushered them into the room. Mulally stood there silently as they studied his handiwork. As he expected, they were as overwhelmed as he was by the dizzying array of cars and trucks. Mulally had no trouble convincing them that Ford needed to radically simplify its global lineup.

Mulally also wanted to streamline Ford's organizational chart.

It was clear to him from the start that too few people reported directly to the CEO. He had already removed one level of bureaucracy by getting rid of Steve Hamp and eliminating the position of chief of staff. But that still left Mulally with a convoluted management structure riddled with overlapping responsibilities and tangled chains of command. The head of communications for Ford of Europe was a good example: He reported directly to the vice president of communications in Dearborn, which meant the president of Ford's European group had little knowledge of what this key subordinate was doing or why. On the other hand, the head of product development for Ford of Europe did report to the head of Ford's European group, but he had little contact with his counterpart in the United States.

Mulally wanted to replace this confusing command structure with a matrix organization like the one he had employed at Boeing. It divided the company neatly into business units and functional areas. Boeing had a matrix organization in place for engineering when Mulally was coming up in the company. He was quick to appreciate its value as a young engineering manager because it kept him informed of what was going on in other aircraft programs. When he was promoted to president of the commercial airplane division, he extended it across the entire organization. At Boeing, Mulally's matrix organization had divided functions by aircraft program rather than region, treating each model as its own business unit. That meant that, in addition to a director of human resources for the entire commercial aviation division, there were separate HR chiefs for the 777, 767, and 747 programs.

As Mulally figured out how to make this system work at Ford, he studied the automaker's past attempts at creating a matrix organization—particularly Alex Trotman's ill-fated Ford 2000 initiative. Trotman had created global functions without mirroring them in each business unit or making them all direct reports to the CEO. That meant that there was a global head of information technology, but no head of information technology for Europe. And the chief information officer did not report directly to the CEO. At the same time, the business units were stripped of their responsibility for profit and loss, effectively eliminating regional accountability. After the failure of Ford 2000, the pendulum had swung back in the other direction. The company that Mulally inherited had once again divided itself regionally. A few functions, such as human resources and legal affairs, were still organized globally, but most of the global positions had been eliminated. Responsibility for things like manufacturing had reverted back to the regions.

Mulally believed his system offered the best of both approaches. It made each business unit fully accountable, but also made sure that each key function of the organization—from purchasing to product development—was managed globally in order to maximize efficiencies and economies of scale. Mulally wanted to create one Ford and fully leverage the company's global assets, but he also wanted the business units to remain in place to stay on top of the unique challenges and opportunities presented by each market. His approach was designed to break down the barriers to communication that existed inside the automaker and involve all of the company's leaders in the task of fixing Ford.

Mulally took another piece of paper and drew a table. He made columns for each of Ford's four business units: the Asia Pacific, European, and Americas groups, as well as Ford Credit. Above these, Mulally wrote "Customers" to signify that these were the parts of the organization that faced the outside world. Down the left side of the table, he created rows for each function, from finance and product development to human resources and information technology.* The

---

* Most of these were obvious, but Mulally wanted to make sure he did not forget any. So he imagined that he was starting a company from scratch and tried to think of all the different people he would need to hire to staff it.

heads of each of these would report directly to him, as would the heads of each of the four business units. Each function would have a regional director in each business unit as well, and these individuals would jointly report to the head of their division and the head of their function. Under Mulally's system, the head of communications in Ford of Europe would report to both the president of Ford's European group and the vice president of communications in Dearborn. This system significantly increased the number of people who reported to Mulally directly and eliminated additional layers of bureaucracy, such as Mark Schulz's position—president of international operations.

The board was impressed by Mulally's new organization. Now all Mulally had to do was decide who should head each group or function.

He also had to deal with Ford's brands. Mulally thought there were too many of these, too. Ford had not been able to manage the Blue Oval, let alone the seven other brands that made up the company. Each of these brands faced unique challenges. Coping with them was spreading the automaker's already weak bench even thinner and consuming precious working capital the company could no longer spare. It had already pumped billions into these brands, and most were still losing money. As he was putting together his plan for the board, Mulally had listed each one: Ford, Mercury, Lincoln, Aston Martin, Jaguar, Land Rover, Volvo, and Mazda. Then he drew a line through each one of them except for Ford.

Getting rid of the rest would be a tougher sell than streamlining the product portfolio and organization chart. He could not get rid of Lincoln or Mercury yet, because too many dealers in North America depended on them. The European brands presented a different set of challenges.

Owning legendary marques like Aston Martin and Jaguar had been a source of pride for the company and the Ford family. These European brands lent an air of worldliness and sophistication to what had always been a midwestern company that produced more utilitarian products for the masses. Many of the descendants of Henry Ford also drove them. So did many Ford executives, as Mulally had noticed to his dismay when he first arrived in Dearborn. That was one more reason he wanted them gone. But Bill Ford and other directors were fond of the European subsidiaries. They had approved massive investments in these brands because they were convinced Ford needed world-class luxury vehicles to truly compete in the global market. Land Rover was profitable, they reminded Mulally. Some also believed that Jaguar was poised to turn the corner. It took a while, but Mulally was able to convince the board that his strategy of focusing on the Blue Oval made sense, given the company's finite resources. By the end of the year he was able to persuade the board to sell Jaguar and Land Rover and consider a sale of Volvo. Bill Ford still wanted to keep it, but said he would not stand in Mulally's way if the new CEO could put together a compelling case to sell the Swedish brand. Lincoln was staying, at least for now, because Mulally had been persuaded that Ford needed at least one luxury marque. Mercury would get a temporary reprieve, but only until the company could make Lincoln strong enough to stand on its own.

The rest was easy. The board fully supported Mulally's desire to better leverage Ford's global scale, negotiate a competitive contract with the UAW, and redouble its efforts in Europe and Asia. In the past, Mulally explained, Ford had been overly dependent on big trucks and its U.S. business. He wanted to change that. He showed the directors a slide with two pie charts. The first represented Ford's global product offerings, and it was divided into three equal slices labeled small, medium, and large. The second represented Ford's global revenue. It, too, was divided into three equal segments, representing Asia, Europe, and the Americas.

"We need to offer a full family of vehicles—cars, crossovers, and trucks," Mulally told the directors, explaining that this was the surest hedge against fluctuating fuel prices and changing consumer preferences. "We also need to split the business evenly among each of the three regions so that problems in one part of the world no longer threaten the entire organization."

This was the essence of Mulally's plan, which he summed up with just two words: "One Ford." As Mulally watched the directors nodding in agreement, he knew he had found what he was looking for—a catchphrase that summed up everything his revolution stood for, a rallying cry. But there was more. On November 14, as he was finalizing his presentation for the board, Mulally finally managed to distill everything down to four simple points, which he now shared with the directors:

1. Aggressively restructure to operate profitably at the current demand and changing model mix.
2. Accelerate development of new products our customers want and value.
3. Finance our plan and improve our balance sheet.
4. Work together effectively as one team.*

These were the four nails that Mulally would hammer home in every meeting, every speech, and every interview. Fields' accelerated Way Forward plan would take care of the restructuring, at least in North America. Smaller cuts would be needed in Europe and elsewhere. Mulally's Thursday BPR meetings were making his executives work together as a team. He was still looking for the right person to lead the development of new products, but that could wait. His next priority was point number three: He had to figure out how to pay for it all.

---

* This was the final wording Mulally presented to the board of directors. What he actually wrote on November 14 was:
1. Aggressively restructure
2. Accelerate the development of competitive new products that people want and value
3. Secure the financing
4. Need working together and leadership

CHAPTER 7

Betting the Farm

Borrowing for expansion is one thing; borrowing to make up for mismanagement and waste is quite another.

— HENRY FORD

I n November 2006, Alan Mulally listened as Ford Motor Company's chief financial officer, Don Leclair, and treasurer, Ann Marie Petach, went over the pitch the automaker was about to make to the nation's largest investment banks. Ford was hoping to borrow at least $18 billion to help pay for the company's turnaround and insulate it against the economic turbulence looming on the horizon. It was a lot to ask for a struggling domestic car company, even in a time of easy credit. But the presentation was persuasive, and Mulally was smiling by the time the pair finished.

"That's really impressive," he told them. "Let me know how it turns out."

Leclair and Petach shot each other a nervous glance.

"We need you to give the presentation in New York," Leclair told Mulally frankly. "You're the only new model we've got."

A few days later, Mulally was on his way to New York. It would be his first pilgrimage to Wall Street as Ford's CEO.

Though he would later claim credit for convincing Ford to take out "the biggest home improvement loan in history," work on the financing deal that helped save the automaker was already well under way by the time Bill Ford offered Mulally the job. Ford had become convinced that, regardless of who he found to lead the company, they were going to need a huge amount of cash to fund any restructuring.

It was an argument Carl Reichardt had been making for years as Bill Ford's finance guru. His mantra was "Cash is king," and he repeated it often—not just to Ford himself, but also to the rest of the finance team and the board of directors. Even when the company still seemed headed for the big profits Bill Ford had promised Wall Street, the veteran banker had urged him to think beyond the next quarter.

"Earnings are important, but what's really important is cash—cash, cash, cash. We ought to be looking at our liquidity," Reichardt told his protégé. "You can never have enough liquidity, particularly if you think you're going to have to restructure."

Something else was also becoming clear to Reichardt in the months before he retired from Ford's board of directors. He told Ford that the days of loose lending were coming to an end.

"You don't know when that window is going to close," Reichardt warned Ford before stepping down in April 2006. "You ought to grab as much as you can while you can."

But the real push for maximum funding was coming from Leclair. Ford's CFO was becoming increasingly concerned about the company's finances. Like Reichardt, he was worried about the state of the credit markets. But Leclair was even more worried about Ford's ability to borrow money. The automaker's credit rating was falling fast, even as demand for its bread-and-butter pickups and sport utility vehicles waned. At the same time, Leclair was convinced that the sales projections for new models prepared by Mark Fields and other executives were far too rosy. Regardless of what might happen with the broader credit markets, Leclair was convinced that Ford's own borrowing window would soon be slammed shut by the banks. In a meeting with Bill Ford that spring, he urged his boss to authorize one last, big push to borrow as much money as possible—even if it meant using secured loans. That was something Ford hoped to avoid. It would be seen as a sign of desperation. But Leclair said Ford was desperate, and he was adamant that the company needed to avail itself of every option. Bill Ford told Leclair to see what the banks were willing to do.

* * *

By the summer of 2006, Leclair and Petach were hard at work on what would become one of the biggest financing deals in the history of the automobile industry. As Bill Ford and Joe Laymon were wooing Mulally, the finance team had already begun feeling out the big investment banks. The news was not good. If the automaker wanted access to serious money, it would need collateral—and not just a few aging factories or pieces of developable real estate. To get the sort of cash Ford was looking for, the banks wanted the automaker to mortgage nearly everything: Ford Credit, Volvo, and all of its domestic assets. The alternative would have been a bundle of asset-specific loans, but the banks were not particularly keen to end up with the title to, say, a car factory in Wayne, Michigan. If Ford defaulted on its new loans, they wanted everything.

Reichardt and Leclair had been right: The borrowing window was closing. It would still be months before mortgage brokers started turning away unemployed roofers with no proof of income, but for the Dearborn automaker the credit crunch had already arrived.

The man whose name was on the building now faced one of the most difficult decisions of his life. Bill Ford was confident he had found the man who could save his company, but he knew that the sweeping, global restructuring he and Mulally were discussing would not be cheap. Ford also knew that Leclair was right. The company was running out of time. If Mulally had not changed his mind and agreed to leave Boeing, it would have been out of options, too. Bill Ford had to make this count. He hated the idea of gambling with his family legacy, but without sufficient financing they would almost certainly lose the company anyway. He decided to risk everything for one last, heroic effort.

"Do it," Ford told Leclair. "Get as much as you can."

The company began informal negotiations with the major investment banks. People were asked to work their contacts to figure out which ones were most likely to lend. Board members with banking ties—such as Sir John Bond, who had just retired as chairman of HSBC Holdings, and former U.S. Treasury secretary Robert Rubin, who was also a member of Citigroup's board of directors, also began making calls. By the time Mulally's hiring was announced, discussions with three of the biggest banks on Wall Street—Citigroup, JPMorgan, and Goldman Sachs—were already well under way. They would become Ford's loan advisers and the core of the lead lending group. And they were already making it clear just what they meant by "everything."

Ford would be required to stake all of its domestic assets: its factories, its office buildings, and its patents. The banks told Ford that its assets were now worth so little that nothing short of an enterprise-wide valuation made any sense. They also wanted Ford Credit and Volvo put up as collateral. They even wanted the Ford logo itself. The banks knew that, even if the company collapsed, some Chinese automaker would pay good money for the right to stamp the Ford name on its cheap subcompacts. If Mulally failed to turn things around, Henry Ford's worst nightmare would come true: The big banks would finally get his company.

Ford's finance team tried to keep anything they could sell off the table in case they needed to raise even more cash. They won a few concessions. The Jaguar and Land Rover brands were excluded from the deal. So was Ford's stake in Mazda, though language was added that would allow the automaker to add its Mazda shares later in exchange for a higher credit limit on the revolving loan that would make up the biggest portion of the package. Volvo could be sold, too, but only with the approval of Ford's lenders—and half the proceeds would have to go toward paying down its loan.

Bill Ford knew that, if he did use the company as collateral, it would be the automaker's last chance to save itself. If Ford defaulted on these loans, the game would be over—at least as far as he and the rest of the Ford family were concerned.*

The business-minded members of Ford's board understood why this was the only option left and were willing to place the bet. So was Alan Mulally. Before accepting Bill Ford's offer, he asked for assurances that he would have the money he needed to pay for his plan. Convincing the Ford family to mortgage their birthright would be a far tougher sell. They had not cashed in their shares when they were worth a fortune, and they certainly were not going to be eager to bet

---

* Under the terms of the final lending agreement, Ford would get the Blue Oval and the rest of its collateral back only after it paid off the revolver and had two of the three major debt-rating agencies elevate its credit rating back to investment grade.

them all on a make-or-break gamble. So Bill Ford decided to package his finance proposition with some more positive news. He held off telling the family about the finance plan until the meeting in September when he presented Mulally to them. Ford knew his new CEO made a great first impression, and he believed the fact that Mulally already had the outlines of a compelling turnaround plan would convince them that he was not risking their patrimony on a long shot. Once they had met Mulally and heard him out, Ford made his pitch.

"You've seen the plan," he told his relatives. "If you want us to execute it, you have to fund for it. This is the only option left to us."

It was a masterful move. In the end, no one in the family opposed the decision. They understood the reasoning behind it. That did not mean everyone was thrilled with the idea. In fact, the dissidents would try to leverage this unease a few months later in one final bid to split the family. But, for now, Bill Ford had the support he needed to send Mulally to New York.

*   *   *

Neil Schloss, Ford's assistant treasurer, and other members of the automaker's finance team spent hours on the telephone with each of the company's existing lenders trying to persuade them to pony up more cash. They made the same argument to each one. These banks were already major investors in Ford. Subscribing to this new finance offering would increase their exposure to the company, but it would also dramatically improve their position because it would transform them from unsecured to secured lenders. Even if this ended up being a case of throwing good money after bad, they would at least end up holding something more than worthless paper.

Though the banks were already receptive before Mulally's name was even mentioned, their attitudes toward the deal improved markedly after his hiring was announced. Mulally's reputation preceded him on Wall Street, and Bill Ford's decision to get out of the way and bring in an outsider with real turnaround experience telegraphed that this would not be yet another halfhearted attempt to save the automaker. By the time Mulally left for New York, Citigroup, JPMorgan, and Goldman Sachs had already pledged $800 million each to the company, as had four other banks that would form the lead group in the financing deal. More important, all of the banks had agreed to allow Ford not only to publicize this fact at the meeting but also to use their names. This was key to convincing other banks to sign up, because it showed that some of the biggest names in finance still believed in Ford.

* * *

On Monday, November 27, Ford announced that it was seeking $18 billion in financing "to address near- and medium-term negative operating-related cash flow, to fund its restructuring, and to provide added liquidity to protect against a recession or other unanticipated events."

Specifically, Ford said it would seek a new five-year secured revolving credit facility worth $8 billion to replace its existing unsecured $6.3 billion revolver, a senior secured term loan of about $7 billion, and a $3 billion unsecured note, convertible into Ford stock. As collateral, Ford said it was prepared to mortgage nearly all of its U.S. assets, in addition to all or part of its stock in subsidiaries like Ford Credit and Volvo. The company said it expected to close the deal by December 31 and hoped to end the year with $38 billion in liquidity.

It was the first time in the company's 103-year history that it had staked its assets as collateral, and Wall Street took it as a sign of desperation. Analysts had expected Ford to seek additional financing, but this went way beyond what any of them had anticipated. Ford's stock tumbled by more than 4 percent on the news, closing at $8.16 a share. More ominously, Standard & Poor's and Moody's dropped their ratings on the company's notes deeper into junk bond territory, saying Ford's move would make it more difficult for unsecured bondholders to recoup their investment if the company defaulted on its debt.

"This is Ford's one last shot to get it right," veteran Wall Street analyst John Casesa told me at the time. "If the restructuring plan is not executed flawlessly, the company will lose its independence. Management is staking the entire future of the company on successfully executing this plan."

But he also said it was the only option left to Ford, "short of finding a well-capitalized partner."

* * *

As Mulally approached the rostrum in the ballroom of the Marriott Marquis hotel in Times Square on November 29, he was confident he could close the deal with the bankers. He had met many in the room as president of Boeing's commercial aviation division, and was certain most of the others knew him by reputation.

These guys know what I can do, he thought. *I just have to convince them that I can do it again.*

"It is a pleasure to be here today to discuss opportunities we think you will want to become a part of," he began. After his introductory remarks, Mulally offered an unflinching assessment of the challenges confronting Ford.

"We face an industry that is increasingly competitive. Consumer preferences are changing, particularly in North America, where higher fuel prices are shifting demand from trucks—our strength—to cars. And excess capacity continues to add downward pressure on prices," he said. "The industry also faces rising health care costs in the U.S., high commodity costs, and a fragile supply base, particularly in North America."

Next, Mulally acknowledged the problems that were uniquely Ford's.

"Ford also faces many company-specific challenges. Our market share has been declining in North America; it is critical we stabilize our share in our home market. Manufacturing capacity exceeds demand, and our cost structure is not competitive. Finally, our business units are not well integrated, resulting in a high level of complexity in the company," he said. "The number-one thing we need to do is to deal with our reality, and tackle these issues head on."

Then Mulally shared the broad outlines of the plan for the first time outside the company.

"A key opportunity going forward is to operate as one company. In my short time with Ford, I have seen that we have many largely separate, regional companies operating around the world," he said.

"There are substantial business opportunities for Ford from leveraging its global assets and integrating the regional business units. Operating as one company also will allow Ford to accelerate our product development efforts, increase scale, and develop more efficient global designs."

Mulally closed with his sales pitch, listing the reasons why the bankers should open their checkbooks.

"We are accelerating actions to improve our cost structure through personnel reductions, capacity reductions, and restructuring our supply base," he said. "While restructuring the company, we must continue to invest in new products. Leveraging our global product development and production systems will enable Ford to develop more products, and to develop these products faster and more efficiently. Developing more new products will mean Ford will be competitive in the marketplace when our restructuring takes hold, allowing the company to deliver profitable growth."

All of this would require money—more money than Ford had on its balance sheet.

"This liquidity is needed to execute the plan I have highlighted to transform the company and provide a cushion to protect for a recession or other unexpected event," Mulally told them. "I hope you will see the opportunity I see at Ford."

Next came in-depth presentations by Leclair and Petach that dissected Ford's public financial data. After that, the bankers had to make a decision. Those who wanted to know more could stay and listen to Leclair and Petach deliver a detailed overview of the company's financial projections for the next five years. By doing so, they would become insiders and lose their ability to trade in the company's stock and bonds. But they would get a much clearer picture of Ford's finances. The rest would have to leave the room.

In the private briefing, Mulally walked the bankers through every element of his emerging plan for Ford. He showed them his new product road map, with its emphasis on small cars and crossovers, and he went over Ford's quality and productivity goals. Mulally also told them he was prepared to take the difficult steps necessary to return Ford to profitability. He would close more factories, cut more jobs, and sell off the money-losing British brands.

From the comments and questions he received after the presentation, Mulally was convinced that many in the room were impressed. That sense was reinforced during a series of private, one-on-one sessions with individual banks held before and after the two group meetings.* By the time Mulally got back on the plane to Michigan, he was confident Ford would get the money he needed to implement his plan—and enough to cushion the automaker from any economic potholes that might lie on the road ahead.

His optimism was not misplaced. Citing "overwhelming support by lenders," Ford announced on December 6 that it now hoped to secure more than $23 billion in financing.† The amount of the unfunded revolver was increased to $11 billion,‡ while the size of the convertible note was increased to $4.5 billion—with a stipulation that Ford could increase that amount to $5 billion if it was oversubscribed. It was. By the time the deal closed on December 31, the automaker had managed to borrow a total of $23.6 billion. The size of the total package far exceeded Ford's expectations. It was a testament to Wall Street's confidence in the company's new CEO.

* * *

Back in Michigan, the automaker's executives waited for the response from the banks and dealt with the fallout. Bill Ford ran into General Motors CEO Rick Wagoner and Chrysler CEO Tom LaSorda at a regularly scheduled meeting of industry leaders, and both expressed their dismay at his decision to bet the company.

"Are you crazy?" Wagoner asked.

---

* These smaller meetings were held at the nearby Waldorf-Astoria hotel.
† Once again the markets would ding Ford for upping its borrowing. This time, Ford's stock dropped another 4.2 percent on the news—falling to $7.36 a share—while Fitch would further downgrade the company's debt rating from B to B−. Most analysts were beginning to see the logic in Ford's moves, though.
‡ The underwriters could also sell an additional $500 million more than originally planned through what is commonly refered to as a greenshoe option.

Ford shrugged.

"We've got a big restructuring ahead of us," he said.

"Well, we've already done ours," Wagoner replied.

Oh? thought Ford. *Really?*

"You're going to regret this," Wagoner insisted, pointing out that the interest expense alone would be a huge drag on Ford's balance sheet—not to mention how it looked to investors.

"Well, to me, it's the only thing that makes sense," Ford said. "It's all going to be in the execution. If we borrow all this money and don't execute, you're right. But if we can execute against the plan, then I think this is absolutely the right thing to do."

While Wagoner remained dismissive, LaSorda listened closely to what Ford had to say and asked him to elaborate.

Wagoner's reaction to Ford's funding request was a bit disingenuous. In July of that year, GM had used some of its own North American assets—including inventory, plants, and property—to secure a $4.6 billion revolving loan. And just a month before, GM had pledged some of its factory equipment to secure a $1.5 billion loan. The company would soon wish it had followed Ford's example and mortgaged everything.

Many industry observers would later opine that Ford owed more to luck than skill in doing the finance deal when it did. After all, who could have guessed that the global credit markets were about to seize up like a bad motor? Bill Ford bristles at that notion. He remembers the tough discussions with Carl Reichardt, Don Leclair, and others in the company about the growing need for more cash and the looming prospect of tighter lending. Mulally has also expressed dismay at the suggestion that Ford was just lucky. After all, he specifically told the bankers in New York that Ford was looking for a cushion against a potential recession.

At the time, analysts recognized that the company was being smart.

"We think Ford is taking advantage of a favorable debt market to grab as much financing as it can, lowering the risk of insolvency as it works to restructure," wrote Goldman Sachs analyst Robert Barry in a note to investors following Ford's initial funding request.

Did Ford see the credit crisis coming? Certainly not the full magnitude of it. But it is clear that Ford knew the game was changing and had the foresight to get as much cash as it could before it was too late. Other automakers would not prove so prescient. In the end, they would have to borrow their money not from the big Wall Street banks, but from the American people. Ford's financing deal would allow it to survive without a government bailout. If Bill Ford had not convinced his family to stake everything, the Fords likely would have lost control of the company entirely. A few months later, such a deal would have been impossible for any American automaker. A year later, even the most profitable companies in the world would have been unable to borrow half that amount.

Mulally now had the money he needed to bankroll his revolution. But the decision to go all in had not just provided Ford with the cash it needed to fund its restructuring—it also made it clear to everyone inside and outside the company that there would be no more half-hearted attempts to save the automaker. This time, Ford would finally fix its fundamental problems, or it would die trying.

CHAPTER 8

Assembling the Team

If everyone is moving forward together, then success takes care of itself.

— HENRY FORD

Mark Schulz was getting on Alan Mulally's nerves. First the head of Ford Motor Company's international operations had tried to get out of the weekly business plan review, or BPR, meetings. Now whenever Mulally tried to understand what was going on in Asia or Europe, he found he had to go through Schulz, who rarely gave Mulally a straight answer.

Schulz did not seem to think he had to. He had forgotten more than Mulally knew about the automobile industry. Moreover, he was one of Bill Ford's closest friends at the company. They were fishing buddies who had worked together for years. Schulz was confident he could deal with the Mulally situation the next time he was alone with Bill Ford on a trout stream. Until then, he remained evasive and bureaucratic.

Mulally never lost his temper with Schulz. He continued to invite him to "join the team," but Schulz refused to play by Mulally's rules. When his new boss put a limit on how many slides each executive could show each week, Schulz brought twice that number. The next week, he went to China and did not call in for the Thursday meeting at all. When Schulz returned to Dearborn, Joe Laymon took him aside and warned him not to test Mulally's patience.

"You're going to get your ass fired," he cautioned Schulz. "Bill can't save you on this one."

"He's still the chairman of the company," Schulz shot back.

"Yes, but he hired a guy to run it for him—and if this guy says,

'I need this team to run the company' and it doesn't include you, Bill's going to give him his team," Laymon said. "Don't impose on Bill's friendship. Don't put Bill in a position where he has to make a decision."

But Schulz was confident Ford would take his side. When they were alone on the company jet during a trip to China in late October, he pleaded his case. But Bill Ford told Schulz he would not help him this time; whatever problems he had needed to be worked out with Mulally. Schulz was devastated. The era of cronyism had come to an end at Ford.

A few days after he returned to the United States, Mulally called Schulz into his office to tell him that his position—president of international operations—was being eliminated. It was one more layer of bureaucracy that would not be needed in the new Ford. Mulally wanted the heads of Ford's Asian and European operations to report to him directly. He asked Schulz if he would consider overseeing global product planning. It was a clear demotion, and Schulz left fuming.

"Maybe it's for the better," his wife told him.

Schulz was a third-generation Ford employee, and his grandfather and father had both died of heart attacks on the job—his grandfather at fifty-seven, his father at forty-seven. Schulz was fifty-three and did not want to end up the same way. It was a bitter pill to swallow, but he announced his retirement in December. He turned down the company's offer of a farewell party.

Schulz had underestimated both Mulally and Bill Ford. He was unable to get past the new CEO's amiable exterior, to see the relentless leader it concealed. Nor did he seem to grasp that Bill Ford had bet everything on Mulally; he was not about to second-guess him or undermine his authority.

＊　＊　＊

Ford Americas president Mark Fields had gotten over his initial anger at Mulally's appointment, which had ended, at least for now, his own shot at the top job. He seemed to be getting with the new program. But Fields went out of his way to make it clear to Mulally that he was in charge of the Americas group and did not need any help running it. Mulally was impressed with Fields' work on the Way Forward acceleration plan, as well as by the courage he had shown in telling the truth in the BPR review about the troubled Edge launch. But Mulally also knew that a big part of why he had been hired to run Ford was that Fields had proven he could not do it alone.

Turf was not the only thing Fields was trying to protect. He was also fighting to keep his jet privileges. Fields' weekly commute from Florida was being held up as a symbol of Ford's hypocrisy as it demanded more and deeper sacrifices from its employees to cope with its mounting losses. Many already viewed Fields as arrogant and aloof; his use of the company plane only reinforced that—particularly when he called for "sacrifices at every level."

On a warm Saturday morning in November, Fields went out to grab a cup of coffee and a newspaper. He was ambling back to his Volvo, enjoying the Florida heat, when Detroit's version of a *60 Minutes* hit squad—WXYZ investigative reporter Steve Wilson—jumped out of the palm trees and thrust a microphone into Fields' face, demanding to know how the Ford executive had made the trip from Dearborn to Delray Beach.

"Listen, it's Saturday morning," Fields said wearily. "I'm here with my family."

"Yeah, but you're down here on the Gulfstream!" Wilson snarled at him. "You're spending what? How much is that every weekend?"

According to Wilson, each of Fields' weekly round-trips was costing the company approximately $50,000. Ford would later put the figure at $30,000. Either way, it added up to a sizable chunk of change for a company that was slashing thousands of jobs.

Mulally ordered Fields to stop using the Ford jet. It was a bit hypocritical, given that Mulally himself was commuting back and forth between Dearborn and Seattle on Ford's friendly skies. But Mulally was not the one being ambushed by reporters. Fields' use of the plane had become an embarrassment to the company. Even the *Wall Street Journal,* which did not usually traffic in such sensationalism, had picked up the story.

Fields tried to hold his ground. Use of the jet was in his contract, which was a legal document that could not be abrogated, except by mutual consent. He threatened to quit if Ford breached it. But Mulally was not about to let Fields go on generating negative publicity for the company. Laymon was asked to deal with the situation. He challenged Fields to make good on his threat.

"If you truly have alternatives, exercise them," he dared Fields.

In the end, Fields reached a compromise with the company. Ford agreed to up his annual cash compensation and Fields agreed to fly commercial.*

* * *

Outsiders saw Mark Schulz's "retirement" as a sign that the blood-letting at Ford had finally begun. In fact, Mulally was remaining true to his word. Instead of figuring out whom to get rid of, he was trying to figure out where each of Ford's executives could make the biggest contribution to the company's turnaround effort. He was focused on filling in the blanks on his matrix organization chart.

Mulally tried to come up with two or three candidates for each position. He was prepared to look outside Ford if necessary, but he wanted people with deep knowledge of the company and its problems. Mulally looked at who was currently in charge of each function and then tried to identify the best people beneath him or her. That way, if his first choice did not work out, he would be able to quickly fill the position with other in-house talent. Mulally moved cautiously. He scheduled one-on-one interviews with executives, talking to them about what they had done at Ford, what they were doing now, and where they thought they could help. He looked not only at their qualifications and technical expertise but also at whether they worked well with others. Mulally also needed to know that they had

---

* Ford announced that Fields would no longer be using a corporate jet for personal travel on January 18, 2007. While the cost of his weekly flights had been significant, it is worth noting—as Fields did to me at the time—that he worked on the way to and from Florida, something that was certainly more difficult to do on a commercial jet.

the stomach for the heavy lifting that lay ahead. Most important, they needed to be able to function in the midst of crisis.

Some of the choices, like Michael Bannister and Mark Fields, were obvious. Mulally decided to give the current heads of Ford's European and Asian divisions a chance to prove themselves as well. With Schulz gone, the company's Asia-Pacific and European operations were reconstituted as separate business units, coequal with Fields' Americas group.

Asia-Pacific, which was also responsible for Ford's operations in Africa, was led by John Parker—a short, soft-spoken South African who had been with the company since the 1960s. An engineer by training, Parker had been Ford's chief technical officer in Taiwan, head of product development in Australia, president of Ford India, and Dearborn's senior representative at Mazda before taking over the entire region just before Mulally arrived. He had good connections throughout Asia, which was vital to doing business in that region. But Mulally made it clear that he was not impressed with Ford's performance there, particularly in the critical Chinese market. He expected Parker to turn things around, and fast.

Lewis Booth was the head of Ford of Europe and the Premier Automotive Group, which were now united in the European group. He was a tough but unassuming Liverpudlian who started his career in the automobile industry as an engineer for British Leyland. Booth also trained as an accountant and had joined Ford in 1978 as a financial analyst for Ford of Europe's product development division. His rise through the ranks was far from meteoric. Booth was short and frumpy and therefore at a significant disadvantage in Jacques Nasser's Ford, where good looks and urbane style were often valued more than leadership skills. He had spent the past several years following in Fields' wake, succeeding him first as president of Mazda, then as the head of Ford of Europe and the Premier Automotive Group. But Booth was smart, had a good sense of humor, and cared about his employees. This made him an effective leader who was regarded by many as one of the company's hidden gems.

Because he had reported to Schulz, Booth did not have an

opportunity to meet Mulally until a few weeks after he joined the company. When he did, Booth was wary. He could tell there was more to the man than his boyish grin and cheerful demeanor suggested. He thought many of his colleagues had been unwise in their early appraisals and he did not want to make the same mistake. It quickly became clear to Booth that Mulally was a man who sincerely wanted to change Ford for the better. Booth was prepared to follow anybody who made that his mission. He hated working for Schulz, whom he found far too easygoing. Booth was a better manager who had more experience running large organizations, and he knew it. But he was not a personal friend of Bill Ford. Booth had continued the European restructuring that Fields had begun, and Ford's operations there were becoming stronger by the month. Its products were the envy of the rest of the company. Mulally told Booth to keep doing whatever it was he was doing and share as much as he could with the rest of the leadership team.

*　　*　　*

With the business units in place, Mulally turned to the functional teams, starting with finance. Mulally had decided to keep Don Leclair around as long as possible. His department already operated globally, but its authority was somewhat limited outside the Americas. That was changing as the walls that divided the company were knocked down.

Joe Laymon would also be staying on as vice president in charge of human resources and labor affairs, at least for now. Though Laymon had proven a valuable ally, Mulally was beginning to see him more as part of the problem than the solution. His real value lay in his ability to do Bill Ford's dirty work. But even Ford had begun to suspect that Laymon started as many fires as he put out. He had done more than his share of fighting in Ford's internal turf wars, and he was a ruthless adversary who was not above leaking damaging information about other executives to the press. Like Leclair, he was never going to be a team player. That worried Mulally. But Laymon was a good friend of United Auto Workers president Ron

Gettelfinger, and Mulally needed him until the critical 2007 contract negotiations were concluded.

Charlie Holleran was a more immediate concern. Though Mulally was impressed with how Ford's vice president of communications handled his hiring, he did not like Holleran's style. Holleran was an old-school public relations manager whose expertise lay in crisis management. If someone lobbed a grenade into the room, he was the guy who would grab it and pitch it back out the window before it went off. But Mulally did not need a crisis manager; he hoped the days that demanded one were over. As with the other functions, Mulally wanted someone who could come up with a plan—in this case, one for improving the public perception of Ford Motor Company—and then rigorously monitor its execution. Holleran ran things by instinct and intuition; he was not one for PowerPoint presentations and media metrics. He would keep his job for the time being, but Mulally had his eye out for a replacement.

Mulally was generally satisfied with the rest of the team that he inherited.

Legal affairs was led by General Counsel David Leitch, a beefy, battle-scarred Beltway veteran with a sharp legal mind. He was a graduate of the University of Virginia School of Law and had clerked for U.S. Supreme Court chief justice William Rehnquist. On September 11, 2001, he was a few months into his new job as chief counsel for the Federal Aviation Administration. He spent the next year exploring uncharted legal waters as the United States locked down commercial air travel. Then he was tapped to be deputy assistant to President George W. Bush and deputy White House counsel, just in time for the invasion of Iraq. Leitch loved being in the White House, even though his work there took him into some unsettling legal areas, such as the debate over "enhanced interrogation techniques." But he knew going in that his position there was not permanent. When Leitch had the opportunity to come to Ford, he took it. He had only been at the Glass House since 2005. Mulally liked him instantly—in part because he was another outsider who was still untainted by Dearborn, in part because he was a good attorney. Mulally would rely on Leitch's counsel a great deal in the months and years ahead.

Ziad Ojakli, Ford's vice president of corporate affairs, was another veteran of the Bush administration. A fast-talking, well-connected Turkish American lobbyist with a knack for political deal making, Ojakli had been deputy assistant to the president for legislative affairs and Bush's chief liaison to the Senate from 2001 to 2004. Bush, who liked to bestow nicknames on his closest advisers, dubbed him "Z-man." Others in Washington referred to him as "the Energizer Bunny," because of his frenetic pace. The smiling, pudgy-faced Ojakli grew up in Brooklyn's Bay Ridge neighborhood and earned a bachelor's from Georgetown and a master's from Johns Hopkins. His unique blend of street smarts, elite education, and stamina made him a real force on Capitol Hill, where he worked behind the scenes to build support for the president's agenda. He got along with Democrats and Republicans alike, and his connections in Washington ensured that Ford's concerns always got a hearing.

Chief Information Officer Nick Smither was a tall, thin Brit who said little but kept Ford's computers running. He would now report directly to Mulally. So would Chief Technical Officer Richard Parry-Jones, a Welsh engineering savant who was considered one of the best vehicle tuners in the industry. Mulally had forgiven Parry-Jones for doubting his ability to grasp the complexities of the automobile business during their first meeting in September.

Mulally thought he had a chief marketing officer in the person of Hans-Olov Olsson, who was also chairman of Volvo. But the sixty-four-year-old Swede announced his retirement on November 30. He had grand plans for a massive marketing campaign that would embrace all of Ford's disparate brands, and it did not take Olsson long to realize that was wholly incompatible with Mulally's new vision for the company. Besides, he missed Sweden. So Booth added the title of Volvo chairman to his growing list of responsibilities, and Mulally began searching for someone else to fill the critical post of marketing chief.

Marketing would be key to Mulally's transformation of Ford, and he quickly concluded that no one inside the company was capable of leading the major push he had planned. He would need to hire another outsider. Mulally tapped Lisa Bacus, the brand manager for the

Lincoln Mercury division, to fill in as the senior marketing executive until he could find the right person.*

Some functions at Ford were already led by people whose titles implied a global purview. In practice, however, few were able to exercise real, direct authority worldwide. Mulally wanted to make sure that they owned all the processes, all the people, and all the responsibility.

Vice President of Global Quality Bennie Fowler was a good example. A stern, African American manufacturing expert from Georgia who looked like a former linebacker, Fowler learned the value of order and structure from his father, an army sergeant, who ran his house with the same discipline that he ran his platoon. As a boy, the other kids in the Augusta housing project Fowler grew up in called him "Streetlights," because his parents required him to return home at dusk. As an adult, he applied that same disciplined approach to manufacturing and was known to mete out wire-brushings to subordinates who failed to live up to his high standards. Quality was a religion for Fowler, and he approached his job with the intensity of a Baptist preacher. He was the sort of guy who could change the way a plant operated by force of will alone. He came to Ford after stints at General Motors and Chrysler, starting as superintendent of Ford's assembly plant in St. Thomas, Ontario. Fowler went on to rattle the teacups of tweed-coated Brits as chief operating officer for Jaguar and Land Rover before the progress he made on their abysmal quality ratings prompted Jim Padilla to call him back to Dearborn in the summer of 2005. He was given responsibility for manufacturing engineering and new product launches on Mark Fields' Way Forward restructuring team.† After a particularly rocky board meeting led to the demotion of the previous quality chief, Fowler added vice president of global quality to his title in April 2006.

Fowler made the mistake of taking his new title seriously. He started by calling a meeting of all the Ford quality chiefs from around the

---

* In the interim, the marketing position was downgraded, and Bacus was never made an officer of the company.

† In this capacity, Fowler worked closely with Joe Hinrichs, then head of manufacturing for North America. Both men reported to Dave Szczupak, who retired shortly after Mulally was hired.

world and asked each one to explain the processes in place in their regions. Every part of the company was handling quality differently. That upset Fowler, because he knew Ford had invested a great deal of time and resources in developing what he thought was one of the best quality control systems in the industry—a system that nobody besides him seemed to be following. When he suggested they start, Fowler's subordinates responded with a chorus of impossibles. Every region found some part of the system it could not implement. Fowler quickly discovered that he lacked the necessary backing to force the issue, so he focused on fixing North America. He had made real progress there by the time Mulally was hired. But Fowler was certain he was going to lose his job. He knew that he was considered one of Padilla's protégés and assumed that was reason enough for Mulally to get rid of him. He was surprised then when he first encountered the new CEO walking down the hall in November.*

"Hey!" Mulally giggled. "I'm your new quality guy!"

The two men spent the next fifteen minutes talking. Mulally assured him that his position was secure.

"We're going to focus on quality and productivity at the company," he told Fowler. "We're going to make it a priority. You're the guy!"

Then Mulally looked at his watch and arched his eyebrows.

"I've got to run!" he said. "I've got to get a home-improvement loan."

A few weeks later Fowler got a call from Mulally, who told the quality chief that he would now be reporting directly to him. Mulally also told Fowler that he wanted him to start taking the "global" part of his title seriously.

Fowler, too, was overwhelmed by his first Thursday BPR meeting. There was just so much information to absorb. He was also daunted by the task of getting his own data together for his part of the presentation. Initially he did not have the quality metrics for the other regions and could only present the numbers for North America. Once he started getting reports from other parts of the world, Fowler

---

* Because Fowler was not part of the senior leadership team, he was not invited to the first executive meeting with Mulally.

discovered that each region measured quality a bit differently and presented its data in different formats. It took about eighteen months before Fowler was able to present a comprehensive snapshot of Ford's quality efforts worldwide. It took several of the other functions just as long to get up to speed—evidence of just how disjointed the company had been before Mulally. Presenting the data in the five minutes that he was allotted each week was a challenge, too. Fowler practiced before each meeting like an actor rehearsing his role. As tough as he was, Fowler was a little intimidated by suddenly finding himself on equal footing with men who had been his bosses until a few months ago. Mulally spent some time with him alone after each of his first few meetings.

"Look, Bennie, you're at this level now," he said. "Just watch the team and observe. I'll give you a little time to do that, and I know you'll figure it out."

Like the other executives, Fowler worried at first that Mulally's talk about honesty and transparency was just a trap, and he waited to see who would be gullible enough to fall for it first. He made sure all of his charts were solid green, even though he knew many of the boxes should have been red. But when Fields survived his first brush with the truth, Fowler decided to show his true colors, too.

✳   ✳   ✳

Fields may have emerged from that meeting with head still attached, but he was still worried about his job. Rumors of his imminent departure were everywhere. In addition to the jet scandal, many outside the company continued to view Bill Ford's decision to bring in Mulally as an indictment of Fields' own abilities. One Dow Jones reporter even tried to start a pool, inviting other journalists to place bets on how much longer Fields would last.* Fields was a tough Jersey boy who prided himself on his ability to shake off just about anything, but this speculation started to get under even his thick skin. When Daniel Howes of the *Detroit News* called Fields and flat out asked him if his days were numbered, he decided to find out. Fields

---

* Many of us thought this was unprofessional and did not participate.

hung up the phone and walked down the hall to Mulally's office, brushed past his secretary, and stood before Mulally's desk.

"Everybody around here seems to think you're planning on canning me," Fields told him. "Is that true?"

"*No!*" Mulally said with evident dismay. "Mark, you're a valued member of the team."

"Can we just have an agreement?" Fields asked. "If you don't think I'm working out for you, let's just have that discussion. I'm okay with that."

"Sure," Mulally said. "But you shouldn't let yourself get distracted by rumors."

Fields said it was hard not to when the city's leading columnist was getting ready to write his obituary. A few minutes later, Howes' cellphone rang.

"Hi, Daniel. This is Alan. I heard you were writing something about Mark."

"I am," said the surprised columnist.

"Well, I just want you to know that I think he is a really, really fine leader," Mulally said. "I have the utmost confidence in him. . . . He's done a great job. And I *really* believe in him."

Mulally meant it, too. He saw plenty of potential in Fields. Mulally had adopted his accelerated restructuring plan and had been deeply impressed by Fields' courage in the Thunderbird Room. Yet he needed Fields to do more than just pay lip service to the new order. He needed him to embrace it. And Fields was starting to do just that. He did not swagger quite so much when he walked, and he had toned down his tough-talking rhetoric. He started to refer to "the team" and "we" instead of "I" and "me." Fields was starting to worry less about scoring points and more about how to fix what was wrong with the North American business. He was beginning to see that Bill Ford had been right—that Alan Mulally was the guy who could teach him to be a world-class CEO. Fields was not only learning everything he could from Mulally; he was also becoming one of his most valued lieutenants.

Fields was not the only one worrying about being replaced. As Mulally worked on his new organization chart, Ford's top executives watched their doors warily and cringed a little each time the phone rang. They knew it was a rare outside CEO who does not bring in at least a few of his or her own people. With each new appointment to Mulally's senior team, they relaxed a bit. Then came news that seemed to confirm their worst fears. In November, Jerry Calhoun—Mulally's head of human resources at Boeing—announced his retirement from the aircraft company. Word leaked that he was coming to Dearborn as a consultant. Many assumed that Laymon's career at Ford would soon be coming to an end. In fact, it was Laymon who had suggested to Mulally that he hire Calhoun. He reckoned that no one knew the new CEO's management style better and thought he could help him figure it out. When it became clear that Laymon was not going anywhere—at least not yet—the other executives finally began to calm down.

That was what Mulally had been hoping for all along. He knew that there had been too much churn at the top of Ford for too long. He needed everyone to settle down and get to work polishing the Blue Oval—not their résumés. His confidence that those who could not be part of the solution would vote themselves off the team had been borne out by the departures of Anne Stevens and Mark Schulz. He just needed to finish finding the right people to round out his roster.

* * *

Most of the positions on Mulally's matrix already existed at Ford, but there was one key position that did not: head of global product development.* Mulally and Bill Ford had agreed during their first meeting in Ann Arbor that weaving the automaker's disparate design and engineering operations together into a single, global team would be central to the success of any restructuring. Now Mulally needed to find someone to lead that effort. He also wanted one person to have ultimate authority—and accountability—for every vehicle program around the world.

One name that kept coming up was Derrick Kuzak's. If Leclair was quiet, the mild-mannered Kuzak was almost mute. A tall,

---

* Chief Technical Officer Richard Parry-Jones did have this title at one point, but in name only.

slouch-shouldered man with a neatly clipped mustache, the engineer usually hung out in the back of the room. He rarely spoke, and when he did, his words came out in a slow whisper—and only after a long hesitation. But what he said would fundamentally change the way Ford built its cars and trucks.

Kuzak was a native Detroiter who was in charge of product development for North America. Before being recalled to Dearborn to join the North American restructuring team in August 2005, he had been the head of vehicle development for Ford of Europe, where he was credited with leading the region's product renaissance. He had also led the development of the second-generation Ford Focus compact—a completely different vehicle than the cheap econobox the company sold under the same name in the United States.

When it was unveiled at the Paris Motor Show in 2004, the European Focus wowed critics and won wide acclaim as one of the best small cars in the world. For Kuzak, it was also a glimpse of what could be accomplished if Ford could manage to unite its balkanized global design and engineering operations. The car had been developed in conjunction with Ford's Japanese and Swedish subsidiaries, Mazda and Volvo. That collaboration also yielded the Mazda3 and Volvo S40, both of which were receiving their own rave reviews. Kuzak knew that none of these brands could have created any of these vehicles on their own, but together they had created all three for a fraction of what it would have cost to do so independently. Kuzak could not stop thinking about what Ford could gain by taking the same approach worldwide. In theory, the company had already tried this once with Ford 2000, though most of the product development functions had remained regionally divided. There was one exception: electrical systems.* And Kuzak had been in charge of it. There, too, he saw how Ford could save time and money by globalizing the design and engineering of its cars and trucks. He had lobbied for that in his own quiet way ever since, but nobody seemed to be listening.†

---

* The reason electrical was different was that Ford realized it simply did not have the engineering talent to maintain separate electrical teams in each region at that time.

† Kuzak had been pushing for a less parochial approach to product development

Until now.

Mulally called Kuzak at home one Sunday. He told Kuzak he had heard about some of his ideas. He asked the engineer to come to his office the next day to talk about them. The two men clicked instantly. They were both engineers, after all. In fact, Kuzak had started in the aerospace industry, while Mulally had once been Boeing's head of product development. They literally spoke the same language. And as Kuzak described his experience during Ford 2000 and his insights from the European Focus program, Mulally liked what he was hearing.

"I think the most important asset we have as a company is the Ford brand," Kuzak told Mulally. "We should devote our resources to that brand globally."

Mulally said he was of the same mind. But he said he had one big concern: Kuzak and his North American product development team did not seem to be aiming high enough. Instead of setting their sights on making Ford's cars and trucks the best, they were simply trying to match the competition. Mulally wanted to know why they were not aiming to make each vehicle the best in its class.

"We never committed to that as a company," Kuzak said calmly.

Mulally nodded. He also wanted to know why Ford was not keeping up with the rest of the industry in terms of new product introductions.

"Because it wasn't part of the plan," Kuzak said. "We never had a leader who believed in this."

"Well, I do," Mulally said. "The biggest opportunity we have as a company is to integrate Ford globally. It starts with product. That's what's going to make us a success—making the best products in the world."

To do that, Ford's cars and trucks had to be the highest quality,

---

ever since he was called back to Dearborn. When Bill Ford had summoned him for a review of the company's hybrid programs, Kuzak had advocated the creation of a common global platform for all of them. But Kuzak's style was so understated and Ford's culture was so impervious to change that it was unlikely that he could have made much of a difference without the backing of a forceful figure like Alan Mulally.

safest, and most fuel-efficient vehicles on the road. Kuzak agreed but told Mulally that not everyone at Ford felt the same way.

"Don't worry," Mulally told him. "I'm not just going to let you do it, I'm going to back you up. I'm going to support you, and I'm going to make sure the whole organization gets behind this. I'm right here for you, Derrick."

The two men shook hands and walked to the door. When they got to the hallway, Mulally stopped and patted Kuzak on the back.

"Remember," Mulally said, smiling, "engineers are the source of all wealth creation."

Kuzak left the CEO's office feeling more inspired than he had in a very long time.

* * *

Kuzak was the perfect choice to spearhead the globalization of product development—and not just because of his obvious engineering talent. He was also the only senior executive at Ford with little ego and no desire to rule. Kuzak was not running for anything, and everybody knew it. That meant none of the business unit chiefs saw him as a threat to their own ambitions. Nor was he seen as a partisan figure who would put the interests of one over another. They might not like giving up some of their authority over product programs, but as long as Kuzak was the one demanding it they were not going to view it as a personal attack.

However, Kuzak was only half of the equation. In keeping with the tenets of Ford's new, Mazda-inspired Global Product Development System, he would be paired with the global head of purchasing, Tony Brown.

Brown was a smooth-talking African American supply expert with a rakish mustache, and he was far better liked by Ford's parts manufacturers than was the company he represented. Brown was sympathetic to supplier concerns but more than capable of dishing out the tough love he knew the parts industry needed. He carried an ace of hearts in his briefcase—a personal totem invoking the heart and courage required to make tough decisions about Ford's supply base. Brown had been vice president of global purchasing at the company since 2002, and unlike most of the other Ford executives who had the word *global* in their titles, he really did have worldwide responsibility for his function. But that function also had some serious issues.

Ford was consistently rated one of the worst automakers to do business with by the industry's leading suppliers. Of the major manufacturers, only General Motors scored worse. Parts producers resented Ford's constant pressure to cut prices, its frequent last-minute design changes, and its grossly inflated production estimates. Suppliers had long ago figured out Ford's game and were charging the company a premium on parts to cover these surpluses. If Ford asked them to set aside 20 percent more capacity for steering wheels than they thought the company would actually buy, they would simply raise the cost of those wheels by 20 percent. As a result, it cost Ford substantially more to build its cars and trucks. To make matters worse, Ford had historically maintained a large pool of suppliers so that it could pit them against one another in an effort to shave a few cents off the price of a particular component. In contrast, Japanese car companies such as top-rated Toyota signed long-term contracts with their suppliers and were often willing to pay a premium to those who could deliver the best quality.

Under Brown's leadership, Ford started trying to reform itself by launching an aggressive new supplier strategy in 2005. Called the Aligned Business Framework, it was a page right out of Toyota's playbook. Brown's plan was to dramatically reduce the number of suppliers Ford did business with, but forge deeper and stronger relationships with those that made the cut. It would take years to implement, but Ford's ratings were already creeping up—albeit at a much slower rate than its Japanese competitors'. Most of Ford's suppliers were willing to wait, partly because they needed the business, but also because they trusted that Brown would make good on his promises.

Despite his important position in the company, Brown was not part of the senior leadership team when Mulally arrived at Ford. That changed quickly, though not before Mulally gave Brown's reform efforts some added impetus. When Brown arrived at his first one-on-one with the new CEO, Mulally had the latest supplier survey from Planning Perspectives Inc. on his desk. It showed that suppliers were increasingly shifting the bulk of their capital investments and research-and-development expenditures to their Japanese customers. Parts manufacturers were making more effort to improve the quality of the components they supplied to these companies as well.

"This doesn't work for me," Mulally said, tapping the report with his finger.

Brown agreed that there was plenty of room for improvement and outlined his strategy for bettering supplier relations. It sounded good to Mulally—particularly the part about it being patterned after Toyota's model. He told Brown to pick up the pace.

*　　*　　*

With Kuzak in charge of global product development and paired with Brown, Mulally now had all of the company's critical functions reporting to directly to him. Ford's three regional divisions were now coequal business units, along with Ford Credit, and all four would now be represented at every Thursday BPR meeting along with each of the functional teams. The layers of bureaucracy that had insulated Bill Ford from the unpleasant details of the business had been eliminated. Just as important, Mulally now had the team he needed to begin transforming Ford from an automaker with operations around the world into a true multinational corporation—one capable of using its global scale and expertise to challenge the best in the business.

On December 14, the automaker announced Kuzak's promotion along with the other changes in the company's management structure. Just before Ford issued the press release, Mulally sent an e-mail to employees explaining the importance of this corporate realignment.

"Working together to make the most of our global talent and resources is critical to our success," he said. "I know I can count on you to join me in supporting the leadership team during this transition. This is a great company. This is a terrific team. We have the right leaders. Together, we can do this!"

*　　*　　*

B ill Ford once complained that his company had more political intrigue than czarist Russia. Now Mulally had stormed the Winter
Palace and was ushering in change at a dizzying pace. He had made
Derrick Kuzak his commissar of product development and ordered
him to liberate Ford's designers and engineers from bean counters
and bureaucratic inefficiency. Major overhauls of manufacturing and
marketing were being planned, and the search was on for new talent to lead them. Whole layers of corporate bureaucracy were being
purged. But Mulally's revolution had been relatively bloodless. Steve
Hamp and Mark Schulz were gone, but those waiting for more heads
to roll—and that included just about everyone following Ford—would
be disappointed.

As 2006 came to an end, the rest of Ford's executives were quietly taking their places on Mulally's team. Those first few months had
been tough. These were people who had risen through the company's
ranks by mastering a game that was now fundamentally changed, and
they were still struggling to learn the new rules. The smiling Kansan
whom many executives had dismissed as a sappy rube had proven to
be a regular radical, hurling bombs into their fortified bunkers and
Molotov cocktails at some of Ford's most cherished delusions. But
Mulally had also proven himself to be an able and inspiring leader
who, in a matter of months, had come up with a comprehensive plan
to save Ford Motor Company from itself. Those who thought they
could wait him out were gone. Those who were left joined Mulally's
team and pledged allegiance to his plan—sometimes gritting their
teeth and cursing under their breath, but doing it all the same.

"I don't care if everyone believes in the plan one hundred percent,
as long as they act like they do," Mulally told them. "Because once
you start acting like you do, you'll find yourself in the light—and you
won't want to go back into the darkness."

He was right. Though the bickering and backstabbing would begin
again every time he left the office, Ford's executives were starting to
realize that these were no longer viable means of career advancement.
At the same time, adherence to Mulally's strict processes was starting
to yield tangible results. Mulally's cause was helped by the deepening

crisis afflicting the rest of the domestic automobile industry. With each passing month, there were fewer and fewer places to go.

But Mulally was taking no chances. Now that he had his team in place, he did not want to risk losing any of his top talent. With the board's approval, he ordered Laymon to put together retention plans for each of Ford's key executives—just in case. Mulally still had concerns about several of them, but he wanted to see if they could be rehabilitated. He knew that Ford did not have any executive talent to spare.

By late December, the old turf wars were finally winding down.

"If I have a technical problem, Lewis will say, 'Hey, I'll send a few guys over from Volvo to help you,'" Mark Fields explained at the time. "You don't hear [Mulally] say the word 'I' a lot. It's 'we.' It's the team."

The cult of personality that had long held sway at Ford was being replaced by a new regime of results. But some privately expressed concern that too much was riding on Mulally's shoulders and wondered if his would be a permanent revolution or just another failed coup.

CHAPTER 9

The Best and Worst of Times

It is failure that is easy. Success is always hard.

— HENRY FORD

O n January 7, 2007, guitars shrieked, spotlights danced, and a hundred camera flashes popped as Alan Mulally rode onto the stage in Detroit's Cobo Arena in a new Ford Five Hundred, an enormous Blue Oval glowing on the screen behind him. He emerged to the cheers of Ford Motor Company employees who laced the capacity crowd of automotive journalists from around the world. This was Mulally's first auto show, and nothing in the aerospace industry had prepared him for it. He had done plenty of air shows, but those were subdued affairs compared to the North American International Auto Show, an annual spectacle of enormous proportions in which the world's automobile manufacturers struggled to outdo one another before the assembled automotive press.

At the first auto show in 1907, Henry Ford had revealed his plans for the Model T — the car that would turn his modest Michigan start-up into one of the biggest manufacturing companies in the world. Now, exactly one hundred years later, the star of Ford's show would not be a car, but a computer. Dubbed "Sync," it was the product of a collaboration between the Dearborn automaker and Microsoft Corporation. It allowed motorists to connect their cellular telephones or MP3 music players to their automobile — either with a USB cable or a wireless Bluetooth connection — and control them using voice commands. Drivers could make calls, answer their phones, read text messages, or choose songs without taking their hands off the wheel.* It was noth-

---

* Later versions would add additional features, including vehicle diagnostics,

ing short of revolutionary, and it drew more attention than most of the cars and trucks shown in Detroit that year.

And it almost did not happen. A month before Sync's scheduled unveiling, working prototypes had not yet arrived in Dearborn. But when Bill Gates is personally overseeing a project, things have a way of working out.

Sync was the common solution to both companies' problems. Ford wanted its own in-car infotainment system to challenge General Motors' OnStar system, a subscription-based service that used live operators instead of computers. Microsoft wanted to establish a beachhead inside the automobile—that elusive space between work and home where millions of people somehow managed to survive without its products. In 2003, the software giant set out to change that, beginning work on a voice-activated system that would allow motorists to control their phones and iPods while driving. It also began looking for partners in each of the world's major automobile markets to put it on the road. Microsoft inked its first deal with Italy's Fiat SpA in 2005.* In the United States, Microsoft initially approached General Motors, for the simple reason that it was the biggest player. But GM already had OnStar and was not interested in swapping it for an untried alternative from a company that was not exactly known for its flawless launches. Ford was next on Microsoft's list. The two companies had been working together since the Nasser era. Though the plug had been pulled on some of those early ventures, the two companies still had a good relationship thanks to the mutual admiration of their respective chairmen. Bill Ford was impressed by Gates' inventiveness; Gates appreciated Bill Ford's "vision for how technology can improve the car experience." That was about as much praise as he could muster for any other business leader. But despite their affinity, Gates said nothing to Ford about Microsoft's new system until GM passed on it.

---

traffic reports, turn-by-turn navigation, and even a program that could call 911 in the event of a crash.
* Fiat's "Blue&Me" system was less advanced than Ford's, offering fewer features. Under the terms of its agreement with Microsoft, it was initially only available in Europe. That changed when Fiat began selling cars in the United States again in 2011.

Then, in April 2005, the Microsoft chairman traveled to Dearborn to present a $1 million donation to the Henry Ford Museum. Bill Ford was there, too. After the ceremony, Gates told him that he had an idea for the perfect collaboration. Later that summer, Ford and Microsoft began getting in sync.*

Ford originally planned to introduce the new system in the Explorer. But when Mark Fields was briefed on the program after taking over the Americas group a few months later, he rejected that idea. Fields recognized that Sync offered Ford something it desperately needed—a way to connect with young car buyers. To do that, Ford had to put it in a car they would actually buy. There was only one such car in Ford's entire North American lineup: the Focus. Sync in a cheap compact was cool. Sync in a big SUV was just another piece of technology to bedevil their parents. Fields made the switch. Sync would debut in the Focus that fall, then spread rapidly to the rest of Ford's showroom.

The only problem with the change in plans was that it made more work for the engineers, who were already struggling to deliver the product on time. Ford's system was originally supposed to use the same hardware as Fiat's. But as the designers added more features and voice commands, it became clear that the processors were just not powerful enough—particularly since Ford wanted a system that could be expanded in the future. In May 2006, both Ford and Microsoft decided a more robust set of chips was needed. The first Sync prototypes arrived in Dearborn on December 21. They were not fully functional, but they were close enough to fool reporters.

*   *   *

Alan Mulally was not fully up and running either. The usually eloquent CEO stumbled through the first half of Ford's press conference at the auto show with an uncharacteristically stilted delivery. Mulally hated prepared speeches, but his handlers insisted that he

---

* The formal negotiations were conducted by Ford director Robert Rubin, Derrick Kuzak, Bill Gates, and Martin Thall, the head of Microsoft's automotive division.

use a teleprompter for this important event. It was a bad idea. But just when it seemed like the jaundiced journalists might start yawning, an image flashed up on the giant screen behind Mulally that drew audible gasps from some in the arena. There was Bill Gates smiling down on his old friend from Seattle like a nerdy Wizard of Oz. The Microsoft chairman was broadcasting via a satellite uplink from the Consumer Electronics Show in Las Vegas, where Sync was being unveiled simultaneously for the world's technology press. Sync would prove the biggest hit of both shows—a lucky break for Ford, since the automaker had nothing else to offer in Detroit other than some mid-cycle product freshenings and a few concepts that would never be built.*

Ford's other big hit was Mulally himself. Though his performance on stage was underwhelming, he was still Detroit's most interesting new model. As soon as Ford's formal press conference was finished, scores of reporters scrambled onto the stage, swarming the wide-eyed CEO like a bunch of Africanized honeybees. The scrum was so intense that more than one journalist was knocked off the stage as reporters from five continents thrust their tape recorders and boom mikes at the beaming executive.

"I have a great team here at Ford," he told them. "The fact that we were able to raise the money to finance the plan just shows you the confidence the people have in us, [and] you're going to see that momentum building quarter after quarter."

When he finally broke away from press conference and began walking the show floor to check out the competition, the rock star treatment continued. Mulally's media handlers held the reporters at bay, but photographers followed him everywhere he went—even into the General Motors and Chrysler stands. When he surprised the

---

* These included the Ford Interceptor concept, a modern reimagining of the muscle car as a full-size sedan, and the Ford Airstream concept, a futuristic space probe on wheels whose chief feature was an LED lava lamp. Once the show was over, both would be rolled into the warehouse, never to be seen again. A third prototype, the Lincoln MK-R concept, would at least provide the framework for the future Lincoln MKS sedan. In addition to the Five Hundred, Ford also unveiled a freshened version of the North American Focus.

leaders of both companies by showing up unannounced, they looked less than thrilled to see him. The puckish Mulally just grinned, relishing their discomfort. GM's Rick Wagoner and Chrysler's Tom LaSorda and the other Detroit auto brass resented the speed with which the industry outsider had become the darling of the automotive press. In their minds, they had been slogging it out in the trenches for years and getting little credit for it. Now the aerospace industry's answer to Howdy Doody had flown into town with a four-point plan and some color-coded slides and quite literally stolen the show. His Cheshire-cat grin was plastered across the front page of every newspaper and on the cover of every magazine. Nor were Ford's competitors the only ones gnashing their teeth. Mark Fields had been the public face of the company in the United States ever since he arrived back in Dearborn. Now he stood awkwardly off to the side as reporters swirled around his new boss.

The intensity of the media coverage took Mulally by surprise. Boeing may have been a big company, but few journalists followed it closely. Ford, on the other hand, was the subject of continuous scrutiny by the local, national, and international media. Scores of reporters followed every twist and turn of the company's travails. Now they also followed Mulally like a pack of hounds. A scribe from the *Detroit Free Press* tracked down his elderly mother in Kansas. Mulally resented this intrusion into his family life and never forgave the reporter. Mulally told his children to be careful about who they talked to and about what they posted on sites like Facebook. But he also loved the attention. He started each day by reading the press clippings, and he had a tough time when reporters drew attention to Ford's many problems.

"Don't make this a scuzzy story," he warned during an early interview with the *Detroit News*. "I'll burn your house down!"

Then he burst out laughing. But no one was entirely sure he was joking.

* * *

The financial results that Ford released a few weeks after the Detroit auto show were certainly no laughing matter. On January 25, the automaker posted a record loss of $12.7 billion for the previous year.* Much of that was due to one-time charges incurred as it idled factories and laid off workers. But the company's loss from continuing operations was still $2.8 billion.

"We fully recognize our business reality and are dealing with it," Mulally said in a conference call with reporters and analysts that morning. "We have a plan and we are on track to deliver."

But Ford was already missing some of that plan's key targets—a fact that came to light a few weeks later when the *Detroit News* obtained a copy of an internal company report card in February. It showed that Ford had fallen short of its January sales goal in the United States by 10,600 vehicles—the equivalent of an entire point of market share. Worse, the report card indicated that the company expected its U.S. sales to remain below plan for at least the next couple of months. Ford had hit its material cost reduction target in January but was not on track to hit its targets for the rest of the quarter. Ominously, the document noted that these metrics were "key indicators of progress toward achieving profitability by 2009 for North American automotive operations." Finally, the report card showed that, according to the latest internal morale survey, Ford employees were not buying into Mulally's revolution. Less than half said they were optimistic about the company's future. That was even lower than the previous year. The goal had been 60 percent.

The report card was another calculated risk by Fields. Mulally had insisted on honesty and transparency—not just in the Thunderbird Room, but throughout the company. Fields decided a monthly report card was a good way to keep employees informed about the automaker's progress, or lack thereof. Before it went out, most at Ford had no real idea of just how bad things were. They knew their stock was not worth as much as it had been, and they could count the empty desks, but there was little communication from the top. Even before Mulally's arrival, Fields had tried to rectify this with weekly webcasts

---

* Before 2006, the most Ford had ever lost was $7.4 billion in 1992. The 2006 figure was far from the worst in the industry, though: General Motors had lost a staggering $23.4 billion, also in 1992, when accounting changes undercut both automakers' earnings.

on the company's intranet. Now he was taking that one step further by sharing some of the actual data from the Thursday BPRs with the U.S. workforce. And he planned to do it every month.

Mulally approved. The report cards would show everybody in the company where Ford was falling short of its turnaround goals, and he hoped this would inspire them to work harder. But not everyone agreed. Not surprisingly, Chief Financial Officer Don Leclair was the lead dissenter.

"This stuff is going to get out," he warned Fields after he saw a draft of the first report card.

Fields knew he was right. After all, Ford leaked like a sieve. Fields himself had been furious when the *Detroit News* printed the details of his original Way Forward plan the day the board approved it, and he knew it was only a matter of time before someone sent the newspaper a copy of his report card, too. But Fields also knew that most of the data it contained would have to be made public eventually, either during the monthly sales briefing* or in the company's quarterly financial filings.

"Listen, we've made the commitment, and I've made the commitment, to communicate regularly with our folks so they understand where we are," he told Leclair. "It gives them the motivation to improve."

Leclair persisted in his objections, but Mulally backed Fields. That did not stop a panicked Leclair from calling his rival when the story broke to say, "I told you so."

"So what? It is what it is," Fields replied. "On balance, there's a lot more benefit to the company in our employees knowing where we are. It's going to become public knowledge anyway, because we can't seem to keep a secret."

The same thing happened in March. Fields sent out his report card, the *Detroit News* got a copy, and Leclair got angry. This time, however, the charts on the report card did not include the actual numbers. Those had been removed. There had also been some thoughtful

---

* Each month, Ford held a conference call with analysts and reporters to go over its U.S. sales results. Most of the other major automakers did as well.

discussions about which metrics to include and which to leave out.*
But there was far more concern about what this data actually showed.

Most things that Ford could control directly—quality, engineering
costs, and the like—were on plan. But the company could do little
about rising raw materials costs. Sales were also tricky. Some of the
levers Mulally was pulling to improve the company's long-term fundamentals were having a negative impact in the short term. Nowhere
was that more obvious than in the sales numbers. For years Ford and
the other Detroit automakers had offered consumers big cash incentives to make up for the shortcomings in their products. As a result,
many cars and trucks were sold at a loss. These deals also eroded the
resale value of those vehicles, making them that much less attractive
compared to the imports. Incentives were a hard habit to break. But
Ford was trying, and that was costing the company some customers.

Ford was also trying to limit sales to rental car agencies. The vehicles it sold to companies like Hertz and the Budget Rent a Car
System were deeply discounted. Ford did not make much money
from these sales, and it lost even more in terms of brand image. In
America, cars and trucks are as much a fashion statement as a means
of transportation. Nobody wants to drive a model they see lined up
like canned food in airport lots. That was a big part of why the first
Ford Taurus fizzled in the end, and Mulally was keen to avoid repeating that mistake. In addition to cheapening the brand, the commercial fleet business further undermined the resale value of Ford's
products, because these customers tended to dump large numbers
of hard-driven vehicles on the used car market. Ford had a team of
scientists and mathematicians figure out exactly how many units the
company could sell to rental car companies before it began having a
deleterious effect, and Mulally told the sales team not to exceed that
number.

In January—the month rental agencies placed most of their big

---

* After a few months, Ford's public relations team realized they could use these
report cards to draw attention to positive news that might otherwise have been
ignored. The communications staff figured that any information we obtained
surreptitiously would be deemed more newsworthy. Once we realized what Ford
was up to, we stopped writing about the report cards.

orders for the year—Ford's sales dropped 20 percent. But that was not the only reason why Ford was missing its market share targets. Despite Mulally's insistence on sticking to the facts, some of the company's sales forecasts were still too optimistic. He continued to hammer home the need for honesty in his Thursday meetings, often devoting special attention review sessions to this topic. Even more troubling developments outside Ford were also on the agenda.

The company's chief economist, Ellen Hughes-Cromwick, was raising real concerns about the economy. Serious and analytical, Hughes-Cromwick was a meticulous East Coaster from upstate New York who always seemed to be crunching numbers in the back of her mind, even in the middle of a conversation. She had a master's in international development and a doctorate in economics from Clark University. She came to Ford in 1996 after teaching at Trinity College in Hartford and putting in six years at Mellon Bank.

Hughes-Cromwick was a member of the Harvard Industrial Economists Group, which had been studying the issue of mortgage-backed securities with growing trepidation since early 2006. The housing market was deteriorating and credit was getting tighter. Ford's own cost of borrowing had gone up astronomically because of its poor credit rating. During her first meeting with Mulally on September 29, Hughes-Cromwick showed him a copy of the letter she had sent to Ford treasurer Ann Marie Petach on September 19:

> There are significant shifts underway in several markets. We're presently in the midst of a significant housing correction in the U.S. More than twenty central banks globally have been tightening policies. Typically, these developments raise the probability of some financial consequences. In the past, the financial consequences have included:
> 1. Devaluation, along with contagion
> 2. Corporate implosion—this time it could be hedge funds
> 3. Companies exposed to the commodity cycle
> 4. Banks with large exposures to selected assets could get devalued

Hughes-Cromwick told Mulally that the odds of a recession were as high as 1-in-3. She was surprised by how little this seemed to worry him.

"You just have to deal with the realities and face it together," Mulally said with a reassuring smile. "You have just got to be relentless in matching production to demand. You can't let those stocks build."

He asked her to stay on top of the situation and make sure any bad news was highlighted in her weekly reports.

Now those reports were getting more dire. After a closed-door meeting with a commissioner from the U.S. Securities and Exchange Commission in February, Hughes-Cromwick wrote a note to senior executives warning that the proliferation of subprime mortgages was posing a real danger to the nation's financial system.

"The subprime market has the potential to instigate volatility across other asset classes. Subprime bonds in equity indexes are plunging," she wrote on February 13. "[There is] potential for this sector, along with hedge funds, to generate systemic risk."

Hughes-Cromwick also said she was concerned that federal regulators seemed to be relying on the financial industry to police itself.

On March 4, she sent another note to Don Leclair listing all the warning signs that had preceded previous recessions, and compared those to the current data for leading economic indicators. She concluded that the economy was "vulnerable" and estimated the risk of another recession at as high as 30 percent. A few days later, she sent another note to Ford's treasurer.

"I remain concerned about subprime and other potential systemic risk," Hughes-Cromwick cautioned.

In their Thursday SAR meetings, Mulally and his team studied her reports with growing anxiety.

＊　＊　＊

Clearly Ford faced a long, uphill battle back to profitability—a daunting prospect for everybody but Mulally. Belying the predictions that the harsh realities of the American automobile industry would soon grind him down, he seemed to be having the time of his life.

In March, Nancy Miner walked into a Ford dealership in Dearborn looking for a new car. A perky salesman stepped in front of her and extended his hand.

"Hi, I'm Alan," he said. "I'm from Ford. I'm just helping out here today."

The woman, a visitor from New York, had no idea whom she was speaking with. She told Mulally she was in the market for a new sedan and had narrowed her choices down to a Ford Fusion and a Toyota Camry. He told her he had owned several Camrys—all good cars—but suggested the Ford was a better bet. A few minutes later, Mulally had made his first sale. In less than an hour, he made two more. Another was pending.

It would not be the last time Mulally played at being a car salesman. This was a way for him to see firsthand how Ford's customers approached its cars and trucks. But it also generated a huge amount of goodwill for the company. Everybody who met Mulally walked away an ambassador for Ford. He had that effect on people.

Consumers were not the only ones being won over by Mulally's charismatic approach. In June, he invited all of the company's dealers in the United States to come to town for three days so that he could look them in the eye and explain the big changes under way at Ford. There were about four thousand of them. To accommodate them all, the company commandeered Ford Field—the sleekly modern indoor stadium Bill Ford and his father had built for the Lions in downtown Detroit. There Mulally outlined his "One Ford" vision and promised to work with the franchise owners to improve relations between the dealers and the company. Then he did something entirely unexpected. He asked all of the Ford employees in the stadium to stand up, turn and face the dealers, and say, "We love you."

"We love you," they mumbled.

"No!" Mulally cried. He knew that many of the dealers hated dealing with the company. They felt like no one in Dearborn cared about them or their businesses. Mulally said that was going to change today.

For Ford to prosper, its dealers needed to prosper. From now on, it was going to be a partnership.

"Look at them and say it like you *mean* it," Mulally insisted. "If you do, it will become a self-fulfilling prophecy."

"We love you!" the Ford employees shouted in unison.

A few weeks later, he did the same thing with Ford's suppliers.

* * *

In January, Mulally made his first visit to Ford's European head-quarters in Cologne. European group chief Lewis Booth and Ford of Europe president John Fleming were eager to show off their latest products and brief their new boss on the progress they were making in the region. Ford's European operations were a poignant contrast to North America. While most of its products were being panned in the United States, the new Ford S-Max had just been named "Car of the Year" in Europe, while a redesigned Ford Transit had taken the "Van of the Year" title. For 2006, Ford of Europe had posted a profit of $469 million, while North America had lost $6.1 billion. This was why Mulally had been in no rush to get over there; he had bigger things to worry about closer to home.

Now that he was in Europe, Mulally worked his usual charm. During a town hall meeting with about 150 German employees, Mulally brought them to their feet with his effusive praise for their products and performance. During the question-and-answer session that followed, one of the engineers asked Mulally if he could get a Blue Oval lapel pin like the one the CEO was wearing.

"You *should* have one," Mulally said. "In fact, you can have mine."

He stepped off the stage, went over to the man, and pinned it on his chest like a medal. German employees were still talking about it a year later.

Booth and Fleming organized a deep dive into the company's European progress, showing Mulally how they had already right-sized the organization there and remade the product lineup. They were careful not to draw too sharp a contrast between themselves and their counterparts in the United States, because they knew Europe had been in the same dire straits only a few years earlier. Mulally was impressed by the presentation.

"You guys have to keep it going while we sort out the rest of the business," he told them. "What's your better plan?"

Booth and Fleming were not entirely sure what he meant. Mulally explained how important it was for them to keep improving and not be satisfied with the success they had already achieved. They needed to keep raising their targets to stay ahead of the competition and the external business environment. That was why all of the charts they put together for the weekly BPR meetings needed to look five years out. It was not just about coming up with a plan, Mulally said, it was also about coming up with a *better plan* at the same time. He left Booth and Fleming feeling upbeat, but with the knowledge they still had a lot more work to do.

* * *

Mulally had made his first trip to Japan as Ford's president and CEO in December. It was something of a pilgrimage—and a surprising one for the head of America's second-largest automaker. He went specifically to see Toyota—Shoichiro Toyoda, that is, the head of the Toyoda family and honorary chairman of Toyota Motor Company.* Mulally had made no secret of his great admiration for the Japanese automotive juggernaut. He believed Toyota had become what Ford had once been: an agile, innovative manufacturer of products that made people's lives better. Toyota was lean, well organized, and immensely profitable.

Officially, the purpose of Mulally's visit was to find out if Toyota was willing to allow its suppliers to sell Ford more of the parts it needed to produce hybrids.† He also wanted to find out if the

---

* The Toyoda family spells its name differently than the company founded by its patriarch, Sakichi Toyoda, in 1926. *Toyota* sounds almost the same as *Toyoda* but has more auspicious connotations in the Japanese language.
† Ford was still dependent on key components from Japanese suppliers that were part of the Toyota keiretsu, and these companies limited the number of parts the Dearborn automaker could purchase annually.

Japanese automaker was willing to work with Ford to develop new powertrain technologies. But Mulally also had a more secret agenda. He wanted to see if Toyota was open to even closer collaboration with Ford. Maybe even an alliance. The answer to all of these questions was a polite, but firm, "No."

At the end of February, Mulally made a second trip to Asia. This time he stopped in Hiroshima to visit the partner Ford already had in Japan, Mazda. The executives there viewed Bill Ford's decision to hire Mulally as a positive development. They knew that Mulally had made many visits to Japan during his years at Boeing and had a real appreciation for the nation's manufacturing prowess. He quickly impressed them with his knowledge of Mazda, too. It was a cordial visit, but Mulally dropped a subtle hint that the relationship with Ford was not something the Japanese automaker should take for granted.

"Ford cannot continue to take care of Mazda forever," he said. "I look forward to Mazda becoming stronger and learning to stand tall."

* * *

Mulally took his role as cheerleader in chief seriously. Ford's employees had been down for so long, they needed someone to show them which way was up. But first he had to show several thousand of them the door.

A total of 8,000 salaried employees had signed up for early retirement or buyout offers after the company announced that it would be eliminating 10,000 salaried positions in the United States by 2008 as part of Mark Fields' Way Forward acceleration the previous September. On February 28, 2007, some 6,000 of those white-collar workers piled their possessions in file boxes, handed their ID badges to their bosses, and shuffled to their cars with heads hung low, a Ford security guard following close behind.* A few whispered the words to a protest song written by an anonymous employee to the tune of the

---

* The rest of the 8,000 would leave later that year. Another 2,000 salaried employees would get pink slips, since there had not been enough takers for the voluntary separation program.

Beatles' "Yesterday" that had been making the e-mail rounds for the past couple of weeks:

> *Yesterday*
> *Unemployment seemed so far away*
> *Now it looks as though it's here to stay*
> *I was employed, just yesterday*
> *Suddenly*
> *My boss said they had no use for me*
> *I walked out with Ford security*
> *My Ford career stopped suddenly*
> *Yesterday*

The same day, Ford announced that its board of directors had voted to increase Mulally's bonus from $5 million to $6 million for his four months of work in 2006. The timing could not have been worse. Suddenly the company's cheerleader in chief was looking more like Ebenezer Scrooge.* The United Auto Workers were already in a huff over Mulally's insistence that some executives continue to receive bonuses, despite the company's staggering 2006 loss. Bill Ford recognized that Mulally's windfall would provide more fuel for that fire, so he asked Joe Laymon to call UAW president Ron Gettelfinger to give him a heads-up before it was announced.

"He was deserving of being recognized," Laymon told the union boss, noting that the recent $12.7 billion loss was not Mulally's fault. "We're not talking about an average guy. We're talking about a guy who we need to help us save the company."

Gettelfinger did not see it that way. The two men agreed to disagree, but the union boss warned Laymon that there would be an outcry from the workers. And there was. Mulally took a few punches

---

* The board also approved a new bonus scheme that tied executive bonuses to the same performance metrics that were used for other salaried employees. Mulally had insisted upon this to make the point that everyone was on the same team and should be judged accordingly. The board also required executives to begin paying their own greens fees when they golfed.

in the press, too, which was already ridiculing his recent decision to revive the Taurus name.

Mulally never got over his initial perturbation at Ford's decision to drop the once-bestselling car from its lineup and had been trying to figure out how to bring it back ever since that first visit to the Product Development Center. Ford's marketing people had explained to him that its replacement, the Ford Fusion, was the best car the company had in North America and was already making a name for itself thanks to positive reviews in *Consumer Reports* and other influential publications. Changing its nameplate back to Taurus would only confuse consumers, they warned.

"Fine," Mulally said. "What about the Five Hundred?"

The Five Hundred was supposed to be Ford's flagship. But its bland styling and an almost total lack of marketing support had made for a weak launch in 2004, and sales had never really taken off. Despite its homely looks, the Five Hundred was actually a decent automobile. It was based on a rock-solid platform from Volvo with a five-star safety rating and was even available with all-wheel drive. And as Mulally had tried to convince reporters at the North American International Auto Show in January, its appearance had been improved—though one of the designers in charge of that makeover had described it as "lipstick on a pig."

It was good enough for Mulally. But when Ford announced that the refreshed 2008 Five Hundred would henceforth be known as the Taurus a month after the Detroit show, there was a great deal of snickering among veteran automotive reporters. It seemed Mulally was the only one who still thought the Taurus name had life in it. It did not help that the new car was also significantly more expensive and a lot larger than the old Taurus. It spoke to a lack of understanding of the more subtle nuances of the automobile business. In fact, sales of the Taurus née Five Hundred would continue to disappoint. But Mulally knew what none of his detractors did: The company's designers were already hard at work on a far better version of the automobile. Mulally ordered them to make this one count—and to get it done in record time.

Derrick Kuzak, Ford's new global product development chief, was already making real progress with the company's engineering and design departments. His teams continued to improve Ford's Global Product Development System, taking the original Mazda approach to new levels. Mulally had been a big proponent of computer-aided engineering and testing at Boeing, and pushed for a more rapid migration to digital design tools at Ford. Kuzak also gave his engineers more time to actually engineer by reducing the number of meetings required at each step of the design process. By the middle of the year, he and his team were well on their way to reducing the engineering cost of a new vehicle by 60 percent and cutting the time to market by 25 percent or more. These gains would have been impressive anywhere. In Detroit, they were unheard-of.

Under Mulally, the status of engineers inside Ford improved dramatically. People in other departments listened to what they had to say, because Mulally had convinced everyone that better cars and trucks were the key to Ford's revival. All employees at every level of the company now knew their most important job was supporting Ford's global product renaissance.

Mulally's new multinational approach even extended to design. Before he was hired, the company was simultaneously developing two distinctly different design languages. In North America, designer Peter Horbury was still focusing on "bold, American design," while his counterpart in Europe, Martin Smith, was winning wide acclaim in automotive circles for what he called "kinetic design." Unlike Horbury's chunky, chrome-heavy approach, Smith's style was all about curves and fluid shapes and making cars that looked like they were moving even when they were standing still.

"Pick one," Mulally said.

Kuzak and his team decided to focus on Smith's kinetic design theme. Though there would be minor variations to account for regional requirements, this look would define all of Ford's globally available vehicles going forward—in other words, most of the company's lineup. A few products that were specific to certain regions, such as the Ford Mustang and F-150 pickup, would retain their local flavor, albeit with a nod to this overarching look.

Agreeing on a common design language made it easier to create vehicles for the world market. But that was not the only reason Mulally insisted on it. It was also about building Ford's brand. He wanted a Ford to be instantly recognizable as a Ford whether it was in Detroit or Dresden, São Paulo or Shanghai. And he did not want it to stop with the exterior. Mulally insisted that this commonality extend to the look, feel, and placement of knobs and switches—even the way a Ford door sounded when it was closed. Kuzak had already been working in this direction in North America before Mulally arrived. He referred to the approach as "Feels right, sounds tight." Now he had the brief to take it around the world. Together, all of these attributes would form what Kuzak referred to as the Ford brand DNA—a genome that was designed and engineered to convey quality, innovation, and style.

"It's all aimed at creating a design that creates a visceral reaction in people," he explained. "We want people to have strong, emotional reactions to our products."

*   *   *

The rapid pace of the revolution in Dearborn began to silence the skeptics who had doubted the ability of an outsider to make sense of such a complex business. But Mulally was finding the automobile industry a lot more complicated than he had anticipated—particularly when it came to labor relations and government regulations.

As he studied Ford's contract with the UAW, Mulally was dismayed to discover that Ford could not close factories in the United States without the consent of the union. Even then it had to continue to pay idled workers and cover their benefits until new jobs could be found for them. Nor could the company force them to relocate. This was a real problem in places like Edison, New Jersey, where about 160 workers remained on the Ford payroll three years after their plant—the only one in the region—had been shut down. The only option was buyouts. Ford was offering generous packages to all of its UAW-represented employees as part of Fields' accelerated Way Forward plan, but the whole idea of paying people to leave the company was hard for Mulally to swallow. When he slashed Boeing's workforce after the September 11 attacks, it had all been accomplished with the stroke of a pen. In the automobile industry, nothing was that simple.

Mulally was also learning about the dizzying array of rules and regulations imposed by governments around the world on Ford and its products. There were no global standards for cars and trucks; the United States followed one set of rules, while most of the rest of the world followed another. Turn signals, for example, were required to be amber in most countries, but in the United States, the rear ones could also be red. In Europe, additional indicator lights were required on the side of the vehicle, but those were optional in the United States. Changing the color of a taillight lens was relatively simple, but changing the position of the front bumper to meet the different standards in Europe and the United States was a major engineering feat. In Europe, the emphasis was on protecting pedestrians; the U.S. rules were designed to protect vehicles and the people riding in them. Crash tests were also conducted differently in different regions, each subject to different standards. All of this made Mulally's dream of homogenizing Ford's global lineup a stretch goal for the company's designers and engineers.

Safety standards were not the only thing the United States and European Union differed on either. E.U. lawmakers were pushing for tighter restrictions on carbon dioxide emissions, while the U.S. Congress was preparing tough new fuel-economy targets. Designing products for worldwide consumption would require Ford to serve both masters.

Mulally found the American mileage restrictions particularly galling. Known as the corporate average fuel economy, or CAFE, regulations, they established sales-weighted mileage standards for all of the automakers. That meant a company could produce as many gas-guzzling SUVs as it wanted, as long as it also made a similar number of fuel-efficient compacts. Most other nations used high fuel taxes to dissuade drivers from choosing inefficient vehicles. CAFE put the onus on the car companies. It appealed to America's libertarian sensibilities, but it forced automakers to produce cars that nobody wanted to buy and then sell them at a substantial loss. In a nation with some of the lowest gasoline prices on the planet, there was little incentive for consumers to choose a small car—particularly when most of their neighbors were tooling around in enormous trucks.

When Mulally studied the data, he found that, despite the billions of dollars spent by automakers to meet the CAFE requirements, the American people were driving farther, using more gasoline, and importing more oil than they were when the first limits went into effect in 1975. He made the mistake of sharing his findings with Congress during a hearing on even tougher proposed standards before the House Subcommittee on Energy and Air Quality on March 14.

"When the CAFE law passed in the 1970s, the goal was to reduce our dependence on foreign oil," he told lawmakers. "Frankly, that did not work."

The members of Congress were not accustomed to this sort of candor—particularly from the CEOs of companies who were the target of new regulations they were about to vote on. One lawmaker asked the representatives of the other car companies on the panel if they agreed with Mulally. Their answers were far more equivocal. But Mulally was not finished. He reminded the legislators that, despite their best efforts, consumers were still the ones who decided what they drove. If Washington wanted them to drive smaller cars, the government should consider other alternatives, such as a higher tax on gasoline. Many of the lawmakers bristled at Mulally's implied criticism of their approach to the problem and made sure he knew it.

Mulally was surprised by the animosity he felt emanating from the dais during this first visit to Capitol Hill as the head of Ford Motor Company. At Boeing he had worked closely with the federal government on a number of issues, and his presence was always welcomed—particularly by politicians eager to get a piece of Boeing's production in their district. There was a lot less love for the American automobile industry.

These guys act like we're running guns or smuggling drugs! he thought as he listened to the legislators rail against Detroit's intransigence on the fuel-economy front. *This is going to make things a lot harder.*

Mulally was not opposed to better gas mileage or reducing greenhouse gases. He proved that a few weeks later by naming the company's first vice president of sustainability, environment, and safety engineering, Sue Cischke, who would also be the first woman on his senior leadership team.

"I firmly believe we are at an inflection point in the world's history as it relates to climate change and energy security. The time for debating whether climate change is real has past," Mulally said in an e-mail to employees announcing Cischke's appointment on April 23. "It is time for a conversation about what we, as a society, intend to do to address it."

✳   ✳   ✳

The task of fixing Ford became Mulally's all-consuming mission. He got to the office early each morning. He was already answering e-mails by 6 A.M. He worked until dinnertime, then went home and spent the rest of the evening reading reports, retiring early. He worked seven days a week. Mulally rarely saw his family, though he scheduled regular telephone calls with his wife, children, and mother.

During one conversation with his mother in early 2007, Mrs. Mulally complained that the Dodge van at the senior center she frequented in Lawrence kept breaking down. Since her boy was now the CEO of one of the world's largest automobile manufacturers, she thought he might be able to help them out. Mulally asked the local Ford dealer to meet with his mother and some of the other ladies at the senior center to pick out a new E-Series van. But she was soon back on the phone complaining that there were too many choices—185 to be exact, and that was not counting all the different colors and upholstery options.

Mulally thought that was ridiculous, but as he studied the order books for other vehicles, he discovered that the problem was not limited to the E-Series. The number of different configurations available for each Ford car and truck was staggering. A customer buying a 2007 Ford Mustang V-6 deluxe model could choose from 16,000 different combinations of colors, upholstery, and features. Building all those different variants taxed Ford's factories and created a huge amount of work for designers, engineers, and suppliers. It also limited the company's ability to achieve real economies of scale. Ford's Japanese competitors offered far fewer choices. Mulally ordered the sales and marketing team to pick the most popular combinations and eliminate the rest. By the time the next version of the Mustang came out a few months later, the number of buildable combinations had been reduced to just 200.

As for the senior center, Mulally personally delivered a fifteen-passenger van on March 17. The oldsters promptly christened it "the Mulally Trolley" as his white-haired mother showed off her successful son, who stuck around to serve as grand marshal for Lawrence's St. Patrick's Day parade. He rode down Locust Street with his mother in the back of a red Mustang convertible, both of them waving to the cheering crowd. No astronaut ever enjoyed a better homecoming.

＊　＊　＊

On March 12, Ford closed on the sale of Aston Martin. Bill Ford had put the bespoke British brand up for sale in August 2006, just before Mulally was hired. It was the one recommendation from the Project Game Plan team that everyone could actually agree on. Mulally wholeheartedly endorsed the move; he would have just as soon put "For Sale" signs on Jaguar, Land Rover, and Volvo at the same time. But at least this was a start. The brand of choice for fictional superspy James Bond was sold to a consortium of investors led by motor racing entrepreneur David Richards and backed by Kuwaiti capital. The deal added another $848 million to Mulally's war chest and began the difficult process of dismantling Ford's house of brands.*

Mulally felt like he was moving at light speed. He had only been at Ford for six months, but he had already fundamentally transformed just about every aspect of the business—and bigger changes were in the offing. Mulally had figured out where Ford needed to go, and he could not wait to get there.

Outside the auto shows and financial briefings, he had been spending much of his time briefing analysts and reporters on his four-point plan to save the company. By the time Mulally took the podium at

---

* Under the terms of the sales agreement, Ford retained a $77 million stake in Aston Martin—not enough to have any say in its operations, but enough to retain a modicum of the prestige associated with the marque.

the New York International Auto Show on April 4, most could re-
cite each point verbatim. When he delivered the same stump speech
there that he had been giving since January, it began to sound a bit
stale — particularly to the Wall Street analysts who were always looking for some new tidbit of information to feed into their models.

During a one-on-one with Mulally shortly after the New York show,
I told him that people seemed to be growing tired of hearing about
his four-point plan and wanted something new.

Mulally looked at me with sincere incredulity.

"But, Bryce, we're still working on *this* plan," he said. "Until we
achieve these goals, why would we need another one?"

He was right. Ford did not need a new plan. But the analysts were
growing impatient. And they were not the only ones. The Ford family
was starting to ask some tough questions, too.

CHAPTER 10

Family Strife

A business which exists to make one man or one family rich, and whose existence is of no moment when this is achieved, is not solidly founded.

—HENRY FORD

On a pleasant Saturday in April 2007, the heirs of Henry Ford once again converged on Greenfield Village to discuss the fate of Ford Motor Company. This time they were not alone. The principals of Perella Weinberg Partners, two of the most well-connected dealmakers on Wall Street, had been invited to address the Fords. Bill Ford had hoped his decision to step aside as the automaker's chief executive would mend the rift that had begun to form inside the family. Now it seemed like those long-simmering tensions were about to boil over.

As he made the short drive to the museum grounds, Alan Mulally tried not to take it personally. Until now, he had paid little attention to the internal politics of the Ford family. He counted on Bill Ford to keep the peace and watch his back. As a condition of taking the job, Mulally had asked him to handle the Ford heirs and keep them out of his hair. He warned Bill that any interference or public disagreement would jeopardize the "consistency of purpose" that was essential to his turnaround plan for the company.

"You've got to support me one hundred percent," Mulally insisted.

Bill had agreed, asking only that Mulally provide his relatives with regular updates on the progress he was making. Ford said these briefings would go a long way toward deflecting the sort of problems he was concerned about. That was not an issue for Mulally, who loved nothing more than sharing Ford's progress on his plan, but the presence of the Wall Street dealmakers at this meeting was hard to ignore. As he pulled into the parking lot, he reminded himself that Perella Weinberg was there because of an internal debate that had begun long before he was even approached by the company.

This isn't about me, Mulally told himself. *They just want to know how this is going to turn out.*

* * *

For years the Ford family had been meeting about once a quarter— often in Dearborn, but sometimes in more exotic locales. These gatherings were part social occasion, part business briefing. They always featured what many participants described as "a healthy amount" of discussion and debate. But the intensity of both had increased dramatically since the beginning of 2006. This was partly a function of the deepening crisis confronting Ford and the broader challenges facing the entire U.S. automobile industry. It was also a testament to the proliferation of new media, which allowed the far-flung Fords to follow every twist and turn of their company's travails like never before. Thanks to the Internet, even the most casually engaged members of the family were familiar with Ford's mounting losses, declining sales, and uncompetitive products. They knew that General Motors and Chrysler each claimed to be far ahead of their company in addressing the industry's collective woes. They had no way of knowing whether these statements were true or false, which only added to their anxiety. It did not help that many of them had never worked a day in their lives and knew little about the car business—or any other business for that matter. Every setback seemed like a catastrophe. Ford's decision to suspend dividend payments seemed to support General Motors' claim that it was in better shape than Ford because GM was still paying dividends to its shareholders. Family members were also getting an earful from their personal advisers. Some had lawyers. Some had financial planners. They all had an opinion about Ford Motor Company, its future prospects, and what those might mean for their clients. However, few of these advisers knew enough to have informed opinions. By the time they arrived at each quarter's meeting, the heirs were bristling with questions.

"What's the company doing about this?"

"How does this compare with what's happening in the global industry?"

"How should we, the family, think of these issues that we're reading about and hearing about?"

By the spring of 2006, these concerns were coming to a head. At the time, the board of directors was actively considering all options and the family knew it. While most trusted Bill Ford and his cousin Edsel—who was still a member of Ford's board of directors—to look out for their interests, a growing minority worried that they were more concerned about saving the company than protecting the family's investment. They voiced these concerns during the conclave. It was "a particularly spirited session," in the words of one attendee, and it ended with the family asking its attorneys to begin a search for a firm that could advise the Fords on their options.

The decision to hire Mulally initially seemed to obviate the need for an outside adviser, but the issue was raised once again shortly after he started at the company. Who was stirring the pot? Many pointed the finger at Bill Ford's sister, Sheila, and her husband, Steve Hamp.

In a family like the Fords, the usual sibling rivalries sometimes escalate into business battles. That was certainly the case between Bill and Sheila. It had long been understood in the family that Ford women would never be appointed to the company's board of directors, let alone to the chairman's post. Friends said Sheila resented this, just as she resented her exclusion from the family's football franchise, which Bill ran with his father. They suggested this made her a more vocal critic of her brother, and that criticism increased after Hamp joined the company as Bill's chief of staff in late 2005.

If Hamp had been pessimistic about Ford and its future when he was chief of staff, the circumstances of his departure did little to improve his attitude. Some family members resented Mulally's move against one of their own. But there were other causes for renewed concern on the part of Henry Ford's heirs.

When Bill Ford took over as chairman in 1999, the family's Class B shares had been worth approximately $2.25 billion. Now they were worth only about $578 million. The bulk of that loss had occurred long before Mulally's name was even discussed in Dearborn, but several family members had hoped the decision to hire a new CEO would spur a rebound. It did initially. However, while Mulally's arrival had sent Ford's stock north of $9, the rally did not last. By the time the family convened on April 21, the company's shares were trading for less than they had been before his hiring was announced seven months earlier. Then there was the matter of the dividends. Those Class B shares generated $130 million for the Ford family back in 1999. These payments were a significant source of income for some of Henry Ford's heirs, many of whom also had sizable holdings of the company's common stock. Now they were getting nothing.

Some were still worried they might end up with less than that. The recently concluded financing deal had required Ford to mortgage all of its U.S. assets. If the company defaulted on those loans, the Fords would lose control of their own name. Of course, they knew that when they approved the deal, but that was before the company posted the largest loss in its history.

✳　✳　✳

Identity was important to the Ford family. If the automaker failed, many of them would still be quite wealthy. Money had married money; wise investments had turned small fortunes into large ones. There was land, buildings, and other businesses. But America was full of millionaires and billionaires. What made the Fords different was the fact that they still controlled Ford Motor Company.

Maintaining that control meant maintaining their exclusive ownership of the company's supervoting Class B shares. The ownership structure that Henry Ford II had put in place half a century earlier ensured that the Fords would always control Ford Motor Company as long as they did not sell those shares. The automaker had issued millions of new shares since its initial public offering in 1956. Now their 70 million Class B shares represented just 3.7 percent of the company's total stock. But they still wielded the same 40 percent of the vote they always had. That was because none of the shares had ever been sold outside the family. If any were, they would convert to regular Class A common stock and lose their supervoting power. However, in doing so they would also reduce the voting power of the remaining Class B shares and break the family's hold on Ford Motor Company.*

Not everyone was thrilled with this arrangement. While most employees—even those on the factory floor—welcomed the stability and long-term perspective that the family brought to Ford, Wall Street did not. Most investment bankers and analysts saw the Ford family's continuing control of the company as an anachronism that stymied the sort of speculation that had made them fantastically rich over the past decade. Some investors also objected, arguing that the dual-stock structure diminished the value of their own shares. In just a few weeks, Ford's shareholders were due to vote on what had become a perennial resolution at the automaker's annual meeting to recapitalize the company and make all shares equal. There was no danger of it passing as long as the family retained its control of all its Class B shares, but the chorus of voices objecting was growing louder. What had begun a few years earlier as a bunch of disgruntled stockholders now included influential institutional investors like the California Public Employees' Retirement System, which owned 9.7 million Ford shares, valued at nearly $80 million, and now called Ford's ownership structure "undemocratic."

Many on Wall Street had been hoping for years that the Ford family would one day split, just like the Gettys and so many other fabled families before them. So far, they had not. But as power shifted from the third generation to the fourth with the ascent of Bill Ford to the chairman's seat, it was becoming more difficult to hold together what now amounted to a very diverse group of more than seventy heirs. One board member compared it to herding cats.

The fourth generation of the Ford family included Bill and a dozen of his cousins, the great-grandchildren of Henry Ford. Some, like Edsel Ford II, were businessmen. Others, like Alfred Ford, were not. He had joined the Hare Krishnas and changed his name to Ambarish Das. It also included New York socialites like Charlotte Ford, author of *21st-Century Etiquette*, and philanthropists like Lynn Ford

---

* For example, if 7 million Class B shares were sold, the voting power of the remainder would only be 30 percent.

Alandt. Increasingly they were joined at family meetings by members of the fifth generation, which numbered more than thirty. Many of these younger Fords had a tenuous connection at best to the automaker. New CEO or not, some of them were beginning to wonder if the money tied up in their Ford shares might not be more profitably invested elsewhere. If just one of them decided to sell his or her shares on the open market, the Ford family's control of Ford Motor Company could be threatened.

✳   ✳   ✳

Ford family attorney David Hempstead believed it would be a good idea to hire someone with no ties to the company to advise the family. After the spring 2006 meeting, he and family adviser Bruce Blythe began putting together a list of potential candidates. They moved cautiously, because they knew that any report that suggested the Ford family might be considering a sale would have major consequences for the company and its stock.

By early 2007, they had narrowed the field to two or three firms. The first was Perella Weinberg Partners, a "boutique investment bank" founded just a few months earlier by Joseph Perella, the former vice-chairman of Morgan Stanley, and Peter Weinberg, the former CEO of Goldman Sachs International, to provide corporate advice and asset management services. They were attractive for a couple of important reasons—the names Perella and Weinberg.

Joseph Perella was widely regarded as a "mergers and acquisitions pioneer" and a key player in one of the biggest corporate takeovers in history—the 1989 leveraged buyout of RJR Nabisco. Peter Weinberg was the grandson of Mr. Wall Street himself, Sidney Weinberg, the legendary Goldman Sachs leader who had developed Ford Motor Company's unique stock structure for Henry Ford II back in 1956.

Hempstead contacted the two men and asked if they would be interested in meeting with the Ford family. They jumped at the opportunity. Now the firm, which offered "sage counsel in the middle of huge decisions," was waiting to make its pitch to the men and women who controlled America's last great industrial dynasty.

But it was Alan Mulally's turn to speak first.

* * *

Mulally was still dazzled by the Fords, though their decision to bring in Perella Weinberg certainly tempered his enthusiasm. He tried to put the presence of the two Wall Street titans out of his head as he detailed the progress Ford was making on its restructuring for the family. He assured them that his plan remained on track, despite missing some sales and cost-reduction targets in the United States.

Then he took their questions.

The Fords were respectful, but he could tell some were concerned about the company and its future. They asked for more information about the terms of the financing deal, seeking a better understanding of what would have to go wrong for them to lose control of the Ford name. They also wanted to know more about his plans for Jaguar and Land Rover now that the Aston Martin deal was finished. Mulally knew that Bill's father, William Clay Ford Sr., drove a Jag, as did many of the other people in the room. So he trod carefully. But what they really wanted to know was if Mulally's turnaround was creating "value" for the company yet. He took that as code for "When are you going to restore our dividends?" Mulally admitted that might take a while.

Then he left them to it.

The presentation from Perella Weinberg was more general and focused on the firm's bona fides. There was no concrete discussion of the state of the company, no predictions about its future, and no alternatives to staying the course that Bill Ford had charted for the automaker and the family. Those would only be offered if the firm was actually retained by the Fords.

Once the bankers left the room, the real debate began. Family members peppered Bill Ford with questions.

"What if Alan can't get it done?"

"What are the alternatives if it doesn't work?"

If Bill Ford was angry about this challenge to his authority, he did not show it. His voice was calm as he addressed the other members of the Ford family, his argument simple and compelling. The company had carefully weighed all of its options before hiring a new CEO and had concluded that was the best course for Ford. The family's own interests would be best served by following that course and lending its support to Alan Mulally. He needed it, and he needed it to be unanimous and unequivocal.

"When the going gets tough, it's time to pitch in," Bill said, "not head for the hills."

He told his relations that he had studied Mulally's turnaround plan carefully. Now Bill went over it once again for their benefit and said it represented Ford's best chance at success in many years. He could not promise it would work, but he had faith that it would. Mulally had already proven he could do it at Boeing. Bill said he understood why some in the room might want a second opinion, but he warned them that hiring a firm like Perella Weinberg to advise the family now would undermine Mulally and everything he was trying to do to save their company.

However, Bill said he would abide by whatever the family decided. He reminded the other heirs of Henry Ford that they had so far managed to remain publicly united. Maintaining unity was essential — now more than ever. He urged them to reflect on the drama then playing out in the Bancroft family. The owners of the *Wall Street Journal*, they were unraveling in the face of relentless advances by media mogul Rupert Murdoch. History was filled with such cautionary tales, Bill reminded them.

"Whatever the family does now or in the future, we're always going to be better off unified rather than divided," he said, urging them to consider what had happened when those other famous families had fractured and split. "There was never a good outcome. It never ends well."

Then he excused himself and left the room so that they could discuss the matter without worrying about his feelings.

* * *

At some point in the discussion, someone asked what the family's Class B shares would really be worth if they were sold on the open market, suggesting it might be time for the Fords to cut their losses and get out while they still could. For many in the room, this was crossing a line.

Elena Ford was one of them.

The daughter of Charlotte Ford and Greek shipping magnate Stavros Niarchos, she was born Elena Anne Ford-Niarchos in 1966. She dropped the *Niarchos* and eschewed the glamorous New York society life of her mother and siblings for the smoky factories and sharp-elbowed corporate politics of Dearborn. With her plain appearance and blunt manner, she fit right in. Though the fortune she inherited from her father made her wealthy even by Ford standards, Elena was no pampered debutante. A self-described "car freak," she asked for a Mustang for her sixteenth birthday. Now in her forties, she still drove one—often to lunch at Miller's Bar, a favorite Ford hangout a few miles down Michigan Avenue from World Headquarters that was famous for its greasy burgers. After joining the automaker in 1995, she began a grand tour of the company typical of the Fords who decided to work there—starting as a communications coordinator for Ford's truck division and making a rapid ascent up the corporate ladder, including brief stints as a finance specialist in product development, brand strategy leader in global marketing, director of business strategy for Ford's international automotive group and director of product marketing for the Lincoln Mercury division. Now she was director of North American product marketing, planning, and strategy.

Unlike some of the other Fords who had taken jobs at the company, Elena had a reputation for being a tireless worker. She was eager to prove herself, but she was also passionate about the company. It was the first place she ever felt she really belonged, and she took immense pride in the respect its employees had for the Ford family. During her time in Dearborn, Elena had developed a respect for her coworkers, too, as well as a modicum of disdain for her relatives who chose to live off their inheritances and did nothing to contribute to the success of their company.

Elena's strong emotions for Ford and its employees were evident as she rose to address her aunts, uncles, and cousins at the family meeting.

"I work inside this company, and I believe in it," she began with characteristic directness. "The people who don't work here have to trust the people who do work here."

Part of Elena's responsibilities included powertrain and product planning. That meant she was more aware than most at Ford of the new products already under development, along with a new generation of engines that promised to get more power out of less gas. These were game-changers, she said, and Ford was committed to bringing them to market even if it had to make deeper cuts to pay for them. In the past, the company had eaten its seed corn. But not this time. Mulally was committed to that.

"It's going to be tough, and it's going to be hard, but we are going to get through it," she insisted. "We have the expertise. We have the product."

Elena choked up when she turned to the family's obligation to the company's employees.

"You've *got* to believe in this company, because the people who work here are so dedicated and so intensely proud that they *will* do everything in their power to make it work," she said, adding that she had already lost many friends to the layoffs and seen others quit because they had given up hope before Mulally was hired. "If you don't live it every day, it's hard to understand. It's not about whether Ford can be saved or not. We have no choice!"

As for the idea of selling out, Elena wanted no part of it. She understood why some of her relations might be uneasy about the challenges still facing Ford. She knew that many did not work for a living and had much of their wealth tied up in a company that had stopped paying dividends and offered little prospect of resuming those payments anytime soon.

"I know times are tough, but this company is going to succeed. I'm going to continue to support it, and I think you should, too. If you don't, that's fine—but I don't think you're making the right choice," she said, reminding them that she and others in the room were more than willing to purchase shares from any family member who needed cash or who no longer had the stomach for it. "I believe in the company, and I'm going to support the company."*

By the time she sat back down, at least a few in the room were dabbing their eyes. Several of Elena's relatives came up afterward and thanked her, including her cousin Bill, who had been told of her impassioned plea.

*   *   *

Bill's father also opposed bringing in Perella Weinberg or any other investment bank. William Clay Ford Sr. was the family's patriarch—the last of Edsel Ford's children, which also made him the last of Henry Ford's grandchildren. He also was the largest individual holder of the family's Class B shares. At the time, he owned 11.1 million of them, worth $90.6 million and accounting for 15.63 percent of the total. It was a tiny fraction of his immense fortune, which also included a significant chunk of the company's regular Class A shares.† He was the invisible hand behind his son's rise to power, and if he said no to something, most of the other family members were not likely to say yes.

Bill also received strong support from his onetime rival for the Ford throne, Edsel Ford II. Hank the Deuce's son had been outmaneuvered by his cousin in the 1990s, but he had taken his defeat gracefully. Though he remained on the board of directors and was the family's designated liaison with the company's dealers, he quit his day job at Ford and bought Chrysler's corporate jet division, Pentastar Aviation, which he turned into one of the region's largest jet charter companies. Edsel also became a major force in Michigan philanthropy, representing both the family and the company in the community. It was an important role, and he excelled at it.

Edsel controlled more of the Class B shares than anyone other

---

* It was not unheard-of for family members to sell some of their shares to other family members to pay for their children's college education or cover other major expenses.

† Bill Ford himself owned 3.4 million Class B shares, then valued at $27.7 million. Like other family members, he also owned a sizable chunk of the company's common stock.

than William Clay Ford Sr., owning 4.18 million, or 5.89 percent, as well as a substantial number of publicly traded Class A shares. More important, he, along with Bill and his father, controlled the family trust, that held the vast majority of its stock—51.7 million shares that were voted as a bloc.

Edsel was traveling and could not be present at the meeting, but he wrote a two-page letter that was read aloud there, urging his relatives not to hire Perella Weinberg, asking them to instead give their full support to Bill and Mulally.

* * *

With the biggest shareholders rallying around Bill, and his cousin Elena ready to buy the shares of anyone who did not believe in the company's future, the dissent was squelched.

There are no votes at Ford family meetings. The emphasis is on consensus, and by the end of the session one had been reached: If anyone could save Ford Motor Company and the family's legacy, it was Alan Mulally. His plan was the right one, and the heirs of Henry Ford owed it to Mulally to give him the time and the space necessary to execute it. They all agreed that hiring an outside adviser—particularly one with a reputation as a Wall Street dealmaker—was a mistake.*

Bill Ford breathed a long sigh of relief that night. For the first time in its history, the Ford family had been faced with a real threat to its unity and to its continuing control of the company. But he had held it together. Some shares would exchange hands, but not outside the family. In the months and years ahead, he would face persistent questioning from his relations about the resumption of dividends, but he would never again face a direct challenge to his authority, or to Mulally's.

At least as far as the family was concerned, Mulally now had the breathing room he needed to execute his turnaround plan. They were on board. So was his senior leadership team. Now he just needed to win over the United Auto Workers.

---

* Ironically, the U.S. Treasury Department would hire Perella Weinberg in 2011 to advise it on the initial public offering of Ally Financial, the reincarnation of General Motors' former credit arm, GMAC.

CHAPTER 11

Watershed

You've been fighting General Motors and the Wall Street crowd.
Now you are in here, and we have given you a union shop and more
than you got out of them. That puts you on our side doesn't it? We
fight General Motors and Wall Street together, eh?

— HENRY FORD to United Auto Workers
leader Walter Reuther

For decades, Ford Motor Company had enjoyed a better relationship with the United Auto Workers than either General
Motors or Chrysler. This was due largely to the mutual respect
between the union and the Ford family, which was a bit ironic considering that their bond was baptized in blood.

Henry Ford's $5-a-day wage may have made him the best friend
the workingman ever had, but his relationship with his employees
was always paternalistic. He cared about their welfare in the same way
a kindly nobleman might have cared about his serfs. But he spurned
their efforts to bargain with him on equal footing. Ford knew he
treated his workers better than any other industrialist in the world,
and he resented the idea that they might need a union to mediate
with him on their behalf. He did everything in his power to block the
early attempts to organize his factories in the 1930s. In 1932, Ford
security guards and Dearborn police officers opened fire on workers demonstrating outside the River Rouge complex, killing four and
wounding more than fifty. The passage of President Franklin Roo-
sevelt's National Industrial Recovery Act in 1933, which gave workers
the right to collective bargaining, did little to change Ford's mind.*

---

* The U.S. Supreme Court ruled the NIRA unconstitutional in 1935. However,

"Labor unions are the worst things that ever struck the earth," Ford declared after the UAW used sit-down strikes to force GM and Chrysler to recognize the union. And he used Harry Bennett's infamous Service Department, with its small army of thugs and spies, to keep them out of his factories even after the rest of the American automobile industry had capitulated. In 1937, Bennett's goons attacked a UAW march led by Walter Reuther on an overpass leading to the Rouge factory—the same pedestrian bridge that had been the scene of the 1932 violence. Reuther and several others were badly beaten in what became known as "the Battle of the Overpass." It turned public sentiment against Ford and brought growing pressure from Washington. After his workers managed to shut down the Rouge in 1941, Ford finally relented and signed his first contract with the UAW.

The adversarial relationship between Ford Motor Company and the UAW began to change at that moment. Henry Ford stunned Reuther by offering him more generous terms than the union had been seeking for its members. If Ford was going to be a union company, it was going to offer the best contract in the business.

Relations between the company and the UAW continued to improve under Henry Ford II, who remained remarkably at ease with the rank and file even as he became a role model for the international jet set. In the boom years after World War II, union workers prospered along with the company. Wages got richer and contracts got fatter as Detroit fell into the happy stupor of prosperity that carried it through the end of the 1960s. Labor agreements that were originally a few pages long morphed into thick tomes filled with arcane rules that governed every aspect of factory operations, from the division of labor to the time allowed for restroom breaks. Like the other Detroit automakers, Ford lost the ability to reassign workers and could not close plants without the UAW's approval. Workers were eligible to retire with full pensions and benefits after just thirty years on the job, making it possible for some to earn more as retirees than they had on the assembly line. The companies also had to fund massive union bureaucracies that

---

that same year Congress passed the National Labor Relations Act, which limited the power of employers to oppose union organizing and industrial action.

Henry Ford with his Model T, circa 1919—the man and
the car that put the world on wheels.

Henry Ford's grandsons—
Benson Ford, William Clay
Ford, and Henry Ford II—
in 1949 with one of Ford's
popular postwar models.
Hank the Deuce had already
been president of Ford
Motor Company for four
years. William Clay's son,
Bill Ford Jr., would be born
eight years later.

Chairman Bill Ford Jr. surveys the damage after a deadly explosion at the Rouge complex on February 1, 1999. Ford, who had only become chairman a month before, would spend the rest of the day comforting the families of the victims.

Ford Americas president Mark Fields shows off a new version of the Ford F-150 pickup, the company's bestselling vehicle. Fields underestimated how quickly American consumers would abandon trucks and sport utility vehicles once gasoline prices began to rise.

A worker leaves Ford's Wixom Assembly Plant in Michigan on January 23, 2006, after learning the factory would be shuttered as part of Mark Fields' "Way Forward" restructuring plan. Wixom was one of fourteen plants in the United States and Canada that were marked for closure as part of the plan. *The Detroit News Archives*

Alan Mulally (*left*) and Bill Ford take questions from the media during a press conference on September 5, 2006. Ford had just informed the assembled reporters that he was stepping aside and giving the CEO's job to Mulally. Ford would continue to serve as the company's executive chairman.

Alan Mulally is mobbed by reporters from around the world at the North
American International Auto Show in Detroit. From the moment he was
hired, Ford's new CEO found himself at the center of the media spotlight—
a position he relished. *The Detroit News Archives*

The 1925 Ford ad that Alan Mulally turned to for inspiration. For Mulally,
this summed up everything Ford stood for, and he was determined to return
to the core values that had guided the company to its early success.

A salaried Ford employee cries as he leaves World Headquarters in Dearborn after being laid off on February 28, 2007. Alan Mulally had to cut even deeper in order to restore Ford to profitability.
The Detroit News Archives

Heiress Elena Ford was more comfortable in Ford's factories than in New York society. She would become a powerful advocate for the company inside the family, urging her relatives to give Alan Mulally the time he needed to turn the automaker around.

Don Leclair, Chief
Financial Officer

Joe Laymon,
Vice President of
Human Resources
and Labor Affairs

Mike Bannister,
Chairman and
CEO, Ford Credit

Derrick Kuzak, Vice
President of Global
Product Development

Bennie Fowler,
Vice President of
Global Quality

Jim Farley, Vice President
of Global Marketing,
Sales and Service

Ray Day,
Vice President of
Communications

Ziad Ojakli, Vice
President, Government
and Community
Relations Quality

Tony Brown,
Vice President of
Global Purchasing

United Auto Workers president Ron Gettelfinger and Alan Mulally begin formal negotiations on a new national contract on July 23, 2007. The two men had actually been talking secretly for months. Ford's lead negotiators, Martin Mulloy and Joe Hinrichs, are seated to Mulally's left.

Ford executives hold one of their daily Special Attention Review (SAR) meetings in the Thunderbird Room at World Headquarters on December 1, 2008, during the depths of the crisis. Pictured (*from left*) are Ford Americas Controller Bob Shanks, President of the Americas Mark Fields, President and CEO Alan Mulally, Chief Financial Officer Lewis Booth, General Counsel David Leitch, and Vice President of Global Manufacturing and Labor Affairs Joe Hinrichs.

Alan Mulally and Bill Ford with the all-new 2012 Ford Focus, the car that would embody Mulally's global "One Ford" vision for the company.

grew inside each factory to ensure the terms of these contracts were being followed to the letter. It was hard for the companies to complain too loudly. The union's bureaucracies were inspired by those on the management side, often matching them person for person, while demands for ever-higher wages were a response to the mushrooming salaries of the automakers' top executives. As Paul Ingrassia put it in his book *Crash Course,* "Detroit's auto industry was built on corporate oligopoly and union monopoly—a combination that had produced decades of astounding success but also sowed the seeds of failure."

When the Japanese invasion of the 1970s sent the automakers scrambling for cover, union bosses were unwilling to cede the gains they had made for their members over the past three decades. As Ford and the other manufacturers demanded concessions to keep their cars profitable, the UAW dug in its heels. The industry entered a new era of labor hostility. Quality began to erode as workers took out their frustrations on the assembly lines, and the automakers began sending more work to factories in Canada and Mexico—particularly after the North American Free Trade Agreement removed the barriers to trade with those countries in 1994.

Even in the face of this increasing animosity between the UAW and Detroit's Big Three, Ford managed to maintain a better relationship with the union. Ford family members often dealt directly with UAW officials, even during the period when there was no Ford in the chairman's seat. None of the company's factories had been struck since 1976. But even Ford could not get the concessions it needed to be competitive with the growing number of foreign transplants setting up factories of their own in the southern United States.

*   *   *

In 2002, Ron Gettelfinger was elected president of the UAW. Gettelfinger was a short, wiry, gravel-voiced man with a white mustache and an intense stare who carried himself with the air of a volcano about to erupt. A puritanical fighter for workers' rights, he had grown up as one of a dozen children on a farm in rural Indiana. Gettelfinger crossed the state line to take a job at the Ford factory in Louisville, Kentucky, in 1964. At night he worked on his business degree at

Indiana University Southeast in New Albany. Gettelfinger graduated in 1976 and began making his way up the union's ranks. He was elected vice president in 1998 and became head of the UAW's National Ford Department. Four years later, he became the head of the whole union.

Despite the often-confrontational relationship between the union and the American automakers, relations between company executives and UAW bosses had remained remarkably chummy behind the scenes. Ford, GM, and Chrysler spent big on golf outings, cigars, and booze to ensure the lines of communication remained open. Gettelfinger was the brother of a Catholic bishop and did not drink, smoke, or play golf. He put an end to all of this schmoozing when he took over at Solidarity House, the union's international headquarters in downtown Detroit. For a while it seemed like things might go from bad to worse, at least as far as the companies were concerned. But Gettelfinger was also a pragmatist. He knew that the fate of the UAW and its members was inextricably tied to the fate of the Detroit automakers.

Bill Ford believed Gettelfinger was someone he could work with. The great-grandson of Henry Ford had spent a lot of time thinking about how to end the decades-long stalemate between his company and the UAW. He had studied labor history in college and was part of the company's bargaining team in the 1982 contract talks that got the UAW to commit to making quality "Job One." When Gettelfinger emerged as the heir apparent to confrontational UAW boss Stephen Yokich in 2001, Ford instructed Joe Laymon to start building a rapport with him. It was the sort of thing Laymon did best. During their first meeting, he offered to pass Gettelfinger confidential information about Ford's competitive position and finances. He also offered to set up secret meetings between Gettelfinger and Bill Ford. During these sessions, Laymon urged Gettelfinger to raise any issues he might have with the automaker. When Gettelfinger did, Ford did his best to see that they were addressed. If lower-level managers lied to the UAW, Laymon told Gettelfinger the truth. Occasionally Ford would call in a favor. But not often. This was all about laying the foundation for a deal that would fundamentally alter the rules of the game in Detroit.

Laymon found himself sitting across the negotiating table from Gettelfinger in 2003, but the timing was wrong. The industry was still making too much money from its sport utility vehicles to demand meaningful concessions from the union. But that did not mean Ford had to wait until that contract expired in 2007.

＊　＊　＊

In October 2005, Bill Ford promoted Joe Hinrichs to vice president in charge of North American vehicle operations, giving him responsibility for all of the company's factories in the United States, Canada, and Mexico. Hinrichs was a young production executive who looked and sounded like a corporate version of Adam Sandler. Like Gettelfinger, he never drank, and he possessed a boundless energy that made him difficult to keep up with—even in conversation. At thirty-eight, Hinrichs was the youngest vice president in Dearborn, but he had already spent enough time in the automobile industry to develop a passionate aversion to the inefficiencies imposed on Ford and the other Detroit automakers by the UAW.

After earning a degree in electrical engineering from the University of Dayton in 1989, Hinrichs had signed on at General Motors. He did stints at a number of plants before being assigned to a joint-venture parts factory in Kentucky that GM had set up with Japan's Akebono Brake Corporation. Like most Japanese-run factories, this plant had only two job classifications for hourly workers: production and maintenance. It was a model of efficiency compared to the American-run factories Hinrichs had worked in where the UAW contract established dozens of different job descriptions and prohibited the company from assigning workers tasks that were not specifically part of their description. He became so frustrated with GM's inability to compete that he decided to get out of the automobile business and give private equity a try. Hinrichs became a partner at a Chicago firm that specialized in manufacturing companies, but returned to Detroit in 2000 as manager of Ford's Van Dyke Transmission Plant. There he heard much about the cooperative relationship Ford was supposed to have with the UAW, but could discern no real benefit from it on the factory floor. There was no question that Ford avoided the nasty skirmishes that perennially plagued GM and Chrysler, but that did not make the Dearborn automaker any more competitive with the foreign transplants. When he was tapped to join Mark Fields' Way Forward team, Hinrichs decided to challenge the UAW to make this so-called special relationship truly special.

Every spring, Ford hosted a meeting with local union leaders from around the country in Las Vegas. It was mostly about wining and dining on the company's dime, but Hinrichs was determined to get a return on Ford's investment when he headed for Sin City in March 2006. During a meeting with Ford's plant managers and their UAW counterparts at the Paris Las Vegas hotel, he delivered a blunt analysis of Ford's automotive operations in the United States. The company had too many employees in its U.S. factories—40,000 more than it needed to meet the current demand for its cars and trucks. Hundreds of these men and women were twiddling their thumbs in the company's jobs bank. Thousands more were being paid assembly-line wages to clean the bathrooms, mop the floors, and mow the lawns. There was an unspoken rule at American automobile factories that, when a worker's body started to pay the price for all those years of toil on the assembly line, he would be given a nice easy job pushing a broom or riding a mower until he was ready to retire. The problem was that many of these new assignments were so cushy that the workers who got them stayed on the job long after they were eligible to retire. This was work that any other company would have outsourced to low-wage contractors at a substantial savings. Hinrichs told the UAW leaders that this model was no longer sustainable. He also presented a series of slides comparing each of Ford's U.S. factories with those of its principal competitors—Toyota, Honda, and GM—on the key metrics of quality, safety, and productivity. Hinrichs translated the productivity data for each plant into a dollar amount, showing the local union leaders just how much more Ford's competitors were getting for their money. He also showed how this gap was forcing Ford to charge more for its cars and trucks and siphoning off cash that could be better spent elsewhere.

"If we had this money, we could be investing in new products—which you say you want for your plants," Hinrichs told the labor leaders. "We could grow market share, which could boost employment. So, let's start talking about how we fix this."

There was a rush for the microphone. The first one to grab it was Mike Oblak, the chairman of UAW Local 900, which represented workers at Ford's stamping plant in Wayne, Michigan.

"You don't respect the UAW!" he shouted, accusing Hinrichs of youthful inexperience and an adherence to the adversarial labor practices he had learned while working at General Motors. "This is how GM thinks, not how Ford thinks."

"The facts are the facts," Hinrichs replied coolly. "We're here to save the company, not appoint blame."

Similar accusations followed from the next couple of speakers. But then something unexpected happened. First one UAW official, then another took the floor to thank Hinrichs for sharing this information with them. For years they had been listening to the company complain that its factories were becoming less and less competitive, but this was the first time anybody had shown them the data that proved it.

"I think we need to talk about it and start working together on what we're going to do about it," said one plant chairman, "because I'm worried about the future."

And the UAW was about to get a lot more scared.

Though few recognized it at the time, Ford and the other American automakers had been handed a big break on October 8, 2005, when Delphi Corporation, the largest automotive supplier in the country, filed for Chapter 11 bankruptcy protection.* Like the companies it served, Delphi was groaning under the ever-increasing burden of providing pensions and health care to thousands of retired factory workers and their dependents while union contracts written in better times saddled it with higher labor costs than its foreign competitors and imposed work rules that made its factories inefficient and uncompetitive. What made Delphi different was the way it decided to deal with these problems. After going back and forth with the UAW for months, Delphi walked into bankruptcy court on March 31 and

---

* Formerly General Motors' parts subsidiary, Delphi had been spun off in 1999 to capitalize on the then-hot market for initial public offerings. Since then, the company had struggled along with the rest of the nation's automotive suppliers.

asked a federal judge to void its contract with the union. For the first time anyone could remember, someone was calling the UAW's bluff.

Hinrichs had left Las Vegas challenging the UAW leaders to negotiate new, more competitive local operating agreements at their factories to close the competitiveness gap ahead of the 2007 national contract talks, warning them that Ford might not make it until then without their help. They were still debating how to respond when they received news of Delphi's move. It pushed the local UAW leaders to the bargaining table.

So did the new head of the union's National Ford Department, Bob King.

King was a gaunt intellectual with messy hair and thick glasses, the son of a Ford labor relations executive who had switched sides at an early age. A quiet Michiganian with socialist leanings, King could rouse himself to a revolutionary fervor when necessary. But like Gettelfinger, King was also a realist, and he soon realized that Ford was in serious trouble. After he was elected vice president in June, King got Ford's usual spiel about how dire its financial position had become. With talks on a new national contract only a year away, he was skeptical.

"If that's the case, I want to have somebody I trust come in and review all the numbers," he told Ford. King knew he was in trouble when the company immediately agreed to open its books to whomever the union designated. The UAW had its own finance whiz, Eric Perkins, crunch Ford's numbers. Chief Financial Officer Don Leclair went over everything with him.

"It's worse than they're telling you," Perkins told King and Gettelfinger when he had completed his analysis.

King knew that if Ford failed, tens of thousands of UAW members would be out of work, and many times that number of retirees, spouses, and dependents could lose their pensions and their benefits. He was prepared to do whatever was required to keep Ford in business. That did not mean he had to like it. King believed many of Ford's problems were the result of catastrophic blunders by the company's management. But the past was suddenly a lot less important than the future. King worked with the automaker to put together the buyout packages that were necessary to meet Mark Fields' downsizing goals and allowed Hinrichs and Martin Mulloy, Ford's vice president of labor affairs for North America, to pitch them directly to workers at each Ford factory.

The two Ford men made a bit of an odd couple. Hinrichs was young and willing to outshout workers who challenged his facts and figures. Mulloy, who went by "Marty," was an older, quieter, and far more easygoing negotiator with a bald pate and quick smile who spent a lot of time unruffling feathers that Hinrichs had ruffled. But they worked well together—a bit like a latter-day vaudeville team—and with King's help managed to exceed the buyout targets established in Ford's Way Forward plan. They were also able to negotiate more competitive operating agreements at all but six of Ford's U.S. factories by September 2006.

Hinrichs was pleased with the progress, but he was also working on a contingency plan. If Ford could not wrest even deeper concessions from the UAW in the upcoming national contract talks, he wanted to move the bulk of its U.S. manufacturing to Mexico. And he was not alone. But Alan Mulally had a different idea.

* * *

Ron Gettelfinger and Bob King were not entirely sure what to make of Ford's new CEO. Mulally was not exactly known as a friend to labor. After all, he was the guy who cut Boeing's factory workforce in half after the September 11 terrorist attacks, went on to outsource much of the work on its flagship 787 airliner, and battled its unions in a series of bitter strikes that were called as a result of these measures. Gettelfinger had firsthand knowledge of all of this. While most of Boeing's hourly workers were members of the International Association of Machinists and Aerospace Workers, employees at some of its facilities were represented by the UAW's aerospace division, which Gettelfinger headed from 1998 to 2002. During that time, he sat across the table from Mulally more than once, and while he had not been a big fan of the painful cuts Mulally demanded to save Boeing, Gettelfinger had always found him to be an honest broker. King was more concerned. He had gotten an earful from the West Coast unions after Mulally was named president and CEO of Ford back in September. But he was willing to follow Gettelfinger's lead.

Both UAW leaders were also a little concerned about Bill Ford's decision to remove himself from the day-to-day running of the company. They were impressed by his humility but valued the long-standing relationship between the Ford family and the union. They knew that he and the other members of the Ford family genuinely cared for the company's workers, and they were not entirely sure what Ford's decision would mean for that relationship. However, those concerns were soon put to rest. Bill Ford contacted Gettelfinger shortly after Mulally was hired and told him that he would continue to hold private, one-on-one meetings with the UAW president. Even Mulally did not know about them, at least initially.

As Gettelfinger and King tried to figure out Mulally, he was trying to figure out the UAW. It quickly became clear to him that this union wielded far more power at Ford than the Machinists had ever known at Boeing. He could not believe the UAW could force Ford to keep factories open, nor could he believe the company had to pay union members to leave. And the jobs bank—that seemed like something out of Kafka. Mulally was not particularly interested in assigning blame for this mess. His predecessors had signed the contracts that made all these things possible, so they were as much responsible for making the company's American factories uncompetitive as the union was. He was more worried about figuring out how both sides could work together to change the equation so that it once again made sense for Ford to build cars and trucks in the United States. Like everything else, labor relations were all about teamwork for Mulally. He rejected the traditional adversarial relationship between companies and unions. To him both sides were in it together. Both stood to lose if the company failed. Both stood to gain if it succeeded. And just like the white-collar workers, those on the assembly line needed to know what the real situation was so that they could make informed decisions about how to respond to it. But he also firmly believed that, if push came to shove, a company had to do whatever was required to stay in business.

Laymon warned Mulally that his track record at Boeing would

worry many Ford workers, and Mulally did his best to assuage those concerns. The day after his hiring was announced, Mulally went on the radio in Detroit and said his mission was to save Ford Motor Company, not destroy the UAW.

"I am absolutely not Mr. Ax Man," he promised.

Mulally also remembered Gettelfinger. When he was overseeing the integration of the Rockwell and McDonnell Douglas aerospace and defense operations in the late 1990s, he had come to Detroit to meet with the UAW president at Solidarity House and hash out details of that transition. Mulally recalled that Gettelfinger had excused himself in the middle of those talks because he was engaged in his own negotiations with the union representing the UAW's office staff. A few minutes later, Gettelfinger returned and dropped into his seat with a sigh.

"Boy!" he exclaimed with a wicked grin. "These unions are tough."

Laymon told Mulally that there was no way he could save Ford without Gettelfinger.

"You might not like the guy," he told Mulally. "But you gotta appreciate the power and influence he has over your ability to produce product."

Laymon urged Mulally to begin a dialogue with the union boss as soon as he arrived in Dearborn and scheduled a meet-and-greet for the two men on September 28, 2006, just a few weeks after Mulally was hired. During that first visit, Gettelfinger spent most of the time listing all of the things the UAW had done to help Ford to date. He talked about the competitive operating agreements, the quality pushes, and the buyouts. Mulally got the message: We've already done a lot, so don't expect us to do much more. But he was impressed with the genuine pride Gettelfinger took in these accomplishments—and with the UAW president's stories about his own time on the Ford line in Kentucky.

He's really got a personal connection with Ford, Mulally thought. *He wants Ford to succeed.*

They agreed to keep talking.

* * *

O n May 11, 2007, Mulally held a secret meeting with Gettelfinger and King at the Dearborn Inn, a stately redbrick hotel hidden behind a screen of trees across the street from Ford Motor Company's proving grounds.* They convened in a large suite with Leclair, Laymon, Mulloy, and Hinrichs, who had recently been promoted to vice president of manufacturing for North America. It was a casual gathering. There was no conference table. The men sat in armchairs clustered around a blank flip chart. Mulally stood next to the easel, a black marker in his hand. It was a beautiful spring day, and a gentle breeze blew through the open windows. A large American flag flapped audibly outside the window as Mulally began outlining his plan to make the United States a manufacturing leader once again.

At the top of the first blank sheet, Mulally wrote "Our World." Beneath it he drew a simple chart plotting the decline of Detroit's Big Three and the rise of their Japanese competitors.

"All three companies have been going out of business for decades. When they finally do, they'll take the UAW down with them," Mulally told the union leaders. "We've got to deal with this reality."

Of course, this was not news to either Gettelfinger or King. The UAW had its own financial advisers. They had reached the same conclusion. The only question was what to do about it. Mulally said he had some ideas.

He drew three intersecting circles. In one he wrote "Customers," in another "Dealers," and in the last one "Ford." Then he wrote "UAW" underneath the automaker's name. These were the company's stakeholders, Mulally explained. They all stood to benefit from Ford's success, and they all would lose if Ford failed.

Mulally drew three more circles, labeling these "Products," "Production," and "People." Under that he once again wrote "UAW." These, he said, were the levers Ford could pull to effect its transformation into a viable company—the inputs into his equation.

Beneath these two diagrams, Mulally charted Ford's finances, projected out over the next five years.

---

* The Dearborn Inn is run by Marriott but owned by Ford Motor Company.

"Look at how much money we're losing," he said, tapping the chart with his pen. "We've got to get to break-even by '09."

But Mulally's chart showed the company losing $4 billion in 2009, the current internal forecast. If Ford could not figure out how to transform that loss into a profit, it might as well turn the lights out.

"We're going to run out of time," he said.

Gettelfinger and King complained that Ford was investing too much in its money-losing foreign brands. Why not start there? Mulally smiled, and wrote the initials of each brand on the bottom of the sheet, starting with "F" for Ford, followed by "L" for Lincoln, "M" for Mercury, "J" for Jaguar, "LR" for Land Rover, "V" for Volvo, "AM" for Aston Martin, and another "M" for Mazda. Then he crossed all of them out, except for the "F" and the "L." The union men were stunned.

"This is our plan. We're going to do this to invest in Ford," Mulally said with a grin. The only question was where to make that investment. The answer was up to the UAW. Right now Ford was losing money on almost every vehicle it made in America. It could keep doing that and go out of business, or it could use the money freed up by selling off the foreign brands to build new factories in Mexico, where it could build cars at a profit.

"What would you do?" Mulally asked. Neither Gettelfinger nor King answered.

Mulally said there was a third option: With the right contract, Ford could profitably build its cars right here, in the good old U.S. of A.

"If we can get back to being competitive, we can grow and we can provide more opportunities for salaried employees and UAW employees," he said. "That's my theme: Profitable growth for all."

Mulally took a step toward Gettelfinger and looked him in the eye.

"We want to prove that we can do this in America," he said solemnly. "Ron, will you hold hands with me? We'll do this together, and we'll go out there and say we did this together. We're going to be able to make products in America and make them profitably and successfully. Or, we'll just go out there and tell everybody it was too hard. We just couldn't do it. It's up to you."

Gettelfinger did not hesitate.

"We agree," he said.

"Great!" Mulally exclaimed. "If we can come to a competitive agreement going forward, here's what we're willing to do."

He flipped the page over and started on a clean sheet. This time Mulally outlined Ford's entire North American cycle plan—every product, every plant—for the life of the next contract. Mulally's biggest carrot was the Ford Focus. The North American version was being built at Ford's Wayne Stamping and Assembly Plant in Michigan. But he had already decided to replace it with the far better European version. The current plan called for the new Focus to be built in Mexico, because that was the only way Ford could make a profit on the inexpensive compact. Now, he told Gettelfinger, he was willing to keep building the Focus in Michigan—if the UAW would give the company the concessions it needed to build it profitably.

"I'm not trying to run away from you," Mulally promised the UAW president. "If we can do that, I'll make it here in the United States. That's my commitment."

＊　＊　＊

What followed was a series of regular, covert meetings between Ford and the UAW. Sometimes it was just Alan Mulally and Ron Gettelfinger in the room, but Bob King was often there, too, as were Joe Laymon, Joe Hinrichs, and Marty Mulloy. Sometimes it would just be the latter two sitting down with the UAW leaders. Sometimes Don Leclair would be the man sitting across the table from Gettelfinger. These informal bargaining sessions were held every week or two. Gettelfinger, who despised the media, was worried some enterprising reporter might notice him coming or going from the Glass House, so they usually met in an empty, nondescript office building Bill Ford owned behind the Detroit Lions' practice facility in nearby Allen Park. It was a scene right out of a bad spy novel. The men would arrive in separate cars early in the morning, wait to make sure the coast was clear, and then hurry into an unlocked side door, taking care not to spill the steaming cup of coffee each brought with him. Once inside, they would gather around a conference table in an otherwise empty room and begin hashing out the details of a new national contract.

It had been a year since Hinrichs first delivered his tough love speech to union leaders in Las Vegas. Since then, Ford and the UAW had negotiated forty-four new competitive operating agreements at facilities around the country. Together they had convinced 38,000 hourly workers to sign up for buyouts or early retirement packages, halving the company's factory workforce in the United States and exceeding the goal set in Ford's original Way Forward restructuring plan. But one enormous problem remained: retiree health care.

By 2007, some in Detroit were joking that Ford, GM, and Chrysler should be reclassified as insurance companies since they were providing health care to hundreds of thousands of employees and retirees, as well as their spouses and dependents. As medical costs skyrocketed in the United States, this was becoming a crushing weight on the three American automakers—one their foreign competitors did not have to shoulder. Even the Japanese, German, and Korean carmakers that opened factories in the United States were comparatively unencumbered, because they had a much younger workforce and few retirees. Nor were they contractually obligated to provide health insurance for them.*

Ford's own obligation for hourly retiree health care totaled approximately $23 billion. It was like a black hole on the company's balance sheet, sucking away all hope of future profitability. And it would only get bigger as more employees retired and insurance premiums continued to increase. Getting it off the books was Mulally's top priority in the upcoming negotiations with the UAW.

The UAW already knew the situation was untenable. In fact, it was the union that first proposed a solution. Back in 2005, Gettelfinger suggested to General Motors—which had the largest liability and was the most eager to get rid of it—that it transfer responsibility for

---

* For years, the UAW had tried to organize these foreign-owned factories, but most were strategically located in the South, where high-paying jobs were scarce and there was little love for organized labor.

hourly-retiree health care to a trust run by the UAW. It would have required GM to pony up a substantial amount of cash, but once the bill had been paid, the automaker would no longer have to worry about providing health insurance for its union retirees or the drag that exerted on its bottom line. It was known as a voluntary employees' beneficiary association, or VEBA, and a similar deal had been negotiated between the UAW and Caterpillar in 1998. It had since run out of money, but the union believed it had learned enough from that experience to put together one that would work for both GM and its retirees. But the price proved too high for GM, and since it was unwilling to pursue a VEBA, Gettelfinger never extended the offer to Ford.

A lot had changed since then. By the end of 2006, the UAW knew all three Detroit manufacturers were careening toward bankruptcy. Ford knew it, too, and even GM and Chrysler were beginning to see that they had grossly underestimated the severity of their own situations. If the companies filed for Chapter 11 protection, the union's retirees could lose everything. And if the companies could not cut a deal with the UAW on retiree health care, that might be their only option. So there was a new impetus on both sides to find a solution.

In Mulally's early discussions with his counterparts at General Motors and Chrysler, the three CEOs had agreed that negotiating a VEBA would be the central focus of their upcoming contract talks with the UAW. All three had agreed to limit their dickering over other issues that might threaten a deal on retiree health care.

Laymon was worried that Hinrichs' efforts to negotiate local competitive operating agreements might do just that, and he asked him to ease off. Changing the work rules was all well and good, he said, but they were not going to save the company. They were saving Ford mere millions at a time when it needed to cut billions of dollars from its balance sheet in order to survive.

"We need twenty-three billion dollars," Laymon told Hinrichs. "There's nothing you've said yet in the plants that can get me there. I'm going to get twenty-three billion from health care. I'm going to get it from one guy—Ron Gettelfinger. So don't piss him off!"

* * *

The terms of Ford's VEBA became the major topic of discussion in the secret meetings between the company and the union. Joe Laymon made Ford's position clear in one of the first sessions.

"You know you're in a position to pick us apart on this thing. You can have three different VEBAs," he told Gettelfinger. "Here's how we want ours constructed. We want to put less money on the table, but we'll give you a lot of leverage. We can't convince the other two companies that this is in their best interest. But this is what we need."

Laymon told Gettelfinger that, while Mulally may have just secured the largest home improvement loan in history, it was the last one Ford was likely to get anytime soon. He brought in Ford's chief economist, Ellen Hughes-Cromwick, to explain the company's growing concern about the global credit markets and the likelihood of a serious financial crisis. The union chief listened, but the Caterpillar experience was too fresh in Gettelfinger's mind. The UAW was willing to accept a discount in each automaker's contribution to its VEBA. The companies would not be required to fund these trusts at 100 percent of their actual liability. But Gettelfinger wanted all three to make their contributions in cash. The reason the UAW was willing to assume responsibility for their retirees' health care in the first place was that the automakers were in serious financial trouble. That was taking its toll on the companies' stock prices. There was no way of knowing how far they would fall, and the union was unwilling to bet its retirees' futures on a rebound.

Ford's labor team was sympathetic to the UAW's position, but Don Leclair was more worried about the company's own cash reserves. Ford needed the money it raised on Wall Street to fund Mulally's revolution. Leclair also wanted to preserve as much of a cash cushion as possible to help the company ride out the economic storm he saw looming on the horizon. Still, as spring turned to summer, both Ford and the UAW felt good about the progress they were making on the VEBA and other issues.

The union was a big believer in pattern bargaining. It picked one company to negotiate with first, then used that contract as a template for the others. Gettelfinger hinted that Ford would be the target company once the formal talks began on July 23, 2007. That meant it would be allowed to set the pattern according to its needs, and General Motors and Chrysler would have to accept more or less the same terms. At least that was how the game had been played for decades.* However, as it became clear that Leclair was the one calling the shots on the VEBA funding, Gettelfinger began to grow impatient. They kept talking, but Leclair refused to budge on how much cash he was willing to put on the table. After the two had gone back and forth for a few hours, Gettelfinger simply slid his chair back, stood up, and left without saying a word.

Leclair was apoplectic. He rushed back to World Headquarters and told Mulally the union could not be trusted. Mulally's secretary called Joe Laymon and asked him to come to the CEO's office.

"That fucking guy walked out on me!" Leclair shouted at the HR chief when he walked in.

"He has a right to do that," Laymon said with a shrug. He told Mulally not to worry; Gettelfinger would be back.

*　*　*

B ut the UAW leader decided to deal with General Motors first. It was a smart move on Gettelfinger's part. GM had been the first of the Detroit Three to appreciate the potential of the VEBA. Its CFO, Frederick "Fritz" Henderson, understood the mechanics of it better than anyone. He would not give the UAW everything it wanted, but he was willing to come a lot closer than Ford was. GM was less concerned about its cash position than it was about its $51 billion unfunded liability for hourly-retiree health care.

Serious negotiations between General Motors and the UAW began on September 14 and continued with few pauses for the next ten days. There were whispers that a deal was imminent. Then, on September 24, Gettelfinger surprised everyone by calling a strike. Within hours, picket lines were up around all of GM's factories in the United States. The company's negotiators were dumbfounded. They thought they had a deal. They did. But Gettelfinger knew the concessionary

---

* A notable exception was Chrysler, which negotiated separate deals with the UAW for several years following its near-death experience in the early 1980s.

agreement he was about to announce would be a tough sell to his members, and he needed their votes to ratify it. The walkout was designed to demonstrate that he had gone to the mat for the workers and to convince them that the deal he negotiated with GM was the best one possible under the circumstances. Two days later, Gettelfinger sent them back to work and announced that the UAW had reached an agreement on a new contract with the automaker.

General Motors got its VEBA. It would have to pay only $35 billion into the union-run trust, and it got three years to do it. That represented a discount of about 70 cents on the dollar. In addition, GM could cover more than $4 billion of its VEBA obligations with a convertible note that the union could cash in for stock. When the last cash payment was made, GM would no longer be responsible for providing health insurance to current or future UAW retirees. That would be the union's problem.

But there was more to the deal than the VEBA. General Motors and the UAW also agreed that the automaker could pay new hires who were assigned to what were now identified as "non-core jobs" substantially lower wages and provide them with fewer benefits. These jobs included most factory positions not directly involved in the production of vehicles or vehicle components. And the agreement changed the rules governing GM's jobs bank. From now on, workers could say no to only one job offer. If they did not accept the next position GM offered after that, they would have to leave the company. In exchange, GM made substantial new product commitments to the UAW and promised additional investment in its American factories.

On October 10, the UAW announced that its members had ratified the agreement. But the vote had been perilously close at several factories. It would be even closer at Chrysler, which announced an almost identical agreement with the union the same day after a brief walkout lasting less than seven hours.*

---

* The strike at Chrysler was more about convincing recalcitrant members of the UAW's own bargaining team to accept the deal that Gettelfinger had already reached with the company.

* * *

Ford had said all along that, if it could not go first, it wanted to go last. By the time formal high-level negotiations between the Dearborn automaker and the UAW resumed on Wednesday, October 31, the terms of the UAW's deals with GM and Chrysler had been published. Ford knew exactly what the union was willing to accept. It also knew that the UAW was willing to bend the pattern, because it had given Chrysler slightly less favorable terms than it had negotiated with GM. Ford hoped it could tweak the contract to better meet its needs. It might even be able to get a sweeter deal from the union, because Gettelfinger would not have to offer the same terms to GM or Chrysler.

Once again, Ford's special relationship with the UAW paid off.

The company successfully pushed for more favorable terms on the two-tier wage system. The deals the union cut with GM and Chrysler were tied to specific job classifications. Ford saw several problems with that. For one thing, many of those non-core jobs were the same cushy positions UAW members aspired to at the end of their careers. Ford suspected that was a big part of why ratification proved so difficult at some of its competitors' factories. Those workers often carried a lot of clout on the assembly line. At the same time, Ford was worried that the system GM and Chrysler had negotiated with the union left the door open to ongoing disputes at every facility over every job. So Hinrichs and Mulloy proposed a less complicated approach. About 20 percent of Ford's UAW-represented workers were employed in non-core jobs. Ford suggested that all new hires come in as second-tier workers regardless of what job they were assigned to do, but agreed that no more than 20 percent of Ford's hourly workforce would be made up of these lower-wage workers. If it reached that cap, some second-tier workers would have to be promoted to the first tier before Ford could hire any more entry-level employees. The UAW agreed. The union also agreed that any new positions the company created by bringing work back into its factories that was currently being performed by outside suppliers could also be filled with second-tier workers without those new employees counting toward the total percentage. The union's ranks were dwindling, and it needed to add more members to survive financially. So Gettelfinger and King viewed this as a win for both sides.

Ford also got a better deal on the jobs bank. Its workers could stay in the program for only one year and had to accept any job Ford offered them, even if it required them to relocate.

In exchange for these more generous terms, Ford not only made good on the product commitments Mulally had made back at the Dearborn Inn earlier that year but also agreed to keep several U.S. plants open that had been slated for closure as part of its Way Forward restructuring plan. These included Ford's Ohio Assembly Plant in Avon Lake and the Wayne Stamping and Assembly Plant.*

Gettelfinger was a big believer in old-school negotiating tactics. He thought the only way to reach the best possible deal was through marathon, around-the-clock negotiations. So that is what he insisted on at Ford, even though most of the heavy lifting had already been done in the secret sessions early that year. Both sides stayed at World Headquarters until almost eleven o'clock on Halloween night, and they were back at the negotiating table by seven the next morning. From that point on, there were no more breaks.

Everything was wrapped up by Friday evening, with one exception—the VEBA. Here, too, the UAW was willing to give Ford slightly more favorable terms than it had negotiated with GM and Chrysler, but it was still not good enough for Leclair. He continued to push for more stock and less cash. As the sun set on Saturday, the two sides were no closer to a deal than they had been that morning. The other Ford negotiators could see that Gettelfinger was losing patience and started to worry that the whole agreement might unravel. Ford's labor team told Leclair that the company had to be more flexible. Leclair refused to budge. Mulally was brought in to mediate.

As Ford's senior leadership debated the issue on the twelfth floor, Hinrichs got word that the UAW bargaining team was getting ready

---

* The Wayne Assembly Plant would later be closed, but the workers there were all reassigned to the Michigan Truck Plant next door. It was retooled to produce the new Ford Focus and other products based on the same platform.

to leave. He ran downstairs to try to keep Gettelfinger and King at the table. Hinrichs launched into a long, rambling presentation outlining all of the product commitments Ford was prepared to make in its U.S. factories if it got the deal it needed on the VEBA. It was all stuff they had heard before. The union men listened, but they were growing impatient. Just when he thought he was losing them Hinrichs got a call from upstairs. He whispered into his phone for a few moments, and then asked Gettelfinger to follow him up to Laymon's office. Mulally was waiting there when they walked in. Leclair was nowhere to be seen. Mulally explained that something had come up at the Jaguar–Land Rover headquarters in England that required the CFO's immediate attention. Unfortunately, someone else would have to take over the VEBA negotiations. Mulally apologized. Gettelfinger grinned. He agreed to wait while Ford controller Peter Daniel drove into the office from his home.

By the time Daniel arrived at World Headquarters, it was about 10 P.M. When the two sides reconvened at the bargaining table, it was closer to midnight. Daniel laid out the following terms: Ford would pay $17.3 billion into the VEBA trust. That was roughly the same percentage of its total liability that GM and Chrysler were putting into theirs. But Ford could cover only 40 percent of that with cash. The rest would have to be paid in the form of convertible notes. That was substantially less cash than the other two automakers were putting up, but it was as high as Ford could go. However, the company would agree to invest the difference in its U.S. factories. It took almost three hours to go over the details. Just before 3 A.M., Gettelfinger pushed back his chair and stood up. Hinrichs thought he was going to walk out again. Instead he looked around the room and then spoke in a voice that betrayed little of the exhaustion everyone else was suffering.

"We need this VEBA structured the way it's proposed, because we need the investments in our plants to keep our people in those plants," he said solemnly. "I take responsibility for what we're agreeing to. We need to get this deal done."

The Ford negotiators looked at each other with wide eyes. It was over. At 3:20 Sunday morning, Ron Gettelfinger and Alan Mulally shook hands in Joe Laymon's office. Joe Hinrichs, who had not even taken a nap since Thursday, found he could not stand up. He had to call for a driver to take him home.

* * *

Voting on the new contract began four days later. Ford had no trouble winning ratification for its deal. Few workers were happy about the concessionary agreement, but most viewed it as a necessary evil.

"I figure in today's economy, this is probably the best we're going to get," said John Kujat, a Michigan Ford worker, as he cast his vote in favor of ratification.

On December 3, the leaders of Ford Motor Company and the United Auto Workers gathered at World Headquarters to sign the formal document. Both sides praised the spirit of cooperation that had characterized their talks since the beginning and expressed their confidence that the deal would lead to a better future for the company and the union.

"This is an historic day for Ford," Bill Ford declared. "The teamwork was amazing, and we came up with a contract that is—in my mind—excellent for the employees, excellent for the retirees, and great for the company."

Mulally did not get everything he wanted. The jobs bank was still there, though there were few workers left in it and those who remained would be gone within a year. But it was close enough. The new deal with the UAW had not only gone a long way toward closing Ford's labor cost gap with its foreign competitors, but also moved a huge chunk of the company's legacy costs off the books. Mulally had done what many inside the Ford believed was impossible: He had figured out a way to profitably produce cars in the United States.

Now he needed to convince the American people to start buying them.

CHAPTER 12

Selling It Like It Is

You can't build a reputation on what you are going to do.

— HENRY FORD

I f Toyota had a rock star in its ranks, it was the gaijin Jim Farley —
the American marketing savant behind its über-cool, youth-
oriented Scion brand, and the man credited with making Lexus
the Cadillac of luxury automobiles. Farley was the cousin of zany,
drug-addled comedian Chris Farley, and it showed. He looked like a
thin version of his more famous relative and had something of his un-
hinged air that, combined with his often out-of-control hair, gave the
impression of a mad scientist probing the outer limits of the Japanese
automaker's staid corporate culture.

Ford Motor Company wanted to help him escape.

Bill Ford had been wooing Farley since 2005. Long before he had
even heard of Alan Mulally, Ford had been eyeing Toyota's rising star
and had learned three very important things about him. First, his
family was from Michigan. Second, his grandfather had been an early
Ford employee who went on to found a parts company that was still
a Ford supplier. Third, Farley's first car was a 1966 Ford Mustang that
he still owned, along with a 1934 flathead Ford hot rod. Bill decided
to reach out to him through a mutual friend, Larry Buhl.

"You should be back at Ford," Buhl told Farley in late 2004, reminding him of his familial connection to the company. "They need
help right now."

Farley agreed to meet Bill Ford at the Detroit auto show in January 2005. Buhl snatched him from the Toyota stand and drove him to
the same office building at the Detroit Lions' training facility in Allen
Park that Ford would later use for its secret meetings with the United

Auto Workers. The conversation was light. At the time, Bill Ford was starring in the company's commercials and Farley asked him how those were being received.

"The research says women in their sixties and seventies think I'm cute," Ford told him with a laugh.

Farley kept waiting for the job offer, but Ford seemed to want to talk about anything but that. Then, as the two men stood up to shake hands, Ford made a quick pitch.

"You know, we'd really like you to seriously consider coming to Ford," he said.

"I'm really happy at Toyota," Farley replied without even a moment's hesitation.

Ford asked him to think about it. He gave Farley his phone number and told him to call if he changed his mind.

Farley doubted that would happen. He *was* happy at Toyota. But a personal tragedy forced Farley to take stock of his life. When he did, he began to wonder just how far he could go at Toyota. His former boss, Jim Press, had become the first non-Japanese on the company's board of directors but was rumored to be chafing at what had turned out to be a largely symbolic promotion.* Farley wanted more than that. He wanted to make a difference. He also wanted to be free. Farley prided himself on being a maverick, but the higher he rose at Toyota, the harder that became. On a spring day in 2007, he was driving down the 405 freeway near Los Angeles, fuming because he had been going back and forth with his masters in Japan for months over issues relating to the upcoming launch of the Toyota Tundra pickup. They kept overruling his decisions about a product he knew they knew nothing about. Toyota had just named Farley head of its Lexus division in the United States, but that now offered little consolation.

This is what it's going to be like for the next twenty years, Jim, he told himself.

He took his cellphone out of his pocket and called Bill Ford.

"I may be interested," Farley said.

---

* In September 2007, Press would resign from Toyota's board and become part of the triumvirate running Chrysler.

"Great," Ford said. "I'd like you to meet our new CEO."

Mulally was still looking for someone to lead Ford's global sales and marketing operations. The lack of a chief marketing officer was the one big hole in his matrix organization. The position had not been filled after Hans-Olov Olsson retired in November 2006. While most of the company's other functions were well on their way to being managed globally, sales and marketing was still largely a regional proposition, and Mulally was eager to change that. He had begun the search for a suitable candidate, taking personal responsibility for it because he knew this person would play a key role in the transformation of Ford. Farley's name was already on the short list Joe Laymon had drawn up for Mulally when the Toyota executive decided to make the call.

During his next trip to Japan, Mulally had the Ford jet land at Los Angeles International Airport and met Farley inside a private terminal. Farley was nervous when he showed up for the lunch meeting. Toyota had been his life for seventeen years, and he felt like he was cheating on the company he loved. But he reminded himself that, unless he suddenly turned Japanese, that feeling would never be mutual.

Farley had no idea what to expect from Mulally. He had read about him in the newspapers but did not even know how to pronounce his last name. Like everyone else who encountered the grinning Kansan, he was immediately disarmed by Mulally's charm—and by his lack of pretension. When Farley looked around for more dressing for his salad, Mulally got up and got it for him. That was something that would never happen at Toyota. But Farley did not think much of Mulally's car company. He did not even consider Ford a competitor, except in the pickup truck segment.

They are totally irrelevant, he reminded himself, *at least on this side of the Atlantic.*

When Farley was the head of sales and marketing for Toyota in Europe, Ford was the company that kept him up at night. At the time, Ford's design still left a lot to be desired there, too, but its products offered the precision handling and driving dynamics that European motorists craved. Toyota's did not. Farley had done his best to forget that after returning to the United States, but he was reminded of it as Mulally pulled out a stack of printouts showing all of the cars and trucks Ford sold around the world and started spreading them out across the table. It was the collection of charts Mulally had pasted together himself shortly after arriving in Dearborn. He pointed to the page displaying Ford's superior European lineup.

"Jim, just think if we could unleash the value of Ford's global assets," Mulally said, passing the sheet to Farley.

Oh my God! What if Ford had the driving dynamics from Europe, the quality of its Asian competitors, and the emotional appeal of cars that I love like the Mustang? Farley thought as he studied the printouts. *If they could put all that together, it would be really cool.*

Mulally liked Farley instantly. As a devotee of Toyota, he had followed his work with Scion and thought it exceptional. He also knew that Farley had a reputation for being the voice of the customer inside Toyota, often challenging its designers and engineers in constructive ways to give the people what they really wanted. It was not adversarial. Farley did not pit marketing against product development. It was about working with that side of the business to make the company's products the best in the world. That was exactly what Mulally was looking for—someone who could work with Derrick Kuzak to make sure Ford's products were even better.

As Farley drove back to Toyota's U.S. headquarters in nearby Torrance, he considered the possibilities. He had grown up loving Ford—not the company that was, but the company that had been. His grandfather had raised Farley on stories of Ford's glory days, and those tales were what drove him into the automobile business in the first place. Farley's grandfather had not opposed his decision to Toyota, but he had asked him to find his way back to Ford if he could. Until now, that had seemed like a road to nowhere, but Farley began to wonder what it would take for Ford to reclaim its former greatness. The idea of helping Ford do that was suddenly incredibly exciting.

We could do this, he thought. *Jim, there's a whole other world you don't know about. You could really leverage your skills.*

Farley went over his own qualifications to make sure he was up to the challenge. He knew the American car business as well as anybody. He knew Europe. He knew the premium segment. He knew dealers.

He knew about product planning. And, most important, he knew how to really shake things up.

If they are smart, they'll give someone like me enough rope to hang himself, he mused. *I think the situation is bad enough at Ford that they will be open to new ideas. But can I fit in, or will I be rejected like a bad organ?*

Fitting in was Farley's biggest concern. He knew Ford's culture was quite a bit different from Toyota's, and he worried that many of the executives in Dearborn might dislike him from the start because of his service to the enemy. But Farley desperately wanted to do something meaningful with his life, and he could think of nothing more meaningful than saving the American icon that his grandfather had helped create.

As soon as he got home that night, Farley's wife knew he wanted to take the job.

"Damn," she said. "I knew you shouldn't have seen that guy."

Farley may have been one of the highest-ranking Americans in Toyota, but his wife's résumé was pretty impressive, too. Lia was a successful script supervisor in Hollywood. She spent her days working beside big-name directors and her evenings attending glamorous parties with Tinsel Town's great and good. Jim and Lia both knew there would be little use for her talents in Michigan. She was also about to give birth again. Farley told her he knew he was being selfish, but said he would regret it for the rest of his life if he turned Ford down. After talking it over for a few days, Lia told him to call Mulally.

Farley had a couple of questions before he accepted the job. One was about compensation. The other was about Mark Fields. Farley knew the president of Ford's Americas group would see him as a threat, and he wanted to make sure Mulally would have his back.

"Will you really let me do my thing, or will you let those guys kind of just squash me in the garage?" Farley asked.

Mulally assured Farley that no one would get in his way. But Ford's CEO could tell there was something else bothering the Toyota executive. Mulally pressed him, and Farley admitted this was a tough decision for his wife. Mulally asked Farley to put her on the telephone. He worked his usual magic. They talked for nearly an hour. Mulally thanked Lia for giving up her career and promised that Farley would have a great one at Ford.

"Okay," she said finally, passing the phone back to her husband.

"I'll join you, Alan," Farley said. Mulally congratulated him, but Farley cut him short. He had to take his wife to the hospital. His son was born a few hours later.*

*　　*　　*

On October 11, 2007, the automotive world was stunned by the news that Jim Farley was leaving Toyota to become vice president of sales and marketing at the still-struggling Ford Motor Company. His defection sent shock waves through Toyota's North American ranks and left its dealers shaken and worried. Ford's dealers could not have been more thrilled. Everyone in the car business knew about Jim Farley, and they could not wait for him to start working his magic at Ford.

"Jim is a car guy, and that means a lot to me as a dealer," said Kent Ritchie, a longtime Toyota franchisee who had recently traded that dealership for a Ford store in Memphis. "I've seen him roll up his sleeves and get dirt under his fingernails. I think my investment just became worth a lot more money."

Mulally was just as ebullient about the newest member of his senior leadership team.

"This is a big deal," he said that afternoon. "I want him to really help me take the marketing capability and that functional expertise to a new level of performance inside Ford, to bring the voice of the customer in—their wants, their needs, what they value—and to use that to help us design cars and trucks."

A month later, Farley was at LAX, waiting for a red-eye to Dearborn. He paced the terminal, thinking about everything he had just given up and the enormous challenge that lay ahead in Dearborn.

---

* During a visit to Japan in 2009, I had dinner with a high-ranking Toyota executive who asked me why Farley left his company in the middle of such a promising career. I told him that Farley could probably see from Press-san's experience that there was a limit to how much authority he would ever have as a gaijin and wanted more than that. The Japanese executive thought for a moment and then laughed over his sake. "It's true," he said. "We are a very homogeneous organization."

After decades of declining quality, product missteps, and corporate blunders, he had to convince the American people that Ford Motor Company deserved another chance. Farley walked into the bathroom, found an empty stall, and threw up.

* * *

Two weeks after it announced the hiring of Jim Farley, Ford sent out another press release announcing the retirement of Vice President of Communications Charlie Holleran. He was replaced by Ray Day, a quiet, calculating public relations executive who could not have been more different from his predecessor. Where Holleran had been easygoing and slightly rumpled, Day was a tightly wound neat freak who could not abide an out-of-place hair. Where Holleran had relied on experience and instinct, Day put his faith in research and analytical reports. That made him a far better fit with Mulally's data-driven approach to management. Under Holleran, the communications department bucked that trend, insisting that what it did could not be quantified in the same way as sales or engineering. Mulally never believed that, and he told Day that he wanted the department to start acting like the rest of Ford. That meant functioning globally and living by its own set of metrics.

"If you can't measure it, you can't manage it," Day agreed, and he quickly developed his own set of slides tracking purchase consideration, press coverage, and social media impact.

Day had been at Ford since 1989, and he had spent much of the past two decades thinking about what he would do if he were in charge of communications. Now that he was, Day ordered a sweeping reorganization of Ford's public relations team and told everyone that their top priorities would now be building and defending the company's reputation. The best way to do that, he said, was by "aggressively communicating" Mulally's plan and Ford's progress against it. Reporters were soon inundated with a relentless barrage of press releases, product briefings, and media dinners. Some journalists complained it was too much, but Day's strategy made Ford impossible to ignore.

Mulally had Day report to Farley initially and told the two men to

work together so that communications could support the new marketing strategy then under development. Farley hoped to unveil that
strategy at the New York auto show in April 2008, but it was proving
far more difficult than he imagined. Farley assumed his biggest challenge would be changing the way the American people thought about
the company. Now his early research was revealing that, at least on
the coasts, they did not think about Ford at all. From a marketing perspective, that was far, far worse.

One group that did care a great deal about Ford was its dealers.
So Farley started with them. As a group, they had decidedly mixed
feelings about the company. On one hand, most of them loved Alan
Mulally and believed that he would deliver on his promise of better
products in the not-too-distant future. On the other, most of them
felt like it had been a long time since they had gotten a straight answer about anything from Dearborn. That was particularly true when
it came to two issues near and dear to them: dealer consolidation and
Mercury.

Though Ford could only claim 14.8 percent of the U.S. market,
it still had roughly the same number of dealerships in the United
States as it had when that figure had been closer to 25 percent. In
big cities, that meant too many dealers were competing for a smaller
slice of a shrinking pie. Many of them, like Ford itself, had been
dying a slow death for years. They could no longer afford to keep
up their stores, and it was hurting Ford's image in the marketplace.
General Motors and Chrysler were struggling with the same problem, and all three companies had launched nationwide campaigns
to consolidate their dealer networks—particularly in major metropolitan areas. The idea was to reduce the total number of stores in
a given area so that those that remained could do more business. In
theory, this was an entirely voluntary process, with the automakers
acting as matchmakers between franchisees who wanted to sell and
those who wanted to buy out their competition. But as the head of
Ford's National Dealer Council, Tom Addis, was fond of saying, "Everybody wants to go to heaven, but nobody wants to die." So Ford
had resorted to arm-twisting.

Mercury was another sore point for dealers. The brand was the brainchild of Edsel Ford, who in 1938 recognized that the company needed a mid-market marque to bridge the gap between its luxury Lincolns and mainstream Fords. General Motors had already developed a comprehensive brand strategy with a different marque for every socioeconomic class that could afford an automobile, and Ford was losing customers to its crosstown rival as a result. Henry Ford, who still thought the world only needed one automobile, was reluctant to expand his lineup. But Edsel won a rare victory and persuaded his father to create Mercury. For decades Mercury did exactly what Edsel hoped it would. It brought in new customers who wanted something more than a Ford but less than a Lincoln. But by the 1990s, as the American market became crowded with foreign brands, it became increasingly difficult to find a niche for Mercury. The brand's annual sales peaked in 1993 at 483,845 vehicles. By 2007 that figure had fallen to less than 169,000.

When Mark Fields returned to the United States at the end of 2005, he considered killing off Mercury. However, two new products—the Mercury Mariner and Milan—were about to arrive in showrooms, and he figured Ford needed to recoup its investment in them before pulling the plug. Dealers learned that Fields was taking a hard look at Mercury, and they wanted to know what Ford planned to do with the brand. The question was more than academic for those who owned stand-alone Lincoln Mercury franchises.* Most of those stores sold more Mercurys than Lincolns, and the dealers who owned them worried they would not be able to stay in business without the added volume that Mercury brought. Fields knew that, if his plan to do away with Mercury got out, sales would collapse. So he decided to string the dealers along until Ford was ready to summon the undertaker. Many of them suspected as much, and they were not happy. When Mulally arrived and started talking about focusing on the Ford brand, their fears were magnified. And while the new CEO was all about openness

---

* Most dealerships sold both Lincolns and Mercurys. There had been a few Mercury-only stores, but the last ones were already in the process of closing or merging with other franchises. The last stand-alone Mercury dealership would shut its doors in 2007.

and honesty, he also knew that the details of his brand elimination strategy needed to remain secret.

Farley embarked on a tour of the country, scheduling meetings with dealers groups in each region. He could offer no more clarity on Mercury and told them the consolidation effort would continue until Ford had right-sized its retail sales network, but Farley did ask for their input in developing his new marketing strategy. He also told the dealer groups that, since they knew best what sold in their part of the country, they would now have a say in how Ford's marketing dollars were spent in their region. Nobody at Ford had ever done that before. Both moves went a long way toward restoring dealer confidence. They also had an almost immediate impact on Ford's sales. Dealers in California, for example, decided the company should focus on its new crossover, the Ford Edge. Ford put up billboard ads across the Golden State and offered more generous incentives on the vehicle there than it did in other regions. By February 2008, California—long a bastion of Toyota and Honda—had become one of the fastest-growing markets in the country for Ford.

Farley really did want the dealers' input as he hammered out his new advertising campaign. He recruited a group of sixty from around the country and flew them to Dearborn to review the creative work and tell him what they thought of it. But he also knew from his experience at Toyota that, when dealers felt like they had a say in an automaker's marketing strategy, they were more likely to support it with their own advertising dollars. And they did, to the tune of approximately $800 million.

At Toyota, Farley had all the marketing money he wanted. At cash-strapped Ford, he would have to do a lot more with a lot less. He decided to rely on the same guerrilla marketing tactics he had used to launch Scion. Early on, he and Day agreed that what they referred to as "earned media" would be the key to getting the most bang for Ford's buck. The idea was to spend more on public relations and less on traditional advertising—to get other people to tell Ford's story for it. They assigned members of Day's communications team to work with Ford's dealers, for example, and used money earmarked for incentives to hire outside agencies to help Day put together a social media offensive. Soon, at Ford press conferences, old-school newspaper and magazine reporters in coats and ties found themselves seated next to unkempt bloggers and twenty-somethings with websites.

✳ ✳ ✳

As Farley pieced together his new marketing strategy, there were more changes at the top of the house in Dearborn. Mulally decided that, just like communications and product development, Ford's factories should also be managed centrally. He was pleased with Joe Hinrichs' role in negotiating the transformational agreement with the UAW and, in December, promoted him to the newly created post of vice president in charge of global manufacturing.

A few months later Vice President of Human Resources Joe Laymon announced that he was leaving Ford. Once the UAW deal was concluded, he had walked into Mulally's office and said his work in Dearborn was finished. Oil giant Chevron Corporation had made Laymon an offer, and he told Mulally he was going to take it. Mulally did not try to change his mind. Like Holleran's, Laymon's skills had been more in demand in the old Ford. Mulally did not need a hatchet man. Laymon was replaced by his second in command, Felicia Fields, a methodical African American woman who was more adept at putting together employee handbooks than Machiavellian plots.*

One of the biggest human resources challenges now facing the automaker was how to improve morale and keep workers focused on their jobs in the middle of the most painful downsizing in Ford's history. Since Mulally had arrived in September 2006, more than 35,000 jobs had been eliminated in North America alone—mostly in the United States. That was on top of the thousands of positions that had been cut in the months before he was hired. In Ford's factories, most of the downsizing had simply gotten rid of excess manufacturing capacity. Mulally's drive to consolidate the company's global operations meant fewer people were needed in other areas as well. But in many parts of the business, the employees who remained were

---

* Felicia Fields was not related to Mark Fields.

being asked to do a lot more. And they were being asked to do it better than ever.

At the same time, Mulally was struggling to extend his cultural revolution deeper into the organization. By the end of 2007, Ford's top executives had embraced his new order. However, lower-level employees reported that the old ways persisted further down inside the bowels of the corporation. Mulally wanted to make sure that everyone understood the aims of his revolution and their role in it. He decided to spell it out for them—not in a little red book, but on a small blue card.

Wallet cards had long been a favorite tool of Ford's human resources department, and Felicia Fields was already working on a new one when Mulally was hired. It took Fields and her team the better part of the following year to finish it. When Mulally saw the final result, he was unimpressed. It sounded like a bunch of generic corporate-speak to him. It was hardly revolutionary. What he wanted was a pocket manifesto.

"Does everybody really like this?" he asked when she presented it to him. As Fields soon learned, that was code for "I don't like this one bit."

She and Mulally began work on a new version that would more accurately reflect the key tenets of his philosophy. Fields knew they had it right when every word on the card sounded like it was coming out of Mulally's mouth. In fact, much of what was on it was lifted directly from his early notes.

On the front of the card, beneath Ford's Blue Oval, was the phrase that, to him, summed it all up—"One Ford"—and three other Mulally catchphrases: "One Team," "One Plan," and "One Goal."* Beneath the first, Mulally spelled out his vision for the company:

**People working together as a lean, global enterprise for automotive leadership, as measured by:
Customer, Employee, Dealer, Investor, Supplier, Union/Council, and Community Satisfaction**

---

* These were all slogans Mulally used to sign his e-mails.

Under "One Plan," he restated his now famous four-point strategy. Beneath "One Goal," he wrote:

An exciting viable Ford delivering profitable growth for all.

The back of the card listed what Mulally called "Expected Behaviors":

> **F**oster Functional and Technical Excellence
> **O**wn Working Together
> **R**ole Model Ford Values
> **D**eliver Results

When the first batch came back from the printer, Mulally was thrilled. It was all there, everything he wanted Ford employees to know and understand. He started passing them out to his executive team at the company's global leadership meeting in January 2008. Soon each employee had one—and was expected to carry it at all times.

"Take two of these and call me in the morning," Mulally would say with a laugh as he passed them out. "This is the cure for what ails you."

* * *

Jim Farley had concluded that far more potent medicine was required to put Ford back on consumers' radar screens. The man tasked with helping him formulate it was Toby Barlow, chief creative officer at Team Detroit, a marketing collective that united the five WPP units—JWT, Mindshare, Ogilvy & Mather Worldwide, Wunderman, and Y&R—that handled Ford's advertising in North America. Barlow was a Chinese puzzle, a mild-mannered practicing Quaker who wrote werewolf novels and did pro bono work on behalf of Detroit in his spare time. He was also an advertising genius, the man responsible for the original Saturn ads that had launched the initially successful GM brand back in 1990. Barlow now brought that same genius to the Ford account, coining a new tagline for the company that sounded like a Mulally quote: "Drive One." It beat out about fifty other candidates that included such cringe-worthy mottos as "Do the Henry."

Next, Barlow and his team turned to the advertisements themselves. Farley knew that he needed to make people care about Ford again. He consulted with a behavioral psychologist who told him the best way to do that would be to put a human face on the company. So Farley told Barlow to use real people in the ads, starting with Ford's own employees. They would talk about cool features like Sync and the soy foam Ford had begun using in its seats, as well as their personal commitment to the company's turnaround. Ford's cars and trucks would appear as bit players in these spots, because Farley thought most of them were still not ready for prime time. But it was an evolutionary strategy. As the first fruits of Mulally's product renaissance emerged from the pipeline, the ads would shift from actual employees to real customers talking about how much they loved their new Fords. Once Ford's vehicles leapt ahead of its rivals', the ads would evolve again to feature owners of competing products test-driving Fords and reacting to their superior qualities and features. All of these spots, from the first to the last, were unscripted and featured real people saying what they really felt. It was all about authenticity.

"We need to have a conversation with the consumer," Farley told Mulally when he unveiled his plan. "It's not talking heads, it's not corporate speak."

Although Mulally loved it, the Drive One campaign was a tougher sell with the board. A few of the directors thought Alan Mulally should be the star. Some members of the Ford family had been lobbying to bring back Bill Ford as the company's pitchman. But Farley succeeded in persuading them all to give his strategy a chance.

In his first focus groups with consumers, Farley discovered that the mere presence of a Blue Oval on a car's grille was enough to reduce what they thought it was worth by thousands of dollars. Participants were shown an automobile with the brand badge masked and asked how much they thought it was worth. Farley watched through a two-way mirror as the tape was removed, and he could see their smiles turn to frowns when they discovered it was a Ford. Again they were asked to put a price on the vehicle. This time the number was a lot lower. When Farley had run the same test at Toyota, it had always gone up.

The Drive One campaign was designed to address the perception issue by focusing on the four areas where Ford had made the most progress: quality, safety, sustainability, and innovation. Farley called these the four pillars of the Blue Oval brand, and told Barlow and his team that every ad had to focus on one of them. More important, every new Ford product had to embody them.

The first television spots debuted during the finale of the supremely popular *American Idol* in April 2008. They were an instant success. For the first time in years, people were talking about Ford. So was billionaire investor and Las Vegas casino mogul Kirk Kerkorian. In fact, he was trying to buy up as much of the company's stock as he possibly could.

CHAPTER 13

Ripe for the Picking

A business which can bring itself to the point where it attracts the attention of money should be able to continue on its own feet without being financed.

— HENRY FORD

Kirk Kerkorian was a gambler, but the risks he took were always carefully calculated. Born in California to Armenian immigrants in 1917, he dropped out of school in the eighth grade and earned his pilot's license by milking cows for a flight instructor. When World War II started, he went to Canada and signed up with the Royal Air Force's Ferry Command—a group of daredevil pilots whose job was flying new aircraft from factories in Canada to their squadrons in embattled England. It would have been a milk run except for the fact that doing so required them to push the planes to the very edge of their operational range. Hundreds died trying, but the pay was a thousand dollars a month for those who made it home alive. Kerkorian did it thirty-three times. He pocketed his pay and used the money to start a small charter service after the war that flew between Los Angeles and Las Vegas.

There he became one of Sin City's original high rollers. In 1962, Kerkorian bought eighty acres on the Strip for just under $1 million, leased it to the builders of Caesar's Palace, and made $4 million off the deal before selling it to the casino for another $5 million in 1968. He used that money to buy MGM, and he used the profits generated by the movie studio to start building casinos of his own. In 1986 he sold the MGM Grand casinos in Las Vegas and Reno to Bally Manufacturing Corporation for $594 million. By 1990, Kerkorian was one of the richest men in America—one with a sudden interest in the automobile industry. He started buying shares in Chrysler and, in 1995, launched a failed takeover bid for the company with its former CEO Lee Iacocca. Later he sued to block the sale of Chrysler to Germany's Daimler-Benz, but was again unsuccessful. In 2005, Kerkorian began buying up shares in General Motors and tried to force the Detroit automaker into a three-way marriage with France's Renault and Japan's Nissan. When that also failed, the billionaire casino tycoon turned his attention to Ford Motor Company.

Kerkorian kept a close eye on Ford throughout 2007. In July, the company surprised Wall Street with a $750 million profit. Just nine months after he arrived in Dearborn, Alan Mulally had Ford back in the black for the first time in two years. But the company's sales continued to slide and Mulally warned that things would get worse before they got better. Ford lost $380 million in the third quarter but still beat analysts' expectations. However, by the end of the year, Ford's domestic sales had fallen 12 percent—the most of any full-line manufacturer, making Toyota the number-two automaker in the United States. Ford fell to third place for the first time in seventy-five years. Ford also missed its sales targets in Asia but reported big profits in Europe and South America, where turnaround efforts were already well under way. Ford lost $2.7 billion for the full year in 2007. That was a big improvement over the $12.6 billion loss the company posted a year earlier, but Mulally and Chief Financial Officer Don Leclair were increasingly concerned about the deteriorating economy and the impact it was having on car and truck sales. In January 2008, they announced another round of belt-tightening. Ford offered more generous buyouts to its remaining 54,000 factory workers in the United States and told salaried employees to prepare for additional downsizing. Ford was bracing for a major recession.

"We are fiscally conservative," Mulally said the day the latest cost-cutting moves were announced. "We wanted to make sure we had enough cash to ride this out."

Ford's stock price fell precipitously in the early weeks of 2008. On January 15, it closed below $6 a share for the first time since 1986. Kerkorian knew a deal when he saw one. The Dearborn automaker was struggling, but it was doing something that its crosstown rivals had refused to do for decades: deal with reality. It might not be pretty, but Kerkorian was sure it would yield positive results in the not-too-distant future.

Or at least Jerry York was sure it would.

Jerome "Jerry" York was Kerkorian's man in Detroit, his adviser on all things automotive since Kerkorian's ill-fated bid to take over Chrysler in the 1990s. York had started his career in the automobile industry as an engineer for General Motors in 1963. He moved to Ford, where he worked in product planning from 1967 to 1970. He joined Chrysler in 1979, worked his way up to CFO under Iacocca, and was the leading candidate to succeed Iacocca when he retired. After being passed over for the top job at Chrysler in 1993, York left the automotive industry for a brief stint as IBM's CFO before joining Kerkorian's Tracinda Corporation in 1995. Since then, he had been Kerkorian's eyes and ears in the Motor City, and he liked what he saw and heard about Ford.

In 2006, Kerkorian had forced GM to give York a seat on its board of directors. In addition to pushing for an alliance with Nissan and Renault, the fiery York had insisted on a comprehensive restructuring plan that included getting rid of non-core brands like Saab, Hummer, and Saturn. GM had rejected York's proposal. Now he noticed that Ford's new CEO seemed to be following it to the letter. Still bitter about GM's brush-off, York had grown to despise the Detroit carmaker, its board of directors, and its CEO, Rick Wagoner. He relished the idea of a resurgent Ford leaving GM in its dust.

"It's pretty damn clear to me that Ford has a huge sense of urgency compared to GM," York told Kerkorian. "They are so fucking far ahead of them it's not funny."

❋   ❋   ❋

In June 2007, Ford asked investment banks Goldman Sachs and Morgan Stanley to begin soliciting bids for its two remaining British luxury brands, Jaguar and Land Rover.

They were two of the most storied brands in automotive history. Jaguar was famous for making drop-dead-gorgeous sports cars, while Land Rover was known worldwide for its high-end sport utility vehicles. They were also about all that was left of the once-great British automobile industry. Both brands oozed class and sophistication, but they were also notorious for their abysmal quality. That had improved markedly under Ford's tutelage, particularly at Jaguar, but Land Rover still had the lowest quality rating of any brand. But at least it was making money—quite a lot of it, actually. During some quarters, Land Rover was Ford's most profitable automotive unit.* Jaguar, on the other hand, was a bottomless pit that Ford had been shoveling cash into for years without any sign of it delivering a return on that investment. Ford had bought the luxury brand for $2.5 billion in 1989. That was significantly more than most analysts thought it was worth at the time. Since then, the Dearborn automaker had poured approximately $10 billion into Jaguar.

Ford was not required to break out Jaguar's financial results, but the *Detroit News* obtained a copy of a secret internal report that revealed it had lost more than $715 million in 2006 alone. Jaguar was improving, but according to that analysis it would be years before it turned a profit. Ford was furious when the newspaper published those numbers. Some employees were subjected to polygraph tests in an effort to find out who leaked the report. Mulally had mostly put an end to this sort of overreaction. It was bad for morale and smacked of the old Ford. But this one was different: It might have cost Ford the sale of the money-losing brand.

With losses like that, no serious buyer would have been willing to take Jaguar without Land Rover. Separating the two brands would have been next to impossible anyway because Ford had consolidated most of their business operations to reduce costs. So Ford put them up for sale together.

Within weeks, dozens of bids were submitted. They came from Russian oligarchs, private equity funds, and a couple of Indian automakers that had not yet made their debut on the world stage. Ford and its bankers sifted through the offers, rejecting those that were too low or came from undesirable elements. Several of the Russians were weeded out simply by inviting them to meetings in the United

---

* It earned approximately $1.5 billion in 2007.

States. They were unable to obtain visas. Kerkorian's Tracinda Corporation was among the early bidders, but it quickly dropped out. The more serious offers came from Cerberus Capital Management, which had just purchased a majority stake in Chrysler*; Ripplewood Holdings, which tapped former Ford president Sir Nick Scheele to lead its effort; TPG Capital, which owned Italian motorcycle manufacturer Ducati; Apollo Management, which specialized in leveraged buyouts; British-based Terra Firma; JPMorgan's One Equity Partners, led by former Ford CEO Jacques Nasser; and the two Indian companies, Mahindra & Mahindra and Tata Motors.

Ford spent the next several months carefully assessing each of these suitors. There was far too much at stake to simply go with the highest bidder. Ford was the largest automaker in Britain. It had been making cars there for so long that most consumers considered it a domestic manufacturer. The United Kingdom was also Ford's second-biggest market after the United States. Executives in Dearborn worried that, if they botched the sale of these two venerable British marques, British car buyers might turn their backs on the Blue Oval itself.†

The man charged with making sure that did not happen was Ford of Europe chairman Lewis Booth. While he understood the business case for selling both brands, that did not make it any easier for the British executive. He had spent much of the past couple of years trying to turn them into something resembling viable automotive enterprises. Many of their employees were close personal friends. Booth was a car guy, too, and no one could claim that title without having a special place in their heart for Jaguar. The last thing he wanted was to go down in history as the Englishman who turned the lights off. As a Brit, Booth knew better than most at Ford just what was at stake and proceeded cautiously. He became Ford's conscience, carefully vetting each bidder and working closely with the British government and trade unions to bring them along every step of the way.

---

* Daimler, which had lost patience with its American "partner," sold about 80 percent of Chrysler to Cerberus for $7.4 billion on May 14, 2007.
† Ironically, Ford executives in Britain were less worried about this. They had watched BMW botch the sale of Rover in 2000 and knew that it had done little to diminish demand for the German luxury brand.

"All of our stakeholders have got to come with us. This has got to be done real well, and I think I'm the person to do it. The unions trust me, the government trusts me, the European Union trusts me and the Jaguar–Land Rover employees trust me," Booth told Mulally, reminding him that Ford's reputation in Britain hung in the balance. "I need to stay in Britain, because I'm the person that can get this done with minimum damage to Ford."

Mulally agreed that negotiating the sale should be Booth's top priority, though as the process dragged on, he began to wonder if the Brit really could bring himself to pull the trigger.

The British government was particularly concerned about the sale because the two brands were both based in the English Midlands — major employers in an otherwise depressed manufacturing region. The trade unions were anxious to see guarantees for workers and their pensions. Booth told both groups that he welcomed their input but said the final decision on whom to sell to would be Ford's and Ford's alone. He took great pains to make sure Ford made the right one. Booth studied the finances of the bidders to make sure they had enough money not just to cover the purchase price but also to keep both brands running. Ford would remain a major supplier to whoever ended up with Jaguar and Land Rover, so ensuring their future viability was critical to more than just Ford's public image. Booth also demanded concrete commitments about how workers at the two brands would be treated by the new owner.

"It's not a fire sale," Booth told his team. "We have to do this right."

By the fall of 2007, Ford had narrowed the field to three finalists: the two Indian manufacturers and Nasser's One Equity Partners. Each was assigned a code name to prevent their identity from being leaked. Tata's was "Tibet," and it quickly emerged as Ford's preferred customer.

Tata not only was one of the highest bidders but also had the clearest vision for what it intended to do with the two brands. Moreover, Booth quickly hit it off with the company's chairman, Ratan Tata. He was a tough businessman but also evinced a great deal of integrity. Booth recognized him as a man Ford could deal with, one who understood the value of both properties and their unique place in the world's automobile market. Like Ford, Tata was a family-controlled company, which also helped. And the huge multinational conglomerate had the resources not just to buy Jaguar and Land Rover but also to invest in their futures.

The unions also came out in favor of Tata. They had been terrified by the mere mention of Jac Nasser's name and were worried a return to his control would mean a new era of deep cuts and layoffs. But Nasser's bid was always a long shot. One Equity Partners had plenty of money, but Bill Ford was not eager to sell the brands to his onetime nemesis. The two men had set aside their differences, but Ford knew Nasser would go out of his way to rub his nose in it if he got hold of Jaguar and Land Rover and managed to turn them into profitable enterprises.

As for Mahindra, Ford quickly realized the Indian tractor company was primarily interested in Land Rover and would probably resell Jaguar as soon as it got a chance. Booth left Mahindra in the mix because it gave Ford leverage with Tata. Tata was a much larger company, and it would not have looked good back home if it lost out to its smaller rival.

On January 3, 2008, Booth announced that the Indian carmaker had emerged as its preferred bidder and said formal negotiations on the terms of a sale were now under way. In the United States, the news was met with some dismay. A few dealers objected loudly, arguing that selling the high-end English brands to an upstart Indian automaker would destroy their luxury image. But it was received rather more calmly in Britain itself, where four centuries of shared history and a love of takeout curry dampened any indignation over a sale to an Indian company. Tata already owned Tetley, one of England's most popular tea companies, as well as the Taj hotel and resort chain. And the Indian conglomerate was well-known to the British government and labor unions because of its recent purchase of Anglo-Dutch steel giant Corus.*

On March 26, Ford announced that it had reached an agreement to sell Jaguar and Land Rover to Tata for approximately $2.3 billion.

---

* That deal was completed in January 2007.

It was less than Ford had paid for Jaguar alone almost twenty years before and did nothing to make up for the billions the automaker had pumped into the brands. But Mulally was glad to see the end of them. For too long, Jaguar and Land Rover had distracted Ford from the more pressing task of getting its own house in order.* Besides, Ford needed the cash. A week earlier, Mulally had warned Wall Street analysts that the growing credit crisis was making it a lot harder for consumers to finance new car and truck purchases.

*   *   *

Despite the accelerating decline of new vehicle sales in the United States and other major markets, York remained bullish about Ford. He told Kerkorian that the Dearborn automaker seemed to be doing everything they had tried to convince General Motors to do back in 2006. And Ford's stock was trading at levels not seen since the 1980s. On April 2, 2008, Kerkorian began buying. Two days later, he sent York to the Glass House to meet Mulally in person.

The get-together was hastily arranged by Don Leclair, who was a longtime friend of York. Not that Mulally needed much persuading; he had read about York's efforts to reform GM and was eager to meet the industry gadfly face-to-face. The meeting ended up being something of a lovefest. York told Mulally how impressed he was with the changes he was making at Ford. Mulally told York how much he had thought of his ideas to save GM. As York stood up to leave, he told Mulally and Leclair that his boss Kerkorian was "interested in investing in Ford." After York briefed Kerkorian on the meeting, Tracinda bought another 6.5 million shares.

On April 24, Ford reported its financial results for the first three months of 2008. Once again the company was back in the black, with a surprise profit of $100 million. But no one in Dearborn was

---

* Extricating Jaguar and Land Rover from Ford would take months. Jaguar of France did not officially become part of the new Jaguar for nearly a year because of the legal hurdles that had to be overcome to separate it from Ford of France. In Russia, Jaguar and Land Rover employees worked side by side with Ford employees in the company's business headquarters. As of 2011, they were still there, though now on separate floors.

smiling. The same day Mulally announced those better-than-expected earnings, he also announced that Ford was slashing production in North America by 100,000 units in the second quarter and said deep cuts to the company's white-collar workforce would be necessary to protect the automaker from the economic crisis it now openly anticipated. The rising price of oil and other commodities was eroding Ford's margins, and 4,200 hourly workers had signed up for the latest buyouts—about half as many as the company needed. Yet another round of buyouts would begin soon, but Ford recognized that its factory workers shared its own concern about the economy. They were reluctant to give up their guaranteed employment in an uncertain job market. Nonetheless, Mulally promised that Ford would continue to do whatever was required to make good on his pledge to deliver a full year of profits in 2009.

Kerkorian played his hand four days later. On April 28, his company issued a press release announcing that he had amassed 100 million shares in Ford since April 2 and planned to tender a public offer for 20 million more at a premium of a buck a share over the latest closing price. That would give Kerkorian more than 5 percent of the company—not enough to force its hand, but too much to ignore.

"Tracinda has been following Ford closely since the company released its fourth quarter 2007 results which indicated that Ford's management was starting to achieve highly meaningful traction in its turnaround efforts. Last week this was reinforced by Ford's first quarter 2008 results, achieved despite the difficult U.S. economic environment," it stated. "Tracinda believes that Ford management under the leadership of Chief Executive Officer Alan Mulally will continue to show significant improvements in its results going forward."

News of Kerkorian's interest in Ford sent shock waves through the company and the family. The Ford heirs were scheduled to hold their regular spring meeting on May 3. Many arrived demanding to know what Bill Ford was going to do to protect them and their investment from one of the most disruptive forces in the American automobile industry. It had been only a year since he had welded the schism in the family shut, and Ford was not about to let it start opening up again. He assured his relatives that there was nothing Kerkorian or anyone else could do to win control of the automaker without their consent. Ford also told them that Kerkorian's sudden interest in their company made it more important than ever for the family to remain united behind Mulally.

Bill Ford did not know it, but York was already making discreet inquiries, asking people how much it would cost to buy out the Ford family. It was not clear that Kerkorian knew about it, either. But York had been salivating ever since he read about the split in the family a year earlier. He was convinced that, once the crack was opened, it would only get wider and deeper. For years York had been dreaming of leading a successful car company. With Kerkorian's money behind him, he just might have a chance to become part of the miraculous comeback taking shape in Dearborn.

On May 9, Kerkorian sent a formal offer to Ford shareholders. In it he revealed that York had met with Alan Mulally and Don Leclair and informed them of Tracinda's interest in Ford. Neither Mulally nor Leclair had mentioned York's comments to Bill Ford, and he was not happy. When the executive chairman learned that Leclair had been having one-on-one conversations with Kerkorian's emissary, he became furious. Ford wanted to know just what Leclair had been up to with York and Kerkorian.

The truth was Leclair was growing increasingly alarmed by the state of the economy and increasingly worried about Ford's ability to ride out a storm of the magnitude he believed was about to strike. Leclair was a master of game theory and wanted to keep Tracinda close at hand in case the company needed to raise additional cash quickly. By the middle of 2008, there were few other options left. Ford also had feelers out to sovereign wealth funds at the time and was even talking to the Chinese. Leclair knew that he could issue additional equity and get Kerkorian to buy it. Mulally, too, was keen to keep every funding option open. But he was also flattered by York's gushing admiration and viewed Kerkorian's interest as a powerful endorsement of his turnaround plan. Mulally insisted that it was all just a big misunderstanding.

The company issued a statement to that effect. Bill Ford told Mulally not to let it happen again, and the board admonished both

Mulally and Leclair to be more careful. The board accepted Leclair's explanation of the situation, but it hurt the CFO's standing with Bill Ford and the other directors. They were well aware of the disruptive role Kerkorian and York had played at GM and Chrysler, and they were not about to let history repeat itself. The directors made it clear that no matter how many shares Kerkorian acquired, he would not be able to buy a seat on Ford's board the way he had on GM's.

*　*　*

On June 17, 2008, Bill Ford and Alan Mulally flew to Las Vegas to find out what Kirk Kerkorian's intentions were from the man himself. They met at his Bellagio casino. When they arrived, they were led through a maze of hallways lined with original artwork to an elegant suite with a private garden and pool. It was an opulent setting that even managed to wow the wealthy Ford. But Ford brought along a surprise of his own—a secret weapon in the form of board member Richard Manoogian. Manoogian was the white-haired chairman of Masco Corporation, a major manufacturer of cabinets and other home amenities. He was also Armenian, and his father had been a good friend of Kerkorian. The Manoogians were hugely respected in the Armenian community, and it was unlikely that Kerkorian would lie to Manoogian's face.

Kerkorian did not seem inclined to lie at all. With wavy steel-gray hair and bushy eyebrows, he was both gracious and charming, and his energy and facile intellect made it hard to believe he had just turned ninety-one. He told Ford he thought his company was on the right path and said he was happy to be along for the ride.

"This is going to be a friendly investment," he assured him.

Bill Ford doubted that.

During the meeting, it became clear that York was not the close personal adviser he had portrayed himself to be. He was a hired gun who got a percentage of the profit off any deals he put together for Kerkorian. He was not Kerkorian's right-hand man, as many in Detroit believed. That job belonged to Alex Yemenidjian, another Armenian who also was present at the meeting. This came as a surprise to Ford, and he could not help noticing that neither Kerkorian nor

Yemenidjian seemed to be paying much attention to what York had to say. Clearly York's ideas were not entirely aligned with his employer's intentions. That would have been more reassuring if Ford had been able to fathom just what Kerkorian's intentions were.

Before they left, Manoogian wrested a pledge from Kerkorian that he would not try to go behind Ford's back as he had done with General Motors and Chrysler. Kerkorian promised him that he had no hidden agenda, that he was only interested in Ford because he thought it had become a good investment with Mulally at the helm.

Despite these assurances, the meeting did little to ease Bill Ford's concern. Kerkorian seemed amiable enough, but Ford did not trust him. Mulally was not worried; he thought York had some good ideas. But Mulally did not have Bill Ford's experience or his memory of the pair's earlier exploits. The executive chairman was not about to let his guard down.

In June, just days after successfully concluding his initial tender offer for 20 million shares, Kerkorian announced that he had purchased another 20 million, increasing his stake in Ford to 6.5 percent.

Bill Ford assembled a team to deal with the Kerkorian threat. His attorneys were confident that there was nothing Kerkorian could do to outmaneuver the family, but given the recent internal debate, he did not want to take any chances. In a war room at World Headquarters, the team began gaming out an array of possible scenarios, trying to figure out what Kerkorian's next move would be and how Ford could block it. In September, Ford adopted a poison pill plan that was aimed at safeguarding $19 billion in deferred tax benefits. It would also kick in if Kerkorian increased his Ford holdings by another 50 percent.

But Ford would never have to worry about that. The economic tsunami that Leclair had long feared finally arrived that fall, battering car companies and casino moguls alike. Ford became too risky for Kerkorian, who was now struggling to shore up his investment in MGM. In October he began unloading his Ford shares. By then Ford had much bigger problems to worry about than Kirk Kerkorian.

CHAPTER 14

Storm Warning

Every depression is a challenge to every manufacturer to put more brains into his business.

— HENRY FORD

On March 5, 2008, Ford Motor Company CEO Alan Mulally placed a call to U.S. Federal Reserve chairman Ben Bernanke.* "We're very concerned about the economy and the credit crisis," Mulally told the central bank chief, explaining that vehicle sales in the United States were falling off fast and credit was drying up. "It looks like there is a recession underway."

Five days later, Mulally called U.S. Treasury secretary Henry "Hank" Paulson and said the same thing.† Neither of the men disputed Ford's assertion, but both said it was too early to tell for certain.

In fact, the United States had been in a recession since December. As Mulally laid out his concerns for Secretary Paulson, rumors were spreading on Wall Street that the giant investment bank Bear Stearns was running out of cash. Five days later, Bernanke was brokering a fire sale of what was left of the bank to JPMorgan Chase. The unraveling of the subprime mortgage market that began in 2007 was bringing down Wall Street. The credit markets began to seize up, unemployment rose, and nervous consumers kept a tight grip on their wallets. Many of those still willing to buy a big-ticket item like a new car found it difficult to get a loan as banks and finance companies turned their

---

* Ford Chief Financial Officer Don Leclair was also on this call.
† This was actually Mulally's second call to Secretary Paulson. The first had been on January 11, 2008. In that conversation, Mulally had warned that the tightening credit supply could trigger a recession.

backs on the riskier consumers they had been trying so hard to woo just a few months earlier. Used car prices began to fall as more cars were repossessed, making it hard to get a good price for trade-ins. The collapse of the housing bubble that had precipitated the crisis in the first place was also having a more direct impact on automobile sales. In 2007, some 2 million Americans had used the equity in their homes to purchase new vehicles. That represented one out of every nine purchased in the country. Now that equity was evaporating.

The end of the housing boom was also accelerating the demise of the truck market because so many of the pickups sold had been purchased by companies and individuals employed in the construction sector. Truck sales had been trending downward since the end of 2005. Ford, in keeping with Mulally's dictum to match production to demand, had been reducing factory output accordingly. But in January, the price of crude oil passed $100 a barrel for the first time ever, and demand for pickups and sport utility vehicles began to fall far faster than Ford had forecast. In April cars outsold trucks for the first time in the United States since 2000. Consumers were trading in their gas-guzzling trucks and SUVs in record numbers, and Ford still had nothing more economical to offer them besides a couple of money-losing hybrids and the same old North American version of the Focus. The company's designers and engineers were hard at work on a new generation of fuel-efficient cars and crossovers, but the first of these would not arrive in U.S. showrooms for more than a year. It was 2006 all over again. Mulally's turnaround plan was about to jump the tracks just like Mark Fields' Way Forward plan had done exactly two years earlier.

By May, Ford was in crisis mode. Mulally's weekly SAR meetings had become daily sessions. The average price of gasoline in the country was $3.50 a gallon, and the truck market was in free fall. In the first two weeks of the month, full-size pickups tumbled from about 11 percent of the U.S. market to just 9 percent. That represented the loss of approximately 10,000 sales a day in Ford's most profitable segment. And every day the numbers got worse. As sales plummeted, the price of steel and other raw materials was rising, further eroding Ford's margins. Before each meeting, the latest data was plugged into

Ford's projections. Each day, Ford's financial forecast fell further and further below Mulally's targets. The team struggled to find additional cost savings to offset these mounting losses, but by Friday, May 16, they were out of options. The next day, Mulally called Ford of Europe chairman Lewis Booth one more time to see if there was anything else he could do to boost sales on the other side of the Atlantic. The answer was no. Though Ford was still making money in Europe, the market was beginning to sag there, too.

On Tuesday, May 20, Ford's senior executives gathered in Mulally's office to go over the numbers one more time. They squeezed in around his rectangular conference table. It was more cramped than the Thunderbird Room, but this would be a short meeting. There was no need for slides, either; they all knew how bad the numbers were. Mulally could read it on their faces. They were each given a draft of a press release that summed up Ford's situation.

"Have we looked at all the data?" Mulally asked. "Does this reflect everybody's view?"

All the executives nodded.

"Is there anything else we can do?"

They all shook their heads.

Two days later, on a conference call with industry analysts and reporters, Mulally began reading one of the most difficult statements of his career.

"Based on everything we can see on the outlook for fuel prices, we do not anticipate a rapid turnaround in business conditions. We have analyzed the data, and our best judgment is that a large part of the recent changes are structural as opposed to cyclical," he said. "We have assessed our ability to find other offsets internally, and we believe we have identified about as much as we can without damaging the long-term health of our business. As a result, our judgment is that it will be extremely unlikely we can achieve profitability in 2009 for either North America or for our automotive business in total."

Once again, it looked like Ford was going back on its word. And that was something Alan Mulally had promised it would never do again.

Mulally went on to announce even deeper production cuts in North America and said further downsizing moves would be necessary. But he said that the one thing Ford was not going to do was curtail its investment in new vehicles.

"The most important thing we do for the long-term success of the Ford Motor Company is deal with this reality and structure ourselves to deliver the vehicles that the customers want, in the amount that they want, and also to absolutely continue to invest in the new, more fuel-efficient smaller and midsize cars and utilities that people really do want," he said. "So as tough as this is, by taking these steps now and continuing the acceleration of our transformation, it's exactly what we need to do to create an exciting and a viable, profitably growing Ford for the long term."

That evening, Mulally received the 2008 Manufacturing Achievement Award from the Society of Automotive Engineers at a banquet in Detroit. The day's news cast a pall over the dinner. As Mulally accepted his award, his media handlers glanced warily at the throng of reporters waiting in the back of the room. There would be no softball questions tonight. To pass the time, the Ford PR people tried to tally all the promises the company had broken. They hoped this would be the last. When Mulally finished with his speech, he stepped off the stage and made his way through the still-admiring crowd of engineers with a smile on his face. But as the journalists leapt to their feet and readied their recorders, his smile began to fade. When a reporter asked Mulally if the decision to abandon his 2009 profitability pledge had damaged his credibility, the otherwise ebullient executive simply snapped, "No comment," and turned away.

* * *

It was a rare hint of frustration from a man who was so relentlessly upbeat. Just when it seemed like he had finally got Ford firing on all cylinders, the engine was running out of gas. But Mulally remained steadfastly optimistic. He was disappointed, but he refused to dwell on it. He knew that he and his team had done everything they could. The market was just deteriorating too fast for Ford to catch up.

Our plan is working, Mulally reminded himself as he rode home to Dearborn that night, past the glowing smelters of the Rouge. *It's just that nothing else is.*

Though the cars and trucks in Ford's showrooms were mostly the same vehicles that had been there when Mulally was hired back in 2006, their quality had improved dramatically. With Mulally's backing, Bennie Fowler had taken his show on the road—preaching his gospel of quality across the United States and around the globe. He started with Ford's existing quality procedures, personally traveling to each region to make sure they were being followed. If someone had a better idea about some aspect of the process, he incorporated that into his canon. But Fowler expected every Ford factory around the world to rigorously adhere to the same quality practices. Fowler began deploying a global computer system to track customer complaints worldwide and make sure they were routed to the appropriate facility.* The system allowed each plant manager to review warranty claims within forty-eight hours of a customer bringing a vehicle into a dealer. In most cases, these reports reached the factory that had made that car or truck in less than twenty-four hours. Once they did, a manager would go to the station on the assembly line responsible for that part of the vehicle and speak with the worker responsible for installing it. Whenever possible, fixes were made right there on the factory floor. The manager would also visit the final inspection area of the plant to figure out how the problem had been missed before the vehicle left the plant. A company-wide report was generated every day identifying the top quality issues around the world, allowing Fowler and his team to give these special attention. The system also tracked data from third-party sources like J.D. Power and Associates, as well as the warranty costs associated with each vehicle component. These were ranked to make it easy to identify problems with a particular part or supplier. It made a big difference. Each Thursday, there were fewer red boxes on Fowler's BPR slides.

As Ford's quality improved, Fowler began publicly planting some very ambitious flags that raised more than a few eyebrows in the automobile industry. In 2007, he vowed that Ford would close the quality gap with its Japanese rivals by the end of 2008. That bold claim raised

---

* It would take until 2010 to roll out Fowler's tracking system worldwide, with the Asia-Pacific region being the last one to come online.

some eyebrows internally as well. But Fowler had the data to back up his boast. His team had done regression analysis to figure out where Toyota would be in 2008 and made certain Ford's own quality gains were trending ahead of that mark. Some of Ford's public relations staff worried that he was giving the press a bat to beat Ford with later, but Fowler was not doing it for the media—he was setting a goal to motivate his team.

"We don't play to be second place," he reminded them.

In June, J.D. Power announced that Ford's Mercury brand now outperformed Honda in initial quality and was just a few points behind Toyota. It was the first time anyone could remember a nonluxury American brand beating one of the big Japanese automakers. And the Blue Oval itself was not far behind.

"Ford has shown consistent improvement for the past five years, despite its restructuring," said David Letson, the vice president in charge of automotive quality at the influential firm. "No other full-line manufacturer has done that."

Derrick Kuzak had not been idle, either. Under his leadership, Ford's Global Product Development System had been improved and expanded. New and better digital design processes had been rolled out worldwide, further reducing development times and engineering costs. By 2008, the ninety-seven different nameplates that Ford and its affiliated brands offered when Mulally joined the company in 2006 had been reduced to just fifty-nine. Ford was on track to reduce the number of vehicle platforms it used worldwide by 40 percent over the next five years, with more than two-thirds of Ford's entire lineup built off just ten platforms. Then the real economies of scale would kick in.

Mulally's team approach to product development was a key enabler of all these gains. The internal realignment that began with matched pairs in 2007 had evolved into matched quints. In addition to a representative from product development and a representative from purchasing, these teams now included representatives from Joe Hinrichs' new global manufacturing organization, Bennie Fowler's global quality team, and Jim Farley's global marketing, sales, and service organization. This structure cascaded down Ford's organizational chart. At the highest level, the heads of each of these global functions formed the ultimate matched quint. Below them, teams were formed around each major vehicle system. For example, Barb Samardzich, the vice president in charge of global powertrain engineering, was teamed with her counterparts in global powertrain purchasing, manufacturing, quality, and marketing. Teams were also formed to manage each vehicle segment, from small cars to pickups. Beneath these, other teams were formed for each individual vehicle program and for key components such as four-cylinder engines and automatic transmissions.

All of these teams had global responsibility. For example, the manual transmission team was based in Europe but was responsible for all of the manual transmissions used by Ford worldwide, while a different team based in the United States was responsible for all hybrid powertrains. Europe was responsible for small cars, even the ones sold in North America. The United States was responsible for pickup trucks, even those sold in South America. Every member of every team had a voice in every decision, but ultimate authority and responsibility resided with Kuzak as head of product development because it was product that would save Ford Motor Company and ensure its future success. All of the other departments understood that their role was to support that effort. These teams also played an important in role in Ford's continued quality improvement. Thanks to Fowler's tracking system, they were able to review the quality data for their particular product, vehicle system, or vehicle segment every day and were required to do so. Each team was in constant contact with a representative from each relevant supplier, too, so that any problems with that company's parts could be addressed quickly.

In October, *Consumer Reports* declared that Ford was now equal to both Toyota and Honda in quality. The magazine also rated the Ford Fusion and Mercury Milan the best-made nonhybrid family sedans in America.

By then Fowler had moved the flag forward once again. At a high-profile industry conference in August, he declared that Ford would not rest until it had snatched the quality crown from Toyota. And he promised to do it by the end of 2010.

"That's right, I said it. Ford Motor Company will be the quality leader," Fowler promised, drawing audible gasps from some of the industry veterans in the audience. "This time, we're playing for all the marbles—and we aim to win."

* * *

However, just figuring out how to survive until 2010 was becoming a real challenge.

In May, the Detroit Three were outsold by their Asian rivals for the first time ever. Ford's F-Series pickup, long the bestselling vehicle in America, was unseated by the Honda Civic. Ford's bread-and-butter truck was not even number two, three, or four. Sales of the pickup plunged nearly 31 percent. Overall Ford sales fell more than 15 percent. Those numbers were bad, but the results were far worse at General Motors and Chrysler. GM's sales were down nearly 28 percent. Chrysler's were down more than 25 percent. The industry as a whole dropped almost 11 percent. Even Toyota was down more than 4 percent.

By June, oil was nearing $150 a barrel and the average price of gasoline in the United States was over $4 a gallon. On June 20, Ford issued a formal warning to Wall Street that its financial results for the second quarter and the remainder of 2008 would be significantly worse than expected. Ford Credit was also losing money as the declining value of used pickups and SUVs ate away at its lease portfolio. That was particularly troubling, because the automaker had usually been able to rely on its lending subsidiary to provide some black ink even when the rest of the company was in the red. Ford responded with additional production cuts at its truck plants. It also delayed the launch of the new version of its F-150 pickup by two months because there were so many of the current model still sitting on dealer lots.

That afternoon, Mulally was asked when he expected the slide in U.S. sales to bottom out.

"It's too early to say," he said, explaining that the entire external environment seemed to be conspiring against Ford. "It's the economy, it's fuel prices, it's consumer confidence—it's everything."

Ford was still on track to meet Mulally's goal of reducing annual operating costs by $5 billion in 2008, thanks in part to another 15 percent reduction in its North American salaried payroll that had been

announced two weeks earlier and the lower labor costs it wrested
from the UAW in the new contract. But Mulally acknowledged that
these gains were dwarfed by declining sales and rising raw materials
costs.

Many analysts thought Mulally was being overly pessimistic—
perhaps even underpromising so that he could overdeliver when Ford
reported its second-quarter financial results, which were due out in
a month. The consensus on Wall Street was that Ford would lose 27
cents a share. The consensus was wrong.

On July 24, Ford posted a staggering loss of $8.7 billion for the
second three months of 2008. It was the company's largest quarterly
loss ever and amounted to a whopping $3.88-per-share hit. The mag-
nitude of the automaker's loss was primarily due to one-time charges
and the write-offs associated with Ford Credit, but the tectonic shift
away from trucks and SUVs to more fuel-efficient cars had not helped,
either. Ford's core automotive operations in North America lost $1.3
billion, compared to just $270 million a year before. Though this was
partly offset by the still-impressive numbers Ford was able to post
from Europe and South America, it meant Mulally's push to fix the
company's car and truck business in the United States was faltering.
And Volkswagen was about to pass Ford to become the third-largest
automaker in the world.

Thanks to the massive financing package Leclair and his team had
worked so hard to secure before the gates of the global credit market
slammed shut, Ford was no longer the subject of bankruptcy speculation. That had shifted to General Motors and Chrysler. But analysts
were still worried about Ford's ability to withstand a serious industry
downturn.

"Ford's liquidity remains adequate despite the prospective cash use
and despite ongoing restructuring efforts," the ratings agency Standard & Poor's stated in a May report. "But if lower-than-expected U.S.
light-vehicle sales persist through 2009 or higher fuel prices cause
an even more dramatic shift away from light trucks, Ford's liquidity
could reach undesirable levels by late 2009."

* * *

If things were bad at Ford, they were worse at GM and Chrysler. After insisting for years that they were far ahead of the Dearborn automaker in their own restructuring, the truth was finally coming out. They had just done a better job of hiding the magnitude of their woes—from Wall Street as well as from themselves.

General Motors would soon post a second-quarter loss of $15.5 billion. Three years earlier, CEO Rick Wagoner had assumed personal responsibility for GM's struggling North American car and truck business, promising a sweeping restructuring that would return it and the entire company to profitability.* Since then, America's largest automaker had lost more than $70 billion. And GM had less cash than Ford. In May, GM's share of the U.S. market fell below 20 percent. It had started the year at 24 percent. In June, Chrysler's market share fell below 10 percent and now lagged behind both Toyota's and Honda's. Because it was now privately held, Chrysler did not have to report its financial results, but they were presumed to be grim.

Any doubts about the depth of GM's distress were dispelled in July when Bill Ford's secretary appeared in his doorway to announce an unexpected phone call.

"It's Rick Wagoner," she said. "He wants to talk to you."

Bill Ford was surprised. He nodded, hit the remote control he carried in his pocket that closed the door, and picked up the telephone. GM's CEO got right to the point.

"You know, I think it's really time we put our companies together. We should talk," Wagoner said. "We could come over there."

Ford was stunned. He asked Wagoner to repeat what he had just said.

A few days later, Wagoner arrived at the Glass House with GM president Fritz Henderson and Chief Financial Officer Ray Young. They were whisked up the executive elevator to Bill Ford's personal conference room on the twelfth floor. The executive chairman was waiting there, along with Alan Mulally, Controller Peter Daniel, and Deputy Counsel Peter Sherry. Once again Wagoner got right to the

---

* Unlike his counterparts at Ford, Wagoner did not say when GM would accomplish this feat.

point. He wanted to know if Ford would consider a merger. Together, he said, they could create an American automotive powerhouse strong enough to withstand the crisis that now threatened to take down the entire industry. Wagoner and the other GM executives were clearly worried. They were running out of money. They did not come right out and say it, but it was there between the lines.

Mulally had no desire to marry Ford to another struggling automaker. When he took the job, he had told Bill Ford that he was only coming to Dearborn to fix his company—not sell it, dismantle it, or merge it. That was still his intention. Moreover, his plan was all about narrowing Ford's focus, not expanding it. But the world was changing. With the entire automotive industry falling apart, Mulally knew that he had to seriously consider every option. So he listened to what GM had to say and asked a lot of questions.

What would they do about all the overlapping brands?

Where were the synergies? What could they combine, consolidate, and eliminate?

How would the new company be governed?

Wagoner's answer to that one made it clear that, although General Motors was the one coming to Ford, its old arrogance remained intact. He said that, since GM was the larger of the two—both domestically and internationally—it would obviously be in charge.

"In most mergers, market cap is what counts," one of the Ford men pointed out, noting that Ford was worth about $10 billion, while GM was only worth about $7 billion. GM also had far less cash and much greater liabilities.

Wagoner suggested that they could work that out later. If not, GM would take its proposal to another automaker.

Mulally did not think much of that threat, nor did he think much of Wagoner's pitch. It did not take him long to conclude that a merger with General Motors would be a step back to where Ford had been, not a step forward to the leaner, more focused company he was striving to create. As he listened to Wagoner and the others describe the challenges facing GM and the ways they were trying to deal with them, he became more confident than ever that his plan was the right plan for Ford. He and his team just needed to stick to it, no matter how hard that became. Bill Ford agreed. He thought Wagoner was being incredibly arrogant, but that was GM's way. But both Ford and Mulally were deeply distressed by what Wagoner's proposal said about the state of his company.

The next call was for Mulally. This time it was from Chrysler chairman and CEO Robert Nardelli.* The two men were both outsiders in Detroit and had developed a decent rapport over the past couple of years. Nardelli said he needed to talk to Mulally face-to-face, and soon. He brought Chrysler president Tom LaSorda to the Glass House. Mulally had Ford's corporate counsel, David Leitch, at his side. Like Wagoner, Nardelli did not beat around the bush.

"Why don't the two of us—or all three of us—get together and keep our separate storefronts, but combine our back offices?" he asked. "We could get a lot of efficiency and reduce a lot of cost."

This was a more interesting idea, but as they talked through it Mulally realized that there was no way to do what Nardelli proposed and still maintain the clarity of brand focus that he was trying to achieve at Ford. It would certainly save money, but it would also make everything that much more complicated.

Once again he decided to stay the course. But both meetings made Mulally a little nervous.

Wow! he thought. *If these guys are coming after us, it's getting much worse than we realized.*

*   *   *

It was not just the American car companies that were suffering. In June, Toyota announced that it was slowing truck production and warned of lower-than-expected profits. Honda and Nissan also announced production cuts and profit warnings. As truck sales continued to plummet, GM and Chrysler began idling their pickup, SUV, and minivan plants. But Mulally did not believe demand for these

---

* Robert "Bob" Nardelli, a General Electric alum and former head of Home Depot, was appointed chairman and CEO of Chrysler by Cerberus in August 2007. Tom LaSorda was demoted to co-chairman and president. Nardelli, who had left Home Depot in disgrace, would later be named one of the "Worst American CEOs of All Time" by *Portfolio* magazine.

vehicles was ever going to return to its previous highs. He had a far more radical solution in mind—one that would finally break Ford's decades-long dependence on trucks.

On the same day Ford reported its record second-quarter loss, the company announced that it would retool pickup and SUV factories in the United States and Mexico to produce small cars and crossovers from Europe.* Bringing these vehicles to North America had always been part of Mulally's plan to create a global product lineup and achieve greater economies of scale. But with the price of gas pushing past $4 a gallon in the United States, it became more urgent than ever to get these fuel-efficient vehicles into U.S. showrooms. Importing them was not an option. With the United States now in the midst of a serious recession, exchange rates made that prohibitively expensive. However, just as Mulally had promised, the game-changing contract that Ford negotiated with United Auto Workers in 2007 now made it possible to build those cars in the United States profitably. Mulally acknowledged that this rapid retooling would be a challenge—particularly given the company's dwindling cash reserves—but the alternative was to keep making the same old gas-guzzlers that consumers were abandoning in droves.

"We're doing it faster, which gets us to a profitably growing Ford even sooner," he said optimistically. "It's using proven products that we know and proven technology. It's utilizing all the assets that Ford has—and that other people don't have."

Ford's Michigan Truck Plant, which produced the full-size Ford Expedition and Lincoln Navigator SUVs, would close in December and be retooled to produce the new global Ford Focus and other vehicles based on the same compact platform. Production of the big SUVs would be moved to Ford's Kentucky Truck Plant in Louisville. Another Ford factory in Kentucky that was currently producing Ford Explorer SUVs, the Louisville Assembly Plant, would also be converted to manufacture additional models off the new platform. Finally, Ford's Cuautitlán Assembly Plant near Mexico City, which produced

---

* Ford's retooling plan was finalized in June. The *Detroit News* had actually broken the story on June 11.

F-Series pickups, would be converted to produce the new Ford Fiesta for the American market. Ford also announced that its Twin Cities Assembly Plant in St. Paul, Minnesota—scheduled to close in 2009—would remain open until at least 2011 to continue production of Ford's aging but fuel-efficient Ranger compact pickup.

In addition to the six new models it promised to bring to the United States from Europe, Ford said it would double both hybrid production and the number of hybrid models it offered in 2009. The company would also double its North American four-cylinder engine capacity by 2011. All of this would go a long way toward making Ford's lineup one of the most fuel-efficient in the industry. But the automaker had something even better in the works for consumers seeking relief from the prices at the pump.

*　　*　　*

On a beautiful summer evening in August 2008, I was riding with Ford Americas president Mark Fields in a heavily modified Lincoln MKS sedan at a leisurely pace down a country road running alongside Lake Michigan.

"People think environmentally friendly cars are boring," he said, glancing over at me with a wicked grin. "Watch this."

He punched the accelerator and the Lincoln leapt forward with an explosive burst of power that threw me back against the passenger's seat.

"This will put a smile on your face," Fields said, as the trees on either side of the road became a blur. "But you get twenty percent better fuel economy with fifteen percent less CO_2. I call it the great taste, less filling school of powertrain technology."

Underneath the hood was Ford's secret weapon in the war against rising fuel prices—a new engine technology called EcoBoost that combined turbocharging and direct fuel injection to produce more power from a smaller motor. It would not arrive in showrooms for another year, Fields explained, but the company was sending a message to worried consumers: Ford felt their pain. Help was on the way.

Ford had begun work on EcoBoost more than seven years earlier. Neither of the underlying technologies was new. Turbochargers are centrifugal compressors driven by an engine's exhaust gases that increase the pressure of the air entering the motor, resulting in more power. The French began using them on their fighter planes in World War I. GM first began using them in high-performance automobiles such as the Chevrolet Corvair in 1962. Direct fuel injection allows for better dispersion of gasoline inside the cylinder, which in turn allows for higher compression and more aggressive ignition timing, both of which translate into better performance. German automakers were already combining the two technologies in high-end sports cars to boost horsepower and torque. Kuzak and others at Ford recognized that, instead of making powerful engines more powerful, the same sort of system could be used to make smaller, more fuel-efficient motors as powerful as larger, thirstier ones. They began developing four-cylinder engines with the power of a V-6 and V-6 motors with the power of a V-8.

By the end of 2005, Kuzak was pushing EcoBoost as a cheaper, better-performing alternative to hybrid powertrains. But it was a tough sell. Many Ford executives doubted that consumers would embrace the idea that smaller was better, particularly in the United States, where customers were conditioned to believe that more cylinders equaled better performance. Others thought Ford's money would be better spent on more hybrids, pointing to the breakout success of Toyota's Prius. But Kuzak had done the math. An EcoBoost engine would only add a few hundred dollars to the price of vehicle. Hybrids might boast better mileage numbers, but they also cost thousands of dollars more. Both technologies would raise the price of a vehicle, but customers would recoup the added cost much more quickly with EcoBoost.* Moreover, Kuzak argued that Ford could actually do more to reduce greenhouse gas emissions and fuel consumption with the system because it would be accessible to many more motorists. That made a lot of sense to Bill Ford, who saw EcoBoost as a return to Ford's roots as democratizer of technology. His great-grandfather had not invented the automobile, but he had made it available to the

---

* In December 2007, Ford estimated that it would take the typical motorist two and a half years to recoup his or her investment in an EcoBoost engine, compared to eleven years for a hybrid.

masses. EcoBoost was a way to do the same thing with green technology. He approved the EcoBoost program in early 2006.

Marketing vice president Jim Farley had also become a big proponent. His research had identified fuel economy as Ford's greatest opportunity. Despite the company's impressive quality gains, consumers were still wary of the brand. However, if Ford could promise them unbeatable gas mileage, too, Farley was convinced they would be willing to give its cars another chance. As gasoline prices continued to rise, he pushed for an even more aggressive rollout of EcoBoost.

A month after announcing its retooling plan, Ford declared that EcoBoost—slated to debut on the MKS in 2009—would be made available on 90 percent of Ford's other cars and trucks by 2013. Mulally also authorized additional investment in new transmissions, including fuel-saving dual-clutch designs. He ordered a new push to accelerate the introduction of more hybrids, plug-in hybrids, and electric vehicles.

All of this would require massive investment at a time when other automakers were cutting their product development budgets to offset the dramatic decline in sales. Ford would have done the same thing a few years before. Mulally knew that he could probably still make good on his promise to return Ford to profitability in 2009 if he curtailed investment in new vehicles, as GM and Chrysler were doing. But he had not come to Dearborn to keep Ford on life support. If Ford kept its foot on the gas while everyone else slammed on the brakes, it could leap ahead of the competition and emerge from this economic crisis with one of the strongest product lineups in the industry.

"That is the plan," Mulally reminded everyone who questioned his strategy. "Long-term profitable growth."

Accelerating Kuzak's product time line would require a heroic effort on the part of Ford's designers and engineers. It would also require other departments to cut deeper. It was a testament to how much Mulally had changed the culture inside the Glass House that they were willing to do so. Fields expressed this new spirit in a speech to his troops that summer.

"I know this is really a kick in the teeth, but this is not Ford Motor

Company not delivering—this is the external environment. This is an egalitarian knock to the industry, and what's going to separate the winners from the losers is how those companies approach this setback," he said. "It's easy to be a victim. It's harder to say we're going to take this and we're going to make lemonade out of lemons."

CHAPTER 15

The Sum of All Fears

Bankers play far too great a part in the conduct of industry.

—HENRY FORD

J ust when it seemed as though Ford Motor Company had figured
out a way to stay on course and ride out the downturn, the economic crisis in the United States turned into a global financial
meltdown.

On September 15, 2008, Lehman Brothers—America's fourth-
largest investment bank—filed for Chapter 11 protection. It was the
biggest bankruptcy in U.S. history, and it pushed the world's economy
over the edge. Already-tight credit markets froze, making it nearly impossible for customers to get car loans. Not that many were interested
in making big purchases with unemployment skyrocketing and no
sign of relief in sight. In May, Ford had worried that demand for cars
and trucks in the United States would fall from the 16.1 million units
sold in 2007 to less than 15 million in 2008. A week after Lehman
collapsed, Jim Farley warned that number could fall to 13 million—a
level not seen since 1992.*

After returning to Alan Mulally's regular weekly meeting cadence
that summer, Ford was now back in crisis mode. The entire leadership team convened at least once a day, either in Mulally's office or in
the Thunderbird Room. Much of the attention was focused on sales,
which continued to plummet. Fewer than 1 million cars and trucks
were sold in the United States in September. That had not happened

---

* Farley's prognostication was nearly perfect. Actual light vehicle sales in the
United States in 2009 totaled 13,194,493, according to Ward's Autodata. It was
the lowest annual tally since 1992.

since 1993. Ford's own sales plunged by more than a third, falling nearly 35 percent from a year before. By October, even the daily meetings were not enough. Mulally's team began huddling several times a day. They worked through lunch, taking quick bites of Caesar salad as they struggled to find a way through the worst financial crisis since the Great Depression.

Ford was running out of money, and it was consuming cash at alarming rate—$7.7 billion in the third quarter alone. That translated into more than $83 million a day. At that rate, Ford would be broke in a year.* But unless something changed soon, it would not even survive that long. Ford needed between $8 billion and $10 billion just to keep the lights on and the factories humming.† At its current burn rate, the automaker would fall below that critical level before summer. And sales were still declining—not just in the United States, but now in Europe and Asia as well.

Chief Financial Officer Don Leclair began planning for bankruptcy, despite the Ford family's adamant insistence that it would never allow that to happen. But Ford's board of directors insisted on preparing for the worst. Mulally's turnaround plan seemed to be working, but several of the directors now feared that the gains he had made would be unsustainable in the face of the global financial cataclysm.

"Alan may have gotten here too late," one director whispered during a break in the October meeting. The others said nothing, but they were all thinking the same thing.

With the credit markets now frozen shut, Ford's treasury staff struggled to keep Ford Credit funded. When Mulally took over, the automaker's lending arm was in surprisingly good shape—especially considering the state the rest of the company was in. Ford Credit had a good balance of secured and unsecured funding from both public and private sources. And because Ford's sales were in a perpetual nosedive, its loan and lease portfolios were shrinking, meaning it needed less cash to keep up with demand. But it still needed some.

---

* The company ended the third quarter of 2008 with $29.6 billion in cash and available credit.
† The amount varies because of the seasonality of demand.

By early 2008, borrowing had become prohibitively expensive. Now it was becoming impossible. Getting rid of Aston Martin, Jaguar, and Land Rover reduced Ford Credit's capital needs, but by October the situation was becoming critical.

For years, Ford Credit had pursued an aggressive expansion policy, aiming to build a brick-and-mortar presence in every market where Ford's cars and trucks were sold worldwide. As cash became tight, those expansion plans were reevaluated and, in many cases, abandoned. Leclair wanted to preserve that money for the parent company.

Initially, Ford Credit CEO Mike Bannister agreed. He shuttered Ford Credit's offices in Chile, closed up shop in Venezuela, and transferred the retail lending business in Brazil to Banco Bradesco. He unwound the Ford Credit's Mexican operations, too. Bannister focused his support on critical products and critical areas like Ford's home market in the United States. The second priority was Europe, but Bannister and his team decided that they would fall back to the five most important markets there if necessary—France, Germany, Spain, Italy, and Great Britain. The third priority was protecting Ford's growing business in China. It was still small, but it was vital to the company's future. Ford had been late to the game in Asia and could not afford to pull back now.

"That's not enough," Leclair told him. "We have to cut more."

Bannister shook his head. Additional cuts would cost Ford sales it could not afford to lose. Soon it might have no choice. Until then, he wanted to keep moving as much metal as possible. But Leclair kept pushing. He wanted to get rid of more international operations and even cut back on domestic lending. Bannister warned they were already in danger of losing critical scale.

"You've got to deal with the fundamental issues that are causing the automotive company not to be profitable," he told Leclair.

Leclair also wanted to sell the company's controlling stake in Mazda, despite the fact that Ford was still working closely with the Japanese carmaker on several key projects—including the new compact car platform that would provide the underlying architecture for the global version of the Ford Focus and other key products. Now it was Derrick Kuzak's turn to push back.

"We can't do that," he told Leclair. "We still need Mazda."

"There's no other way!" the CFO insisted.

As that crisis deepened, Leclair even began calling for cuts to the product plan that Mulally had insisted on protecting. Given the dramatic drop in demand for pickups, Leclair argued that Ford should curtail future investment in its F-Series trucks. GM had announced that it was halting work on its next-generation pickups and Chrysler was cutting back on all product spending, so Ford had little to lose by doing the same. Leclair also wanted to scrap Mulally's costly retooling plan. The small cars and crossovers he wanted to bring over from Europe might be far superior to the vehicles Ford was currently peddling in North America, but with few buyers for cars of any kind, Leclair argued that that no longer mattered. These European models were far more fuel-efficient than the ones currently in Ford's U.S. showrooms, but as economies around the world ground to a halt, demand for oil was falling. So were prices at the pump. In the past Americans had always demonstrated an almost insane eagerness to jump back into big cars and trucks as soon as gasoline prices retreated to a level they could tolerate. Why should this time be any different? But Mulally would not pull back on his product plan.

"No way," he said firmly. "That's our future—building vehicles that people want and value."

Leclair had never been particularly interested in anyone else's opinion; now he steadfastly refused to discuss other options. He had always been pessimistic, but now he was talking openly about bankruptcy and demanding deeper cuts that he insisted were the only way to avoid it. One by one, the other top executives decided that they had had enough.

Ford Americas president Mark Fields had never gotten along with Leclair, so Mulally was not surprised when he showed up at his office door with an ultimatum.

"I can't productively work in this environment anymore," Fields said. "It's either him or me."

Mulally was surprised when Bannister told him the same thing. The Ford Credit chief had known Leclair since 1988, and they had been friends. They lived two blocks from each other and would often race to work in their Mustang GTs. Their kids went to school together. But now Leclair was second-guessing Bannister's plan to downsize Ford Credit, and Bannister was convinced he was going too far. He reminded Mulally of their conversation two years earlier, when the new CEO had asked him to reconsider his retirement plans. Bannister had only agreed to stay because he was convinced Mulally wanted to save Ford. However, if Mulally was going to let Leclair eviscerate what was left of it, Bannister would just as soon not stick around for the last rites.

Mulally knew most of the other senior executives felt the same way as Fields and Bannister. And unbeknownst to anyone besides Bill Ford and the other members of Ford's board of directors, Mulally had identified a replacement for Leclair more than a year earlier—Lewis Booth, the head of Ford's European group. Mulally thought Booth would be the perfect CFO. He had a huge amount of operational experience and was known throughout the industry as a real car guy, but he also had a financial background. Most important, he was a team player who was both liked and respected by the other Ford executives. The board agreed. But Booth was also the man in charge of selling Ford's European brands. When Mulally asked him to consider the CFO job back in 2007, Booth had asked to stay in Europe until the Jaguar–Land Rover deal was completed. Once it was, Booth had promptly turned his attention to readying Ford's Swedish brand, Volvo, for sale. Mulally knew that, given the state of the world's economy, that was unlikely to happen anytime soon.

The situation came to a head just before the October board meeting.

Don Leclair was right about one thing—Ford was in an existential crisis, and the board was looking for a clear plan to address it. But as the team worked around the clock to hammer out a strategy to keep Ford solvent, Leclair dug in his heels and refused to cooperate with the other executives. The night before the board meeting, they had still not reached an agreement. Leclair walked into the boardroom on the twelfth floor clutching his financial projections and glowering at the other executives. Fields and Bannister scowled right back. Mulally tried to remain positive, but he was embarrassed: His team had failed to deliver. When the board found out, the directors were dismayed. Where was the action plan they had asked for? The executives traded recriminations before being sent out of the room. When the doors closed behind them, the directors told Mulally they were disappointed. This sort of infighting smacked of the old Ford. The board told Mulally to get his team in line before the next meeting.

After the board recessed, Alan Mulally and Bill Ford walked down the hall to Ford's office and closed the door. They knew what had to be done, but it was a difficult decision for both men. Mulally still got along well with Leclair and continued to admire his financial acumen and grasp of the business. He was reluctant to lose such a valuable intellectual asset. But he was far more concerned about the disruption Leclair was causing at the top of the Glass House. Bill Ford knew that, if it were not for Don Leclair, the automaker never would have secured the financing that was now the only thing standing between his family's company and bankruptcy. Leclair had devoted his life to Ford and worked as hard or harder than anyone else in the building to save it. But he was dividing the company at a time when it needed to be united like never before. He had to go, and go now.

On October 10, Ford announced that Leclair was retiring at the age of fifty-six. The company also announced that Lewis Booth would replace him as CFO. The same day, the price of Ford's stock fell below $2 a share for the first time since 1982.

Mulally did not have time to worry about that.

If we make it through this crisis, it'll rebound, he thought. *If we don't, it won't matter.*

* * *

At the end of October, Lewis Booth sat alone at a table in the bar of the Ritz-Carlton across from Ford World Headquarters, studying his laptop screen as he nursed a pint. He was not supposed to be here. He would not even officially become CFO until November 1. But here he was, stuck on the wrong side of the pond, looking at the grimmest financials he had ever seen in his life. If there was a worse time to become the chief financial officer of a major multinational, Booth certainly could not imagine it.

Mulally had asked him to come to Dearborn early to prepare Ford's third-quarter results. Those were due out on November 7, which also happened to be Booth's sixtieth birthday. He had planned to celebrate it with his twin brother back in Blighty. Instead he would be here, coming to grips with Ford's stark fiscal realities.

As a participant in the weekly BPR meetings, Booth was already well aware of the company's financial situation. He appreciated Leclair's focus on conserving cash and was grateful to his predecessor for having insisted on obtaining as much financing as possible before the days of easy credit came to an end. Booth was also grateful for the stellar team he inherited. He was a bit worried about his ability to master the technical aspects of his new job. But his staff made him look smart. They knew what needed to be done; he just needed to let them do it.

The last thing people need is a new CFO coming in and saying, "Fuck me! Have you seen how bad the company's financials are?" he thought. *I'm the oldest member of the senior leadership team next to Alan. I need to set an example.*

So Booth cultivated an air of calm confidence. A few weeks after he arrived, he called his new team together.

"I believe in the plan, and I believe we are going to get through this," he told them. "Trust us. We'll find a way."

* * *

The room looked like it belonged at some NASA facility. The walls were covered with computer printouts, each one a dark mass of data. Every few minutes, someone would enter the room with a new bundle and begin replacing old charts with new ones. When they did, men and women stood before them, eyeing the numbers nervously, pointing here and there with pens and shaking their heads. But this was not Houston or Cape Canaveral. It was Conference Room 3B007 in Ford's redbrick Product Development Center—the secret headquarters of Project Quark.

By the fall of 2008, the Detroit Three were not the only ones struggling to stay in business. Most of their suppliers were also on the brink of bankruptcy. Several had already crossed it. And the failure of either GM or Chrysler would push many of the rest over the edge. Without parts, nothing else Ford did would matter. Its factories would wheeze to a halt, and even Alan Mulally would be unable to jump-start them.

To make sure that did not happen, Vice President of Global Purchasing Tony Brown proposed setting up a cross-functional team to monitor parts manufacturers, prevent supply chain disruptions, and accelerate Ford's effort to shrink its supply base. He code-named the effort "Project Quark" after the family dog in the movie *Honey, I Shrunk the Kids.* Mulally did not get the reference, but he got the point. The team would include representatives from all of Ford's business units and all of its departments. Human resources would be there in case Ford needed to assign some of its own employees to help a supplier sort out its problems. Treasury would be on hand to authorize loans or other financial aid. IT would manage the computer system the team would use to monitor Ford's business partners. Communications would be ready to manage the public relations fallout from a supplier bankruptcy or parts shortage. And legal would be there to make sure everybody played by the rules. It would be a perfect example of Mulally's matrix organization in action.

"Let's do it," Mulally told Brown. "I want regular reports every Thursday."

Ford was now three years into Brown's supplier consolidation campaign. Since the end of 2005, the company had been working its way down its long list of suppliers, deciding which ones to keep and which ones to let go. Now that effort shifted into high gear. The Project Quark team set up its war room in the Product Development Center and began a detailed analysis of each of the more than 2,000 suppliers that fed Ford's factories. Scientists from Ford's advanced engineering and research division developed sophisticated software to track and analyze each supplier in real time. The walls were soon covered with printouts listing each company, its financial condition, the plants it supported, the specific parts it provided, and all of its other customers. These were broken down by percentage of the supplier's total business so that the team could see at a glance which ones were most dependent on other automakers. The team created a risk profile for each supplier, based primarily on how much of its business was with Chrysler or GM and how much was with Ford's stronger foreign competitors. Priority was given to those companies that were heavily dependent on work from Chrysler because it was seen as the most likely to fail first. Ford tried to end its relationship with these suppliers as quickly as possible. But Ford also weighed the complexity of the products each company provided. It was relatively easy to find another company to make plastic trim; it was a lot more difficult to find another supplier for exhaust systems.

Similar rooms were set up at Ford's regional headquarters in Europe and Asia, each reporting back to the main team in Dearborn.

Together, they pared the list down to 850 suppliers that Ford wanted to keep. Making sure these companies survived the current crisis became Project Quark's top priority. But that did not mean Ford could simply sever its ties with the rest.

Switching automotive suppliers was not like switching paper vendors. The components these companies provided were often highly engineered and involved proprietary technology. Extricating Ford from these relationships required a carefully coordinated strategy. If the company in question was in relatively good shape, Ford might simply continue with them until the vehicle they provided parts for was due to be replaced or refreshed, then switch to another manufacturer. The team's task became a lot more complicated when it was dealing with suppliers that had not made the cut and were also on the verge of collapsing.

All of this work had to be conducted in the utmost secrecy. If a bank learned that Ford was planning to ditch a particular supplier, it might call that company's loans. Other automakers might take their own business elsewhere. Or the supplier might retaliate by withholding parts before Ford was ready to make the jump to its competitor.

The real heavy lifting came when a supplier ran out of cash. If the company in question was already marked for elimination, Ford would usually try to shift its work to another manufacturer and let that supplier go bankrupt. If Ford could not—or if the company was one that Ford had committed to for the long haul—the Project Quark team had to figure out a way to keep it afloat. In many cases Ford would provide direct financial support in the form of early payments or out-right loans. Sometimes things got ugly. Though automakers usually owned the tools and dies used to make parts for their vehicles, sup-pliers had been known to refuse to turn these over when a company canceled its contract, and making new ones could take weeks. So Ford would sometimes order duplicate tools made ahead of time if it thought that might happen. In a few cases, Ford was forced to make "hostage payments" to suppliers that, as a last desperate gamble, re-fused to ship Ford's parts unless they received cash.

The Project Quark team met every day, often gathering before 7 A.M. and working late into the night. The situation was so fluid that they briefed Brown two or three times a day. They were constantly war-gaming a series of scenarios, updating them throughout the cri-sis as the situation evolved and new data became available. These in-cluded the collapse of Chrysler, the failure of GM, and a decision by Toyota or Honda to close one or more of their U.S. factories. Other gambits included a move by GM to close or sell its Opel and Vauxhall subsidiaries in Europe. Brown's team tried to predict how each sce-nario would impact each of Ford's suppliers and recommended spe-cific actions that would be necessary to support those deemed worthy of saving.

From the beginning, Brown knew that Ford could not prop up the global automotive supply base on its own. He reached out to other manufacturers for help. General Motors refused. It claimed that what Ford was proposing violated U.S. antitrust laws. GM was also a lot more concerned about saving itself. Chrysler was more receptive, but it was losing people so fast that Ford had a hard time even knowing whom to talk to in Auburn Hills. But the American automakers were not the only ones who were worried, and Ford soon found some un-likely allies on the other side of the Pacific.

Thanks to globalization, all of the world's automakers had become mutually dependent on a complex web of suppliers that fed one an-other across oceans and national boundaries. Ford bought parts from members of Toyota's keiretsu partners, and those suppliers bought components from American parts manufacturers like Delphi, which also supplied Toyota's plants in the United States. By late 2008 that web was in danger of collapsing, and everyone in the industry knew it. The fear was as palpable in Tokyo and Nagoya as it was in Dearborn and Detroit.

Both Toyota and Honda were just as concerned as Ford about the impact that the failure of GM or Chrysler could have on their suppliers, as well as about the growing number of parts producers who were already in trouble. When they heard about Ford's effort to support its suppliers, they wanted in. So Brown forged a tripartite alliance with Ford's archrivals to prevent a cascading collapse of the entire automobile industry.

All three companies agreed to coordinate their efforts to support the suppliers that were critical to each of them. In many cases, they agreed to share the cost of keeping a particular supplier in business. At times it got down to real horse-trading. Ford might agree to keep doing business with a parts manufacturer that was vital to Toyota in exchange for Toyota maintaining its relationship with a supplier that was critical to Ford. All of these deals had to be carefully vetted by Ford's antitrust attorneys. The Japanese did not have to worry about this to the same degree; their system allowed far more latitude in relations between competing companies.* Ford, Toyota, and Honda even sent a letter to the U.S. Treasury Department explaining how interconnected the automotive supply base was and urging the federal government to take concrete steps to protect it. They persuaded Nissan to sign it, too.

A year earlier, this would have been unthinkable. It was like Protestants and Catholics coming together to work on a downtown redevelopment plan for Belfast. These companies had been trying to kill one another for the better part of forty years. Industry veterans like Bill Ford had a hard time stomaching it, but Mulally was thrilled: It was his working together philosophy taken to its logical extreme.

*   *   *

One day that November, a junior manager in Ford's communications department went to the supply cabinet, looking for some

---

* U.S. law even required Ford to seek the approval of a supplier before it could begin discussions with Toyota and Honda about that company.

paper clips. There was just one box, and when she opened it, it had just one paper clip in it. She grabbed it with a frustrated sigh and marched to the nearest administrative assistant.

"We're out of paper clips," she said curtly.

The woman looked up from her filing.

"I know," she said.

"Well, are you going to order some more?"

"I can't," said the secretary. "You'll have to get approval from Ray Day."

"You want me to ask the vice president of communications to buy paper clips?" the manager asked incredulously. "You've got to be kidding!"

"I'm sorry," the younger woman said evenly. "But there's a new policy. All office supply requisitions require the approval of a vice president."

The older woman shook her head and went to Staples.

Meanwhile, at Ford Credit, a group of employees were standing around a dying philodendron, plucking brown leaves from its stem. One man poked his finger in the soil and shook his head.

"It's bone dry," he said. "Nobody's been watering it."

Another administrative assistant came over with a bottle of drinking water and emptied it into the sere soil.

"They've canceled the plant service," she said. "We have to water them ourselves."

Similar scenes were playing out across the company as fall turned to winter in Dearborn. Employees who had been working amid empty cubicles found their departments consolidated with others so that entire floors—and in some cases, whole buildings—could be closed off and shut down. Lights were turned out, instead of left on all night long. Thermostats were nudged down, even as the first snowflakes began to fall outside. Trips were canceled, as travel was restricted to essential business only. They even stopped washing the windows. At every level of the company, managers were being told to find ways to save money. They required little convincing. The newspapers told the story every morning: The American automobile industry was collapsing.

Ford had always been at its best when things were at their worst. The end of 2008 was no exception. Though sales continued to fall along with Ford's bank balance, Mulally's leadership team gelled like never before. For the first time in the automaker's history, all of the senior executives were working together as a team—not just Monday through Friday, but on Saturdays and Sundays, too. Mulally did not have to twist anybody's arm to get them there. With the entire industry falling apart around them, most would have been too nervous to be anywhere else than around the big table in the Thunderbird Room, studying one another's charts and fine-tuning the plan. They showed up each morning offering to help one another, suggesting ideas and volunteering personnel and resources. They did not try to hide the true extent of the problems they were grappling with, nor did they try to blame them on others. Each came prepared with the latest data and, with the others, figured out how to deal with its ramifications.

Some of these sessions focused on the economy, the banking system, and the U.S. government's efforts to aid both. Others concentrated on Ford's suppliers, dealers, and competitors. The status of GM and Chrysler was also a frequent topic. At one point the list of issues being covered each day ran thirty items long.

Instead of waiting for each Thursday's BPR meeting, the entire leadership team was now reviewing Ford's finances every day. Ford's cash position was that precarious. Lewis Booth made sure that each of the four business unit leaders knew exactly where they stood financially. He also made sure that they understood how important it was to try to find cash flow offsets for the losses they were incurring. He emphasized the word *try*, because he knew there was no way to match the mounting losses. But he kept pushing people into doing a little bit more than they thought they could. So did Mulally.

"Find a way," he said. And he said it a lot.

With the effort to globalize product development continuing, Derrick Kuzak challenged the directors of each engineering facility and design studio to figure out what else they could cut in light of these newfound efficiencies. Other executives did the same thing in their own departments. Joe Hinrichs and his team began a careful study of Ford's most efficient plants to figure out what they were doing differently and see if it could be applied elsewhere. A year earlier, the company had opened a new joint-venture factory in Nanjing with its Chinese partner, Chang'an Motors. The Chinese automaker had introduced some money-saving tooling practices at the facility. Now Hinrichs ordered the rest of Ford's factories to adopt them. The team also came up with a plan for yet another round of salaried job cuts in North America, shaving a further 10 percent off the payroll. After three years of aggressive cost cutting, there was not much fat left to trim at Ford. These cuts went right to the bone. Bonuses paid to Mulally and other executives were also eliminated, merit pay increases were frozen, and benefits for white-collar workers were cut. Jim Farley reduced advertising spending. Another 3,300 salaried positions were axed at Volvo, too, along with 700 outside contractors. Finally, Ford's treasury team began preparing equity-for-debt swaps aimed at reducing interest expenses. Ford had been on track to meet its 2008 cost-reduction goal of $5 billion. These new cuts almost tripled that figure.

People were scared, and getting more so every day. But Alan Mulally still walked the corridors of World Headquarters with a smile on his face. If he passed people looking glum, he would pat them on the back, maybe even give them a hug, and tell them to cheer up.

"Is our plan still going to work?" one executive asked him, giving voice to the same doubt that was growing in everyone's mind but Mulally's.

"Of course," Mulally said.

"But what if it doesn't?"

"I said it's going to be okay."

"Well, what does that mean?"

"It means that we are doing everything we can to look at the world the way it is, and modify our plan as required. So, whatever happens, we'll have given it our very, very best," Mulally said. "You don't have to go home and worry. You don't have to stay up at night. You're not isolated. You're not by yourself. We're going to come back together in the business plan review and get it right."

Booth spent a lot of time trying to estimate GM's and Chrysler's cash flows. The finance staff went over every public statement and

SEC filing with a magnifying glass trying to figure exactly when they were going to run out of cash. At the time, some observers thought Rick Wagoner was playing up GM's woes in order to get government aid. Booth and his team believed GM's situation was actually worse than its CEO was letting on.

Though Ford began to plan for the bankruptcy of both General Motors and Chrysler, Mulally could see no way to prevent the uncontrolled collapse of his crosstown competitors from bringing down the entire automobile industry. The recession would turn into a full-scale depression. Toyota and Honda shared his concern. With Ford's Project Quark team, they were doing their best to prepare for it and limit the damage. But Mulally knew it would not be enough. The industry could not save itself. It needed Washington's help.

CHAPTER 16

Mr. Mulally Goes to Washington

When you get a whole country — as did ours — thinking that Washington is a sort of heaven and behind its clouds dwell omniscience and omnipotence, you are educating that country into a dependent state of mind which augurs ill for the future.

— HENRY FORD

During the congressional hearings on the new CAFE standards back in 2007, Alan Mulally had learned to his dismay that the United States government did not think much of the nation's automobile industry. The Republicans who controlled the White House saw Detroit's automakers as a pack of stumbling dinosaurs, hamstrung by a union that they were too timid to take on, ceding the market to foreign rivals that built better products for less money. The Democrats who controlled Congress regarded the three car companies as peddlers of polluting products who had spent thirty years resisting regulations that would have made them cleaner, greener, and more competitive. To politicians of both parties, the Detroit Three were an embarrassing counterpoint to the innovation of Silicon Valley and the profitability of Wall Street. Instead of iPods and IPOs, they had given the nation blighted cities and rusting factories.

Since that eye-opening trip to Washington, Mulally had done what he could to convince the Bush administration and Congress that Ford Motor Company wanted to be part of the solution, not part of the problem. It was in that spirit that he had reached out to Treasury secretary Hank Paulson and Federal Reserve chairman Ben Bernanke, offering to be their canary in the coal mine — their eyes and ears on the bleeding edge of the Great Recession. And it was in that spirit that Ford had dropped its opposition to the tough new mileage mandates Congress had been calling for in exchange for help financing the cost of developing the new technologies necessary to meet them.

The result was the Energy Independence and Security Act, which Congress passed and the president signed in December 2007. It established a new CAFE target of 35 miles per gallon by 2020. Such fuel-economy gains would only be possible through a broader rollout of hybrids, electric vehicles, and other innovative technologies like Ford's EcoBoost system. So the legislation authorized the U.S. Department of Energy to provide low-interest loans to automakers, both foreign and domestic, to help cover the cost of creating the manufacturing infrastructure necessary to produce these more advanced products. Then Congress refused to fund the loan program it had authorized.

When automobile sales began to fall in early 2008, Ford and the other American car companies quietly began looking for help from Washington. All three agreed that it would be more effective to work together to build support for one proposal. Ford suggested they make funding the Energy Department loans their top priority. The program was an ideal complement to Mulally's product strategy, which was all about shifting production to more fuel-efficient vehicles. Ford could finance the investment necessary to do that through the federal loan program and save its own money for operating expenses. The other companies would enjoy the same benefit if they took advantage of the program. Ford saw it as a way for Washington to help without giving direct aid to the industry. After all, the loan program had been set up to help the automakers cope with the cost of new federal mandates.

But General Motors and Chrysler had their own ideas. GM wanted Washington to provide big tax breaks for customers who bought its Chevrolet Volt, a plug-in hybrid that it hoped would make Chevy cool again. The Volt was still a work in progress and was likely to cost far more than most consumers could afford—unless Uncle Sam was willing to help them out. Chrysler was in such a state of flux that it was not entirely sure what it wanted. Unable to reach an agreement, each automaker pursued its own agenda.

Ford stuck with the Energy Department loans. On June 21,

Representative John Yarmuth, a Democratic congressman from Kentucky, visited Ford's Louisville Assembly Plant with House Speaker Nancy Pelosi. Yarmuth was a vulnerable freshman, and the plant tour was designed to shore up his support among union members. Ford did it as a favor to Pelosi, but the automaker made it clear it wanted something in return. Sue Cischke, Ford's vice president of sustainability, and Joe Hinrichs, Ford's vice president of manufacturing, asked Pelosi to do what she could to get the loan program funded. She promised to make that happen, but as the months went by there was still no progress. And the economy was only getting worse.

Despite a growing sense that the entire domestic automobile industry was now fighting for its life, General Motors continued to downplay the severity of the situation and lobby for the Volt. Ford's Washington office concluded that GM's senior executives were not giving an honest assessment of the company's situation to their own lobbyists. Chrysler's team in Washington was beginning to sound alarm bells, but remained too distracted by the perpetual churn at the top of their own house to make much of an impact.

Everything changed a few days after GM's merger meeting with Mulally. On July 30, the three CEOs convened for a previously scheduled caucus to discuss their efforts in Washington. Mulally had decided to try one more time to convince GM's Rick Wagoner and Chrysler's Bob Nardelli to make common cause with him on the Energy Department loans. In typical Mulally style, he spent several days preparing for the meeting. This time he would overwhelm the other two CEOs with a barrage of irrefutable data that he was convinced would leave them with no choice but to join Ford. He was just getting started when Wagoner interrupted him.

"This is really important," GM's CEO agreed. "Let's get behind this. Let's do this together."

Nardelli was nodding. Mulally never got to finish his presentation.

This sudden change of heart made it clear to Mulally that his competitors were desperate for aid of any kind. If he had any doubts that GM and Chrysler were in real trouble, they were gone now.

* * *

For a Detroit automaker, Ford enjoyed a decent rapport with the administration of President George W. Bush. Two of the company's top executives—General Counsel David Leitch and Vice President of Government and Community Relations Ziad Ojakli—had been respected White House staffers and maintained close connections with their former colleagues. But with two wars and an imploding housing bubble, Bush had little time for the automobile industry. That began to change in 2008. Administration officials were grateful for Ford's insights into the state of the economy and supported the company's effort to win funding for the Energy Department loans, but when and how to fund those loans was up to the Democrat-controlled Congress. However, there would soon be someone else in the White House, and Ford did its best to ensure that the next president was sympathetic to the automobile industry.

Senator Barack Obama certainly did not seem to be, at least not at first glance. During a speech to the Detroit Economic Club in May, he had delivered the typical Democratic critique of the industry.

"For years, while foreign competitors were investing in more fuel-efficient technology for their vehicles, American automakers were spending their time investing in bigger, faster cars," said the charismatic candidate. "And whenever an attempt was made to raise our fuel efficiency standards, the auto companies would lobby furiously against it, spending millions to prevent the very reform that could've saved their industry."*

But Ojakli and his political operatives were hearing a lot about Obama's willingness to listen to new ideas. On June 25, Mulally put that to the test. He and a small group of business leaders met with the senator from Illinois—now the presumptive Democratic nominee—in Chicago to discuss the state of the U.S. economy and their ideas for fixing it.† Mulally did his best to convey the severity of the deepening

---

* This was a bit hypocritical. After that speech, it was revealed that Obama drove a gas-guzzling Chrysler 300C. He traded it in a couple of months later for a Ford Escape Hybrid.

† The other attendees, according to the campaign, were Jamie Dimon, CEO of JPMorgan; Mark Gallogly, founder of Centerbridge Partners; Jim Rogers, CEO of Duke Energy; Ronald Williams, CEO of Aetna; Brian Roberts, CEO of Comcast;

crisis that now threatened his company, telling Obama that the rising cost of capital and declining car and truck sales had brought the entire industry to "an inflection point."

"What is really important?" Obama asked. "How can we help you contribute to the economy?"

Mulally talked about the need to restore liquidity to the credit markets and the importance of developing a national energy policy, one that included a single standard for fuel mileage and carbon dioxide emissions. At the time, California and a number of other states were preparing their own, more stringent mandates. Complying with these different standards would be difficult, time-consuming, and costly for an industry already at the breaking point. But Ford was not opposed to greener technologies. Mulally outlined ways the federal government could help spur the development of the advanced batteries needed for hybrid and electric vehicles. He also talked about the imbalance of trade with South Korea and the restrictions that nation put on U.S. automobile sales. And, of course, he talked about health care reform. Mulally explained how insurance costs widened Ford's competitive gap with foreign automakers. He thought Obama was a good listener. The candidate was clearly working out the details of his agenda and was genuinely interested in hearing what Ford and other major corporations had to say.

Ford's CEO had already had a similar meeting with Republican presidential candidate Senator John McCain when he visited Michigan in February.

As Mulally worked through official channels, the company's executive chairman was working behind the scenes to put the plight of the American automobile industry on the agenda in this election. Bill Ford believed Barack Obama had a good shot at becoming the next president of the United States. He made his first call to the candidate back in December 2007, planting the seeds for a future dialogue. By the middle of 2008, it seemed like Ford's hunch might be correct. When it became clear that Obama had clinched the Democratic

---

Robert Glaser, CEO of RealNetworks; and Mulally's old colleague James Bell, CFO of Boeing.

nomination, Bill Ford asked Joe Laymon to call in one more favor for him.

Though Laymon now worked for Chevron and lived in California, he still considered himself Ford's guy, and he would do anything for his former boss. He picked up his cellphone and dialed Ron Gettel-finger's number. The United Auto Workers still wielded plenty of power in the Democratic Party, and Laymon asked the union presi-dent to broker a face-to-face meeting between Bill Ford and Obama away from the cameras.

On August 4, the candidate's plane landed in Lansing, Michigan. A black limousine was idling on the tarmac. When Obama got in, Bill Ford was waiting for him. On the way to his campaign speech at the Lansing Center, the two men talked about the state of the economy and the American automobile industry.

"Do you think you will need a bailout?" Obama asked Ford.

"No. I think we can get through this on our own. But I think GM and Chrysler could go bankrupt without one," Ford said. "If that hap-pens, they could bring down the whole industry—and the rest of the economy with it."

Obama nodded.

Ford thought the meeting went well. Obama was receptive to his concerns, and the two men seemed to hit it off. Bill Ford was already a big donor to the Obama campaign. So were many of the other Ford heirs. Laymon, also a Democrat, urged Bill Ford to publicly endorse the candidate—not as a private citizen, but as the head of Ford Motor Company. If he did, Laymon believed it would be worth a cabinet ap-pointment, something Ford had long coveted. Together, they began to put together a plan to invite Obama to the company's advanced research-and-development lab in Dearborn, let him give a speech about green technology, and then publicly announce the automaker's support for the Democratic candidate.

Ojakli argued against it. He told Bill Ford that it was a dangerous gamble to endorse any candidate. If Obama lost, Ford would have no chance of working with McCain. If he won and became unpopu-lar, Ford would be tainted by its association with the new president. Mulally also opposed the move, as did David Leitch. Some in the company accused them of only doing so because they were Republicans, but Ojakli told Ford his recommendation would be the same if he were contemplating a McCain endorsement.

"Either way," he said, "you're going to alienate half the voters."

Ford decided Ojakli was right and decided not to pursue Laymon's plan.

*   *   *

On August 15, Ojakli met with Keith Hennessey, director of the National Economic Council and one of President Bush's most trusted advisers. They knew each other from the West Wing.

"Keith, let me just tell you what's happening. We're borrowing at rates approaching twenty percent," Ojakli said. "If we're in this position now, I can't imagine where GM and Chrysler are. You've got a big problem."

Hennessey agreed to see what he could do about the Energy Department loans.

In the weeks leading up to both parties' national conventions, the newly aligned Detroit Three launched an aggressive grassroots campaign to convince Congress to fund the program as quickly as possible. They had dealers write letters to their representatives and asked suppliers to work their own connections. They hit both conventions hard, passing out literature and talking up delegates. Their message was clear: "The road to the White House goes through midwestern auto states."

After securing the nomination of his party on August 28, Obama expressed his support for the loan program. He not only called for funding it, but also suggested doubling the amount authorized by the legislation from $25 billion to $50 billion. McCain, who became the Republican nominee on September 4, was less receptive. McCain had developed a deep disdain for the American automobile industry during his years as chairman of the Senate Commerce Committee, and he was not convinced the American taxpayers should be helping an industry that had done so little to help itself.

But after the collapse of Lehman a few days later, the Detroit Three were not the only ones pushing Congress to fund the Energy

Department program. Some of the biggest banks on Wall Street began quietly lobbying lawmakers on their behalf. They were heavily exposed, particularly with Ford, and wanted Washington to shore up their investments. The automakers kept up the pressure, too. On September 16, Bill Ford traveled to Washington to meet with the House of Representatives' automotive caucus. It was a standing-room-only gathering in one of the side chambers off the House floor that including more than twenty members of Congress, along with numerous aides and advisers. Ford explained why his company needed access to the loans and needed it now. Lawmakers from states with Ford factories began pressuring McCain to throw his weight behind the Energy Department program, too. He finally relented.

With the support of both presidential nominees, Congress finally approved funding for the $25 billion loan program on September 29. But it would be nine more months before any of that money was actually allocated to an automaker.

*   *   *

Ever since General Motors netted some $14 billion by selling a majority stake in its finance company to Cerberus Capital Management back in 2006, Ford had been under constant pressure from Wall Street to do the same with its lending arm. But Bill Ford and Alan Mulally were convinced that Ford Credit's real value lay in its ability to support the sale of the automaker's cars and trucks. Now, with the global credit markets dried up, Ford's strategy looked downright prescient. In the wake of Lehman, banks began abandoning the automobile industry. Customers—even those with good credit—could not get loans or leases. Dealers could not get the financing they needed to cover their inventory. This began to have a real impact on Ford's competitors. But since Ford still owned its own finance company, it could continue to provide credit to dealers and customers alike—as long as it still had money to lend.

But by the end of September, keeping Ford Credit funded was becoming nearly impossible. Mulally appealed to Bernanke and Paulson, asking them to do whatever they could to restore liquidity to the credit markets. Ford also sent Neil Schloss—who had been promoted to treasurer back in 2007 — to Washington to see what he could shake loose. Schloss was surprised to find receptive audiences at both the Federal Reserve and the Treasury Department. The nation's central bank was preparing two important programs designed to provide credit to companies of all types.*

The first, known as the Commercial Paper Funding Facility, allowed businesses to borrow money from the Federal Reserve using secured or unsecured commercial paper as collateral. When it began accepting applications on October 20, Ford Credit was one of the first in line. Ford's finance company signed up to sell as much as $16 billion worth of asset-backed short-term notes to the Fed.†

The second program, known as the Term Asset-Backed Securities Loan Facility, or TALF, was announced on November 25. It was designed to restore liquidity in the asset-backed securities market. The TALF program did not begin backing investments in securities until March 2009, but once it did, Ford was ready. Over the next twelve months, Ford Credit issued more than $12.5 billion in TALF-eligible bonds. Both foreign and domestic companies were eligible for TALF backing, and most of the Japanese and German automakers also issued TALF-eligible securities.

These programs were instrumental in keeping Ford Credit funded and allowed the automaker to continue to support its dealers and customers with loans and leases throughout the crisis. It would give Ford a real edge over General Motors, which no longer owned its own credit company, leaving its dealers and their customers at the mercy of increasingly stingy banks.‡

But these Fed programs were small change compared to the unprecedented bailout of Wall Street that Congress authorized on

---

* Ford Credit's president of global marketing and sales, John Noone, and assistant treasurer, Scott Krohn, also participated in some of these meetings. It is worth noting that the Federal Reserve made solid returns on all of these loans.

† Though Ford Credit was eligible to sell up to $16 billion worth of notes through the program, its peak utilization never came close to that amount. All of Ford's notes had matured by September 30, 2009.

‡ In some cases, Ford Credit even provided financing for GM and Chrysler products at Ford dealerships that carried those brands because Ford wanted to make sure those stores stayed in business.

October 3. Known as the Troubled Asset Relief Program, or TARP, it gave the Treasury Department, $700 billion to purchase so-called toxic assets from the nation's failing financial institutions. It also allowed the federal government to purchase equity in these firms to bolster their finances and protect the financial markets.

Detroit wanted in on it, too.

*   *   *

On October 13, GM CEO Rick Wagoner met with Hank Paulson in Washington and told him that General Motors could collapse as early as November 3—the day before the presidential election—if it did not receive financial aid from the federal government. He asked for $10 billion of the $700 billion Congress had just authorized to save the banking sector. The Treasury secretary said no. He believed GM was trying to blackmail the federal government by threatening to bring down the economy on the eve of the election. However, after the meeting, Paulson ordered his aides to begin putting together a contingency plan to help the automaker just in case Wagoner was telling the truth.

With less drama, Chrysler was making it clear that it, too, was running out of money. Like GM, it wanted a piece of the TARP pie.

Ford now found itself in a difficult position. The automaker had gotten what it most wanted from Washington. Congress had funded the Energy Department loans, and the company was confident it would be able to borrow several billion dollars through that program to help cover the cost of its ambitious retooling plan and other capital expenditures that its product renaissance would require. The Federal Reserve programs would keep Ford Credit funded for the foreseeable future. Ford's cash position was still precarious, but Mulally believed the company could now make it through the crisis without additional government aid—provided that neither GM nor Chrysler went into an uncontrolled bankruptcy. If that happened, all of Ford's bets would be off. Ford wanted the government to do whatever it could to keep its competitors afloat, but it was also increasingly wary of any moves by Washington that would leave it at a disadvantage. Ford's solution was to ask for additional help for the entire industry—direct aid to GM and Chrysler and guarantees that Ford could get the same consideration if it needed it down the road.

Ojakli shared Ford's concerns with Hennessey and other administration officials. They said the White House was willing to allow the automakers to divvy up the $25 billion Congress had authorized for the Energy Department loan program and use that money for general operating expenses to see them through until January, when the next administration could decide what to do about the industry. Ojakli welcomed this but asked if the president would consider giving the Detroit Three access to the TARP fund as well. Once again the answer was no.

So Ford turned to Congress. Lawmakers were focused on the banking crisis and the election, but Ojakli called in some favors and managed to schedule a meeting with Pelosi and Senate Majority Leader Harry Reid for November 6. General Motors and Chrysler found out about it and asked if they could come, too. Since Ford was asking for aid for the entire industry, Mulally agreed. First he arranged a private meeting with Wagoner, Nardelli, and UAW president Ron Gettelfinger.

"We need to present a united front to the Democratic leadership," Mulally told them. "Let's work together."

The other Detroit CEOs no longer thought of Mulally as a capering bumpkin. He had proven himself to be a worthy competitor—and an important ally in their own fight for survival. Together they drafted a paper explaining the importance of the domestic automobile industry to the United States economy. It presented the footprint of each of the three companies—how many people they employed, how many factories they had in how many different states, how many suppliers depended on them. It also showed how interdependent the industry was, with the vast majority of each company's suppliers also providing parts for at least one of the other two U.S. automakers. The aim was to demonstrate how important the industry was to America, and how devastating the failure of even one of the Detroit Three would be for the nation. The three CEOs agreed that they would support the administration's idea of using the Energy Department loans as a source of short-term liquidity. However, they wanted to double the amount of money available through the program to ensure that they did not lose the retooling money in the process. GM and Chrysler would reiterate their request for TARP funds, and all three automakers would seek authorization to borrow additional money from the Federal Reserve at the same low rate it offered banks. In addition, Gettelfinger suggested that they ask Congress for yet another $25 billion in loans to cover the companies' initial contributions to the three VEBA trust funds that were assuming responsibility for hourly-retiree health care as part of the 2007 UAW contract. Finally, all three companies agreed that they would split whatever money they got from Washington according to their relative share of the U.S. market.

On November 4, Barack Obama was elected president of the United States. The Democrats also maintained control of both houses of Congress. When the three CEOs and Gettelfinger met with Pelosi and Reid two days later, they were meeting with the people who held the nation's purse strings. And the two Democratic leaders were surprisingly receptive.

The delegation from Detroit sat on one side of a large rectangular table. Reid and Pelosi and their aides sat across from them and asked what they could do to help. The automakers laid out their proposals. It was a lot to ask. As they drilled down into the details of each request, Mulally could tell the lawmakers were becoming frustrated. The automakers were asking for too many different things. He could tell they were losing their audience.

Mulally reached into his folder and pulled out a piece of paper that charted the dramatic decline in car and truck sales in the United States from January 2006 through October 2008. During that time, the seasonally adjusted annualized selling rate had fallen from 18 million units to less than 10 million. He slid it across the table to Pelosi.

"Madame Speaker, we have a *really* serious problem in the United States," he said, pointing to the graph. "This could take down the industry."

Pelosi's eyebrows arched as she studied the chart.

"Can I keep this?" she asked.

Mulally nodded.

* * *

As if to underscore Mulally's point, General Motors announced a third-quarter loss of $2.5 billion the next day and admitted that it was running out of money. The same day, Ford posted a third-quarter loss of $129 million. That was nothing in the new math of the Great Recession, but Ford's financial results were much worse than that number suggested. During the quarter, the automaker received a one-time gain as result of the VEBA. Without that, Ford would have lost $2.7 billion. Analysts were concerned about Ford's mounting losses. They were even more concerned about the company's cash burn rate, which was far higher than any of them had predicted. Ford was going through more money each month than General Motors, which was a much larger company. Much of this represented the cost of taking out all that excess capacity and matching production to the actual demand, no matter how far it fell. None of Mulally's predecessors had really been able to do that, because they could not stomach the losses required. They held the blade in trembling hands and tried to make the incision, but they could not bring themselves to cut deep enough. Yet Mulally knew that this was the only way to extricate Ford from the vicious cycle of overproduction and deep discounting that had undermined its profitability for decades.

"In these challenging times, our plan is more important than ever: aggressively restructure the business, accelerate the development of vehicles people want and need, finance our plan and improve our balance sheet, and work together as one team, leveraging our global assets," Mulally said during a conference call with analysts and reporters that morning. "We remain absolutely convinced that we have the right plan and are taking the right actions to weather this difficult period and emerge as a lean, globally integrated company poised for long-term, profitable growth."

Ford was now engaged in a delicate balancing act, trying to convince consumers and investors that it was in better shape than its crosstown competitors while at the same time trying to persuade Washington that it was just as deserving of help. When Mulally was asked why Ford needed taxpayer assistance if it was not in dire financial straits, he said Ford would need help if either GM or Chrysler failed.

"It's just prudent to be prepared together. There's a lot of issues that we're all dealing with," he said. "We are very interdependent, and we're all dependent on the U.S. economy. If any one of us gets in trouble in a big way, then that's going to have major ramifications for the entire value stream—for the suppliers, for the (automakers), for the dealers."

Later that day, President-elect Obama addressed the industry's woes in his first press conference since winning the election.

"The news coming out of the auto industry this week reminds us of the hardship it faces—hardship that goes far beyond individual auto companies to the countless suppliers, small businesses, and communities throughout our nation who depend on a vibrant American auto industry. The auto industry is the backbone of American manufacturing and a critical part of our attempt to reduce our dependence on foreign oil. I would like to see the administration do everything it can to accelerate the retooling assistance that Congress has already enacted. In addition, I have made it a high priority for my transition team to work on additional policy options to help the auto industry adjust, weather the financial crisis, and succeed in producing fuel-efficient cars here in the United States of America," Obama declared. "I have asked my team to explore what we can do under current law and whether additional legislation will be needed for this purpose."

A day later, on November 8, Reid and Pelosi called on the outgoing Bush administration to give Ford, General Motors, and Chrysler access to the $700 billion. They sent a letter to Treasury secretary Paulson reminding him that, in authorizing the TARP fund, they had given him broad discretion to use it in whatever way was necessary to stabilize the financial markets.

"A healthy automobile manufacturing sector is essential to the restoration of financial market security," they said.

Paulson disagreed. He and other Bush advisers maintained that letting the three Detroit automakers tap that money would set a dangerous precedent. Soon a host of other industries would be lining up for their share, each one insisting that they were vital to the health of the broader economy. Paulson continued to push for wider use of the Energy Department loans to see the companies through until January, when Obama could decide how best to deal with their problems. Pelosi and Reid began drafting legislation that would give the Detroit Three another $25 billion from the TARP fund, whether Paulson wanted to or not.

However, before Congress would vote on that, it wanted assurances from the automakers that the money would be well spent. On November 17, Mulally, Wagoner, Nardelli, and Gettelfinger received letters from Senator Christopher Dodd and Congressman Barney Frank asking them to come to Washington the next day to testify before the Senate Banking, Housing, and Urban Affairs Committee and the House Financial Services Committee. When Mulally finished reading his letter, he breathed a deep sigh of relief. They had finally gotten Washington's attention.

✻ ✻ ✻

On November 18, as Mulally headed for the nation's capital, Ford demonstrated just how dire the situation in Detroit had become, announcing that it was selling most of its stake in Mazda for $538 million. For that price, it hardly seemed worth it. But Ford was desperate.

Mulally had always thought Ford was using the Japanese automaker as a crutch. He had wanted to get rid of it from the start, but Derrick Kuzak had talked him out of it. Ford's product development chief believed the two companies complemented each other. Ford's new small cars would be based on platforms jointly developed by both automakers, and they had already begun working on even more advanced architectures. Kuzak argued that Mazda gave Ford a valuable window into the world of Japanese manufacturing and automotive engineering—one that Ford shut at its own peril. Mazda alums like Mark Fields and Lewis Booth had also made powerful arguments for maintaining Ford's controlling stake in the Hiroshima company. But Don Leclair had lobbied hard for selling Mazda before he left Ford, contending that Ford's need for cash trumped all of these concerns. Almost all of Ford's other assets had been pledged as collateral. Ford could sell them, but there were restrictions on how it could use the proceeds. Mazda was one of the few assets that could still be turned into cash. And Ford now needed all the cash it could get.

As usual, Mulally did not force the issue. He allowed a consensus to develop organically. The team agreed on a compromise: instead of selling all of its shares, Ford would retain 13 percent of Mazda.* Both companies hoped that would be enough to guarantee future collaboration. With characteristic pluck, Mazda chose to view Ford's decision as an endorsement of the progress it had made since Mulally-san's first visit to Hiroshima back in 2007. But Japanese analysts were skeptical of its ability to stand on its own.

✳   ✳   ✳

Later that afternoon, Mulally and his entourage arrived at the Dirksen Senate Office Building, an imposing 1950s edifice across the street from the U.S. Capitol. Ojakli was confident his boss was about to deliver another great performance. He and other members of Ford's government affairs team had spent days preparing Mulally for his testimony before the two congressional committees. They had worked their sources on Capitol Hill to find out what sort of information the legislators were looking for, then spent hours closeted with Mulally inside Ford's Washington office going over the various personalities on each committee and putting him through a regular murder board until he could manage the toughest questions with ease. They role-played every conceivable scenario and threw out tough questions, trying to trip him up. But Mulally handled everything they threw at him with characteristic aplomb.

He's going to be fabulous, Ojakli thought as Mulally—wearing his customary blue blazer, button-down blue shirt, and red tie—strode through the door and smiled confidently at the phalanx of cameramen and photographers who had crammed themselves into Room 538. Senator Dodd took one look at the crowd and joked that he

---

* Before the sale, Ford owned just over 33 percent of Mazda. More than a third of the 20 percent it sold went to Mazda itself; the rest went to a consortium of Japanese banks, suppliers, insurers, and trading companies that did business with Mazda.

should have held the hearing at nearby RFK Stadium. Mulally took his place between Nardelli and Gettelfinger at the long witness table in front of the raised dais where the senators sat, and then read a succinct opening statement that focused on the progress Ford had already made on its own turnaround plan.

"Much of the recent commentary has suggested that our companies need a new business model. I completely agree. In fact, we at Ford are well on our way to transforming our company and building a new Ford that I believe has a very bright future," he said, pointing out that Ford had already closed seventeen factories, reduced its workforce by 51,000 employees in North America, negotiated a game-changing contract with the UAW, sold off foreign brands, and begun the process of remaking its entire vehicle lineup to break its dependency on big trucks and SUVs. "The speed and the breadth of our transformation is evident by actions just this week alone. Tomorrow at the Los Angeles Auto Show, we will introduce two all-new hybrids. Our new Ford Fusion Hybrid beats the Toyota Camry Hybrid by at least six miles per gallon. Today, we are submitting our application for direct loans, authorized by Congress last year, to help us speed advanced technologies and vehicles to the market. On Friday, we end large SUV production at our Michigan Truck Plant and we begin converting to fuel-efficient small car production."

As crouching photographers snapped away by his feet, Mulally pointed out that Ford had returned to profitability before the economy imploded and was still trying to deal with the unprecedented industry downturn on its own.

"We believe we must join our competitors today in asking for your support to gain access to an industry bridge loan that will help us navigate through this difficult economic crisis," he said. "We at Ford are hopeful that we have enough liquidity. But we also must prepare ourselves for the prospect of further deteriorating economic conditions in 2009. In addition, the collapse of one of our competitors would have a severe impact on Ford and our transformation plan, because the domestic auto industry is highly interdependent. It would also have devastating ripple effects across the entire U.S. economy."

The message was clear: We are not in trouble, but the other guys at this table are. And if they go down, we could, too—unless you help us out. But it soon became clear that few on the committee were inclined to do that, at least not until they made the three CEOs and their colleague from the UAW pay for their sins.

"Why should we believe that your firms are capable of restructuring now when you were unable to do so under better conditions—more benign conditions?" drawled Senator Richard Shelby, a Republican from Alabama, home to more foreign automobile factories than any other state. "A lot of people think you've already failed, that your model has failed, that you're here to get life support. You've burned billions collectively—the three of you—you've burned billions and billions and billions of dollars trying to turn around your industry."

Shelby's face contorted into a grimace of disgust as he addressed the three CEOs. He looked like a man surveying a pile of rotting corpses.

"I'm sure if you got twenty-five billion [dollars] you'd want twenty-five or thirty or forty more," he sneered.

Even the supposedly sympathetic committee chairman got in a few licks.

"I support efforts to assist the industry," Dodd said. "[But] their boardrooms and executive suites have been famously devoid of vision."

The sharpest criticism was leveled at General Motors and Chrysler. A few senators came right out and said they thought that Ford had done more to address its faults than GM and Chrysler had. But Mulally was clearly taken aback by the sheer venom of the senators' attacks. He did his best to respond to the committee's often pointed questions amicably, but he was not his usual eloquent self. By the time Dodd gaveled the hearing to a close, Mulally was exhausted. He hoped the next day's House hearing would go better. But it would prove far worse.

On November 19, America awoke to the news that all three CEOs had traveled to the nation's capital on private corporate jets. From the reaction that sparked, one would have thought they had been carried there on the backs of Bangladeshi children.

"The CEOs of GM, Ford, and Chrysler will be back before Congress today to ask for twenty-five *billion* dollars they say they need or will go out of business. Yet, that hasn't stopped them from traveling in style. Even *first class* isn't good enough for those three," declared an ABC News reporter on *Good Morning America,* shaking his head in disdain before cutting to a hazy shot of Rick Wagoner boarding a GM Gulfstream, followed by shaky footage of Mulally leaving the Senate hearing the day before, apparently ignoring the questions being shouted at him by the reporter. It was Fields in Florida all over again. Only this time, there was a long line of grandstanding politicians waiting to pile on, too.

"There's a delicious irony in seeing private luxury jets flying into Washington, D.C., and people coming off of them with tin cups in their hands," observed Representative Gary Ackerman, a Democrat from New York, during the House hearing later that day. "It's almost like seeing a guy show up at the soup kitchen in high hat and tuxedo. It kind of makes you a little bit suspicious as to whether or not, as Mr. Mulally said, 'We've seen the future.' And it causes at least some of us to think, 'Have we seen the future?' I mean, there's a message there. I mean, couldn't you all have downgraded to first class or jet-pooled or something to get here?"

Ackerman had not felt the need to ask the Wall Street bankers who precipitated the economic crisis how they traveled when he voted for their $700 billion bailout a month earlier. But at least he was civil. Other representatives actually shouted at Mulally and the other two CEOs, launching verbal assaults that made the previous day's questioning seem genteel.

"We're not sure we trust you!" bellowed Michael Capuano, a Democrat from Massachusetts. "My fear is, you're going to take this money and continue the same stupid decisions you've made for twenty-five years!"

Once again, most of their fury was directed at Wagoner and Nardelli, but Mulally took his share of abuse, too. It got to him—particularly the endless jabs about the jets. He kept reminding himself that the lawmakers had a right to be angry at the American automobile industry, but his answers started to take on an arrogant edge.

When Democrat Emanuel Cleaver of Missouri asked how much

of the $25 billion Ford needed, Mulally simply said Ford would take whatever was left after GM and Chrysler took what they needed.

" 'Whatever's left, I'll take?' " asked the congressman, shaking his head. "This is loosey-goosey."

It got worse when Representative Peter Roskam, an Illinois Republican, asked the three CEOs if they would be willing to work for one dollar a year, as Chrysler CEO Lee Iacocca famously had after negotiating a government bailout back in 1980. Nardelli said he would. Wagoner said he had already cut his own salary in half, but would not rule it out. Roskam gestured toward Mulally.

"We have eliminated our bonuses also, and any salary increases," said Ford's CEO.

"Okay. Are you willing to go down to the dollar?"

"I understand your point about the symbol and clearly the intent of what you're asking," Mulally replied wearily. "But we're trying to field a skilled and motivated team also. And it's just so important that, as we do this plan, we have the team that we need. So, I understand the intent, but I think where we are is okay."

"Okay. Just so I'm clear, I'm not asking about the *team;* I'm just asking about *you*," Roskam said, glaring at Mulally over his glasses.

"I understand."

"And the answer is no?"

"Uh, I think I'm okay where I am."

Ojakli, who was sitting behind his boss, cringed.

✳　✳　✳

After spending most of that fall saving Wall Street from itself, Congress had lost its appetite for helping the private sector. Many lawmakers were already getting an earful about "corporate welfare" from angry constituents. Congress went home for the Thanksgiving holiday without acting on the automakers' request, but it did offer them the consolation prize of a second chance. Pelosi and Reid would summon their colleagues back for a lame-duck session and hold a second round of hearings in December. But this time, each of the companies would be required to submit a "credible restructuring plan."

There would be no Thanksgiving recess at Ford.

Mulally flew back to Michigan on the Ford Gulfstream, still reeling from the drubbing that he and the other two CEOs had taken at the hands of Congress. He understood why lawmakers were disappointed in the American automobile industry. He understood why they were reluctant to help. But he resented the way so many of them lumped Ford together with General Motors and Chrysler. Under his leadership, Ford had acknowledged its problems and was well on its way to fixing them when the economy fell apart. GM and Chrysler had stubbornly insisted that they knew better until it was too late. Ford was a sober alcoholic. They were two stumbling drunks. But all Congress saw was three winos.

Ford had to make a clean break. It had to banish "Big Three" from the American lexicon. It had to prove to Congress and the American people that it was different. And the best way to do that was to stop asking for their money.

We have a choice, Mulally thought as his plane circled Detroit International. *GM and Chrysler don't, but we do.*

CHAPTER 17

Breaking with Detroit

Our help does not come from Washington, but from ourselves.

—HENRY FORD

The next morning—Thursday, November 20, 2008—found Alan Mulally back at the head of the round table in the Thunderbird Room, watching the weekly slide show and wondering if Ford Motor Company could make it through the worst financial crisis since the Great Depression on its own. The numbers were still horrible. Overall industry sales were down sharply in North America and Europe. But something was happening. Ford's sales in both regions did not appear to be down quite as much as its competitors'. It had started in October. Ford's sales analysts cautioned it could be a fluke. Now, three weeks into November, it was beginning to look like a trend.

In the United States, the new version of the Ford F-150 pickup had finally arrived in dealer showrooms, and demand was surprisingly strong. The economy was still in a nosedive, but if there was one thing Ford knew, it was truck customers. The latest model proved that. It offered a host of new features that spoke directly to their needs and wants, including things like a retractable side step for easy bed access, a high-tech system that kept trailers from swaying, and even an optional dashboard office—complete with keyboard, printer, and a special mobile version of Microsoft Windows for folks who worked out of their trucks. The new F-150 also boasted better gas mileage than the previous model. It was an eye-pleaser as well. And the decision to delay its launch had only made customers want it more.

In Europe, Ford's new Fiesta subcompact was also off to a strong start. It was peppy and fun to drive and got 40 miles to the gallon. It was also more stylish and much better built than most of its competitors. Ford was actually selling more of the sexy new models in some markets than it did of the previous version a year earlier, when the European economy was still strong.

Neither the F-150 nor the Fiesta was going to save the company by itself. Overall sales were still down sharply. But the early success of these products did suggest that Mulally's strategy was fundamentally sound. By continuing to invest in new cars and trucks while other automakers cut back to control costs, Ford was leaping ahead of the competition. If it kept it up, it just might emerge from this recession faster and stronger than its rivals. Ford's chief economist, Ellen Hughes-Cromwick, told the team that she believed the economy would bottom out within the next three to six months in the United States. She predicted that car and truck sales would rebound in the second half of 2009. People could only put off buying a new vehicle for so long, she said.

Even Chief Financial Officer Lewis Booth had a little bit of good news. Ford's cash burn rate was beginning to slow. All of the cost cutting was starting to make a difference. The philodendrons had not died in vain.

Our plan is working, Mulally thought. *We just have to make it through this trough.*

After the slides were finished and the executives had refilled their coffee cups, Mulally reassembled his team for the special attention review session. The agenda was full, but it could wait. There was a more pressing question that Mulally wanted answered first. As he looked around the table at his team, he could not help glancing over at the wall of old photographs of the company's founder and his early automobiles. A giant blowup of Mulally's pocket card had been added to the wall, right next to a picture of Henry Ford and his hero, Thomas Edison. There was the Dearborn plowboy who had put the world on wheels through sheer force of will and strength of vision. If there was an archetype for the self-made man, he was it. And Mulally did not want to let him down.

"Can we make it without the government's money?" Mulally asked his team. "Can we get through this without their help?"

There was silence as the other executives weighed the risks and potential rewards of going it alone. If Washington was writing checks, Ford would be foolish not to take one. But if it could somehow make it through this crisis on its own, it would make up for a lot of years of bad products and broken promises. Jim Farley could see the marketing potential immediately.

"This can be a moment that really separates Ford," he said. "It can be a moment that really differentiates us."

General Motors and Chrysler had already made it clear they would have no choice but to file for bankruptcy without a bailout.

"We're not there yet," Booth said. "We still have options."

"Let's look at them," Mulally said.

First, there was the revolver. Ford still had not tapped its $11 billion credit line. The actual amount available was closer to $10 billion now because Lehman had been underwriting a tenth of it, but it was still there. No one wanted to touch it—partly because it would raise Ford's interest expenses, but mostly because Wall Street would view it as a last, desperate act before bankruptcy. The fact that Ford had not significantly scaled back its investment in new vehicles also gave the company a cushion that GM and Chrysler did not have. Treasurer Neil Schloss and his team were exploring the possibility of a debt-for-equity swap to reduce the amount of interest Ford was already paying. Then there was Volvo. Selling the Swedish brand had always been part of Mulally's plan, but he had decided to wait until it was making money again. It was still not there yet, and the global economic crisis made it unlikely that Ford could get anything near what it had hoped to for the brand, but it could get something. Finally, there was the United Auto Workers. President Ron Gettelfinger was hinting that the union might be willing to renegotiate the terms of the VEBA to allow Ford and the other Detroit automakers to cover a greater portion of their upcoming obligations to the health care trust fund with stock instead of cash. The UAW was even willing to let them borrow back some of the money they had already set aside for those trust funds.*

---

* The terms of the 2007 Ford-UAW contract required Ford to establish a

By the time the team had finished going over all of these options, Mulally was beaming.

"We're going to figure out how to do this on our own," he said. "I believe in you, and I believe in the plan. And I believe it's the right thing to do."

✳   ✳   ✳

That night, some of Ford's executives lay awake wondering if it really was. They were not convinced the company could survive the recession, even with government aid. Most were worried Ford was about to close a door that would never open again. The automakers were already trying Washington's patience, and Congress had made it quite clear during the first two hearings that the last thing it wanted to see was any of the companies coming back in six months or a year asking for help again. If they wanted money from Uncle Sam, the time to ask for it was now.

Even if it looked like Ford could make it on its own today, there was no guarantee that it could tomorrow—particularly with the fate of the other two domestic automakers still undecided. It was still far from certain that any of the automakers would get a penny from Washington, and if General Motors or Chrysler collapsed, all of Ford's assumptions would have to be reevaluated. With the capital markets frozen, there was nowhere else the company could turn.

When the team reconvened the following day, Mulally could read the fear on many of the faces. Ford's blunt Australian controller Peter Daniel got right to the point.

"What if GM were to go down or Chrysler were to go down?" he asked.

There was awkward silence. He broke it with a have-your-cake-and-eat-it-too solution. What if Ford asked for a $9 billion line of credit but promised that it would only use it as a last resort? If it did,

---

temporary asset account with $2.3 billion in marketable securities. In January 2009, Ford replaced those with a promissory note that matured on December 31, 2009, and paid the VEBA 9 percent interest.

the company would submit to whatever terms the government had already imposed on GM and Chrysler. Otherwise it would continue to follow its own turnaround plan. Ziad Ojakli said it would be a tough sell, particularly in the middle of a transfer of power when politicians were looking for simple solutions, but he agreed to see what he could do.

* * *

B ill Ford was thrilled when Mulally told him he thought the company could make it on its own without a bailout. It was what he wanted. It was what the family wanted. It was what his great-grandfather would have insisted on, regardless of the risk. He also was worried that Washington would insist on the family ceding its control of the company to the regular shareholders as a condition of direct financial aid.

The board of directors was a little more concerned about the plan. It wanted to know what Ford was giving up and whether it could return to Washington later if the situation got worse. The outside directors were reluctant to exclude any option—including bankruptcy. As Ford's cash reserves dwindled, they were once again worrying about their fiduciary responsibility to Ford's investors. A Chapter 11 filing would wipe out all of the stockholders, but the secured bondholders might walk out of federal court with at least a portion of their investment. Normally directors are not legally required to worry much about bondholders, but that changes when a company is on the verge of insolvency. Corporate counsel David Leitch assured the board that the threshold had not yet been reached, but the directors were still nervous. A couple of them had already resigned.

Sir John Bond and Jorma Ollila both left the board in October, saying they needed to focus on their own companies. With the global economy imploding, that was understandable. Bond was the chairman of Vodafone Group, and Ollila was the chairman of both Nokia and Royal Dutch Shell. The crisis at Ford was requiring frequent trips across the Atlantic at a time when their own corporations also were contending with the global economic catastrophe. But bankruptcy also carried a much bigger stigma in Europe. If Ford failed, their careers might be in jeopardy. Senior director Irv Hockaday tried to talk them out of resigning. He knew it would not look good to Wall Street. But Bond and Ollila could not be swayed.

Now, a month later, Hockaday was more sympathetic. He and the other independent directors decided the time had come to hire outside counsel to advise them on bankruptcy, the bailout, and related issues. After all, Bill and Edsel had the family's attorneys advising them; the independent directors wanted someone at the table looking out for their interests, too. They also wanted to be certain that all the possibilities were being thoroughly evaluated. They hired Richard Beattie of Simpson Thacher, who specialized in helping boards navigate crises. They also made certain he understood whom he was working for.

"You are not representing anybody but the independent directors," they told Beattie. "That means you are *not* representing the Ford family."

They told the same thing to Goldman Sachs, which was also advising the outside directors.

All of this made for a crowded boardroom. It also meant Leitch had to work extra hard, fulfilling his regular duties while also acting as an intermediary between the various legal factions. But he understood why the board wanted the extra insurance. Bill Ford did, too, although he hated it. It felt like the summer of 2006 all over again—particularly with all the talk about bankruptcy.

A Ford bankruptcy would be the end of America's last great industrial dynasty. The family would be wiped out along with the rest of the shareholders. Ford Motor Company would almost certainly survive, but the descendants of Henry Ford would no longer control it. For Bill Ford and his relatives, it would be an ignoble end to their ancestral legacy. Bankruptcy would be a huge blow to Mulally as well. If Ford filed for Chapter 11 protection, he would not be remembered as the man who saved Boeing, only as the man who lost Ford. The independent directors could no longer afford to be sentimental, though. They wanted to know what bankruptcy would mean for the company as a whole.

Mulally and his team had been studying that issue for a while. A

Chapter 11 filing would erase Ford's debt and perhaps even void its contract with the UAW, but it would also do incalculable damage to the company's image and the Ford brand. All the hard work of the past two years—the quality gains, the new products, EcoBoost and Sync—would be lost behind a cloud of epic failure. It was a real question whether anyone would even buy a car from a bankrupt automaker. That same question was being asked throughout the American automobile industry, as well as in Washington. The general consensus was that the answer was no. At the time, the idea of a "prepackaged" or "quick-rinse" bankruptcy had yet to become part of the public discourse. The board still thought of bankruptcies as slow, messy affairs. For now, at least, they were willing to give Mulally and his team more time to prove Ford could fix itself.

*　*　*

The only problem with asking for a line of credit was that it required Ford to return to Washington for the second round of hearings in December. After the public pillorying that Mulally and the other CEOs had endured during the first round, some on the team wondered if the company should bother asking for anything at all. But Mulally felt strongly that Ford needed to be there to support General Motors and Chrysler in their request for funding. The hearings would also provide an ideal stage for a very public split with the other Detroit automakers. If the first round was any indication, media coverage would be intense.

Having decided to withdraw its request for a bridge loan, there was no need for Ford to plead poverty this time. But Mulally knew he still had to tread carefully. Ford needed to trumpet its own relative success without making its competitors look so bad that Washington would find them unworthy of a bailout. Getting GM and Chrysler the help they needed was the best way to ensure that Ford did not need any help of its own.

Congress had given the automakers until December 2 to submit complete details of their restructuring efforts and their time lines for restoring profitability. Mulally and his team worked feverishly to prepare a comprehensive filing that would meet these requirements but also highlight the difference between their company and the other two American automakers. It would be Ford's declaration of independence from old Detroit. Mulally decided to share the entire plan. It was the best way to show Congress and the American people that Ford got it, that it recognized its past mistakes, had learned from them, and was in the middle of a top-to-bottom transformation that would allow it to compete with all comers and prove to the world that the United States was still a great manufacturing nation.

They worked through the Thanksgiving holiday. Mulally split up the task, asking all of the executives to prepare the portions pertaining to their specific areas. He asked Leitch to stitch the pieces together, vet them legally, and make sure the tone was correct. The entire team met at World Headquarters on November 24, 25, and 26. They took off Thanksgiving Day itself, but most of them spent it working on their portion of the document at home, glancing up from their laptops to watch the Detroit Lions lose to the Tennessee Titans or putting them aside for a quick bite of turkey and stuffing. They were back in the Thunderbird Room on November 28 and continued to meet several times a day until December 1. That morning, Ford announced that it had begun a review of Volvo's future with an eye toward selling the Swedish carmaker. That evening the team huddled around the conference table in Mulally's office going over the latest draft one more time. They continued tweaking it until they were all satisfied. Mulally thought it struck exactly the right note:

> As a company and as an industry, we readily admit that we have made our share of mistakes and miscalculations in the past. We would ask Congress to recognize, however, that Ford did not wait until the current crisis to begin our restructuring efforts, and that much of what we describe below are actions we have taken and decisions we have made about the future that have already put us on a path to long-term viability. . . . We note that Ford is in a different situation from our competitors, in that we believe our Company has the necessary liquidity to weather this current

economic downturn—assuming that it is of limited duration. If the downturn is longer and deeper than we now anticipate, however, access to government financing would be important to help us be able to continue to implement our Plan and benefit when the economic recovery inevitably arrives. While we hope we do not have to access the loans, we believe it is critically important that loans are available to us and the domestic auto industry.

In addition, the credit markets currently remain frozen and are not available to finance the industry's cyclical needs. This means that our liquidity through 2009 could come under increasing pressure if a significant industry event, such as a bankruptcy of one of our competitors, causes a disruption to our supply base, dealers and creditors.

We are acutely aware that our domestic competitors are, by their own reporting, at risk of running out of cash in a matter of weeks or months. Our industry is an interdependent one. We have 80 percent overlap in supplier networks. Nearly 25 percent of Ford's top dealers also own GM and Chrysler franchises. That is why the collapse of one or both of our domestic competitors would also threaten Ford.

For Ford, the availability of a government line of credit would serve as a critical backstop or safeguard against these conditions as we drive transformational change in our Company. Accordingly, given the significant economic and market risks that exist, Ford respectfully requests that government funding be made available to us, in the form of a "stand-by" line of credit, in the amount of up to $9 billion. This line of credit would be a backstop to be used only if conditions worsen further and only to the extent needed.

Mulally was satisfied, but Booth was still frowning.

"We really need to have this page look better," he said. "Could we have some boxes that kind of call out key points or quotes?"

It was late. All the secretaries had gone home for the night. There was no one left in the building but the top executives and a few of their aides. Leitch was exhausted and he knew next to nothing about desktop publishing, but he agreed to try. He went home and spent the entire night trying to figure out how to create text boxes in Microsoft Word.

This is what I went to law school for? he thought as he worked his way through the thirty-one-page document, picking out the best quotes. But Leitch had spent enough time in Washington to know they were the only part of the document most of the lawmakers would actually read.

✳　✳　✳

The next day, Mulally left for Washington. There was no corporate jet this time, just a kiwi-green Ford Escape Hybrid and more than 500 miles of blacktop.* Mulally piled in with his press aide, Karen Hampton; Ford Americas group controller Bob Shanks; and John Kostiuk, the head of Ford's motor pool. Bodyguards traveled in two other vehicles ahead and behind Mulally's Escape. The inconspicuous motorcade spent ten hours on the road, stopping only for bathroom breaks. Mulally himself took the last stretch through Pennsylvania. A secretary packed turkey salad sandwiches, chips, and soda for the group. When he was not behind the wheel Mulally did telephone interviews. He called U.S. Treasury secretary Hank Paulson and Federal Reserve chairman Ben Bernanke to tell them about Ford's decision to go it alone. Given the security escort the trip required, it probably would have been cheaper to take the Gulfstream. But Ford had learned the hard way that appearance counted for more than reality inside the Beltway. That morning, the automaker announced that it was selling all of its corporate jets.†

---

* The CEOs of General Motors and Chrysler also prudently elected to drive this time.

† That would prove far easier said than done. Given the state of the economy, there were few buyers for a fleet of used corporate jets. As they sat in Ford's hangar waiting for one, the company still had to spend a considerable sum maintaining the planes. And because Ford's security people would not countenance Mulally using a commercial carrier, the company had to spend even more money chartering jets whenever he traveled. Because Edsel Ford owned the local

Having made it to the nation's capital without getting lost, they drove to Ford's Washington headquarters. Ojakli was waiting for them. He had spent much of the time since Thanksgiving working his contacts on Capitol Hill, finding out how they would react to the idea of Ford passing on a bailout. The response was positive. It was clear by now that most of Congress's ire was focused on GM and Chrysler. This made it all the more important for Ford to distinguish itself from those companies as clearly as possible. Ojakli prepped Mulally for the next day's session like a coach readying his boxer to get back into the ring after losing the last fight.

"Don't answer any questions that aren't directed at you," he said. "Be short and to the point, and don't get into it more than you need to."

Then they turned to his opening statement.

"You're talking to the American people. You're not just talking to the Congress here," Ojakli told Mulally. "You have a few minutes to tell the Ford story."

It was an opportunity Mulally was eager to seize. But by now, everyone was exhausted. They just could not find the right words to say what Mulally knew needed to be said. He was getting frustrated.

"Alan, what are you really thinking?" Hampton asked her boss. She had developed an uncanny ability to refocus Mulally whenever his train of thought jumped the tracks. For the next five minutes, he delivered a brilliant extemporaneous speech that hit all the points that had eluded them.

"So, Alan, why don't you just say that tomorrow?" she asked. "You don't need any notes."

"Let's put it on a piece of paper," Mulally said. Fortunately, everyone else in the room had been taking notes. Ojakli gathered them up, went into his office, and started writing.

* * *

charter company, the company paid a premium to use a service from out of the area. In the end, Ford's jet costs actually went up substantially as a result of the debacle, and dozens of Ford transportation employees lost their jobs. But at least Congress and the media were satisfied.

The next morning, December 4, Mulally and his entourage arrived back at the Dirksen Senate Office Building for round two. This time, the room was bigger, but there were also more witnesses. Mulally, along with GM's Rick Wagoner, Chrysler's Robert Nardelli, and the UAW's Ron Gettelfinger, were forced to sit and listen to a panel of pundits detail all of Detroit's sins before it was their turn to speak. It was two hours before Mulally was asked to deliver his opening statement. But he made sure it was worth the wait.

"Since the last hearing, I have thought a great deal about the concerns that you have expressed. I want you to know I heard your message loud and clear," he began, striking a note of contrition before launching into an eloquent speech that stood in sharp contrast to Wagoner's excuses, Nardelli's mea culpas, and Gettelfinger's defensiveness.

You were clear that the business model needs to change. I *couldn't* agree more. And that's exactly why I came to Ford two years ago to join Bill Ford in implementing his vision to transform our company and build a greener future using advanced technology. Let me share with you what we have done to change from how it used to be doing business to how we do business now.

It *used to be* that we had too many brands. Now we have a laser focus on our most important brand, the Ford Blue Oval. In the last two years, we sold Aston Martin, Jaguar, and Land Rover, and we have reduced our investment in Mazda. And this week, we announced we are considering a sale of Volvo.

It *used to be* that our approach to the customers was "If you build it, they will come." We produced more vehicles than our customers wanted, and then slashed prices, hurting the residual values of those vehicles and hurting our customers. Now we are aggressively matching production to meet the true customer demand.

It *used to be* that we focused heavily on trucks and SUVs. Now we are shifting to a balanced product portfolio, with

even more focus on small cars and the advanced technologies that will drive higher fuel economy in *all* of our vehicles.

It *used to be* that our labor costs made us uncompetitive.
Now we have a groundbreaking agreement with the UAW to
reduce our labor costs, and we appreciate the UAW's continuing willingness to help close the competitive gap.

It *used to be* that we had too many suppliers and dealers.
Now we are putting in place the right structure to maximize
the efficiency and the profitability of all of our partners.

It *used to be* that we operated regionally, European cars for
Europe, Asian cars for Asia, and American cars for the U.S.
market. Now we are leveraging our global assets—innovation,
technology, and scale—to deliver world-class products for
every market.

It *used to be* that our goal was simply to compete. Now we
are *absolutely* committed to exceeding our customers' expectations for quality, fuel efficiency, safety, and affordability.

This is the Ford story. We are more balanced; we are more
efficient; we are more global; and we are *really* focused. . . .
Ford is an American company, and an American icon. We
are woven into the fabric of every community that relies on
our cars and trucks and the jobs our company supports. The
entire Ford team—from our employees to shareholders, suppliers to dealers—is absolutely committed to implementing
our new business model and becoming a lean, profitable
company that builds the best cars and trucks on the road
for our customers. There is a lot more work to do, but we are
passionate about the future of Ford.

Mulally closed by inviting the senators to Dearborn to see what he
was talking about and "kick the tires." He was actually smiling by the
time he was done. It was, many felt, his finest hour. And once he had
finished telling Ford's story, he shut up and got out of the way.*

---

* It was the same story the next day at the hearing before the House Committee
on Financial Services, but by then Ford was barely part of the debate.

* * *

As Ford's executives were putting together the company's viability plan, Ray Day's communications team had been working with Ford's advertising agency to develop a new public relations campaign to further distance the company from GM and Chrysler and capitalize on its decision to forgo a bailout. To underscore the urgency of their mission, Day pointed to a recent *Saturday Night Live* skit that had lampooned Mulally along with other Detroit CEOs.

"We are all being painted with the same brush," he said. "We need to tell our own story. We need to tell people that Ford is different."

Day's people spent their Thanksgiving holiday building an entirely new website from scratch—www.thefordstory.com—that included detailed information about everything Ford had accomplished in its turnaround, the proof points of its progress, product information, congressional testimony, and videos starring Bill Ford, Alan Mulally, and other executives talking about Ford's transformation. When the site was finished, they e-mailed the link to dealers and employees, encouraging them to pass it on to their friends and customers. They also encouraged dealers to take out advertorials in their local newspapers talking about why Ford was different.

Day began coaching the other executives to make sure they missed no opportunity to underscore the difference between Ford and the other American automakers in their conversations with policy makers, analysts, and reporters. He warned them to avoid the temptation to talk smack about GM and Chrysler.

"Don't gloat," Day said. "If they ask you about what's going on with them, just say, 'I can tell you about Ford.' "

Bill Ford did a masterful job of doing just that on *Larry King Live* later that month, turning every question about why the American automobile industry deserved a bailout into an opportunity to remind the host and his viewers that Ford was different.

"Our plan is working. Our market share is picking up. I believe we're headed exactly where the country wants us to go," he told King. "We're not asking for any federal money. We're trying to pull ourselves up by our bootstraps and make it on our own."

* * *

B y the time the second hearing recessed, it was clear that General
Motors and Chrysler were going to get something, but it was not
at all clear what.

On December 10, the House approved $14 billion in emergency
funding to keep the two automakers afloat until the incoming Obama
administration could figure out a more permanent solution. It was
supposed to keep their lights on until the end of March. But the Senate rejected it the next day after the UAW refused to accept wage concessions that were part of the compromise deal. With concern over
the fate of GM and Chrysler now threatening to make the already dire
economic situation in the United States worse, President Bush reluctantly stepped up and wrote a check.

"In the midst of a financial crisis and a recession, allowing the U.S.
auto industry to collapse is not a responsible course of action," said a
visibly frustrated Bush when he announced his decision on December 19. "It could send our suffering economy into a deeper and longer
recession, and it would leave the next president to confront the demise of a major American industry in his first days of office."

The president gave GM and Chrysler a $17.4 billion loan* and told
them they had until March 31, 2009, to put together comprehensive
restructuring plans that proved they could become viable companies. If they could not, they would be forced to file for Chapter 11
reorganization. Bush also demanded "meaningful concessions" from
"management, labor unions, creditors, bondholders, dealers and suppliers." The terms were somewhat vague, but it was a long list. The
government ordered caps on executive compensation, an end to bonuses for the top executives at both companies, the immediate sale of
all corporate aircraft, and strict limits on expenses. GM and Chrysler
were required to trade two-thirds of their debt for equity and extract

---

* The money would come from the TARP fund that Secretary Paulson had fought
so hard to prevent the automakers from accessing. This was partly to ensure that
the Democratic Congress released the other half of the $350 billion authorized
for the fund. In fact, $4 billion of the $17.4 billion short-term bailout would only
be given to the automakers if those monies were released.

painful concessions from the UAW. They had to get the union to agree to end the jobs banks, align wages and work rules with the Japanese transplants, and restructure their VEBAs to allow the two companies to cover at least half of their outstanding obligations with stock instead of cash. GM and Chrysler were also required to demonstrate their ability to meet the government's tough new CAFE requirements and begin manufacturing green vehicles in the United States. Finally, both automakers had to seek the government's approval for any expenditure of $100 million or more.

There was no mention of a line of credit for Ford. However, after studying the terms Washington was imposing on GM and Chrysler, no one in the room was keen to join them on the dole. But many thought it would sure be nice to have Uncle Sam pointing a gun to the head of the bondholders and the UAW and demanding concessions on the company's behalf. Mulally told them to get over it.

"We, through our own wits, have to participate in this historic restructuring of American automobile industry that the government is leading at GM and Chrysler, and we have to make sure that we are not disadvantaged in the process," he said before breaking out in a smile and waving his copy of the terms sheet in the air. "And we have their plans!"

CHAPTER 18

By Their Own Bootstraps

Then why flounder around waiting for good business? Get the costs down by better management. Get the prices down to the buying power.

— HENRY FORD

The e-mails and telephone calls started coming in right after Alan Mulally's speech on Capitol Hill. Ford Motor Company noticed a huge jump in traffic on its websites as well. The letters began arriving a few days later. They all said the same thing. Thank you. Thank you for not asking for our money. Thank you for fixing your problems on your own. Thank you for showing us that the can-do spirit that made America great is not dead.

A letter Mulally received from Donna Benner in Carnelian Bay, California, was typical. "I was very impressed with your recent refusal to request tax payer funds for your company in the form of bailout money from the government," she wrote. "In fact, I was so pleased with your stance on the matter that I decided then and there to buy a new Ford."

Benner traded in her Infiniti QX4 for a Ford Escape Hybrid in January.

James Saultz Jr. from Deer Park, Texas, wrote admiringly to Mulally. "I appreciate your stand for capitalism, and hope that you can make it last," he said, adding that he had just finished writing a very different letter to General Motors' CEO, Rick Wagoner. James said he planned to trade in his BMW for a Mustang.

Others bought stock instead of a car to show their support. Dealers were hearing the same thing. They began phoning in urgent orders for more brochures because so many people were coming into their showrooms to express their support for Ford and take another look at its cars and trucks. One dealer in Texas told how a woman pulled onto his lot in a brand-new Jeep and asked to trade it in for a Ford. She said she was embarrassed to be seen in a vehicle built by a company that could not survive without a government handout.

Ford's pollsters reported that, within ten days of the second round of hearings on Capitol Hill, 95 percent of the American people knew that General Motors and Chrysler were asking Washington for a bailout. Fifty-two percent knew that Ford was not. Two weeks after the hearings, 48 percent of consumers surveyed said they were more likely to consider a Ford product for the next car or truck as a result. Mulally had never been prouder. His team had come together like he always knew they would. Together they had found a way to fix Ford. And the American people were giving the company credit for doing it.

"This has turned out to be quite an opportunity for us, because it has put a real spotlight on Ford. We just need to continue to tell our story," Mulally said a few days after the December hearing. "It's going to help people know that they've got great choices with Ford—that we're well on our way, that we're financially viable, that we've got great products, a great production system and that we're making tremendous progress."

As if to underscore that point, the U.S. Environmental Protection Agency released its official mileage number for the new Ford Fusion Hybrid that December. With 41 miles per gallon in the city and 36 miles per gallon on the highway, it was a big blow to archrival Toyota, roundly beating the Camry Hybrid to claim the title of most fuel-efficient mid-sized sedan in America.* The knockout blow came a couple of weeks later when the agency announced that the nonhybrid version of the new Fusion also beat the nonhybrid versions of both the Camry and Honda Accord. The previous version of the Fusion had been one of Ford's strongest products since its launch in late 2005, but with dramatically improved styling and mileage numbers

---

* The Fusion Hybrid got 8 more miles to the gallon than the Camry Hybrid on the highway and 2 more miles per gallon in the city. Ford also offered a Mercury version in the form of the Milan Hybrid.

like these, Ford was now taking the fight to the Japanese—challenging them in the segment they had owned since 1997, when the Camry lapped Ford's aging Taurus.

And Ford had a new one of those, too.

On January 11, 2009, a beaming Mulally unveiled a completely re-designed version of the Taurus at the North American International Auto Show in Detroit. It was the car he had been dreaming about re-viving since his first visit to Ford's design studio back in 2006. Ford's designers had done the impossible. They had transformed the lack-luster Ford Five Hundred into a jaw-dropping new flagship that trum-peted Ford's reemergence as a leader in automotive styling. And they had done it in record time. The new Taurus was originally planned as a 2011 model, but with the company fighting for its life, Mulally had ordered an unprecedented acceleration of the program. Derrick Kuzak's team cut an entire year out of the development process. They actually dispensed with clay models and designed the entire vehicle virtually. That and a lot of late nights allowed them to push Ford's new Global Product Development System to its limits.

These new Fords were the first fruits of Mulally's promised prod-uct renaissance. And they were just the beginning. The same day that Mulally pulled the sheet off the new Taurus, Bill Ford announced an aggressive new electrification strategy, detailing plans to bring a new hybrid, a plug-in hybrid, and two battery-powered electric vehicles to market by the end of 2012. It was more of what America wanted to hear.

* * *

B ut no one at World Headquarters was celebrating yet.
On January 29, the automaker announced a staggering loss of $14.6 billion for 2008. It was Ford's biggest loss ever. But there were a few pieces of good news hidden in the otherwise dismal numbers. In the fourth quarter, Ford's core North American automotive opera-tion lost only $1.9 billion—just $400 million more than it lost during the same period a year before, when the economy was still relatively strong. Analysts had been expecting a much deeper decline, given the

dramatic drop in sales. It was proof the company's cost-cutting efforts were working. In the United States, Ford's sales were down more than 20 percent for the full year. That was worse than the industry as a whole, which was down 18 percent. But for the last three months of 2008, the company's sales were down less than the industry average. That meant the automaker had gained market share in October, November, and December. At the same time, Ford's cash burn rate had cooled to $5.5 billion in the last three months of 2008. But the automaker only had $24 billion in cash and credit combined left at the end of the year—including the $10.1 billion still left in its revolving credit line.

Mulally said that would be enough. Despite the grim figures, he told analysts and reporters that Ford would not cut back on product spending, nor would it reconsider its decision to forgo a bailout in the United States.

"Our pipeline is full," Mulally said during a conference call after the results were released. "Ford has sufficient liquidity to make it through this global downturn and to maintain our current product plans without the need for government bridge loans."

But Ford would pull its revolver.

At 7:45 that morning, the Ford CEO had called Timothy Geithner, who had just been confirmed as the new secretary of the Treasury three days earlier. Mulally started by congratulating the grandson of a former Ford vice president* on his appointment, went over the company's financial results, and then told him that he was going to take more than $10 billion out of the nation's fragile banking system.

"We've talked to everybody," Mulally said, uncertain of how the new Treasury secretary would react. "We think it's okay."

Before making its decision to draw down the revolver, Ford treasurer Neil Schloss had personally called each of the fifty banks underwriting it to let them know what was coming and make sure they could fund their portion. Given the state of the economy, he was

---

* Geithner's maternal grandfather, Charles Moore, was Ford's head of public relations from 1952 to 1963.

not certain all of them could. All of the banks funded—except for Lehman, which was no longer among the living and had taken $900 million worth of Ford's liquidity with it to the great beyond.

The loss of Lehman had a lot to do with Ford's decision. Internally, the company's executives had always agreed that they would call the revolver only as a last resort. Many of them—including Chief Financial Officer Lewis Booth—would later say this was the toughest decision they had to make during the crisis, because it meant Ford was playing its last ace. Under normal circumstances, Wall Street would have taken it as a sign that Ford's end was nigh. But the Great Recession had created a new normal. Ford had already lost a tenth of its credit line when Lehman failed in September, and several of the banks that were underwriting the remaining $10.1 billion were barely hanging on. Schloss was spending a good portion of each day checking up on them, and he was worried that Ford's line of credit was about to get even smaller. Pulling it was the only way to preserve it. Ford hoped most analysts would understand that, and the company promised not to use any of the funds to cover operating expenses.*

"I understand," Geithner said.

Mulally was relieved. The last thing he had wanted was to tick off the secretary of the Treasury during their first conversation.

"We continue to manage the business on our own," Mulally assured him. "We started our restructuring a while back, and we plan to keep going."

After Ford's CEO got off the telephone with Geithner, he called Federal Reserve chairman Ben Bernanke and told him the same thing. Bernanke, too, understood.

✳   ✳   ✳

Keeping Ford's promise not to use the money from the revolver to cover operating expenses would require the finance team to monitor the company's cash position in real time. Schloss and his staff were constantly reassessing how much money they were going to

---

* The revolver would have to be paid back or refinanced by the end of 2011.

need for near-term operations and shifting whatever they could forward until sales began to rebound. Ford needed between $8 billion and $10 billion to keep the lights on and the factories humming. Not counting the money from the revolver, its bank balance dropped to right around $10 billion before sales and revenue began to rebound. At best, Ford had only a couple of billion dollars' worth of breathing room.

As precarious as Ford's finances remained, they were a lot better than GM's and Chrysler's. Both companies had retained bankruptcy counsel and were struggling to meet the requirements set forth as a condition of their bridge loans. The Bush administration had given them until February 17 to prove that they could negotiate the concessions from their bondholders and the United Auto Workers, and meeting that deadline was supposed to be a condition for further federal funding. But January was almost over and there was still little sign of progress. It was not looking good for either of the automakers.

Ford's labor team was growing impatient. Joe Hinrichs and Marty Mulloy* had made it clear to the union that Ford needed similar concessions if it was going to make it without taxpayer assistance. UAW president Ron Gettelfinger was sympathetic to Ford's position but refused to negotiate anything with the company until he had signed deals with both of its competitors. His position was understandable. Gettelfinger was only at the bargaining table because Washington had a gun to his head. And Washington had said nothing about Ford. All Hinrichs and Mulloy could do was watch and wait.

That was exactly what they were doing one night in Mulloy's office inside World Headquarters when Hinrichs suddenly leapt out of his chair, grabbed a marker, and started doing math on a blank flip chart. Mulloy looked over his shoulder and saw that Hinrichs—who had come to Ford from General Motors—was adding up GM's debt, the amount it still owed to the UAW-run VEBA health care trust, and the company's unfunded pension liabilities. When Hinrichs was finished with his calculations, he stepped back and shook his head.

---

* After Joe Laymon left Ford in 2008, Hinrichs assumed responsibility for labor affairs, in addition to global manufacturing. Mulloy now reported to him.

"They're going to go bankrupt!" he said.

"What about the government?" Mulloy asked. "Washington will give them more cash once they meet the requirements of the term sheet."

"Yeah, but they can't," Hinrichs said. "Ron's not stupid. He's never going to let GM cover its VEBA obligations with stock, because it's worthless."

If GM could not convince the UAW to do that, the automaker would not be eligible for additional federal funds.

"It's going to be a massacre," Mulloy agreed. "And they'll take the whole industry down with them."

Meanwhile, Booth had been salivating over Ford's bonds. The company's debt was trading at 28 cents on the dollar. At that rate, Ford could make quick work of its debt—if it had some cash to spare. Unfortunately, Booth still had to hold on to every penny. Then Hinrichs showed up in Mulally's office with a proposal.

"What if we can beat GM and Chrysler to the punch?" he asked. "What if we can negotiate our own deal with the UAW first?"

It would not only keep Ford from being disadvantaged, but also free up cash that Booth could use to buy back debt. Mulally was not sure. He was afraid it might look like Ford was taking advantage of the situation, risking the ire of the federal government and undermining the goodwill that it was starting to build with the American people.

But Hinrichs persisted, and the talks between the UAW and the other two automakers continued to drag on. Gettelfinger was clearly hoping the Obama administration would step in and offer better terms for his members, which had done their part to put the new president in the White House. Yet with each passing day, the union was looking more like the villain in this drama. By early February, Hinrichs was convinced that Gettelfinger would jump at the chance to demonstrate his willingness to compromise.

"See what you can do," Mulally told him.

Hinrichs almost ran down the hall to Mulloy's office, catching him just as he was leaving for the night.

"We gotta go see Ron," he said with a triumphant grin.

Despite Gettelfinger's unwillingness to begin negotiations with

Ford, Hinrichs had never stopped talking to the UAW president. In fact, they called each other almost every day. Sometimes Gettelfinger gave him an update on the negotiations with GM and Chrysler. Most of the time he just vented. And Hinrichs let him. That night he called Gettelfinger and asked him to come to the table.

"You have this deadline coming up, Ron, and if you don't have a deal done with either of them by then, it's going to look like the UAW was the one at fault here," Hinrichs told him. "The UAW is going to be viewed as unreasonable."

He said Ford was hearing that the Republicans were just waiting for GM and Chrysler to declare an impasse so that they could take another swing at the union. But Gettelfinger knew when he was being pushed and gave Hinrichs both barrels.

"I don't want to hear what Ford wants to do!" he shouted into the phone. "I'll tell *you* what the UAW wants to do!"

Then he hung up.

But Hinrichs was undaunted. On Saturday, January 24, he sat at his home computer composing a long and carefully worded e-mail to Gettelfinger and his lieutenant, Bob King:

Ron and Bob,

I've been thinking about our conversations about the industry's and Ford's restructuring efforts. It's clear to all of us that our company needs to restructure the business to get our North American business back to ongoing profitability and to get back to investment-grade status so we can fund our product programs, provide for our active and retired employees, and keep Ford Credit part of our family. We look forward to working with you and all the stakeholders to make this happen. I know Ron has told us that you weren't interested in our "wish list" for these restructuring discussions. Respecting that, we have not tabled any kind of formal offer or list of demands. However, I do think we need to get a dialog going on the kinds of things we should look at to fix our business. Clearly, there are many areas of business that need to be improved. We are working on our debt restructuring. We are developing plans for our dealers, both on the costs and the right number of dealers. We're studying what we should do with our supply base, and we have taken very decisive and difficult actions in regard to our salaried employees, including many takeaways and involuntary separations. All the stock options our employees have are worthless, and there are no raises or bonuses this year. The current equity holders of our stock will be diluted in a big way as we work through all these issues. Everyone will contribute to making this company great again.

Hinrichs then outlined Ford's cost disadvantage versus the foreign transplants. It came to approximately $700 million a year.

I know this sounds like a lot of money, and it is. That's why it's so important that we collectively work to address these costs together. Below are some thoughts on where we can work together to eliminate this gap.

He then listed twenty-five changes to the current contract that he thought Ford and the UAW could agree on, with the dollar amount each would save the company annually. It included things such as reducing break time and eliminating the Easter Monday holiday. Most of the savings were small, but they added up to well over $500 million annually. By comparison, a 5 percent wage cut would save the company only $110 million. Together Ford and the UAW could show Washington a way to close the labor cost gap without cutting workers' base wages. In exchange, Ford wanted the same deal that GM and Chrysler were trying to get on the VEBA: half the company's remaining obligation payable in stock instead of cash.

Hinrichs hit "Send" and waited, checking his BlackBerry every few minutes. But by Monday morning, there was still no reply. He waited a few more days before calling Gettelfinger to make sure he had actually received the message.

"I did," the gravel-voiced UAW leader said.

"Well, why don't you let Marty and I come down to Solidarity House and make our pitch to you and Bob?" Hinrichs asked. "Why don't you let us show you why it makes sense for the UAW and why it makes sense for Ford?"

Gettelfinger agreed to meet the two Ford men at the union's headquarters on Friday, February 6.

Solidarity House is a modern office building that sits on a piece of riverfront real estate in downtown Detroit. Hinrichs and Mulloy pulled into the gated parking lot, past the sign informing visitors that foreign automobiles were not allowed on the property. They knew they would get only one chance to convince Gettelfinger and King to come to the table, so they prepared a thorough presentation that they hoped would answer all of the union's questions and address all of its objections. When they arrived at the UAW's headquarters, neither Gettelfinger nor King seemed to be in a particularly good mood, so Hinrichs got right to the point.

"You're never going to get a deal," he told the union leaders. "General Motors is carrying too much debt. They're going to have to go into bankruptcy."

He reminded Gettelfinger and King what had happened when Delphi filed. The UAW had already discovered just how hard it would be to protect its members' interests in bankruptcy court. It would be better to negotiate with Ford now, while they still could. Once they reached an agreement, the union could take it to GM and Chrysler and challenge them to match it. If the automakers refused, they would be the bad guys, not the UAW.

"Go on," Gettelfinger said.

"You've been talking about shared sacrifice since the first hearing," Hinrichs told the union boss. "We're prepared to give it to you."

The company had already announced that it was cutting another 10 percent of its salaried workforce in January. Some 1,200 Ford Credit employees were about to lose their jobs, too. Ford would put together a debt-restructuring deal that would give bondholders a short haircut and dilute stockholders in the process. Everything else would be on the table, include executive compensation and board pay. It took Hinrichs and Mulloy ninety minutes to go over all the details. When they were done, they thanked the UAW leaders for their time and left them to think about Ford's proposal.

Mulloy received a call from King that night.

"We'll be there Monday to start negotiating," he said.

Talks began on February 9. They continued all week, with plenty of back-and-forth wrangling over issues like job security and the jobs bank program. The company and the union bargained through Friday without making much progress. Then, on Saturday morning, Gettelfinger and King arrived with a proposal that would change everything. For the first time ever, the union said it was willing to consider an end to the jobs bank. One of the Ford negotiators—a veteran finance guy who had been brought out of retirement to help hammer out a deal—summed up the company's reaction.

"I worked for the company for thirty-seven years, and I never thought I would see this day!" he exclaimed when Hinrichs told him what he had just heard from the two union bosses. "This is historic!"

Negotiations proceeded quickly from that point on, and the final deal fell into place over the next twenty-four hours. Hinrichs gave Gettelfinger an office a few doors down from his own on the twelfth floor of World Headquarters. King and Mulloy were in a conference room downstairs with the rest of their respective bargaining teams. Each time they reached an agreement on something, Gettelfinger and Hinrichs would calculate the cost savings and see how much more they needed to close the gap with the Japanese transplants. By two in the morning on Sunday it was finished—or so Ford thought. The company had already agreed to eliminate bonuses for all salaried employees, but Gettelfinger wanted more. He wanted to make Alan Mulally share the pain, too.

"He has to work for one dollar a year," Gettelfinger insisted.

Hinrichs was expecting the UAW president to demand a pay cut for Mulally, but he had no idea that Gettelfinger was going to go this far. Hinrichs had already asked Mulally how much latitude he had. Mulally gave him a number, but it still had seven figures. Hinrichs told Gettelfinger to think about what he was asking for, to consider the ramifications.

"First, we need Alan, and none of us want Alan to leave—so let's keep that in our minds. Secondly, I don't think the CEO should be making less than everyone else in the company," Hinrichs said. "Alan would be willing to take a $600,000 pay cut for two years. That's $1.2 million, which is a big deal. The board will also agree to forgo compensation."

Gettelfinger tried hard not to smile.

"What about Mark, Lewis, and the others?" he asked.

"The salaried team has already taken a big hit. They're giving up their bonuses. You've got your shared sacrifice."

Gettelfinger nodded and shook his hand.

Now all that was left was for Hinrichs to make one of the most awkward telephone calls of his entire life. He went to his office, closed the door, and dialed Mulally's cellphone. There was no answer, so Hinrichs left a message, sheepishly informing his boss that he had just negotiated away nearly a third of his salary. When Mulally listened to it later that morning, he was just glad Hinrichs had been able to work out a deal.

But there was still the matter of the VEBA. Hinrichs and Mulloy wanted to finish the negotiations that weekend, but Gettelfinger wanted to take what they had already agreed on to GM and Chrysler first and try to get them to match it ahead of the fast-approaching February 17 deadline.

"I'll be back," he promised.

✳   ✳   ✳

The crisis in the American automobile industry had officially become Barack Obama's problem on January 20, when he was sworn in as the forty-fourth president of the United States. In practice, Obama and his team had been dealing with it ever since the election. Obama had already tapped a former reporter turned Wall Street billionaire, Steven Rattner, to be his "car czar" weeks ahead of the inauguration. Rattner was a managing principal at the Quadrangle Group, a private equity firm, and had no automotive experience. When news of Obama's choice leaked on January 7, Bill Ford was one of the first to express concern.

"It would be really helpful to have somebody in there who would take the time to have a deep understanding of our industry," he said at the Detroit auto show, the implication being that Rattner would not.

Obama had hinted that he would also establish an automotive task force, but as the due date for GM and Chrysler to submit their viability plan approached, even Rattner's appointment remained unofficial. On February 16, reporters on Air Force One were pestering the new White House press secretary, Robert Gibbs, about the task force. They reminded him that the deadline was only a day away. Gibbs assured the scribes that a formal announcement could come later that day. It did not, nor did it come the following day. After the two failing automakers submitted their reports on February 17, the administration issued a short statement saying only that "more will be required from everyone involved—creditors, suppliers, dealers, labor and auto executives themselves—to ensure the viability of these companies."

* * *

By the end of the week, the UAW had come back to the table and resumed negotiations with Ford on the VEBA. They reached a tentative agreement over the weekend and announced it on Monday, February 23. The final deal changed the way overtime pay was calculated, reduced break times, and eliminated cost-of-living adjustments, the Easter Monday holiday, and a $600 Christmas bonus. It required all employees to take company-paid physical exams to lower insurance costs and allowed the company to offer yet another round of buyouts. It also did away with the jobs bank program, though Ford agreed to provide supplemental pay to laid-off workers for up to a year. Most important, it allowed the automaker to use Ford stock to cover half its remaining VEBA obligation.*

By now, the Presidential Task Force on the Auto Industry had finally coalesced and held its first meeting. The group was cochaired by Treasury secretary Geithner and Larry Summers, the director of the President's National Economic Council. It included the secretaries of commerce, transportation, energy, and labor as well as the director of the Office of Management and Budget, the chair of the Council of

---

* The company also agreed to new product commitments for certain plants and promised to keep the UAW informed of its efforts to secure comparable sacrifices from its bondholders, suppliers, and dealers.

Economic Advisers, the director of the White House Office of Energy and Climate Change Policy, the administrator of the Environmental Protection Agency, and Ron Bloom, another investment banker from Lazard.* He and Rattner would lead the day-to-day operations of the ad hoc group and oversee its small team of young technocrats.

General Motors and Chrysler made urgent calls to both men when they heard that Ford had negotiated its own deal with the UAW. Chrysler was particularly upset and accused the Dearborn automaker of trying to force it into bankruptcy. Rattner was not pleased, either. He called Ziad Ojakli after hearing the news.

"Let us handle this," the still-unofficial car czar said.

Ojakli told him that Ford had to look out for its own interests.

Gettelfinger and King briefed local UAW leaders on the deal on February 24. In addition to Mulally's pay cut, Bill Ford—who was still not getting paid—also had agreed to give up a portion of his deferred compensation. Union leaders were impressed. They endorsed the agreement unanimously and urged their members to vote in favor of ratification. With two of the three American automakers teetering on the verge of bankruptcy, it was not a hard sell. The amendment to the 2007 labor agreement was ratified on March 9.

Richard Linz, a worker at Ford's Ohio Assembly Plant in Avon Lake, summed up the prevailing sentiment.

"We feel like we're over a barrel," he said. "I want to retire from Ford. I don't even know if that's possible anymore. I want to keep working. I want to keep my job."

He said the news that Mulally and Ford were taking pay cuts did make his own sacrifices a bit easier to digest.

The agreement was a coup for Ford. The concessions would save the company well over $500 million in 2009 alone, and the VEBA deal would give it another $3.7 billion in cash to use to buy back debt. Booth and his finance team wasted little time getting started on that. They had to. The UAW had agreed to these concessions only because Ford had promised to wrest similar sacrifices from its

---

* Bloom also served as adviser to the United Steelworkers and Airline Pilots Association.

other stakeholders—the bondholders in particular—just as Washington was demanding of GM and Chrysler. Hinrichs and Mulloy gave Gettelfinger and King their word that Ford would do that, and the union leaders trusted them enough to do the deal on the strength of that promise. Now Ford had to make good on it.

* * *

O n March 4, Ford did just that. As GM and Chrysler continued to haggle with the union, the Dearborn automaker announced a three-part debt restructuring program. First, it offered bondholders $80 in cash and nearly 109 shares of Ford stock for every $1,000 in senior convertible notes they sold back to the company.* Second, Ford Credit issued a $1.3 billion cash tender offer of 30 cents on the dollar for unsecured, nonconvertible Ford debt, which was then trading at just 20 cents on the dollar.† Finally, Ford Credit issued another $500 million cash tender offer—later increased to $1 billion—for Ford's senior unsecured term debt, with the price to be set at auction. This mix of cash and stock deals was designed to prevent investors from working together to get better terms from the company. Each component of the program played to a different investor base.‡

It succeeded beyond Ford's most optimistic expectations. Over the next month, Ford and its lending subsidiary spent $2.4 billion in cash and issued 468 million new shares of stock to retire $9.9 billion worth of debt. Wall Street was stunned by the take rate.

"Investors jumped on the offer like it had slapped their mothers," analyst Shelly Lombard of Gimme Credit declared just before the deal closed.

It was one of the largest debt swaps in U.S. history, but it was not Ford's first. Over the past couple of years, Schloss and his team had

---

* This offer applied to Ford's 4.25 percent senior convertible notes due December 15, 2036. The $1,000 referred to the principal value of the notes, and the actual number of shares was 108.6957 per $1,000.

† The 30-cents-on-the-dollar offer was open to most bondholders who signed up by March 19. After that, most only got 27 cents on the dollar. The final amount subscribed was $1.1 billion.

‡ It was a prescient move. At both GM and Chrysler, investors would later gang up on the company to demand more favorable terms.

been quietly working Ford's balance sheet. In August 2007, they had converted $2.1 billion of preferred securities into equity. Over the next twelve months they exchanged another $998 million worth of Ford debt for company stock. Between August and October 2008, they sold another $434 million worth of stock and used the proceeds to purchase Ford Credit bonds.*

All of these moves hurt Ford's shareholders because they diluted the company's stock. However, since the Ford family's shares could not be diluted, this was largely academic. No matter how upset the other shareholders might get, there was really nothing they could do about it. And as long as they did not sell their shares in anger, investors ultimately benefited greatly from these plays. As for the bondholders, the March offering was entirely optional. It was a sweet deal for the company. Ford was able to buy back its debt at 30 cents on the dollar. At the time, at least, it seemed just as sweet to bondholders. They were able to sell their paper back to Ford for a dime more per dollar than it was currently worth. Given the state of the American automobile industry, many of them were happy to get anything.

* * *

President Obama did not wait until March 31. It was already clear that neither GM nor Chrysler would be able to meet the terms his predecessor had established as a condition for further government aid. But he decided to give them one more chance. Like George W. Bush, Obama had concluded that the uncontrolled collapse of the two automakers would be too big a blow for the already battered economy to absorb.

On March 30, Mulally was presiding over the now-daily SAR meeting in the Thunderbird Room when Ojakli was notified that Obama

---

* Ford's treasury team also demonstrated its financial acumen by moving to de-risk the company's pension funds in 2007, before the global economic crisis began. At the time, these totaled approximately $60 billion, and about 70 percent of that money was invested in equity markets, with the remainder in safer fixed-income investments. Schloss decided to balance Ford's funds evenly between the two—just before the equity markets tanked in the second half of the year. He also hedged on interest rates. Together, these moves saved Ford between $6 billion and $7 billion.

was about to address the nation. The technicians in the control booth got CNN up on the big screen just before 11:07 A.M., when the president stepped into the Grand Foyer of the White House and, flanked by the members of his new task force, delivered his final ultimatum to Detroit.

"Year after year, decade after decade, we've seen problems papered over and tough choices kicked down the road, even as foreign competitors outpaced us. Well, we've reached the end of that road," he said. "We cannot, and must not, and we will not let our auto industry simply vanish. [But] we cannot make the survival of our auto industry dependent on an unending flow of taxpayer dollars. These companies and this industry must ultimately stand on their own, not as wards of the state."

The president gave GM sixty days to produce "a better business plan" that addressed all of its legacy issues and transformed the automaker into a leaner, more competitive company. He also fired Rick Wagoner. Obama said it was too late for Chrysler. Instead he gave the Auburn Hills automaker thirty days to negotiate a marriage with Italy's Fiat SpA.

There was something in it for Ford, too, at least indirectly.

"We must also recognize that the difficulties facing this industry are due in no small part to the weaknesses in our economy as a whole," the president said. "Therefore, to support demand for auto sales during this period, I'm directing my team to take several steps."

Obama said he would speed up the release of funds already appropriated to purchase new government vehicles through the recently passed American Recovery and Reinvestment Act. He would take additional steps to free up liquidity for automotive finance companies so that they could provide credit to dealers and consumers. He would also order the Internal Revenue Service to alert consumers to a new tax break for those who purchased a new car or truck. And he would work with Congress to develop "an even more ambitious incentive program to increase car sales."

"Yes!" shouted Ojakli, punching his fist in the air. He and his staff had been working for months to convince Washington to do something to spur new vehicle sales. Similar programs were already making a big difference in Europe. This was the first sign it might happen in the United States, too.

The president concluded by promising to help communities in Michigan and other parts of the Midwest deal with the consequences of this epic restructuring.

"If we can carry one another through this difficult time and do what must be done, then we will look back and say that this was the moment when the American auto industry shed its old ways, marched into the future, remade itself, and once more became an engine of prosperity not only in Detroit, not only in our Midwest, but all across America," Obama promised.

When the president finished speaking, everyone in the Thunder-bird Room looked at one another and let out a collective "Wow!"

After asking for the video feed to be shut off, Mulally addressed his executives.

"Guys, this is an amazing moment for us to come together around the Ford plan and make history," he said. "You've spent all of your working lives waiting to make a difference. Well, now is your time. This is about the soul of American manufacturing, and you're part of the solution."

The White House had e-mailed Ojakli a copy of Obama's speech while the president was delivering it. Copies were quickly made and passed out to everyone seated around the table. Mulally had been taking notes throughout the speech, listing each of the things that Ford's competitors were going to be required to do. He began going over the details, pausing after each item.

Obama told GM it needed to consolidate its brands.

"Have we done it?" Mulally asked. "Check!"

The president ordered GM to clean up its balance sheet.

"Have we done it? Check!"

Obama told GM it needed to create a credible business model that would allow it to succeed in the global marketplace.

"Have we done it? Check!"

Everyone agreed that it would take a miracle for GM to accomplish these things in the short time allotted to it. Bankruptcy was now inevitable. Several of the Ford executives were ready to declare victory.

"There is no way bankruptcy can work," one of them said. "No one will buy their cars."

Mulally shook his head.

"You better believe that, if the federal government is going to get involved in it, it's going to work," he said. "You can count on it. They can write the rules, and they can rewrite the rules. They can put a man on the moon. It *will* work. We are going to have to stick to our plan and execute with more skill and courage than ever."

The mood in the room was suddenly somber as the executives began contemplating what that might mean for Ford.

"Their debt is going to be wiped out," someone sighed.

"So is ours." Mulally smiled. "We're going to accelerate the implementation of our plan and pay back the loans. Who's going to move faster? Who *can* move faster? Who's going to have to have every one-hundred-million-dollar purchase approved by Washington? *We* are in charge of *our* destiny."

Someone made a crack about Wagoner's posterior and the president's boot. Everybody laughed—except for Mulally. He held up his hand and stopped the snickering.

"We're not going to gloat," Mulally said. "This is our time to be humble and stay focused."

*   *   *

In April, a few days after the debt deal was concluded, Booth led a Ford delegation to Washington for the company's first meeting with the task force. Because Ford had passed on a government bailout, the company decided that there was no need for Mulally to deal with the group directly. With Booth were Hinrichs, Ojakli, and Tony Brown, Ford's global purchasing chief and resident expert on the supplier situation. They met with Rattner and Bloom in a small conference room at the Treasury Department. The two administration officials were still fuming over Ford's decision to negotiate a separate peace with the UAW.

"Why are you guys intervening in this?" Rattner asked again. "Why don't you let us take care of it?"

"We want to make sure we're not disadvantaged," Booth replied.

Rattner wanted to know how Ford was able to negotiate concessions from the union before it got them from bondholders. Hinrichs said it was all about trust.

"That was the foundation of all this," he said. "We showed them our plan, and we committed to that plan."

If Rattner was impressed, he did not show it. Instead he went over the terms of Ford's agreement with the UAW.

"Is this really going to be competitive?" he asked Hinrichs.

"Yeah, by our numbers it gets us there—not today, but over the next couple of years. And it was ratifiable," Hinrichs explained. "It keeps us moving on our plan to restructure the business."

*   *   *

By the end of March, all the tracking data showed that Ford had opened a wide gap in public perception with General Motors and Chrysler. The American people were no longer mentioning the Dearborn automaker in the same breath as the other two manufacturers. After Obama's speech, investors began buying Ford's shares again—despite the fact that they were about to be diluted by the company's massive debt-for-equity swap. On April 3, Ford's stock closed above $3 a share for the first time since 2008. By April 9, it was trading above $4. On April 24, Ford posted a first-quarter loss of $1.43 billion. It no longer seemed to matter. The company's stock ended the day at $5 a share. Wall Street was paying more attention to Ford's cash burn rate, which had fallen to $3.7 billion. The company's shares were knocking on the door of $6 at the end of trading on April 30. April also saw Standard & Poor's boost Ford's credit rating for the first time in a decade. The automaker's debt was still deep inside junk bond territory, but it was finally moving in the right direction.

Since the stock float did nothing to diminish investor enthusiasm for Ford, the company decided to issue another $1.6 billion worth of new shares to further strengthen its balance sheet. This was not part of the plan, but an unexpected benefit that put a lot more distance between the Dearborn automaker and the door of bankruptcy court. Barring another significant downturn, everyone at the top of the Glass House now believed the company really could make it without the government's help.

Sales remained depressed, but Ford continued to outperform the market and gain share. In April, its sales were down more than 31 percent, but Toyota's were down nearly 42 percent. It was the same story in Europe, too, where Ford posted its first double-digit share gain since 2001. The automaker's share for the first quarter in the region was its highest in ten years.

The board was pleased. The directors had hoped that Ford would get credit for forgoing a bailout, but none of them expected the decision to generate as much goodwill for the company as it did. Two days after the UAW agreement was ratified, Ford's board of directors awarded Mulally options for another 5 million shares at a strike price of $1.96. It was a sneaky way of making up for the pay cut he had taken to cinch the deal with the union. The company hoped that no one would notice. But the UAW did notice. Bob King felt betrayed. He had sold these concessions to his members on the principle of shared sacrifice. He would not forget it, nor would many of his rank-and-file members. And it would come back to bite both Ford and King later.

But for now, Ford just needed to steer clear of the cataclysm engulfing the rest of Detroit. The supplier situation had not improved and would only get worse if General Motors and Chrysler filed for Chapter 11 protection. But it was becoming clearer by the day that their losses would be Ford's gains. By May 1, 63 percent of the car-buying public said it had a favorable view of the Dearborn automaker. In the depths of the worst crisis to afflict the American automobile industry in eight decades, Mulally and his team had done what many thought impossible even in the best of times: They had restored the American people's faith in Ford Motor Company. The decision to pass on a bailout was a big part of that, but it would have mattered little if the company's showrooms were still filled with the same old boring products. Fortunately for Ford, transports stacked with new vehicles like the redesigned Fusion and Fusion Hybrid were pulling into dealer lots just as customers decided that the company was worth another look. Once again, Ford's timing was perfect.*

Neither the outgoing Bush administration nor the incoming Obama one could figure out how to give Ford the $9 billion line of credit it requested,† but it no longer needed it. The outpouring of support for the automaker's decision to go it alone would soon become a groundswell. Three years after Mark Fields' Way Forward speech, Alan Mulally had finally made Ford America's car company.

---

* If Ford had waited for GM and Chrysler to conclude their own deals with the UAW, it would have been the middle of summer before negotiations even began. By then, Ford's business had improved to the point that rank-and-file members would never have agreed to such concessions. The company's debt would likely have been trading higher as well, making it harder for Ford to buy back.

† Ford's request for a $9 billion line of credit was actually approved by the House of Representatives.

CHAPTER 19

Turning the Corner

Unless you have courage, a courage that keeps you going, always going, no matter what happens, there is no certainty of success.

— HENRY FORD

Chrysler filed for bankruptcy on April 30, 2009. General Motors followed it into Chapter 11 a month later. Once again, the television was on in the Thunderbird Room when President Barack Obama told the American people that the United States government was going to invest $30 billion in GM and become the owner of the nation's largest automaker.

"I recognize that this may give some Americans pause," Obama acknowledged. "[But] their survival and the success of our overall economy depend on it."

There were audible gasps in Dearborn.

"You mean they're not going to have to pay it back!?" shouted one of the executives. The others just shook their heads.

Alan Mulally had not seen this coming. Neither had anyone else at Ford Motor Company. They all knew that GM and Chrysler were going to get substantial infusions of cash from the American taxpayers. They just assumed the two bankrupt automakers would have to pay it back. Now the president was explaining that the old GM and Chrysler would be allowed to convert this debt into equity in their successor corporations. In the case of Chrysler, it was expected that Fiat would purchase the government's shares to complete its acquisition of the automaker. But in the case of General Motors, the United States would own a majority stake in the new company once it emerged from bankruptcy.

Mulally and the other executives sat in silence as they struggled to digest the president's words. They were no longer competing against two bankrupt manufacturers. They were competing against the United States government. As usual, Mulally was the first one to get over it.

"You have to expect the unexpected, and you have to deal with it," he said. "Whining is not a plan. Wallowing is not a plan. We *have* a plan, and if we need to adjust it, we will."

*   *   *

F ord followed both bankruptcies closely. It hired an outside law firm to study every document its competitors filed with the courts. There were new ones submitted every day—often hundreds, sometimes thousands of pages—and Ford's lawyers dissected them all for details about the two companies and their government-run reorganizations. The task of monitoring Washington fell to Ziad Ojakli. He and his operatives prowled the corridors of power trying to figure out what the government was doing to protect its investment. Mulally and his team continued to meet every day to go over the latest developments. These meetings soon settled into a routine.

"What's everybody hearing?" Mulally would ask once all of the executives had taken their seats.

The answer usually involved some new, unanticipated benefit accruing to one or both of Ford's crosstown rivals. Everyone inside the Glass House knew that GM and Chrysler were going to be able to walk away from most of their debt, but no one had expected Washington to authorize a sweeping purge of their dealer ranks or force the United Auto Workers to grant them even deeper concessions than the ones Ford had negotiated with the union. These things were hard for many of the Ford executives to swallow—particularly those who had been fighting for years to make the sort of progress that GM and Chrysler were now achieving with the stroke of a pen.*

Some of these decisions—like the one absolving General Motors

_____

* Another particularly galling move, at least for Ford, was the judge's decision to let General Motors keep its deferred tax assets. Normally these would have been forfeited entirely, since the company that emerged from bankruptcy was a different legal entity. However, since Washington was a major investor, they were transferred to the new GM.

of all liability for past wrongdoing—put Ford at a real disadvantage. Years earlier, all three American automakers had become the targets of costly class-action lawsuits seeking compensation for mechanics and others exposed to asbestos, which was used on brake pads until the early 1990s.* Early on, Ford and General Motors had decided to make common cause, agreeing to share the cost of defending the lawsuits and split any settlements or judgments against them. One day that summer, one of GM's attorneys called Ford corporate counsel David Leitch and told him a federal judge had just ruled that responsibility for the asbestos claims would not be transferred to the new GM.

"We don't have any more liability in this," the GM lawyer said with barely concealed glee. "It's all yours."

There was stunned silence when Leitch broke the news to his colleagues in the Thunderbird Room the next morning.

"Wait, you mean they're going to get to walk away from their lawsuits?" someone asked. "They're not going to have any asbestos liability? Is that right!?"

"This is the way our bankruptcy system works. They get a fresh start," Leitch said calmly. "Sure they're getting a lot of advantages. Do you want to go there, too? We still can."

Nobody did. As jealous as Ford's executives might have been about the ease with which the two other Detroit automakers were undoing decades of mismanagement, none of them wanted to trade places with their bankrupt competitors. Ford was benefiting greatly from its decision to pass on a government bailout. Though the entire industry continued to struggle, Ford continued to gain market share in the United States and around the world. In May, its U.S. sales were down less than 25 percent—the smallest decline of any of the six largest manufacturers. Both Toyota and Honda reported 41 percent drops. Lincoln sales were actually up year-over-year. It was the only brand to report positive numbers.

Demand was also beginning to pick up. Overall U.S. sales had

---

* Ford and the other American automakers began phasing out the asbestos brake pads in the 1970s, but the pads continued to be used in some vehicles until the early 1990s.

been increasing month-over-month since March. On June 2, Ford announced that it was increasing second-quarter production by 10,000 vehicles and adding another 42,000 to its third-quarter production schedule—this at a time when many GM plants and all of Chrysler's U.S. factories were idle. Washington was now guaranteeing the warranties on GM and Chrysler products, but many Americans were still wary of buying a vehicle from a bankrupt manufacturer. In May, Ford added insult to their injury by introducing a new program to help Chrysler owners pay off their vehicles and trade them for a Ford car or truck.

"There are a lot of people out there that don't like the concept that government is running these companies," explained Ken Czubay, head of U.S. sales and marketing for Ford. "They're also disillusioned by the resale value of their products."

By then, the residual value of Chrysler products had fallen by nearly 50 percent.

Even the government-backed dealer consolidation campaign turned out to be something less than the panacea it initially seemed. In May, Chrysler announced that it would eliminate some 800 dealers under the controversial program. GM axed about 1,100.

Jim Farley was furious when he broke the news to the rest of the team.

"Here we are, fighting it out store by store," said Ford's vice president of global marketing, sales, and service. "We're crawling around on our knees with our rifles, and they wake up and a third of their dealers are gone! They hit the fucking lottery!"

But his anger soon gave way to relief. In their fury over losing their franchises, many of the GM and Chrysler dealers destroyed customer lists and account information. It got even messier in December when Washington—bowing to angry constituents—reconsidered and allowed those dealers who had been cut to appeal. Farley was soon thankful that Ford had been left with its less coercive approach. Most of the Ford dealerships that closed sold out to other franchise owners who usually did whatever was necessary to ensure a seamless transition. They purchased customer lists from the defunct dealership and even offered jobs to best salespeople and service writers. It was slow and still left some dealers feeling like they had been strong-armed by the company, but it was working. The company had already convinced 670 Ford and Lincoln-Mercury franchises to close or merge with another dealer—a 16 percent reduction of its retail footprint in the United States.

Still, each day brought new surprises for Mulally and his team. The U.S. government had never gotten so intimately involved in the operations of private corporations. There was no rulebook for any of this; Washington was clearly making it up as it went along. And that made Ford very nervous.*

The government provided debtor-in-possession financing for both General Motors and Chrysler, which would otherwise have been impossible for either company to get. Washington was now spending taxpayer dollars to pay for advertising touting the benefits of GM and Chrysler products over competing Fords. Those companies were also using taxpayer dollars to offer bigger incentives in an effort to win back sales. Even more troubling for Ford was the fact that the government was using General Motors' former lending arm, GMAC, to offer attractive financing terms to buyers that Ford simply could not match.

The government began taking over GMAC in December, trading $5 billion in cash for preferred stock in the company. By May, Washington had injected another $8.4 billion into the finance company and gained majority control. Meanwhile, the U.S. Treasury Department had transformed GMAC into a bank holding company, giving it access to capital from the Federal Reserve at the same low rates banks were charged. Ford was fuming. Its own application to grant Ford Credit similar treatment had been held up for months.† And Washington did not stop there. At the government's behest, GMAC was now functioning as the lending arm for Chrysler, too. Mulally began

---

* Ford was worried that Washington might start exempting GM and Chrysler from some federal regulations to reduce their manufacturing costs, but that never happened.

† Ford was actually asking the government to allow Ford Credit to become an industrial loan company (ILC). It could not have become a bank holding company, but ILC status would still have allowed it to borrow at more attractive rates.

to openly question whether the government was bending the rules in favor of the companies it now owned.

"We want to make sure we're not being disadvantaged," he told Treasury secretary Timothy Geithner and Federal Reserve chairman Ben Bernanke.

Mulally also took GMAC to task for the sweet deals it was making to GM and Chrysler customers.

"If they're a bank, they need to start acting like one," he said. "They need to put their shareholders—the American taxpayers—first."

Other executives kept making the same points to Obama's Auto Task Force.

"Ford made sure it was never completely out of mind," car czar Steve Rattner later wrote. "Alan Mulally phoned Tim [Geithner] regularly and often sent emissaries to me. Ford's message was always the same: We're struggling too, but we're fixing the problem ourselves. Don't penalize us because we didn't take your money."

But Washington was getting tired of hearing about Ford's concerns. After Mulally complained to one administration official about the special treatment GM was getting, the man just smiled.

"You're always welcome to take the bailout," he said.

＊　＊　＊

As Mulally had predicted, the U.S. government was making quick work of the problems at GM and Chrysler. Both were out of bankruptcy by mid-July. But nothing Washington did could match the gains Ford was making with consumers. In June, Ford's U.S. sales were down just 11 percent, compared to the industry's 28 percent decline. Ford economist Ellen Hughes-Cromwick was now convinced that a recovery was imminent, so the company announced another production increase, boosting third-quarter factory output by another 25,000 vehicles—a 16 percent increase over 2008.

And Ford was finally getting some help of its own from Washington. On June 23, it became the first automaker to receive a loan from the U.S. Department of Energy retooling program. The $5.9 billion gave Ford the capital it needed to make good on Bill Ford's promise to introduce a full family of electric and hybrid-electric vehicles. But this was no bailout. The loan program was set up to help Ford and other manufacturers cope with the costly new mandates Washington had imposed on the automobile industry back in 2007. Nor was this aid limited to the Detroit Three. The same day the Department of Energy authorized Ford's loans, it also announced that electric-vehicle manufacturer Tesla Motors would receive $465 million and said Japan's Nissan would receive $1.6 billion from the program.

Ford got even more help on July 1, when the U.S. government's "Cash for Clunkers" program went into effect. This was something Ojakli and his team had been pushing for in Washington for months.

In January, Germany had launched its *Umweltprämie,* or "Environmental Premium," program to stimulate demand for automobiles and encourage drivers of older, more polluting cars to trade them in for cleaner, greener models. Anyone who owned a vehicle that was more than nine years old could trade it in and receive the equivalent of more than $3,300 toward the price of a new one. It was wildly successful. By March, German car sales were up 40 percent year-over-year. Hundreds of thousands of Germans took advantage of the program, and Ford was the biggest beneficiary.

"The global auto industry may be facing its worst crisis ever, but you'd never know it at Ford Motor's factory in Cologne," *Der Spiegel* reported in May. "There, workers are putting in extra shifts on weekends to cope with demand for the compact Fiesta. In fact, Ford sales have been booming in Germany. Customers have placed orders for 68,500 Fiestas, Ka subcompacts, and mid-sized Fusions in the four months to April, more than triple the year-earlier figure."

Scrappage schemes were soon popping up all over Europe. Each one drew customers to dealerships like pigeons to bread crumbs. Ford began lobbying aggressively for similar incentives in the United States. Ojakli mustered all of Ford's heavy hitters for an unrelenting assault on the halls of Congress. He sent Hughes-Cromwick to Washington to explain how such a program would benefit the entire economy. That spring, she personally met with more than two hundred lawmakers and legislative assistants, explaining to each one how every vehicle sale sent ripples through the larger economy.

Congress finally approved the Car Allowance Rebate System on

June 18. Motorists with eligible vehicles could get up to $4,500 from the government to apply to their purchase of a new, more fuel-efficient car or truck. The effect was immediate. All across America, dealers were deluged with customers eager to trade in their aging gas-guzzler for a new, more economical car. The Japanese were the biggest beneficiaries of the program in the United States, but it helped Ford, too. Though it would still be months before the first of Ford's fuel-efficient European models arrived in U.S. showrooms, the automaker still had plenty of vehicles that qualified for the government program. And none of them came with the stigma of bankruptcy. Ford was still selling the same old domestic version of the Focus, but the cheap compact became the most sought-after American car, coming in fourth after the Toyota Corolla, Honda Civic, and Toyota Camry. Less than three weeks after the program was announced, Ford was well on its way to posting its first year-over-year monthly sales gain since 2007.

"Things have stopped getting worse," a coy Mark Fields told reporters on July 21. "The question is, at what point does it start to turn positive?"

The answer came three days later when the automaker stunned Wall Street with an entirely unexpected second-quarter profit of $2.3 billion. The company's quarterly cash burn rate was now down to $1 billion. Investors were ecstatic. Ford's stock passed the $7 mark in trading that day and was at $8 within a week—a level not seen in a year.

Ford was back in the black. And this time it would stay there. Though sales would remain depressed in the United States and around the world, Ford was finally matching production to demand. It had done what no other American automaker had been able to do before: The company had figured out how to make money in a down market. For Ford, at least, the nightmare was over.

❋   ❋   ❋

For the rest of the American automobile industry, the situation remained challenging. Suppliers were still fighting for their lives, and more of them were losing every week. Tony Brown and his Project Quark team continued to manage the situation masterfully, but it was not always easy. Ford was forced to bail out Visteon for the second time in four years, agreeing to provide debtor-in-possession financing to the parts manufacturer after it filed for bankruptcy on May 28.

The investment bankers who had been handed the keys to the American automobile industry knew nothing about the complex web of relationships that sustained car and truck manufacturing in the United States and around the world. Nor did they understand how working capital flowed through the industry. Brown did his best to school them. He explained how all the major manufacturers depended on the same supply base to keep their factories running. He showed them how the collapse of one major supplier could trigger a cascading catastrophe that might bring down the entire manufacturing system. He helped them understand how difficult it was to change suppliers, particularly when heavily engineered components or proprietary technologies were involved. It took a while, but they got it—at least enough to keep them from making an already bad situation worse.

Brown argued against just throwing money at the suppliers. The sector needed to consolidate in order to create a healthy industry. So he lobbied for a more selective approach that would provide aid only to the most critical companies. But that was too complicated for Washington. The government set up a $5 billion fund for troubled suppliers, though the borrowing rates were so high that most of the money went untouched.

A more effective scheme was channeling federal funds to suppliers through General Motors and Chrysler. Before the Obama administration forced them into bankruptcy, it made it clear that their suppliers would still get paid. This had a calming effect on the entire industry, because it suggested that everyone's biggest fear—the collapse of the American supply base—would be avoided. Washington even gave Chrysler and GM money to pass on to those suppliers who needed it most. That was fine with Ford because many of those companies also provided parts for its cars and trucks.

* * *

Meanwhile, Ford was struggling to play catch-up with General Motors and Chrysler on the labor front. Washington had forced the UAW to give those companies the same concessions Ford had negotiated with the union, but the government had not stopped there. The Auto Task Force also pressured the UAW to accept additional concessions, including a freeze on wages for entry-level workers and even more flexible work rules. More important, the Obama administration ordered the union to waive its right to strike both companies when the current contracts expired in 2011.* This put the resurgent Ford at tremendous risk. UAW president Ron Gettelfinger and Vice President Bob King had no interest in striking Ford—either now or in 2011. They understood that returning to the overly generous terms of the pre-2007 labor agreement would undermine everything Ford had accomplished with their help. They were convinced that the best thing they could do to protect their members' jobs was ensure that the companies they worked for stayed in business. But they were also elected leaders, and Ford was worried that their increasingly militant membership might force the union's hand in the future.

Ford wanted the same guarantees as General Motors and Chrysler. Getting the UAW back to the bargaining table was not hard. After the last agreement was ratified in March, Ford manufacturing chief Joe Hinrichs had asked Gettelfinger to leave the door open.

"The government is involved now, and we don't know how this is all going to play out with GM and Chrysler," Hinrichs said. "If something significant changes, we need to get back together and talk about how we're going to remain competitive."

The two sides quickly hammered out an agreement that would give Ford the same protections as GM and Chrysler. In exchange, Ford would pay each UAW member a $1,000 "quality bonus." But there

---

* The no-strike clause was the idea of Fiat CEO Sergio Marchionne. He told the Obama administration that he would not invest the time, money, and energy required to fix Chrysler only to see his work undone by the UAW in the next round of contract negotiations. President Obama felt the same way. He was expending a great deal of political capital to save these companies and did not want the union to undo all of his heavy lifting in 2011.

was a problem. Gettelfinger and King were not sure they could sell the deal to their members. The rank and file were following Ford's progress closely, and some were beginning to question whether they had already given the company too much. Workers had been willing to make sacrifices when the automaker was fighting for its life, but Ford was making money again. The company was becoming a victim of its own success.

"People I've talked to feel like they've given up enough," said Gary Walkowicz, a member of the UAW bargaining committee at Ford's Dearborn Truck Plant. "They feel they shouldn't have to give up any more."

He and other dissidents began organizing opposition to the new Ford agreement before the terms were even announced. Ford and the UAW leadership decided to wait for the right moment before putting the new accord to a vote. But the news kept getting better.

Thanks to Cash for Clunkers, Ford's sales in the United States were up 2 percent in July. Congress initially appropriated $1 billion for the scrappage program. That money was supposed to last until November, but it had run out by the end of the first month. The White House asked dealers to keep offering the incentive and pressured lawmakers to release another $2 billion in early August to keep Cash for Clunkers going for another month. On August 14, Ford boosted factory output yet again and, two weeks later, added extra shifts at its Dearborn Truck Plant and Kansas City Assembly Plant in Claycomo, Missouri, to keep up with demand. Ford posted a 17 percent increase in August. European sales were up, too, thanks to the scrappage programs on the other side of the Atlantic.

Sales finally dropped in September when the Cash for Clunkers program expired. On October 14, the company and the union announced the tentative agreement, and Gettelfinger hastily summoned local union leaders to Detroit, where he urged them to support ratification. Some, such as Walkowicz, refused. Gettelfinger gave the locals only until the end of the month to vote on the agreement, because he wanted workers to cast their ballots before the October sales results were released.

But Ford's relative success was only part of the problem. UAW members remembered how the company's board of directors had backfilled Mulally's February pay cut with stock options; they wondered what Ford had up its sleeve this time around.

The task of convincing workers to support the latest round of concessions fell to King, who had emerged as Gettelfinger's heir apparent. Like many of his members, King thought Ford was asking for too much. He was an idealist who believed the right to strike was sacrosanct. But he was also a good soldier. King kept his feelings to himself and traveled from plant to plant trying to convince workers to vote for the deal with Ford. At more than one factory, King was booed off the stage.

UAW members formally rejected the deal on October 31. As a result, Ford would have to go into the 2011 national contract talks with a target on its back.

✻   ✻   ✻

On October 28, Ford announced that it had finally found a potential buyer for Volvo. China's Geely Group was named the preferred bidder for the Swedish brand, which Ford had officially been trying to unload for the better part of a year. The truth was that Geely had been trying to buy Volvo for years, but it had taken Ford this long to realize that it could not do better.

Chinese car companies did not rate much higher than Russian oligarchs, and Geely was hardly in the forefront of the Chinese automobile industry. This was no state-owned enterprise backed by the full might of the Communist Party, with all of the clout, connections, and capital that implied. Geely was the brainchild of baby-faced entrepreneur Li Shufu. The son of a farmer from the eastern coastal province of Zhejiang, Li decided to skip college and instead borrowed 2,000 yuan from his father and set up a business making refrigerator components in 1984. By the time he was twenty-one, Li was selling his parts nationwide, but new government regulations put him out of business in 1989. Undaunted, Li decided to try his hand at building motorcycles. In 1994 he took over a failing state-owned motorcycle company and turned it into China's bestselling domestic brand. Finally, he turned his attention to automobiles—a simple commodity he once described as "four wheels and two sofas"—starting Geely Automobile in 1997. Geely soon muscled its way into the largely state-controlled car business with dirt-cheap models such as the Geely KingKong, which sold for less than $6,000.

In 2006, Li decided he was ready for the big leagues. He brought his imaginatively named MR7171A sedan to the North American International Auto Show in Detroit. Unable to rent space on the show floor, he set up his stand in the hallway outside and passed out mustard-yellow day planners to the few journalists who wandered by to chuckle at his embarrassing excuse for an automobile. It was so cheaply put together it made a Yugo look downright bespoke.

That was the image of Geely that Ford still had in mind when Li came to Dearborn two years later and asked if he could buy Volvo. The answer was no—even Ford was not that desperate.

Yet.

By the end of 2008, Ford was no longer in a position to be picky. No one else had expressed any real interest in Volvo—at least no one with cash. And after the collapse of Lehman, that included just about everyone. Li's products were improving, and he was earning a reputation in China as a real businessman. Director John Thornton approached Li during a visit to Beijing and told him Ford had reconsidered. Chief Financial Officer and former Volvo chairman Lewis Booth would head up the negotiations. He still had serious reservations about selling to Geely.

"These guys aren't going to be able to run a company like Volvo," Booth told his team. He ordered them to slow-walk the talks, hoping to draw out another, more respectable buyer.

Even the Chinese government was concerned. China was on a buying binge, and the last thing Beijing wanted was for an inexperienced Chinese company to botch the purchase of a well-known brand. A few already had. But Li was ready. He had assembled a team of advisers capable of addressing each constituency's concerns. It included Rothschild's top automotive banker, Meyrick Cox, and Jennifer Yu, the daughter-in-law of former Chinese president Jiang Zemin.

Geely also hired former Volvo CEO and onetime Ford marketing boss Hans-Olov Olsson. Li knew this was his chance to make a name for himself outside of China, and he was determined not to blow it. Over the next several months, he did everything Ford demanded and more to prove that he was serious. Booth actually started to like him. Li was youthful, extroverted, and charismatic. And he was trying so hard to make everyone happy—Ford, the increasingly anxious Swedes, and the Chinese Communist Party.

It became apparent to Booth that Li was spending a huge amount of time, energy, and probably resources convincing the Chinese government that he was worthy of owning what would become China's first global automotive brand. During one meeting with Booth, Li got a call from Beijing. He excused himself, walked over to a corner of the room with his mobile, and spent the next ten minutes shouting into it and waving his hands. When he was finished, he slipped the telephone back into his pocket and returned to the table as though nothing had happened.

"Is everything okay?" Booth asked.

"Oh, yes," Li smiled.

Booth decided that Ford could do a lot worse than a man like Li. But there were still real concerns about selling Volvo to a Chinese company, and most of those concerns dealt with intellectual property. Many of Volvo's products included important proprietary technology that Ford also used in its own cars and trucks. Geely wanted it all. Ford said no. Geely relented, but Ford was still concerned it might take it anyway once it had the schematics. And Ford did not want to fight it out in the Chinese courts, which were notorious for their utter disregard for international patent law. David Leitch came up with a novel solution. He proposed that any disputes over intellectual property would be resolved outside of China through binding arbitration.

Once Geely agreed to that, it all came down to the details. Negotiations between Geely and Volvo's unions began in earnest after Ford formally announced that the Chinese automaker was its preferred bidder in October. As with Jaguar and Land Rover, Booth was the conscience of the sale, constantly raising questions about how Geely planned to deal with Volvo's employees. He also spent a lot of time dealing with the Swedish government, which bristled at the idea of such an iconic Swedish brand being sold to a Chinese company. But there really was no other option. A group of Swedish investors, the Jakob Consortium, tried to jump into the fray, as did a group of Americans led by former Ford executives, but neither of these groups could muster enough financing to make a serious bid. Geely still had not completed its own financing, but by the end of 2009 Ford was confident that it could. In December, Mulally announced that Ford hoped to sign a formal agreement with Geely in the first quarter of 2010 and close on the deal by the end of June.

✳   ✳   ✳

Ford's sales were back up in October even without government incentives, increasing 3 percent year-over-year. Ford had now gained market share in twelve of the last thirteen months. The industry as a whole was up, too, though not as much as Ford. The worst was over. The recovery would be slow, but the market was coming back. And not just in the United States. Ford continued to gain ground in Europe and South America. The company now had enough cash and enough confidence in the future to announce a $2.3 billion investment to expand production in Brazil. Ford was no longer just surviving. It was starting to grow.

The good news kept coming. November was up, too, with sales of the Ford Fusion leaping 54 percent after *Motor Trend* magazine named it "Car of the Year." European sales were up nearly 20 percent. December was Ford's best month since May 2008 in the United States. Sales were up a whopping 33 percent. Ford gained more than a point of market share in the United States in 2009—the company's first full-year gain since 1995. And 2010 was looking even better. The company announced that it would increase North American factory output to 550,000 vehicles in the first three months of 2010—58 percent more than the same period in 2009.

On December 2, Ford's shares closed above $9 for the first time in more than two years. Taking advantage of the rally, the company issued another $1 billion worth of new stock. Once again the market did not seem to mind. Three weeks later, the price passed $10. It was the first time since 2005 that Ford's shares had traded in the double digits.

That month, I had dinner with a small group of Wall Street financiers in Detroit. They represented the investment banks and private equity firms that, along with the American taxpayers and the UAW,* now owned the new General Motors. They were already frustrated with Ed Whitacre Jr., the man Washington had just tapped to lead the still-struggling automaker after firing former CFO Fritz Henderson, whom it had asked to replace Rick Wagoner less than nine months before.

"What they need is another Alan Mulally," one of the bankers opined, drawing vociferous agreements from the rest of the table.

It had become a common sentiment, both in Detroit and on Wall Street. But in Dearborn, Mulally and everyone else in the Glass House knew it was not that simple. Under his leadership, Ford's once-fratricidal executive corps had been transformed into a team, and that team had just saved the company from the biggest crisis in its long and difficult history.

Every December, Ford's board of directors hosted a dinner for the company's senior management. That December, Irv Hockaday toasted them all, invoking the memory of Henry V at Agincourt and quoting from the famous band-of-brothers speech that Shakespeare had him deliver before the English army, outnumbered six to one, faced the French onslaught and emerged victorious.

"Those are the kind of odds you guys have overcome," Hockaday said as he raised his glass.

A few weeks later, Ford reported its financial results for 2009: a full-year profit of $2.7 billion. Mulally had kept his word after all.

---

* The UAW became part owner of the new GM when it accepted stock in lieu of cash to cover a portion of its VEBA obligations.

CHAPTER 20

Proof Points

Wealth is nothing more or less than a tool to do things with. It is like the fuel that runs the furnace or the belt that runs the wheel—only a means to an end.

— HENRY FORD

On August 28, 2009, off-duty California Highway Patrol officer Mark Saylor, his wife, their thirteen-year-old daughter, and his wife's brother, Chris Lastrella, were traveling on State Route 125 near San Diego in a 2009 Lexus ES 350 when Saylor discovered that he could not stop the car. In fact, it was accelerating. As they passed the "End Freeway" sign going 120 miles per hour, Lastrella pleaded with a 911 dispatcher for help.

"Our accelerator's stuck!" he cried as the car literally ran out of road. "We're in trouble. There's no brake!"

A few seconds later, they were all dead. So was Toyota's once-unassailable reputation as the automobile industry's quality leader.

The Japanese automaker blamed the problem on faulty floor mats. On November 26, it recalled 4.2 million vehicles in the United States to address the problem. But crashes continued. On January 16, 2010, Toyota informed the National Highway Traffic Safety Administration that the real problem might be defective accelerator pedals. Five days later the company recalled another 2.3 million vehicles. Four days after that, the U.S. government ordered Toyota to stop selling the affected products until it could resolve the problem. A day later the automaker pulled eight of its most popular models from the market, including the bestselling Toyota Camry. But the scope of the problem continued to widen. It would become the largest automobile recall in U.S. history, even surpassing the Ford-Firestone fiasco. Investigators began looking at what Toyota knew and when. It soon emerged that the automaker had ignored mounting evidence of the problem for years. Toyota executives were called to Washington to explain and found themselves facing the same sort of grilling from Congress that the CEOs of the Detroit Three had endured back in 2008. With few products left to sell and its name plastered across the top of every newspaper in the land, Toyota's sales plummeted. And Ford Motor Company rushed in to fill the void.

* * *

As Toyota fell from grace, Ford was wowing the world's automotive press with the car Alan Mulally and Derrick Kuzak had been talking about since their first meeting in 2006.

The new Ford Focus was finally unveiled at the North American International Auto Show in Detroit on January 11, 2010. It had been only three years since Mulally made his own debut in Cobo Arena. There were no smoke machines this time, just Mulally's motto projected beneath an enormous Blue Oval: One Team. One Plan. One Goal. One Ford. And instead of a bland full-sized sedan, there was a sleek candy-red hatchback rotating in the spotlight.

"How beautiful and cool is our *new* Ford Focus?" shouted a triumphant Mulally, far more at ease in front of a stadium full of the world's automotive press than he had been in 2007. "To us, this is actually more than a car. Focus is the next great example of 'One Ford,' brought to life in steel, glass, and technology. Focus is proof of how we are changing as a company."

In addition to being the hottest small car ever to come out of Detroit, the new Focus was truly a global automobile, a latter-day Model T that would create economies of scale Henry Ford would have been proud of. Though the cars would be built at four plants on three continents, about 80 percent of their parts would be common worldwide—and 75 percent of those would come from the same suppliers.* In addition to the Focus itself, the underlying architecture

---

* There would be minor variations to account for regional tastes and local requirements.

would provide the foundation for at least ten different cars and cross-overs, ranging from a new global version of the C-Max crossover to the Focus Electric. A total of 2 million vehicles would be built off this same compact platform and sold around the world each year by 2012.

The compact segment was now the largest, accounting for one out of every four vehicles sold worldwide. The cost savings realized by globalizing development and production would allow Ford to capital-ize on this growing market and make big money off small cars. Instead of being known for its gas-guzzling trucks and sport utility vehicles, Ford would be known for its stylish compact cars and crossovers.

Even the usually sedate Kuzak was excited.

"It will make us globally competitive like never before," he averred.

There was no more poignant symbol of Ford's transformation than the old Michigan Truck Plant in Detroit's industrial suburb of Wayne. Ford had gutted the SUV factory that had once been its most profit-able plant in the world. The company had rechristened it the Michi-gan Assembly Plant, and it was spending more than $550 million to retool the factory to produce the new Focus and Focus Electric. A few days before the auto show, Ford Americas president Mark Fields led a group of journalists on a tour of the cavernous facility—a space so large, its far walls were lost in shadow.

"Just a year ago in this plant, we were producing Navigators and Expeditions. And one year from now, we're going to be producing the new Ford Focus," Fields said, his voice echoing off the bare concrete. "Our intent is to have a strong manufacturing presence here in the U.S."

Ford had crunched the numbers, and Fields proudly announced that the new American-made Focus was expected to turn a solid profit for the company. A few years earlier, that would have been impossible. But the labor agreements Ford had negotiated with the United Auto Workers in 2007 and 2009 had fundamentally altered the arithmetic. Mulally had promised Ron Gettelfinger and Bob King that he would build small cars in the United States if they would let him. Now he was making good on that pledge. The plan to shift U.S. production to Mexico had been round-filed.

The new Focus was not due to arrive in showrooms until 2011, but other new Fords were already available, such as the Fusion Hybrid, which had just been named "2010 North American Car of the Year," and the Transit Connect compact van, which won "Truck of the Year." Ford became one of the biggest beneficiaries of Toyota's troubles. Its sales soared 24 percent in the United States in January. February sales were up a stunning 43 percent, as were March's. And Ford was making more money off every vehicle it sold, thanks to lower incentives and higher margins.

*   *   *

None of this was lost on investors. Ford's stock price closed above $11 a share on January 6—the first time since 2005. It passed $12 on March 2. And the numbers just kept getting better. Ford made $2.1 billion in the first three months of 2010. Though the automobile market remained weak, each of Ford's business units—North America, South America, Europe, Asia-Pacific, and Ford Credit—posted operating profits that were substantially higher than a year before. The company's share of the U.S. market increased by two and a half percentage points, to 16.6 percent, Ford's largest quarterly share gain since 1977. Sales were up in the rest of the world, too. And Ford was no longer burning cash.

"We are encouraged by our continued progress this quarter, and remain focused on delivering the key aspects of our plan, which have not changed: Aggressively restructure to operate profitably at the current demand and the changing model mix, accelerate the development of a new products our customers want and value, finance our plan and continuously improve our balance sheet, and work together effectively as one team leveraging our global assets," Mulally told analysts and reporters when the results were announced on April 27. "The recovery is gradual, consumer confidence remains relatively weak, and the global auto industry continues to wrestle with excess capacity. But we are committed to remain absolutely focused on executing our business plan while developing even a better plan for the future."

Mulally's focus was now on improving Ford's balance sheet and beginning the long, slow march out of junk bond territory. The terms of

Ford's massive 2006 financing deal stipulated that all the assets it had pledged to secure those loans would be released once its revolving line of credit was paid off and two of the three major agencies restored the company's credit rating to investment grade. So Ford continued to chisel away at its debt, which was the one advantage General Motors and Chrysler still had over the Dearborn automaker. Those companies had shed theirs in bankruptcy court; Ford had to do it the old-fashioned way—by paying it back. Bill Ford was coming under increasing pressure from some of his relatives to restore dividends, but he backed Mulally's decision to focus on fixing the balance sheet first.

On April 6, Ford made a $3 billion payment to the revolver. On June 30, the automaker made a $3.8 billion payment ahead of schedule to the UAW's retiree health care trust, or VEBA. Ford also announced that it had reached an agreement with the union that would let it pay off the rest of its VEBA obligation with cash at a 5 percent discount. A year earlier, the company had convinced the UAW to let it cover half those obligations with stock. Now Ford had enough cash to make that unnecessary. Not that the UAW would have minded. The VEBA made a nice profit off the stock warrants Ford had already given the fund when it sold them at the end of March, netting $1.8 billion for union retirees.

Current employees were also sharing in Ford's success. Ford restored profit sharing with its U.S. factory workers in January, writing each of its approximately 43,000 UAW-represented employees a check for $450. The automaker also lifted a freeze on merit pay increases for salaried workers and began restoring some of the benefits that they had given up in the depths of the crisis.

Dealers were also benefiting from Ford's turnaround. In 2009, their average profit in the United States was fifteen times higher than it was in 2008. It was a poignant contrast to the hundreds of GM and Chrysler dealers fighting to get their franchises back, as well as to the Toyota dealers whose mechanics were working around the clock to replace accelerator pedals.

Mulally was not doing too bad, either. In March, Ford revealed that his compensation for 2009 totaled almost $18 million in cash, stock, and stock options. Even Bill Ford was finally getting paid. Five years after he gave up all compensation, it was announced that the company's executive chairman would receive $4 million in cash and more than $11 million worth of stock options. He immediately donated $1 million of that to a college scholarship fund for the children of Ford employees.

*   *   *

Just as Mulally had promised his team back in 2006, the ride back up was turning out to be a lot of fun. All their hard work was finally paying off. Each week, each month, each quarter was better than the last. Instead of fighting to survive, they were now playing to win. Ford's quality ratings were the highest of any nonluxury brand. Ford no longer had to discount its products in order to convince buyers to test-drive one; customers were now willing to pay more for a car that had a Blue Oval on the grille. And new ones were arriving in dealer showrooms at one of the fastest rates in the industry.

On July 26, Mulally pulled the wraps off the all-new Ford Explorer in New York City's Herald Square, which Ford had filled with dirt and pine trees for the occasion. This reinvention of Ford's bread-and-butter SUV got 30 percent better fuel economy than the old Explorer and cost $1,000 less. Just like Henry Ford a century before, Mulally had figured out how to make Ford's products more efficiently and was passing the savings on to consumers.

The company was in growth mode again. In the first six months of 2010, Ford announced billions of dollars' worth of new investments in Asia, Africa, Europe, South America, and the United States. These were all about delivering on Mulally's vision of a more balanced global footprint for the company—one that would end its long dependence on the North American market. The world was changing. The United States was emerging from the Great Recession, but it now seemed unlikely to reclaim its former economic supremacy. Ford's future lay elsewhere.

*   *   *

With the problems at home largely fixed and Ford's North American business restored to profitability, Asia became Mulally's top priority. China and India were fast becoming the center of a new economic order, but Ford had been late to the game in both countries and was still struggling to catch up.

Mulally decided it was time to export his revolution. At the end of 2009, he tapped Joe Hinrichs to lead a top-to-bottom transformation of Ford's Asia-Pacific group modeled after the turnaround in North America. The young manufacturing chief replaced the aging John Parker, who had done little to make up for the years of mismanagement that preceded him. It was just the sort of opportunity the ambitious Hinrichs had been waiting for, and he threw himself into it with his customary zeal. He flew back and forth between Dearborn and Shanghai, figuring out what Ford needed in China, then returning to World Headquarters to lobby for it in person.

China was now the world's second-largest automobile market, and Ford had neglected it for too long. The first problem Hinrichs identified was a lack of product. The company was doing well in the segments it competed in, but Ford sold only five models in China. He put together a plan to bring more than a dozen new vehicles to market. He ordered a major expansion of Ford's manufacturing base in the country, breaking ground on two new assembly plants and an engine factory. He also began drawing up plans for a new transmission plant. Finally, Hinrichs launched an aggressive expansion of Ford's Chinese dealer network, adding a hundred more stores—mostly in smaller cities and inland provinces where demand was growing.

In March, Alan Mulally arrived to sprinkle his pixie dust on unsuspecting Chinese customers. When Harriet Luo arrived at the Dongchang Ford dealership in Shanghai to pick up her new blue Focus, Mulally was waiting there with the keys and a hug. The poor woman was almost speechless.

"This is totally beyond my expectations," she stammered.

Ford's share of the Chinese market was just 2.6 percent. Volkswagen was the market leader with 13 percent, and General Motors came in second with an even 9 percent. Even Suzuki sold more cars in China than Ford did. But Mulally was undaunted, as usual.

"Now we are here," he declared at the Dongchang dealership. "I have made [Asia] the highest priority for Ford."

India was next on Ford's to-do list. It was a challenging market where Ford had to compete with some of the cheapest automobiles in the world. Three-wheelers were still considered an attractive transportation option by many middle-class consumers. So Ford took the tooling for the old Fiesta that had just been retired, moved it to a factory in Chennai, slapped a fresh face on it, slashed the price to about $7,700, and reintroduced it as the Ford Figo. It was a breakout success, racked up more awards than any other car in the market, and nearly tripled Ford's sales in India by the end of 2010.

Mulally was there for the launch, being serenaded by sitars, decked out in floral garlands and anointed with vermilion. During the trip, he also took time to address more than 5,000 Ford of India employees.

"Ford India rocks!" he declared to the startled crowd, which was unaccustomed to this sort of informality. "It could not be going better! That's my report!"

Mulally left them smiling in his wake.

Europe was also posing new challenges for Ford. The end of scrappage programs across the region brought a decline in sales, followed by increasingly fierce competition that saw most automakers stacking ever-larger piles of cash on the hoods of their cars to lure buyers. Unlike in the United States, the economic crisis had not brought a fundamental restructuring of the automobile industry there. In fact, the help manufacturers had received from the various European governments during the downturn was contingent on them keeping their plants open and workers employed. As a result, all of the automakers—including Ford—emerged from the Great Recession with too much capacity and too few customers.

By April, Ford's sales in Europe were beginning to slip. At Mulally's insistence, Ford tried to resist joining the incentive war even though that meant ceding market share to rival brands. He knew enough of Ford's history by now to understand the role incentives had played in bringing down the Big Three in the United States. They undermined resale values, cheapened the brand image, and ate into profits. But the pricing pressure in Europe would prove impossible to resist.

Mulally decided it was time for a change there as well. He gave Joe Hinrichs' old job to European Group president John Fleming and promoted Volvo chief Stephen Odell to chairman and CEO of Ford of Europe once the Volvo deal closed.* Mulally had been impressed with Odell's tough-love approach to the Swedish brand. He had cut thousands of jobs in a socialist country and gotten away with it. More important, Odell had almost returned Volvo to profitability by the time Ford handed the keys to the Chinese.

On March 28, Ford had reached a definitive agreement to sell Volvo to China's Geely for $1.8 billion. It was less than half of what Mulally had hoped to get for the brand, but even this amount proved to be a stretch. In the end Geely was barely able to come up with enough cash to close the deal. Ford accepted a $200 million note in order to leave the new owner with enough money in the bank to keep Volvo running. The important thing, at least as far as Mulally was concerned, was that Ford had eliminated its last major distraction. When the Volvo deal closed on August 2, all of the foreign brands were gone. Most of Ford's stake in Mazda was, too, and the company would sell another 7.5 percent before the year was finished.† That left one more name on Mulally's hit list: Mercury.

*   *   *

On June 2, Ford summoned reporters to a hastily organized press conference at the Product Development Center in Dearborn. Rumors were once again circulating among dealers that Mercury's demise was imminent. This time the rumors were true. Mark Fields explained the rationale behind Ford's decision to kill the seventy-two-year-old brand. Mercury sales were declining and now accounted for less than 1 percent of the U.S. market. Ford was not spending much on the brand, but what it was could be better spent on Ford's luxury marque.

---

* With Volvo gone, there was no longer a need for a European Group and responsibility for the entire region reverted to Ford of Europe.
† That deal, which reduced Ford's stake in the Japanese company to just 3.5 percent, was announced on November 18, 2010. Ford made about $372 million from the sale.

"We are very proud of [Mercury's] history, but we are now looking forward," Fields said. "We've made a lot of progress with the Ford brand. Now's the time to do that with Lincoln."

Privately, Ford executives acknowledged that the only reason they had kept Mercury alive for this long was that the company lacked the resources to revive Lincoln. Jim Farley had been plotting a top-to-bottom transformation of Lincoln ever since he was hired away from Toyota's Lexus division in 2007. Now he finally had the money to do it. His goal was as ambitious as any Ford had set. Having bested Toyota on the quality front, Farley wanted to out-Lexus Lexus in the luxury segment. Ford began spending big on a major makeover of its luxury lineup. But Farley knew that new products would not be enough. Toyota had entire assembly lines dedicated to Lexus production where cars were put together to the most exacting standards in the industry. Lincoln was too small for its own factories, so Ford would have to raise the bar at its existing plants. It would also have to convince dealers to invest in their showrooms. Farley wanted them to exude luxury, just like the products he planned to fill them with.

Ford's previous attempts to restore Lincoln's lost luster had made little headway. Under Mulally, the brand's products had improved. Some of them, like the Lincoln MKS sedan and MKT crossover, could already compete with the best in the world in terms of styling and features. But they were overpriced—particularly for a brand that still had a lot of explaining to do. Mulally was still not convinced that Ford needed anything but the Blue Oval, but he was willing to give Farley one more shot at Lincoln.

* * *

On July 23, the company reported earnings of $2.6 billion for the second three months of 2010—its best quarter since 2004. Ford's stock closed above $13 a share four days later. But some on Wall Street began to suspect that they were being played. Quarter after quarter, the company was beating analysts' estimates. Some were now wondering if Ford was purposely managing down expectations so that it could exceed them. The truth was that everyone inside Ford was just as surprised. Each quarter was coming in ahead of the company's projections. At lower levels of the company, there may have been some fudging going on: Some regional managers had figured out that, in Mulally's Ford, it was better to lowball their estimates than risk being held accountable for missing their targets. That was the downside of his insistence on accountability. But after years of overpromising and underdelivering, it was better for Ford to err on the side of restraint.

The changes Mulally had made to Ford's culture were no longer limited to the upper echelons of the organization. At each level of the company, managers tried to emulate his inclusive and data-driven approach. Every department now held its own weekly BPR meeting, and similar sessions were held regularly at the national and regional level. Morale soared to an all-time high as Ford employees saw their work recognized and found managers increasingly willing to listen to their ideas and concerns. Reporters noticed the change, too. Ford had stopped leaking.

The press still had plenty to write about, though.

Ford's success had made its CEO a celebrity. On January 15, Mulally was named "Industry Leader of 2009" by the Automotive Hall of Fame, which called him "the overwhelming and obvious choice." *Automobile* magazine had already named Mulally "2010 Man of the Year." *Barron's* added him to its annual list of the thirty most-respected CEOs in the world, while *Automotive News* lauded him as "Industry Leader of the Year." Mulally was voted "Businessperson of the Year" by the readers of *Fortune* and "CEO of the Year" by those who followed *MarketWatch.* The *Detroit News* named him "Michiganian of the Year." Even the president of the United States jumped on the Mulally bandwagon, naming Ford's CEO to his Export Council on July 7.

But Mulally's biggest fan was Jim Cramer, host of CNBC's *Mad Money.*

"[Mulally] is the greatest turnaround artist of all time—not *our* time, *all* time," the hyperactive host declared on June 30. "The guy has already worked his turnaround magic at Boeing, and now at Ford he's taken a laggard and turned it into an industry leader!"

Cramer did not stop there. He had an enormous hundred-dollar bill printed with Mulally's mug replacing Benjamin Franklin's and emblazoned with the motto "In Mulally We Trust." When he was done using it on his show, Cramer sent it to Mulally, who displayed it proudly in his office.

On August 4, Mulally turned sixty-five—the unofficial retirement age at Ford. In Dearborn, few executives ever made it that far. But Mulally insisted that he was not going anywhere yet. Though he had brought Ford back from the brink in the middle of the most serious crisis to confront the automobile industry in eighty years, his work in Dearborn was not yet finished. Mulally still wanted to redeem Ford's mortgaged assets. And once he had done that, he wanted to give the Ford family and the rest of the company's shareholders their dividends back.

Bill Ford seemed inclined to let him.

"He's staying until 2025," the executive chairman joked when asked if he had thought about a successor.

With all the press Mulally was getting, it was the sort of joke Ford found himself making a lot. But his laughter masked some real concerns about who would replace the man some were beginning to regard as one of the greatest CEOs ever.

Bill Ford saw no reason to bring in another outsider. He was convinced that each of the company's top executives had internalized Mulally's revolution and made his precepts their own. Because of Mulally's matrix organization and Thursday-morning BPR meetings, they each knew everything there was to know about every aspect of the business. Vice President of Human Resources Felicia Fields could rattle off the names of the three bestselling Ford cars in China just as surely as quality czar Bennie Fowler could detail the latest debt action.

By the end of 2010, it was Mark Fields' job to lose. Mulally initially had high hopes for Jim Farley, but the marketing maven had turned out to be something of a mad scientist—a true genius who was capable of coming up with big ideas, but who had demonstrated some serious shortcomings in the people-skills department. Mulally also saw a lot of potential in Joe Hinrichs, but he was a generation behind Fields. There was still time for him to hone his skills in Asia. More important, Bill Ford himself made no secret of the fact that his money was on Fields. The chairman was impressed with the way Mark Fields had swallowed his anger at being upstaged by Mulally, embraced his cultural revolution, and become his keenest student. Ford was equally impressed with Fields' loyalty.

"It's my decision," Ford reminded me when I asked about it.

A much bigger concern for Bill Ford was complacency. He had seen Ford become a victim of its own success before, and he was determined to break that cycle.

"It's something that I think about all the time," he confided. "How do we not go back to where we were? How do we stay lean and hungry? And how do we continue to foster innovation? A lot of that does fall to me. I am the institutional memory around here."

✳   ✳   ✳

In September 2010, Alan Mulally marked his fourth anniversary at Ford Motor Company. With the automobile sales slowly recovering around the world and the worst of the supplier crisis subsiding, there was no longer a need for daily meetings. But Mulally and his team still gathered every Thursday in the Thunderbird Room for their weekly BPR and SAR meetings. By now the entire process had been refined to the point of routine.

The first meeting in September was typical. The team convened at 7 A.M. sharp, taking their places at the round table. There were now fourteen black leather executive chairs—one for each of the regular attendees: Chief Financial Officer Lewis Booth, President of the Americas Mark Fields, Ford Credit CEO Mike Bannister, Vice President of Global Product Development Derrick Kuzak, Vice President of Global Manufacturing and Labor Affairs John Fleming, Vice President of Global Purchasing Tony Brown, Vice President of Quality Bennie Fowler, Vice President of Sustainability, Environment and Safety Engineering Sue Cischke, Chief Information Officer Nick Smither, Vice President of Human Resources and Corporate Services Felicia Fields, General Counsel David Leitch, Vice President of Global Marketing, Sales and Service Jim Farley, Vice President of

Communications Ray Day, and, of course, Mulally himself.* He took
his usual seat directly opposite the big projection screen. Joe Hinrichs was at Ford's new Asian headquarters in Shanghai but participated through the company's teleconferencing system. Steve Odell
did the same from Cologne, while Vice President of Government and
Community Relations Ziad Ojakli tuned in from Washington. There
were chairs for each of them off to the side for the times they were
present in Dearborn.

Thirty more utilitarian chairs lined the perimeter of the room—ten
on each wall, except for the western one, which was dominated by
the projection screen. These were for guests. Each executive was allowed to invite a couple of guests to each meeting. A few were there
because they needed to hear what was being discussed, but for most
it was a big honor—the reward for some special service or outstanding achievement. There were mid-level managers, engineers, even
a factory worker. Most looked nervous and uncomfortable as they
filed into the Thunderbird Room, but Mulally quickly put them at
ease.

"We're glad you're here," he said with a big smile. "We hope you
enjoy the meeting, and we'd also like to hear what you think of the
meeting at the end."

The guests served two important purposes. First, they were expected to take what they learned back to their workplaces, allowing
that information and the experience of the BPR process to cascade
down through the organization. Second, Mulally believed their presence kept everyone on their best behavior, just as the documentary
film cameras had at Boeing on the 777 program.

Once everyone was seated, Mulally called for the first slide. There
were now 320 of them, though not every slide was shown every week.
Many of them rotated according to a fixed schedule. Mulally went
first, going over the agenda, explaining the point of the meeting to the

---

* All of these leaders had a designated representative who would attend the
meeting in their place if they were sick, on vacation, or traveling. If Mulally was
unable to attend, Booth filled in for him and led the meeting.

guests and providing his own high-level assessment of the state of the company.

"On plan," it read this week. "No change."

Mulally went over the current cash, sales, revenue, and profit projections for the next five years. They all showed steady increases.

"It's going up because we're making products and services that people want and value, using less time and resources than the competition," Mulally explained. "That creates value for the company and all its stakeholders."

Then he went over the current business environment, listing geopolitical developments that might impact Ford, looking at the state of the global economy, energy issues, environmental concerns, labor issues, and top-level news about Ford's competitors. He went over the two pie charts showing the regional distribution of Ford's business between the Americas, Europe, and Asia and its split between small, medium, and large vehicles. These were still not evenly divided into thirds, but they were getting more balanced all the time. Mulally reminded everyone that this was the goal. He also went over the four-point plan again, just in case anyone had forgotten it. Mulally closed by listing the issues that would be discussed in that day's SAR meeting.

Booth was up next. He presented a more detailed report on the company's finances. Things were looking good for the third quarter, and Ford's cash and debt would be close to parity by the end of the year. Booth also went over the latest data from Ellen Hughes-Cromwick. The global economy continued to strengthen, albeit slowly. The car and truck market in the United States was improving, too, though demand for new vehicles remained well below historic highs. The four business unit leaders—Bannister, Fields, Hinrichs, and Odell—were each given ten minutes to go over their slides, which covered the business environment in their areas, their financial forecasts, and their progress against the plan. When they were done, the function leaders each got five minutes to present an overview of the latest data from their departments. The color-coding system was now well understood and employed by everyone. There was a lot more green these days, but still some red and yellow, too. That was okay; as long as problems were highlighted, the team could deal with them.

When it was over, Mulally summed things up and asked if there were any more issues that needed to be added to the SAR agenda. He closed the meeting by going around the room and asking the guests what they thought of the proceedings. Most said they were reassured to see that everything they had heard about honesty and openness and working together was real.

So were the results. On October 26, Ford posted another $1.7 billion profit for July, August, and September. The company also announced that it would pay off the rest of the money it owed to the UAW's VEBA trust. Ford was now completely absolved of all responsibility for hourly-retiree health care in the United States. One of the most crushing burdens in business history had been lifted from its shoulders. No one inside Ford had ever imagined it would be paid off so quickly.

Neither had anyone on Wall Street. Ford's stock was now trading north of $14 a share. It broke $15 on November 3 and closed above $16 two days later. By the end of 2010, it was flirting with $17. The lucky few who had purchased Ford's stock when it bottomed out at $1.01 on November 20, 2008, had now made a nearly 1,600 percent return on their investment in just two years—assuming they were smart enough to hold on to it. And the price would go even higher.

On December 15, Morningstar Equity Research became the first agency to raise Ford's credit rating back to investment grade. It was not one of the Big Three agencies, but they had all raised their ratings for Ford, too, and set its outlook to "positive." The company continued to pay back the money it had borrowed. Booth, Treasurer Neil Schloss, and the rest of the Ford finance team were smiling when Mulally passed them in the hall on the twelfth floor of World Headquarters at the end of December. And with good reason. Ford had cut its automotive debt almost in half during the year, paying off $14.5 billion. It ended the year with more cash than debt.

"*Great* job, guys!" Mulally exclaimed, giving them an emphatic thumbs-up. "*Fabulous!*"

* * *

O ver the past twelve months, Ford had invested billions around the world. In the United States, the company was hiring again—luring engineers to Dearborn from places like Silicon Valley and insourcing factory jobs that had been outsourced to foreign suppliers years earlier. Ford had passed a still-struggling Toyota to reclaim its historic position as America's number-two automaker, and it now topped the list of car companies that suppliers most wanted to do business with.

The changes Mulally had wrought since his first day at World Headquarters went far beyond what anyone—including Bill Ford—had expected. Ford had been transformed from a company clinging to life on the strength of a few big trucks and SUVs to one that now made money on everything from subcompacts to heavy-duty pickups. Instead of lagging behind the rest of the industry, Ford was now a leader in technology, design, quality, and fuel economy. Farley and Day had succeeded in separating Ford from GM and Chrysler. Toyota's own television ads now compared its cars to Fords instead of Hondas, proof that the Japanese giant now viewed Ford as a direct competitor. And Ford's own consumer clinics now revealed that consumers were actually willing to pay more for a car with a Blue Oval.

But the biggest changes were those that had taken place inside the Glass House. Ford's executives no longer spent their days plotting one another's demise or defending their turf. Instead they spent their time working together to ensure the company's continued success. They offered one another help and sought help when they needed it themselves. They measured their success not by personal victories, but by their progress against Mulally's plan.

Ford still faced challenges, both at home and abroad. In Europe, it was now slogging it out for share with the rest of the world's automakers, cutting prices to keep customers from defecting to other brands. In the United States, its voice-controlled Sync system was coming under fire from federal officials who worried it was too distracting to drivers. Sync was now part of a much more cutting-edge system that replaced many of the old analog dials and buttons on Ford dashboards with customizable computer screens and touch-sensitive controls. These efforts to keep up with the consumer electronics industry continued to attract younger buyers to the Ford brand, but they were causing real problems for older motorists who found the new interfaces cluttered and confusing. Analysts were tired of getting beaten by Ford and began to inflate their profit estimates. Though still making more money every quarter, Ford was now falling short of their marks on occasion. The company's stock took a beating whenever it did. But these were not existential crises. They were the sorts of problems every corporation dealt with all the time.

On January 28, 2011, Ford posted a full-year profit of $6.6 billion for 2010. It was the most money the company had made in more than a decade. Alan Mulally and his team had not just saved an American icon; they had made Ford Motor Company the most profitable automaker in the world.

CHAPTER 21

The Road Ahead

The only history that is worth a tinker's damn is the history we make today.

— HENRY FORD

The tidal wave that overwhelmed the American automobile industry in 2008 had been building for decades. Detroit was a fault line straining under the colliding forces of foreign competition and legacy costs, groaning under the weight of overly generous union contracts, chronic mismanagement, and insular thinking. Ford Motor Company is where the fault failed first. Fortunately, the Dearborn automaker could still do something about it when it did. Despite their persistent insistence that they were well ahead of Ford in their own turnarounds, General Motors and Chrysler were actually slower to appreciate the full magnitude of the impending crisis and the full extent of their own contributions to it. By the time they did, it was too late. The credit markets were closed and anyone with skills necessary to save a major automobile manufacturer no longer wanted anything to do with Detroit. But those who attribute Ford's turnaround to luck or timing ignore two important facts. First, Alan Mulally had already done this before at Boeing. Second, Ford itself had done it before in Europe and South America.

Bill Ford and Don Leclair did not begin putting together the mammoth financing package that kept Ford solvent through the lean months of 2008 because they were lucky. They did so because they knew that saving Ford would require a huge amount of cash and could see that the days of easy credit were coming to an end. Nor did the Dearborn automaker win over Toyota customers just because the Japanese giant stumbled and fumbled its stellar reputation, but because Ford's own vehicles had improved so much that they now represented an attractive alternative. The collapse of Chrysler and GM, Toyota's quality crisis, and the March 2011 earthquake and tsunami, which brought the entire Japanese automobile industry to its knees, certainly created huge opportunities for Ford. But the company was able to take advantage of them only because it already had the products, the resources, and the strategy in place to do so. If any of these had occurred five years earlier they might have helped, but Ford would still be a stumbling dinosaur mired in its own history.

There are some who will point to the loans Ford received from the U.S. Department of Energy and the money it borrowed from the U.S. Federal Reserve and say the company did take taxpayer dollars. This is true, but in this sense, so did the rest of the major automakers—and not just the American companies. Japanese and German manufacturers benefited from these programs as well, in addition to receiving support from their own governments. But these were loan programs set up to address systemic problems beyond these companies' control. What made Ford different from GM and Chrysler was that the U.S. government actually bailed those companies out—not just with loans, but with direct financial aid that they needed merely to keep the lights on. Both of those automakers died on the operating table and were revived by Washington. Ford saved itself.

It is also easy, and not necessarily incorrect, to say that Alan Mulally saved Ford Motor Company. But the truth is more complicated than that. One could just as easily say that Bill Ford saved the company by having the humility and self-awareness to step aside and make way for someone who could do what he had been unable to, or point out that Mark Fields put together the Way Forward plan that provided the framework for Mulally's own restructuring of Ford's North American automotive operations, or credit Don Leclair for having the foresight to pursue the financing package that paid for it all. All of these things are also true. Ford was not saved because a hero rode into town on a white horse. But if he had not, Ford would not be here today. Certainly not the proud, profitable, and independent automaker that has become a symbol of American resilience and resourcefulness for the second time in a century.

While many of the pieces of Ford's turnaround were already in place, the company's own culture was preventing them from being implemented with the speed and scope necessary to effect real change. Fields' plan may have been fundamentally sound, but it did not go far enough fast enough, and he lacked the gravitas and experience necessary to make it work. Derrick Kuzak knew what needed to be done to transform Ford into a world-class automobile manufacturer that took full advantage of its design and engineering resources, and he was already pushing the company in the right direction with the new Global Product Development System. But Ford would have run out of time and money before it got to where it needed to be if Mulally had not been there to put the pedal to the metal. Leclair understood how precarious Ford's position had become and had put together a financing plan to buy the company enough time to fix itself, but he never could have sold it to Wall Street. The big banks no longer trusted anyone from Dearborn. Bennie Fowler was making progress on quality in North America, Tony Brown was trying to make things right with the suppliers, and Ford's labor team—Joe Laymon, Joe Hinrichs, and Marty Mulloy—were making real progress with the United Auto Workers. But all their efforts were still stuck in the muck of infighting and turf warfare that had held the company back for so long. No one inside the Glass House could figure out how to extricate themselves or the company from this miasma, nor could they bring themselves to take a hard and unflinching look at the full gamut of problems Ford faced. At best they were just trying to stop the bleeding.

Mulally ripped off the bandage, cauterized the wound, and cured the disease. Only an outsider could do that. But not just any outsider: It had to be someone who understood the complexities of global manufacturing, labor relations, and heavily engineered products. Chrysler's experience with former Home Depot CEO Robert Nardelli was a cautionary tale about the perils of putting someone with no manufacturing experience behind the wheel of major automobile company. Nardelli believed he could switch suppliers of stamped steel components as easily as he had once changed plywood vendors. He was wrong, and his mistake created major problems not only for

Chrysler, but for a number of other automobile manufacturers as well—including Ford.

Mulally knew enough to avoid such blunders. He combined in one person an exceptional engineering mind with exceptional financial acumen. His experience as an aeronautical engineer taught him the importance of shedding weight and streamlining the edges to make planes lighter and faster. He applied that same approach to the automotive business and made Ford soar. Mulally also brought a relentless determination to Dearborn that had been lacking at the top of the Glass House. He had not been nursed on the mythology of the American automobile industry. Ford's executives, like those at General Motors and Chrysler, could not see beyond their own shared experience. The cyclical nature of the business was internalized. They took it for granted that every success would be followed by failure. It became a convenient excuse. They tinkered with the spark plugs and tightened the belts because none of them believed it was possible to tear apart the entire motor and rebuild it.

But that is exactly what Mulally did—and he got all of them to help him do it. His disciplined approach cut through the company's caustic culture and forced everyone to march in the same direction. He was tough when he had to be, but Mulally's primary means of motivation was a shared vision—a vision of what Ford had been and could be again. He taught the other executives how to make decisions based on data instead of boardroom politics. And once he had, most of the decisions that saved Ford were made by the team as a whole.

"We were not organized for success," Chief Technical Officer Paul Mascarenas told me. "Alan changed that with One Ford."

*   *   *

Other men and women have taken broken corporations, fixed their flaws, and set them back on the road to success, but few have had as good a time doing it as Mulally. He led Ford through one of the most painful and far-reaching restructurings ever and guided it through the global conflagration that was the Great Recession with the same goofy grin on his face that he had when he walked in the door. I once asked his media handler, Karen Hampton, if she had ever seen him stressed. She laughed, and told me about the day in 2008 when she had come into Mulally's office and found him staring out the window, squeezing a stress ball.

"Oh no!" she exclaimed, pointing to the rubber ball. "If you're stressed, we must be dead!"

Mulally started laughing.

"Don't worry," he said. "I hurt my wrist playing tennis."

Once Mulally came up with his plan, he never doubted it would succeed. From the start, he evinced an almost religious conviction in its four points. It was a belief born of an engineer's faith in numbers.

"The data says, if you take these actions it'll work," Mulally said when asked how he could be so certain, even in the midst of a crisis that was toppling his competitors. "Running a business is a design job. You need a point of view about the future, a really good plan to deliver that future, and then *relentless* implementation."

Alan Mulally has now saved not one, but two American industrial giants. His success at Boeing alone would have been enough to ensure his place in the annals of American business history. With the turnaround of Ford added to his list of credits, many would rank him among the greatest CEOs ever.

Mulally's serial success also proves that his unique approach to management—the weekly meetings, devotion to data, and emphasis on working together—is portable. Mulally always believed that. He used the same system to raise his family and run his tennis club. Now he is more certain than ever that the Mulally method is as applicable to small nonprofits as it is to major multinational corporations.

"What I have learned is the power of a compelling vision, a comprehensive strategy, a relentless implementation process, and talented people working together based on those commitments," he told me during our last interview for this book, in May 2011. "We laid out a plan, and for four and a half years, we have been relentlessly implementing that plan."

That meant dealing with reality, no matter how harsh it might be. It meant sowing the seeds of future growth even as the company struggled to make it to tomorrow. And it meant staying the course, no matter how difficult that became.

"You've got to trust the process. You need to trust and nurture your emotional resilience," he said. "Do you have a point of view about the future? Check. Is it still the right vision today? Check. Do you have a comprehensive plan to deliver that? Check. If you get skilled and motivated people working together through this process, you're going to figure it out. But you've got to trust it."

The leader's job is to remind people of that vision, make sure they stick to the process, and keep them working together.

"Working together always works. It *always* works," Mulally stressed. "Everybody has to be on the team. They have to be interdependent with each other."

* * *

At Ford, the ultimate interdependency was the one that existed between Mulally and the man whose name was on the side of the building. He and Bill Ford made a great team. Mulally had the business and leadership skills that Ford lacked. Ford understood the history of his company and knew what it needed to do to save itself. But Ford did not spend a lot of time telling Mulally what to do. If his CEO had concerns, he listened to them and handed them back as questions. Most of the time, Mulally was just looking for someone to validate what he already believed. Ford helped him with the board, too, offering advice about when to pitch ideas and how to sell them. And of course, he kept the family out of Mulally's way.

The Ford family as a whole deserves a great deal of credit for keeping its faith in the company through the biggest crisis in its long history. It was the Fords' determination not to sell out that kept the board of directors from moving forward with "other options." Their continuing control of Ford through their supervoting Class B shares is much maligned, but regular investors would have abandoned the company long ago and left it for the bankruptcy attorneys to pick apart. The Fords brought stability and a long-term view that other corporations secretly envied.

"I am very proud of the family and our board. They hung together through an almost impossibly difficult time, where everything that they were picking up and reading every day was worse than the prior day," Bill Ford told me. "Every indicator was that this company was not going to make it. Our board and our family refused to accept that. They said, 'If that's true, we're going to go down swinging.' And that was certainly my thinking."

Bill Ford's own substantial contributions to the company's turn-around have often been lost in the glare of the spotlight that shined so brightly on Alan Mulally. If the great-grandson of Henry Ford had not stood up and taken back his company, Jacques Nasser would have surely run it into the ground. And while he could not bring himself to cut deeply enough, Ford began the difficult and painful process of downsizing his company. He also understood the primacy of product. He personally approved many of the cars and crossovers that would become synonymous with Ford's turnaround, including the Ford Fusion, Edge, and Escape Hybrid. And Bill Ford not only okayed Leclair's borrowing plan, but also convinced the board and the family to mortgage the entire company to secure those loans. Without his dogged determination to preserve the Ford legacy—not just for his family, but also for Ford's employees, its shareholders, and the nation as a whole—Ford's story might have had a very different ending. It was not just Bill Ford's willingness to step aside and make way for Mulally that helped save the company. It was also his unceasing effort to give him the time, the space, and the resources he needed for his revolution to succeed. Without that, Mulally may well have become just another victim of a company and a culture that seemed impervious to change.

✳   ✳   ✳

I once asked a group of Wall Street bankers what they thought the biggest threat to Ford's future was, now that the company had turned the corner. Was it the ongoing instability of its suppliers, the increasing price pressure in Europe, or the threat of a second Asian invasion from China? Before I could even finish listing all the risks, a guy from BlackRock cut me off.

"The biggest threat to Ford Motor Company is that Alan Mulally steps off the curb tomorrow and gets nailed by a bus," he said.

"Yep," the others agreed. "That's it. They can manage everything else."

That was at the end of 2009. Concern about the end of Mulally's tenure at Ford would increase as the months went by. Those concerns became all the more pressing after he turned sixty-five in 2010. By 2011, hardly a press conference went by without someone asking Mulally when he planned to retire.

"I haven't thought about that at all," he insisted when reporters pressed him on that point after the company's annual shareholders meeting in May.

But everyone knew the clock was ticking. Few outside the company saw an obvious successor inside the Glass House, and many industry observers openly doubted whether the changes Mulally made in Dearborn could endure once he had left the building. Many Ford employees shared these concerns. The questions of when Mulally would leave and who would replace him were enough to make any room in Dearborn fall silent.

The ultimate test of Mulally's revolution will be its ability to endure his absence. Boeing has suffered major setbacks since Mulally left Seattle in 2006. Insiders say that is because his successors have failed to maintain the processes Mulally put in place to guarantee success. When asked if the same thing could happen at Ford, Mulally says simply that he has given Ford the tools it needs to prosper. What the company does with them after he retires is beyond his control. Ford's history is a long list of stunning successes followed by epic failures, of against-all-odds comebacks that turn into retreats back into mediocrity and mismanagement. But there are important differences this time that augur well for Ford's future.

Many of Ford's previous comebacks were based on breakout hits like the Model A, the Mustang, and the Taurus. Mulally's plan was predicated on a sweeping transformation of Ford's entire product portfolio. It was also about changing the way the company designed and built its cars and trucks. Henry Ford used mass production to cut costs and boost efficiency, then passed the savings on to consumers.

Mulally and his team globalized product development, shared platforms, and introduced new vehicles that looked better, drove better,
and cost less than the ones they replaced.

Ford's earlier recoveries were driven by strong leaders who too
often became the objects of sycophantic devotion and slavish obei-
sance. These men inevitably became so concerned with preserving
their power and positions that they drove away other talented executives or pitted them against one another in order to prevent a worthy
successor from rising to the top. A cult of personality certainly developed around Mulally, too. Men and women throughout the company would rise to their feet and cheer when he walked into a room.
They would blush when he hugged them in the hall and shyly ask
for autographs. They would thank him with quavering voices at town
hall meetings for saving the company and their jobs. But for all that,
Mulally himself never ceased talking about the team. He constantly
thrust forward other executives at press conferences, praising their
contributions to Ford's turnaround and making sure they got a share
of the credit for it. Away from the public eye, he was constantly pushing his subordinates to share in the decision-making process and lead
their own divisions the same way he led Ford as a whole.

But the biggest and most important difference between Mulally
and his predecessors is that he attacked the root of the problem:
Ford's corporate culture. He took a sledgehammer to the silos that
had divided the company into warring fiefdoms for generations. He
forced everyone to stare reality in the face without flinching or turning away. It was not easy, nor instantaneous, but in the middle of a
truly existential crisis, Ford's executives finally stopped making decisions based on what was best for their own careers and started trying to figure out what was best for the company as a whole. That was
something that had never happened before in Dearborn, and it was
the key to Ford's phenomenal resurgence. But only time will tell if
Mulally has actually cured the disease or simply driven it back into
remission.

✸   ✸   ✸

In 2011, at least, there was no evidence of the complacency that inevitably followed earlier rebounds in Dearborn. Instead of resting on their laurels, Mulally and his team were still toiling to improve Ford's balance sheet, raise its credit rating, redeem the Blue Oval, and restore dividends. The stalled recovery in the United States and new economic problems abroad meant none of these things would come easy. And there were still bigger goals beyond those. Ford was now competing to stand beside companies like Toyota and Volkswagen at the forefront of the global automotive industry. In June 2011, Mulally vowed to double sales worldwide by 2015.

"Keep your foot on the gas!" became his constant refrain.

Ford's aggressive growth strategy is not without its risks. Toyota's problems began when it decided to challenge General Motors for the title of world's largest automaker. The company that was once content to be the most admired in the world began cutting corners and getting sloppy. There is no sign of that happening at Ford today, but making sure it does not will require constant vigilance.

Still, the real challenge facing Ford Motor Company today is institutionalizing Mulally's revolution. Mulally has given the company a system that, if rigorously adhered to, should prevent Ford's chronic disease from reasserting itself. He has also given it a bench of leaders who know how to win.

"We've been through the trenches. We saw the setbacks. And we saw it work," Mark Fields told me. "Everybody just benefits so much when you develop a plan, you implement it, you work through the issues, you work through the setbacks, and you see the points start going on the board."

On January 12, 2011, Bill Ford asked Lewis Booth to deliver the keynote speech to Ford's senior executives from around the world who had convened for the company's annual global leadership meeting in Dearborn. He started by listing everything Ford had achieved over the past year—paying down the debt, paying off the VEBA, and shifting the entire organization back into growth mode.

"This is I think the best thing I've seen in my thirty-something years at Ford, the opportunities ahead of us. This is absolutely the best thing. And if this doesn't make you break out into a sweat, you should, and give yourself a good shake because this is just a fantastic opportunity ahead of us," he said, his voice heavy with emotion. "This is our moment to change the business forever."

* * *

Henry Ford once said, "A business that makes nothing but money is a poor kind of business."

Ford Motor Company has certainly made a great deal of money since Alan Mulally started there in 2006. But it has also made people believe that the highest principles of American enterprise—ingenuity, innovation, and integrity—have not deserted us entirely. In an economic era marked by avarice and greed, Mulally's Ford has demonstrated that a company can still succeed by building a good product and selling it at a fair price. As the big Wall Street banks tried to hide their mounting failures, Mulally was exposing Ford's shortcomings and challenging his company to overcome them. Wall Street's obfuscation and trickery would ultimately drag the entire world into the Great Recession. With Mulally's relentless determination to succeed, Ford would defy that downturn and once again become an engine of prosperity.

From the day he arrived in Dearborn, Mulally said he was fighting for the soul of American manufacturing. If Ford had failed, a little bit of America would have died, too. But Ford did not fail. Under Mulally's leadership, it showed the entire world that at least one American automaker could pick itself up, shake off the rust, compete with the best in the business, and win.

ACKNOWLEDGMENTS

This work would never have been possible without the help of many extraordinary individuals. There are too many to name, and some of them would prefer to remain anonymous. But among those whom I can name publicly, I must begin with Bill Ford Jr. and Alan Mulally, for without their cooperation it would have been impossible to tell this story in such detail. Both men gave generously of their valuable time, offering a perspective on the events chronicled herein that would have been unobtainable from any other source. Their support for this project also gave me access to the rest of Ford Motor Company's executives, the automaker's archives, and other important sources. That they were willing to sanction it without any promise of editorial review or influence is a powerful testament to their faith and confidence in the Ford story.

I am also indebted to many others at Ford, beginning with Mark Truby. Before he joined Ford's corporate communications staff in 2007, Mark was my editor at the *Detroit News*. He hired me to cover the automaker back in 2005, taught me everything he knew about its secrets, and showed me how to extract more. Mark was the best newshound I have ever met, and I owe much of whatever skill I possess as a reporter to his tutelage. At Ford, he was a powerful advocate for this project and an invaluable aid in my work on it. He and his staff set up many of the interviews I conducted for *American Icon* and spent a great deal of time and energy assisting me with my research—at least until he was transferred to Germany in early 2011. That burden then shifted to Karen Hampton, who had already been a tremendous help as Mulally's media liaison. Karen and her staff did far more than any author could have hoped for, often spending hours or even days tracking down the most minute detail or checking the most obscure fact. My seemingly endless requests would have tried anyone's patience, but not Karen's. She answered them all promptly and cheerfully, and for that I am truly grateful. I am also indebted to Mark and Karen's boss, Ray Day, who first discussed the idea for this book over lunch with me more than two years ago. It was Day who presented this project to Ford and Mulally and urged their cooperation. To him and to the other Ford executives, both current and former, who participated in this project, as well as their assistants, I offer thanks.

I would also like to thank my friend Eric Selle of J.P. Morgan Chase & Company for making me smart about the more arcane financial matters covered in this book.

I am, of course, forever indebted to my fantastic agent, Jane Dystel. Jane has proven an invaluable ally, counselor, and advocate. Her help in navigating the complexities of the publishing business is cause for near constant thanks. I would also like to thank her partner, Miriam Goderich, for her help in preparing my book proposal, along with the rest of the staff at Dystel & Goderich Literary Management for their help in making this happen.

Of course, it never would have happened without Roger Scholl, my editor at Crown Business, who made a big bet on an unknown author and also proved a great collaborator. His enthusiasm for this project and patience with me has been beyond anything I could have hoped for. I would also like to thank his assistant, Logan Balestrino, as well as Paul Lamb, Dennelle Catlett, and everyone else at Crown who believed in this project and has worked to make it a success.

I am also indebted to the *Detroit News* for allowing me to cover this amazing story and giving me the time off to write this book. That was no small thing in this era of ever-shrinking newsrooms. I would particularly like to thank publisher Jon Wolman, managing editor Don Nauss, and business editors Sue Carney and Joanna Firestone for their patience and support, as well as the other members of the *Detroit News* autos team, who were forced to pick up the slack during my long absence. I have been fortunate at the *News* to have worked with and learned from some of the best automotive journalists in the business, including Christine Tierney and Bill Vlasic. But it is to Daniel Howes that I owe my biggest thanks. He has been my mentor and · confessor through some very trying times, has always been there to poke holes in my hypotheses with his encyclopedic knowledge of the automobile industry, and has helped me to become the writer that I am today.

In that, I am also forever indebted to the author Herbert Kohl, who was the first to see my potential as a writer and the first to encourage me to pursue this path in life. I was still in high school when I first met Herb. He helped me hone my talents, showed me what I could do with them, and gave me a kick in the pants when I needed it. And he has been there for me whenever I have needed him ever since.

So have my parents, who have supported me in this and just about everything else in life, even when that was hard.

All of these contributions were enormous, yet they were dwarfed by the help rendered to me in this and in all things by my amazing wife, Gretchen Meyer-Hoffman. Proofreader and editor, cook and collaborator, shrink and soulmate, she was my constant companion at every stage of this project, just as she has been every step of the way for more than eighteen years. She has always believed in me, even when I have not believed in myself, and this book was no exception. Gretchen's name really deserves to stand next to mine in the credits, but she is far too modest for that. So instead I say simply, "Thanks."

NOTES

PROLOGUE

2 five of every six vehicles:
James M. Rubenstein, *Making and Selling Cars: Innovation and Change in the U.S. Automotive Industry* (Baltimore: Johns Hopkins University Press, 2001), p. 188.

1. THE HOUSE THAT HENRY BUILT

5 "Business men go down with their businesses": Henry Ford, with Samuel Crowther, *My Life and Work* (Garden City, NY: Doubleday, 1922), p. 43.

6 the company's billboards: Douglas Brinkley, *Wheels for the World* (New York: Viking, 2003), p. 115.

6 the average time: Paul Ingrassia, *Crash Course: The American Automobile Industry's Road from Glory to Disaster* (New York: Random House, 2010), p. 17.

6 nearly 200,000 fewer: James M. Flammang and David L. Lewis, *Ford Chronicle: A Pictorial History from 1893* (Lincolnwood, IL: Publications International, 2000), pp. 54–57.

6 peaked in 1921: Ibid., p. 52.

7 demand had fallen: Brinkley, *Wheels for the World*, p. 351.

7 Thousands placed orders: Ibid., pp. 356–57.

7 Within two years: Flammang and Lewis, *Ford Chronicle*, p. 64.

8 He even rehired: Brinkley, *Wheels for the World*, p. 256.

8 "Mr. Couzens said": Charles E. Sorensen, with Samuel T. Williamson, *My Forty Years with Ford* (Detroit: Wayne State University Press, 2006), pp. 43, 153.

8 leading it past Ford: Ford R. Bryan, *Henry's Lieutenants* (Detroit: Wayne State University Press, 1993), pp. 154–56.

9 "Mr. Knudsen was": Norman Beasley, *Knudsen: A Biography* (New York: Whittlesey House, 1947), p. 109.

9 largest private police force: Ibid., p. 30.

9 "a dark, almost gothic place": Brinkley, *Wheels for the World*, p. 421.

10 But in September: Ibid., pp. 464–501.

10 a new openness: Ibid., p. 504.

10 "Henry Ford II's": Alex Taylor III, *Sixty to Zero: An Inside Look at the Collapse of General Motors—and the Detroit Auto Industry* (New Haven, CT: Yale University Press, 2010), pp. 71–72.

11 Iacocca as a threat: Brinkley, *Wheels for the World*, p. 676.

11 "I'm not a caretaker": Alex Taylor III, "Fords for the Future," *Fortune*, January 16, 1989.

12 more than $87 million: Brinkley, *Wheels for the World*, p. 271.

12 more than 61 percent: Flammang and Lewis, *Ford Chronicle*, p. 52.

13 lost $120 million: Ibid., pp. 69–72.

13 without losing a cent: William Pelfrey, *Billy, Alfred, and General Motors: The Story of Two Unique Men, a Legendary Company, and a Remarkable Time in American History* (New York: AMACOM, 2006), p. 265.

13 "I frankly don't see": Jerry Flint, "Henry Ford Pessimistic on Foreign Autos; Doubts Detroit Can Compete," *New York Times*, May 14, 1971.

14 more than a hundred deaths and nearly 2,000 injuries: Brinkley, *Wheels for the World*, pp. 670–74.

15 more than all of the Japanese and European carmakers: Ibid., pp. 715–16.

15 "the perfect complement": Ingrassia, *Crash Course*, p. 100.

18 "Everything we did": David Magee, *Ford Tough: Bill Ford and the Battle to Rebuild America's Automaker* (Hoboken, NJ: Wiley, 2005), p. 3.

18 Ford's fondest childhood memories: Ibid., p. 4.

19 managing to get himself elected: Ibid., p. 6.

20 "rich dilettantes": Ingrassia, *Crash Course*, p. 144.

20 "So now you have your monarchy back": Alex Taylor III, "The Fight at Ford: Behind Bill's Boardroom Struggle," *Fortune*, April 3, 2000.

21 board saw him: Mark Truby, "Nasser Out: Chairman Bill Ford Assumes CEO Post," *Detroit News*, October 30, 2001.

22 "a guilt-ridden rich kid": Keith Bradsher, *High and Mighty: The Dangerous Rise of the SUV* (Cambridge, MA: PublicAffairs, 2002), p. 284.

27 asked for their support: Mark Truby and Bill Vlasic, "How Ford Family Saved Dynasty," *Detroit News*, June 2, 2003.

2. BROKEN

28 "The internal ailments": Henry Ford, with Samuel Crowther, *My Life and Work* (Garden City, NY: Doubleday, 1922), p. 158.

29 the company's jets: Mark Truby, "Ford Cuts Advisers, Exec Perks," *Detroit News*, January 24, 2002.

30 climbed two slots: Kathleen Kerwin, "Bill Ford's Long, Hard Road," *BusinessWeek*, October 7, 2002.

32 "I can't say I'm having fun": Ibid.

38 took nearly 36 hours: 2006 Harbour Report.

40 youngest person ever: Daren Fonda, Toko Sekiguchi, and Joseph R. Szczesny, "Ford's Young Gun," *Time*, July 1, 2002.

41 axed 20 percent: Garry Emmons, "Mazda's Main Man Eases into the Fast Lane," *Harvard Business School Alumni Bulletin*, April 2002.

42   **dressed as a boy:** Dee-Ann Durbin, "Gearhead Has the Drive," *Houston Chronicle*, April 8, 2006.

47   **"devastating news":** Bill Vlasic and Bryce G. Hoffman, "Painful," *Detroit News*, January 24, 2006.

47   **$3 a gallon:** U.S. Energy Information Administration.

51   **required a separate vote:** This is established in Ford's certificate of incorporation.

54   **"The stock price":** Betsy Morris, "Driven to the Brink," *Portfolio*, April 16, 2007.

3. THE MAN ON THE WHITE HORSE

57   **"Coming together is a beginning":** Attributed. The source is unknown.

58   **"Mr. Nice Guy":** Kyung M. Song, "Boeing's Mr. Nice Guy: Alan Mulally Steps into the Limelight," *Seattle Times*, April 8, 2001.

59   **Alan grew up:** Rick Montgomery, "Under Kansas Native Alan Mulally, Ford Has Not Only Survived, but Thrived," *Kansas City Star*, November 13, 2010.

59   **Kappa Sigma fraternity:** Ibid.

59   **school's annual engineering exposition:** Song, "Boeing's Mr. Nice Guy."

61   **$500 million under budget:** James P. Lewis, *Working Together: 12 Principles for Achieving Excellence in Managing Projects, Teams, and Organizations* (Washington, DC: Beard Books, 2006), p. 3.

61   **an estimated $5 billion:** Karl Sabbagh, producer and director, *21st Century Jet: The Building of the 777*, PBS, 1996.

61   **"There was resistance":** Ibid.

62   **At about $100 million a plane:** Ibid.

62   **new production records:** Song, "Boeing's Mr. Nice Guy."

64   **"a crime":** Quoted from an article by the author that appeared in the *Detroit News* on September 7, 2006.

79   **"Let me take a crack":** Bill Vlasic, *Once Upon a Car: The Fall and Resurrection of America's Big Three Auto Makers—GM, Ford, and Chrysler* (New York: William Morrow, 2011), p. 153.

80   **"Alan, you've done everything":** Ibid.

80   **"It's not over":** Ibid., p. 154.

4. THE BOLDEST MOVE YET

84   **"Failure is simply an opportunity":** Henry Ford, with Samuel Crowther, *My Life and Work* (Garden City, NY: Doubleday, 1922), p. 19.

95   **"Ford and the Detroit auto industry":** Daniel Howes, "Bold Gamble on Outsider Is Risky Move," *Detroit News*, September 6, 2006.

5. THE REVOLUTION BEGINS

101   **"We do not make changes":** Henry Ford, with Samuel Crowther, *Today and Tomorrow* (Garden City, NY: Doubleday, 1926), p. 51.

104   **"I look at that as nothing but**

opportunity": Bryce G. Hoffman, "Mulally's Job One: Global Overhaul," *Detroit News*, November 11, 2006.

113 **for the third quarter:** Ford press release, October 23, 2006.

6. THE PLAN

126 **"Progress is not made":** Henry Ford, with Samuel Crowther, *My Life and Work* (Garden City, NY: Doubleday, 1922), p. 134.

127 **"It is disappointing":** Alex Taylor III, "Consumer Reports Engineers Are No Test Dummies," *Fortune*, June 13, 2007.

128 **on the fast track:** Paul Ingrassia, *Crash Course: The American Automobile Industry's Road from Glory to Disaster* (New York: Random House, 2010), p. 138.

129 **"An outsider could never":** Alex Taylor III, *Sixty to Zero: An Inside Look at the Collapse of General Motors — and the Detroit Auto Industry* (New Haven, CT: Yale University Press, 2010), p. 156.

130 **"They make products that people want":** Bryce G. Hoffman, "Mulally's Job One: Global Overhaul," *Detroit News*, November 11, 2006.

130 **it would reduce:** Ford press release, September 15, 2006.

131 **closer to 3 million units:** This according to comments made by Chief Financial Officer Don Leclair during Ford's January 25, 2007, earnings call.

131 **Some 70 percent:** Ford press release, September 15, 2006.

131 **similar to the one used by Toyota:** This according to Jeffrey Liker, an engineering professor at the University of Michigan and author of *The Toyota Way*, quoted in a story by the author that appeared in *The Detroit News* on June 21, 2006.

139 **"There's not one Ford":** The quotes from this interview are taken from a story by the author that appeared in *The Detroit News* the following day.

140 **had grown organically:** Douglas Brinkley, *Wheels for the World* (New York: Viking, 2003), pp. 201–3.

140 **foreign subsidiaries:** Ibid., pp. 369–73.

140 **no longer made sense:** Ibid., pp. 545–49.

140 **tried to eliminate these regional organizations:** Ibid., pp. 726–27.

140 **drove costs higher:** Alex Taylor III, "Ford's Fight for Survival," *Fortune*, January 20, 2006.

7. BETTING THE FARM

147 **Borrowing for expansion:** Ford, *My Life and Work* (Garden City, NY: Doubleday, 1926), p. 158.

152 **"to address near- and medium-term negative operating-related cash flow":** Ford press release, November 27, 2006.

152 **"This is Ford's one last shot":** Bryce G. Hoffman, "Ford Bets the House," *Detroit News*, November 28, 2006.

155 **"overwhelming support by**

lenders": Ford letter to prospective lenders, December 6, 2006.

8. ASSEMBLING THE TEAM

158 "If everyone is moving forward": Attributed. The source is unknown.

160 "sacrifices at every level": This quote is from Fields' speech announcing his first Way Forward plan on January 23, 2006.

164 he was tapped: Ford press release, March 24, 2005.

165 "the Energizer Bunny": Luis Perez, "Bay Ridge Boy West-Wings It," *New York Daily News*, January 10, 2003.

169 "I have the utmost confidence": Daniel Howes, "Mulally Shows Faith in Fields," *Detroit News*, January 12, 2007.

173 carried an ace of hearts: Mark Truby, "Ford Leans on Suppliers," *Detroit News*, July 11, 2002.

174 only General Motors scored worse: This according to the influential annual survey conducted by Planning Perspectives Inc. of Birmingham, Michigan.

9. THE BEST AND WORST OF TIMES

178 "It is failure": Henry Ford, with Samuel Crowther, *My Life and Work* (Garden City, NY: Doubleday, 1922), p. 220.

179 "vision for how technology": This is from an e-mail exchange I had with the Microsoft chairman in December 2006. It was originally quoted in the *Detroit News*

article by the author titled "How the Two Bills Got in Sync," which ran on January 8, 2007. Much of this information also appeared in that piece.

183 had been 60 percent: Bryce G. Hoffman, "Ford Fix-It Plan Off Track," *Detroit News*, February 16, 2007.

188 A perky salesman: Amy Wilson, "Mulally Drops by Dealership, Sells Some Cars," *Automotive News*, March 27, 2007.

195 "We want people": From an interview with the author during the Detroit auto show in 2007.

10. FAMILY STRIFE

201 "A business which exists": Henry Ford, with Samuel Crowther, *Today and Tomorrow* (Garden City, NY: Doubleday, 1992), p. 38.

203 only about $578 million: Bill Vlasic and Bryce G. Hoffman, "Ford Family Unity Tested," *Detroit News*, May 8, 2007.

204 generated $130 million: Ibid.

205 "undemocratic": Vlasic and Hoffman, "Ford Family Unity Tested."

205 joined the Hare Krishnas: Mark Truby and Bill Vlasic, "How Ford Family Saved Dynasty," *Detroit News*, June 2, 2003.

206 "boutique investment bank": Jenny Anderson and Landon Thomas Jr., "Boutique Bank Lands Ex-Goldman Star," *New York Times*, January 14, 2006.

206 "mergers and acquisitions pioneer": Adrian Cox, "Perella

Weinberg Raises More Than $1B for Boutique," Bloomberg, June 15, 2006.

206 **"sage counsel"**: Andrew Ross Sorkin, "The Pressure of Great Expectations," *New York Times*, April 27. 2007.

11. WATERSHED

213 **"You've been fighting"**: Quoted in William C. Richards, *The Last Billionaire* (New York: Bantam Books, 1951), pp. 285–86.

214 **"Labor unions are the worst"**: Douglas Brinkley, *Wheels for the World* (New York: Viking, 2003), p. 426.

215 **"Detroit's auto industry"**: Paul Ingrassia, *Crash Course: The American Automobile Industry's Road from Glory to Disaster* (New York: Random House, 2010), p. 8.

223 **"I am absolutely not"**: This was on WWJ-950 on September 6, 2006.

227 **convinced 38,000 hourly workers**: Bryce G. Hoffman, "How 38,000 Were Enticed to Leave Ford," *Detroit News*, December 4, 2006.

231 **a discount of about 70 cents**: Bryce G. Hoffman and Daniel Howes, "Ailing Ford Gets a Deal That Fits Its Needs," *Detroit News*, November 5, 2007.

12. SELLING IT LIKE IT IS

236 **"You can't build a reputation"**: Attributed. The source is unknown.

241 **"I've seen him roll up his sleeves"**: Quoted in a piece by the author that appeared in the *Detroit News* on October 12, 2007.

241 **"This is a big deal"**: Ibid.

13. RIPE FOR THE PICKING

251 **"A business which can bring itself"**: Henry Ford, with Samuel Crowther, *Today and Tomorrow* (Garden City, NY: Doubleday, 1992), p. 32.

251 **did it thirty-three times**: Dial Torgerson, *Kerkorian: An American Success Story* (New York: Dial Press, 1974), p. 65.

252 **"We are fiscally conservative"**: Quoted in an article by the author that appeared in the *Detroit News* on January 25, 2008.

253 **"It's pretty damn clear"**: Bill Vlasic, *Once Upon a Car: The Fall and Resurrection of America's Big Three Auto Makers — GM, Ford, and Chrysler* (New York: William Morrow, 2011), p. 269.

14. STORM WARNING

263 **"Every depression is a challenge"**: Henry Ford, with Samuel Crowther, *My Life and Work* (Garden City, NY: Doubleday, 1922), p. 136.

263 **in a recession since December**: Emily Kaiser, "Recession Started in December 2007: Panel," Reuters, December 1, 2008.

263 **rumors were spreading**: Bryan Burrough, "Bringing Down Bear Stearns," *Vanity Fair*, August 2008.

264 **one out of every nine**: Eric Dash, "Auto Industry Feels the Pain of Tight Credit," *New York Times*, May 27, 2008.

264 about 11 percent: This information was provided by Ford during a briefing on May 22, 2008.

268 "Ford has shown": Quoted in an article by the author that appeared in the *Detroit News* on June 5, 2008.

269 "That's right, I said it": Quoted in an article by the author that appeared in the *Detroit News* on August 12, 2008.

270 over $4 a gallon: U.S. Energy Information Administration.

272 "You know, I think it's really time": Bill Vlasic, *Once Upon a Car: The Fall and Resurrection of America's Big Three Auto Makers—GM, Ford, and Chrysler* (New York: William Morrow, 2011), p. 286.

275 "We're doing it faster": Bryce G. Hoffman, "Ford Revs Up Big Move to Smaller Cars," *Detroit News*, July 25, 2008.

15. THE SUM OF ALL FEARS

280 "Bankers play far": Henry Ford, with Samuel Crowther, *My Life and Work* (Garden City, NY: Doubleday, 1922), p. 176.

280 biggest bankruptcy in U.S. history: Sam Mamudi, "Lehman Folds with Record $613 Billion Debt," *MarketWatch*, September 15, 2008.

16. MR. MULALLY GOES TO WASHINGTON

295 "When you get a whole country": Henry Ford, with Samuel

Crowther, *My Life and Work* (Garden City, NY: Doubleday, 1922), p. 7.

298 "For years, while foreign competitors": This quote is taken from the official text of Obama's speech.

304 GM was trying to blackmail: Steven Rattner, *Overhaul: An Insider's Account of the Obama Administration's Emergency Rescue of the Auto Industry* (New York: Houghton Mifflin Harcourt, 2010), pp. 20–24.

17. BREAKING WITH DETROIT

316 "Our help does not come": Henry Ford, with Samuel Crowther, *My Life and Work* (Garden City, NY: Doubleday, 1922), p. 7.

330 emergency funding: Dan Milmo, "Bush Sanctions Last-Ditch Rescue Plan for General Motors and Chrysler," *Guardian*, December 12, 2008.

330 The president gave: Jeremy Pelofsky and John Crawley, "Bush Throws Lifeline to Auto Industry," Reuters, December 19, 2008.

18. BY THEIR OWN BOOTSTRAPS

332 "Then why flounder": Henry Ford, with Samuel Crowther, *My Life and Work* (Garden City, NY: Doubleday, 1922), p. 136.

333 "This has turned out": Quoted in a story by the author that appeared in the *Detroit News* on December 31, 2008.

343 "It would be really helpful": Steven Rattner, *Overhaul: An Insider's Account of the Obama Ad-*

ministration's Emergency Rescue of the Auto Industry (New York: Houghton Mifflin Harcourt, 2010), p. 47.

344 reporters on Air Force One: Ibid., p. 64.

345 "We feel like we're over a barrel": Quoted in a story by the author that appeared in the *Detroit News* on February 26, 2009.

347 Obama had concluded: Rattner, *Overhaul*, p. 46.

19. TURNING THE CORNER

354 "Unless you have courage": From *Theosophist* magazine, February 1930.

359 "Ford made sure": Steven Rattner, *Overhaul: An Insider's Account of the Obama Administration's Emergency Rescue of the Auto Industry* (New York: Houghton Mifflin Harcourt, 2010), p. 205.

361 most sought-after American car: U.S. Department of Transportation press release, August 26, 2009.

365 son of a farmer: This information is taken from a profile prepared by the *China Daily* on March 27, 2006. It has been confirmed by Reuters and other sources.

366 Geely KingKong: Doug Young, "Geely's Folksy Li Known as China's Henry Ford," Reuters, July 22, 2010.

366 a team of advisers: Kevin Krolicki, Niklas Pollard, and Fang Yan, "Saving Volvo," Reuters, July 22, 2010.

368 first full-year gain: Ford press release, January 5, 2010.

20. PROOF POINTS

370 "Wealth is nothing": From *Theosophist* magazine, February 1930.

370 August 28, 2009: "Timeline—Toyota's Rise and Run-up to Its Recall Crisis," Reuters, February 9, 2010.

372 "It will make us globally competitive": Quoted in a story by the author that appeared in the *Detroit News* on January 11, 2010.

377 "Now we are here": Bruce Einhorn, "Alan Mulally's Asian Sales Call," *Bloomberg Businessweek*, April 1, 2010.

385 more cash than debt: Ford press release, April 1, 2011.

386 now topped the list: According to quarterly surveys by the Swiss investment bank UBS.

21. THE ROAD AHEAD

388 "The only history": Quoted in the *Chicago Tribune*, May 25, 1916.

BIBLIOGRAPHY

Beasley, Norman. *Knudsen: A Biography*. New York: Whittlesey House, 1947.

Bradsher, Keith. *High and Mighty: The Dangerous Rise of the SUV*. Cambridge, MA: PublicAffairs, 2002.

Brinkley, Douglas. *Wheels for the World*. New York: Viking, 2003.

Bryan, Ford R. *Henry's Lieutenants*. Detroit: Wayne State University Press, 1993.

Byrne, John A. *The Whiz Kids: The Founding Fathers of American Business — and the Legacy They Left Us*. New York: Doubleday, 1993.

Flammang, James M., and David L. Lewis. *Ford Chronicle: A Pictorial History from 1893*. Lincolnwood, IL: Publications International, 2000.

Ford, Henry, with Samuel Crowther. *My Life and Work*. Garden City, NY: Doubleday, Page, 1922.

———. *Today and Tomorrow*. Garden City, NY: Doubleday, Page, 1926.

Halberstam, David. *The Reckoning*. New York: William Morrow, 1986.

Hickerson, J. Mel. *Ernie Breech: The Story of His Remarkable Career at General Motors, Ford, and TWA*. New York: Meredith Press, 1968.

Ingrassia, Paul. *Crash Course: The American Automobile Industry's Road from Glory to Disaster*. New York: Random House, 2010.

Lewis, James P. *Working Together: 12 Principles for Achieving Excellence in Managing Projects, Teams, and Organizations*. Washington, DC: Beard Books, 2006.

Liker, Jeffrey K. *The Toyota Way: 14 Management Principles from the World's Greatest Manufacturer*. New York: McGraw-Hill, 2004.

Magee, David. *Ford Tough: Bill Ford and the Battle to Rebuild America's Automaker*. Hoboken, NJ: Wiley, 2005.

Pelfrey, William. *Billy, Alfred, and General Motors: The Story of Two Unique Men, a Legendary Company, and a Remarkable Time in American History*. New York: AMACOM, 2006.

Rattner, Steven. *Overhaul: An Insider's Account of the Obama Administration's Emergency Rescue of the Auto Industry*. New York: Houghton Mifflin Harcourt, 2010.

Rubenstein, James M. *Making and Selling Cars: Innovation and Change in the U.S. Automotive Industry*. Baltimore: Johns Hopkins University Press, 2001.

Sorensen, Charles E., with Samuel T. Williamson. *My Forty Years with Ford*. Detroit: Wayne State University Press, 2006.

Taylor, Alex, III. *Sixty to Zero: An Inside Look at the Collapse of General Motors — and the Detroit Auto Industry*. New Haven, CT: Yale University Press, 2010.

Vlasic, Bill. *Once Upon a Car: The Fall and Resurrection of America's Big Three Auto Makers — GM, Ford, and Chrysler*. New York: William Morrow, 2011.

INDEX